1984

MODERN SPOKEN SPANISH:

An Interdisciplinary Perspective

Ronald P. Lombardi
Amalia Boero de Peters
West Chester State College

University Press
of America™

Copyright © 1981 by

University Press of America, Inc.™

P.O. Box 19101, Washington, DC 20036

Library of Congress Cataloging in Publication Data

Lombardi, Ronald P.
  Modern spoken Spanish.

  Bibliography: p.
  Includes index.
  1. Spanish language--Pronunciation.
2. Spanish language--Dialects--Phonetics.
I. Peters, Amalia Boero de. II. Title.
PC4137.L6   461'.5   80-1442
ISBN 0-8191-1513-4 (pbk.)   AACR2

ACKNOWLEDGEMENTS

We wish to thank Dr. Madelyn Gutwirth of the Department of Foreign Languages and Dr. William Henry of the English Department, both of West Chester State College, for their careful reading, helpful comments and insightful criticism. Moreover, we would like to thank Prof. Joan Fayer of the English-Linguistics Department of the University of Puerto Rico, Río Piedras, for her expert proofreading, helpful comments and generous encouragement. Above all, we gratefully acknowledge the indefatigable efforts of our former graduate student, Mrs. Helen V. Subbio, for her patience as a proofreader and her expertise as a typist. We also thank our graduate and undergraduate students at West Chester State College who cooperated so generously in our attempts at using these materials experimentally in the classroom.

Whereas we are genuinely grateful to the above persons for their kind assistance and encouragement, we fully acknowledge the fact that all errors of omission and commission are ours and ours alone.

Ronald P. Lombardi, Ph.D.
Amalia Boero de Peters, M.S.Ed., M.A.

TABLE OF CONTENTS

CHAPTER FIVE

CHAPTER SIX

ix

LIST OF FIGURES

xi

PREFACE

     This textbook is intended to be a general introduction to a linguistic approach to spoken Spanish. It is designed to be used as a primary text in college-level courses on Spanish Phonetics and Spanish Linguistics. In addition, it may serve as a secondary text in courses on Bilingualism, Teaching of English to Speakers of Other Languages, and in workshops and seminars on various aspects of the spoken language. Finally, it may be used as a comprehensive reference work for students and teachers of Spanish alike. The available texts to date have been, to our knowledge, Tomás Navarro Tomás' traditional Manual de pronunciación española, John B. Dalbor's contrastive Spanish Pronunciation: Theory and Practice, and I. R. Macpherson's dual-focused Spanish Phonology: Descriptive and Historical. Moreover, the branches of theoretical and applied linguistics can boast of a myriad of publications--both theoretical and practical. The present text is not aimed at supplanting any of the aforementioned works in phonology and morphology, nor does it have the breadth of scope of many commendable theoretical and applied studies in the area of structural linguistics. Instead, its main purpose is the integration of the essential aspects of the traditional approach to spoken Spanish and the valuable insights of the structuralists.

     It is our contention that many praiseworthy investigations and texts are utilized to great advantage in the areas of descriptive and applied linguistics, articulatory phonetics, phonology, morphology and other branches of linguistic science--normally with direct application either to English or little known "exotic" languages. On the other hand, much of the emphasis in Hispanics tends to be either philological in nature or traditional in approach. Our primary aim has been to introduce the basic notions of applied linguistics as they pertain directly to spoken Spanish. Even though contrastive English/Spanish aspects have been included to an extent, the objective has remained consistently the oral production of native Hispanics. The secondary purpose of

xiii

the work is to provide information and analysis of a
number of relevant aspects which go beyond the scope
of descriptive linguistics: forms of address and
levels of speech; variant forms; peninsular languages
and dialects; pidginization and creolization; Spanish
in contact with other languages. Whereas an ideal-
ized version of Spanish is frequently the aim of language specialists, our goal has been to present variant forms of the language encountered in Europe and
the New World. Although an overview of Spanish in
the United States has been included, it is hoped that
this text will point to the need for further investigation in this area.

This work consists of two main divisions--Part
One (Chapters One through Four): basic notions of
sound, vowels, consonants, grouped sounds, linkage,
suprasegmentals, and intonation patterns; Part Two
(Chapters Five through Eight): levels of speech,
forms of address, jargon, local color, characteristic
features of certain speech zones, dialects, the language in Latin America, and Spanish in the United
States. Since we believe that drill in sound production should rarely, if ever, be separated from
meaning, the Así Se Dice section has been included
in each chapter and provides a rich collection of
proverbs, idioms and tongue twisters taken from traditional Hispanic speech and folklore. Insofar as
possible, the Spanish equivalent of each linguistic
concept has been included in parenthesis after its
first appearance in the text. Appendix One contains
sixteen original versions of representative Hispanic
speech patterns in the form of narration or dialogue,
followed by phonemic transcriptions. The phonetic
symbols used in all transcriptions are based on the
International Phonetic Alphabet with occasional modifications. Even though it is understood that unstressed diphthongs and triphthongs are normally relaxed both in speech and in transcription, we have
chosen not to relax them in the transcriptions for
purposes of simplicity of presentation. Appendix
Two consists of translations of the proverbs,
sayings, idiomatic and figurative expressions encountered in the text. After the Bibliography there

is a Suggested Reading List containing a valuable, up-to-date collection of studies and reference works related to the principal subject areas presented in the book.

Part One may be used, in conjunction with Appendixes One and Two, as a completely integrated basic course on Spanish Phonetics, Phonology and Morphology. This segment of the work may be utilized along with the Theory and Practice Exercises in each chapter to provide adequate drill in both areas. This may be followed by intensive and extensive practice with the phonemic transcriptions in Appendix One. The First Part may also be used as a secondary text in Basic Phonetics with applications to Spanish by making use of the Theory Exercises only.

Part Two may serve as a secondary text in courses on Bilingualism, Teaching of English to Speakers of Other Languages, and seminars for students and teachers of Spanish by making use of either the Theory Exercises or the Practice Exercises or both. The Así Se Dice section may or may not be used at the discretion of the instructor.

A one-year course on Spanish Phonology, Morphology and Its Variants may be based on the textbook in its entirety. The latter has been tested in both undergraduate and graduate classes with meaningful results. It is suggested that the course be divided into three distinct series of objectives: presentation of theory (the theoretical aspects of the text followed by the Theory Exercises); practical application (textual examples and Practice Exercises); phonetic and phonemic transcription and oral drill (Appendix One, repitition drills based on the Así Se Dice sections and "free" oral practice). Ideally, all examples of sound segments, words, utterances, intonation patterns and variants should be presented orally both by the instructor and available native informants.

CHAPTER ONE

SOUNDS AND HOW THEY ARE MADE

INTRODUCTION. BASIC NOTIONS. Utterances of one
sort or another are the chief source of human communication. They are transmitted by sounds produced by a number of body organs which all normal
human beings possess. People do not really make
use of words as such as the primary units of
speech since they communicate most often in utterances and not in words or sentences. We are
traditionally drawn to think in terms of words,
which increase almost daily as a result of advances
in technology, science, the arts, and the business
world. These developments are in turn reflected
quite rapidly by the mass media, such as the
theatre, movies, radio, television, and other forms
of modern communication. Because of the speed with
which new advances and events are reported daily,
the level of communication is not always of the
highest quality. This, of course, is one of the
many problems encountered in the study of any language. Words which are commonplace today like
adicto a drogas, drogadicto, astronauta, tele-es-
pectador, telenovela, computadora, transformista,
medio ambiente, contaminación del aire, secuestración de aviones, transmisión por satélite, retransmisión televisual, aerosol, desaventajado,
niño marginado, minusválido, aparejo antihurto,
misil televidente, and the like would have been
virtually unknown to Spanish speakers of several
generations ago. In addition, it should be kept
in mind that speech as such is not the only form of
human communication.

Among other forms we find sign language,
subtle uses of flags, grimaces, gestures, body language, and various other types of non-verbal communication. Strictly within the world of sounds,
some audible code is used like morse-key, drum tapping or beating, other kinds of tapping, and
whistling in order to convey basic messages which

1

remain essentially invariable regardless of the
means used. When we deal strictly with the sounds
which humans make in order to communicate, we
limit ourselves to a purely linguistic consideration. A more specific focus upon such sounds and
messages and the countless relationships between
the two brings us much closer to the aim of the
present work--the study of the sounds of spoken
language with particular application to the language used by hispanohablantes or Spanish-speaking
peoples of the world.

PHONETICS AND RELATED FIELDS. The field of phonetics (la fonética) deals with physical and physiological aspects of sound produced by human beings
in conveying messages. A branch of linguistics
(la lingüística), phonetics includes the analysis
and classification of sounds in isolation and in
groups and a systematic representation of their
distinctive features. This field includes the more
concrete, material and acoustical aspects of sound,
but it does not concern itself with meaning per se.
For example, if one pronounces carefully a word
like bata, one produces a very respectable phonetic
(fonético) rendering of the word. However, there
is a second equally important aspect of language
and that is the phonemic (fonemático) level, in
which sound is inextricably linked with meaning.
In other words, while phonetics deals with sounds
in isolation and in groupings without any focus
upon meaning, phonemics (la fonemática) or phonology (la fonología) deals with the various phonic
differences which are normally associated with
meaning per se. When dealing with functional language, phonetics and phonemics are very closely
linked since human beings rarely convey messages by
uttering sounds in isolation. Both points of view
are essential to the work of linguists and language
specialists alike.

One of the most useful aspects of phonology is
the concept of the phoneme (el fonema)--a minimal
unit of sound. For instance, in English the words

2

bed and bad and boot and boat are distinguishable
strictly on the basis of the change in vowel sound
or phoneme. The same occurs with consonants as in
pit and bit, code and goad. Any sound variant of a
basic phoneme is referred to as an allophone (el
alófono) since the phoneme per se is really the abstraction of the sound and the phone (el fono), the
concrete unit of sound in isolation. Therefore, on
a purely theoretical level at least, the basic phoneme is written between slash bars (las líneas in-
clinadas). Thus, phoneme A is rendered /A/. All
variants or allophones of the basic phoneme are
written between brackets (los corchetes)[ ]. For
example, in English the pairs sat and sad, bet and
bed, cot and cod, bit and bid, pluck and plug all
have identical vowels in written form but have
slightly modified vowels as a result of the influence of the consonant which ends the syllable.
Thus, while the vowels in sat and sad seem identical, the vowel in the first word is short and the
one in the second, long. In the example sat and
sad one finds that the phoneme /A/ provides the
allophones [ae] and [ae:], the first being the
short variant since it is followed by a voiceless
consonant, the second being the long one as a result of the final voiced consonant. The same explanation may be given for the remaining pairs.
While in English vocalic phonemes in allophonic
distribution frequently depend on vowel length as a
result of the voicedness or voicelessness of the
consonants which follow, in Spanish vowel length
per se is not especially distinctive.

Although phonemes are really abstract concepts
and cannot really be articulated in isolation as
such, they are very useful in classifying sounds
and their variants and are used to great advantage
in a number of ways. Minimal pairs (los pares con-
trastantes) are derived from the concept of the
phoneme. They are pairs which by contrast prove
whether a change in basic sound will create either
a completely new word or a nonsense syllable.
English has many such pairs sip/zip, tot/top,
ship/sheep, pip/pit, cat/cot, cap/cop, loose/lose,
noose/news, racer/razor. Spanish also admits of

3

many such contrastive pairs cama/gama, pata/bata,
gata/cata, cero/cerro, pero/perro, cata/cada, pa-
nal/penal, peña/pena, año/ano, masa/mesa, gala/gu-
la. In any case, if a change in phone does not
alter the meaning as perceived by the hearer, the
result is only peculiar pronunciation. If, instead, the change is sufficient to cause the
hearer to perceive a new meaning within the internal logic of the language, the result is a new phoneme. The minimal pair is a valuable barometer of
the changes which any given language will accept.

ORGANS USED IN THE PRODUCTION OF SOUND. The organs
involved in producing the accurate, modulated
chains of sound which we normally identify with
speech are the lungs (los pulmones), the windpipe
or trachea (la tráquea), the larynx (la laringe)
with the vocal cords (las cuerdas vocales), the
pharynx (la faringe), the nasal cavity (la cavidad
nasal), and the mouth (la boca) or the buccal
cavity (la cavidad bucal) with the tongue (la lengua), the lips (los labios), the teeth (los dien-
tes), the soft palate (el paladar blando), the
hard palate (el paladar duro), and the alveolar
ridge (los alvéolos), where the teeth meet the gum
line. The tongue itself may be divided into the
apex (el ápice), the frontal portion (la parte anterior), and the posterior portion (el dorso).
Most sounds are produced by breath coming up from
the lungs, enclosed by ribs at the bottom of which
the diaphragm (el diafragma) is found. The action
of the ribs and the diaphragm causes air to flow into and out of the lungs. The stream of air expired
does not go out with an even degree of pressure.
The latter varies according to the corresponding
sound articulated. For example, in the production
of a word like especialmente, the pressure or articulatory thrust is greater on the syllable -men-[1]
than on the rest of the syllables in the word.
Sounds become audible when the stream of air encounters some kind of resistance from the other
organs involved in the production of speech. The
windpipe or trachea is a single tube which links

4

the lungs with the throat through the bronchial tubes (los brónquios). The vocal cords or bands are two pairs of folds of mucous membrane which extend into the larynx. Normally, they remain apart in order to allow for proper breathing. The space between the vocal bands is commonly called the glottis (la glotis). When the vocal cords come together they obstruct the passing air, thereby producing a voiced sound (el sonido sonoro)--one in which there is vibration with or without obstruction in the buccal cavity. For instance, the sound of d in the Spanish word dama is voiced since the vocal cords come into play in its production. A voiceless sound (el sonido sordo) is one in which there may be friction or vibration in the buccal cavity or elsewhere, but there is no obstruction produced by the vocal cords. For example, the t's in the Spanish word total are voiceless since there is a tapping sound produced in the mouth but no obstruction in the glottis, where the vocal cords are located.

If the air is released through the mouth, the result is an oral sound (el sonido bucal). If the air passage is blocked in the mouth and released through the nose (la nariz) or nostrils (los orificios nasales or las narices), we have a nasal sound (el sonido nasal). Generally the position of the tongue determines the types of sound produced. If the stream of air is blocked in the middle but released laterally, a lateral sound (el sonido lateral) results--the l in lado. The apex (el ápice) of the tongue against the teeth produces a dental sound (el sonido dental)--the d's in duende. The tongue flapped against the alveolar ridge produces a vibrant sound (el sonido vibrante), which may be either a simple vibrant (el vibrante simple) as in the r of pera or a multiple vibrant (el vibrante múltiple) as in the rr in perra. The position of the lips is important since it affects the type of articulation also, especially with reference to vowels--open vowels (las vocales abiertas), close vowels (las vocales cerradas), medial vowels (las vocales medias) and others.

5

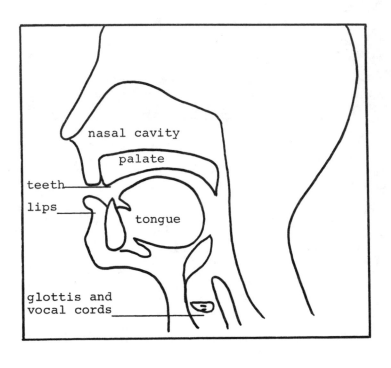

FIGURE 1. SOME ORGANS USED IN THE PRODUCTION OF
SOUND.

6

THE WRITTEN VERSUS THE SPOKEN WORD. In any language there is considerable difference between formal orthographic division of words into syllables, on the one hand, and phonetic syllabication, on the other. The latter is based on the manner in which natives divide words or groups of words when speaking. The traditional orthographic rules of division into syllables are as follows:

1. A single consonant between two vowels becomes the initial consonant of the second syllable.

   a-la-me-da   ba-ta   E-le-na
   pe-rro   pa-ta-ta   ge-ne-ra-li-za

2. The combinations ch, ll, and rr (considered single consonants or digraphs in Spanish) also become the initial consonant of the second syllable.

   ce-rro   e-cho   e-llo
   le-che   o-lla   ta-rro

3. The combinations consonant plus l or consonant plus r always begin the syllable (exceptions: r+l, s+l, t+l, and s+r, which always split as in #4 below).

   a-gra-de-ce   a-pre-su-ra   a-cla-ro
   o-fre-ce   re-pli-ca   ta-bla

4. All other groups of two consonants (including the exceptions in #3 above) separate when they come between vowels, one consonant going with the preceding syllable and the other with the following one.

   ac-ta   bas-ta   can-tar
   Is-ma-el   op-ta   pre-cep-to

5. With more than two consonants between vowels the last consonant initiates the following syllable (including the combinations in #3 above).

   com-pren-de   ex-pre-sión   ins-pi-rar
   trans-pi-ran-te mez-cla   trans-por-te

6. Prefixes are considered a category unto themselves and must always remain separate entities even though they may violate the above rules.

   ab-ne-gar   des-u-nir   en-gran-de-cer
   en-re-dar   sub-en-ten-der   sub-ma-ri-no

7. The vowels present a slightly simpler pic-

7

ture provided one bears in mind that a, e, and o are strong vowels and i(y) and u are weak ones, and that two strong vowels separate into two syllables.

a-ho-rra	a-se-o	cre-a
fe-al-dad	Jo-a-quín	lo-a

8. A strong vowel and a weak vowel coalesce to form one beat or a diphthong (el diptongo).

au-to	bai-le	cau-te-la
deu-da	gai-ta	trai-go

9. If a weak vowel is followed by any vowel (a weak or a strong vowel), it no longer functions as a vowel but assumes the role of a semi-consonant.

bui-tre	ye-rro	tie-ne
pue-de	sien	yun-que

Although this traditional type of division into syllables based on the historical development of the language and conventions of spelling did originally derive from notions of the spoken language, phonetic division into syllables branches out on its own and brings about two changes.

1. The final consonant of one word forms a liaison (el enlace) with the vowels of the following word within the same breath group.

tus años	tu-sa-ños
con un ojo	co-nu-no-jo
un enano	u-ne-na-no
el abrigo	e-la-bri-go

2. Rules pertaining to the prefixes which result from etymological development do not apply.

desunir	de-su-nir
desarraigar	de-sa-rrai-gar
subarrendar	su-ba-rren-dar
subentender	su-ben-ten-der

THE PHONETIC ALPHABET. The characters shown below are based on the International Phonetic Alphabet (el Alfabeto Fonético Internacional). The symbols show in written form what traditional alphabets

8

normally do not show--namely that there are more
vowel and consonant sounds within the sound system
of a language than its traditional alphabet indicates. The Spanish sound symbols are as follows:

[a] a in madre
[b] b in hambre
[ƀ] b in llamaba
[č] ch in techo
[θ] c in centavo (th sound variant)
    z in zapato (th sound variant)
[d] d in dar
[đ] d in nido
[e] e in dedo
[ε] e in cerro
[f] f in feo
[g] g in gato
[ǥ] g in jugo
[i] i in fino
[į] i in perejil
[k] c in carpa
    qu in quema
    qu in quita
[l] l in lana
[ḷ] ll in llama
[y] ll in llama (Latin-American variant)
[m] m in mesa
[m̦] n in enfriar
[n] n in nene
[ɲ] ñ in peña
[o] o in loco
[ɔ] o in tos
[p] p in pata
[r] r in caro
[ř] initial r in Rosa
    rr in tierra
[s] s in peso
    z in vez, c in cien (s sound variant)
[z] s in desde
    z in hallazgo (s sound variant)
[ẕ] z in hallazgo (th sound variant)
[t] t in tapa
[u] u in duda
[ų] u in pulso
[h] j in ojo
    g in gente (Latin-American)[2]

9

[x] j in <u>o</u>jo
g in <u>g</u>ente
[w] u in c<u>u</u>ando
[j] i in h<u>i</u>erro
[ʋ] u in a<u>u</u>n
[ḭ] i in ba<u>i</u>le
y in ho<u>y</u>

The principal use of phonetic alphabets is to aid in a variety of ways in bringing about greater clarity and precision in articulation.

ACCENT OR STRESS (<u>LA ACENTUACIÓN</u>). In Spanish the stressed syllable carries the main emphasis or articulatory thrust. Even though the other syllables in a word do not carry the major stress, they are still pronounced with clarity. Since Spanish is a syllable-timed language, the slurring of syllables is therefore in direct contradiction to its appropriate articulation. In no case does one encounter in Spanish the <u>schwa</u> sound [ə] or [ə], heard so often in English words like <u>again</u>, <u>epaulet</u>, <u>enough</u>, <u>annoy</u>.

Conventionally, one uses the symbol ´ to indicate that the stress of the word is on a particular vowel, should the word be an exception to the two basic rules of Spanish stress.[3] For example, in the word <u>murciélago</u> the vowel e is stressed and this is indicated by the use of the stress accent. Thus written accents in Spanish generally indicate that the words in which they appear are exceptions to the two basic rules. There is, in addition, the <u>acento diferenciador</u>, which is used in the case of monosyllabic words which exist in pairs with completely different meanings--<u>te</u> (you) and <u>té</u> (tea), <u>se</u> (oneself) and <u>sé</u> (I know), <u>si</u> (if, whether) and <u>sí</u> (yes), <u>de</u> (of, from) and <u>dé</u> (give). There is also the accent of interrogation and exclamation (<u>el acento de interrogación y exclamación</u>)--¡qué bueno!, ¿Adónde <u>vas</u>?, ¿Con <u>quién irá</u>?, ¡Quién <u>pudiera</u>!, but like the differentiating accent, it in no way affects articulation.

10

The native uses a change in stress from one
syllable to another in the same word to indicate a
change of meaning. In other words, it is often not
simply a matter of pronouncing words correctly
since this would be merely a phonetic matter. For
instance, Papa stressed on the first syllable means
pope and only pope. In Latin America and elsewhere
it could also be understood to mean potato as in
papas batidas and papas fritas. However, papá
stressed on the second syllable means dad or papa
and nothing else. Aun articulated as one syllable
means even while aún with the stress on the second
syllable means still, yet. The word período
(stressed on the i) generally means epoch, historical period; when stressed on the o, however, it is
frequently understood to mean period of time, a
time interval or the female's time of the month. A
similar case is found in the articulation of océ-
ano, theoretically stressed on the e, but pronounced
oceáno by many of the world's speakers of Spanish.
Pairs like tome and tomé, grite and grité, pague and
pagué, hable and hablé, estudie and estudié, to mention only a few, are all verb forms whose meaning is
changed drastically as a result of the one change in
accent. Therefore, it should be remembered that all
syllables are enunciated clearly and distinctly, but
only one receives a principal emphasis within isolated words. To shift the emphasis from one syllable to another may mean that one is guilty of error
in one of two ways--either by saying one word when
another is intended (critica instead of crítica or
calle instead of callé) or by creating a nonsense
syllable which communicates nothing.

Stress in the spoken language is traditionally
referred to as the prosodic accent (el acento pro-
sódico). Words are normally classified according
to the number of syllables which they contain and
where the stress falls. Acute words (las palabras
agudas) or oxytones (los oxítonos) are stressed on
the final syllable--andar, verter, partir, parlanchín, baladí, chillón, holgazán, londinés. Grave
words (las palabras graves or llanas) or paroxytones (los paroxítonos) are stressed on the penultimate syllable--como, enseña, establece, ensimisma-

11

do, zigzaguea. Proparoxytones (las palabras esdrú-
julas) are stressed on the antepenultimate sylla-
ble--ánimo, luciérnaga, Guantánamo, Málaga, Nérida,
murciélago. Preproparoxytones (las palabras sobres-
drújulas) are stressed three syllables from the end
and are relatively rare in Spanish--lavándoselo,
mandándoselos, peinándosela, refiriéndoselo. Ante-
preproparoxytones are stressed three syllables before the penultimate and do not occur in Spanish.

OPEN AND CLOSED SYLLABLES. (LAS SÍLABAS ABIERTAS
Y CERRADAS). Open and closed syllables are basic
to Spanish pronunciation. We speak of an open syllable as one which ends in a vowel or diphthong.

bo-a	co-mo	deu-da
feu-do	he-chi-za-do	lo-a
lla-ma	pei-ne	rei-na

A closed syllable is one which ends in one or more
consonants.

can-tar	dor-mir	en-ten-der
her-vir	plan-tar	pren-der
vol-car	ver-ter	vis-lum-brar

In order to determine whether a syllable is open or
closed, one must keep in mind the rules that govern
Spanish syllabication. A word or group of words
divides into syllables very differently when pronounced from the way in which they seem to divide
when seen in written form. By way of example, one
of the characteristic features of Spanish is a
shift from open to closed syllable and vice versa in
the formation of the plural (llano > llanos; viudo > viudos; actor > actores; salchichón > salchi-
chones).

HIATUS, SYNAERESIS AND SYNALEPHA. According to the
basic rules of pronunciation, certain vowels come
together to form one syllable in carefully articulated speech. The strong vowels a, e, and o form
separate syllables, and the weak vowels i and u
come together to form one syllable under normal
conditions (pronounced either [wí] or [új]). Also,

12

any combination of a weak and a strong vowel forms
one syllable--guapo, bueno, puerta, ya, yeso, deuda, Souza, hay. The native speaker, however, is
often tempted to glide over two successive identical strong vowels to form one syllable. This phenomenon is called synaeresis (la sinéresis). The
opposite phenomenon is known as hiatus (el hiato).
In fact, both occur frequently. In formal speech
or in cases of contrast or emphasis, hiatus is the
prevailing tendency. In rapid informal speech,
especially if there are two successive identical
vowels, the practice tends to be synaeresis--al-
cohol (ɛlkɔ́l), aprehender (ɛprəndɛ́r), creer (krɛ́r),
leer (lɛ́r), loor (lɔ́r), nihilismo (nɪlízmɔ), zooló-
gico (sɔlóxɪkɔ). Any two vowels, despite rules of
pronunciation and traditional stress, may be reduced to a single syllable. This is often the case
with identical vowels in rapid speech, unstressed
segments, and in other types of careless or popular
speech. To overuse this native tendency frequently
produces undesirable results. In fact, exaggerated
use of synaeresis by speakers who are not comfortable with the language makes for "fake fluency,"
which should be avoided.

Vowels in hiatus often provide a clarity and
precision which are desirable. Hence verbs with
two identical vowels may be pronounced with separate stress on each without producing an artificial
effect. For example, it is legitimate to say
[ləɛ́r] and [krəɛ́r] for leer and creer, especially
when emphasis or formality is desired. The tendency to reduce or close the e in -ear forms such as
costear, regatear, palmotear should be avoided.
Thus the versions [kɔ̀ʃtəɛ́r], [fəqɛtəɛ́r], [pɛlmɔ-
təɛ́r] are preferred to more popular renderings such
as [kɔ̀ʃtjár], [fəqɛtjár], [pɛlmɔtjár]. There is a
point at which relaxed, informal speech falls into
the category of the unacceptable or the substandard.
While its use should not be exaggerated, hiatus in
articulation frequently adds dimensions of clarity
or contrast.

Synalepha (la sinalefa), while somewhat more
complex, is in essence synaeresis between words of

13

the same breath group. One should take into account rules of vowel openness and closeness in linking words between pauses.   In other words, when combining a final vowel of one word with the initial vowel of the next word, the sequence always goes from the more close to the less close vowel or from the less open to the more open vowel. We have already said that if a word within a breath group ends in a vowel and the next word begins with the same vowel, one hears these vowels as only one sound.

puerta abierta   [pwérteɓjértɐ]
buena alma   [bwénálmɐ]
olvidada acción   [ɔlbiðáðɐksjɔn]
rostro ofensivo   [rɔ́strɔfənsíbɔ]
ensanche exterior   [ənsánčəṣtərjɔ́r]

A similar synalepha is possible in the case of vowels from most open to less open--here from a to e

amada esposa   [ɐmáðeəspósɐ]
querida estudiante   [kəríðeəṣtnðjántə]
puerta entreabierta [pwértɐəntrɐ̈ɓjértɐ]

or from a less open vowel to an even less open one

danzante inútil   [dənsánteinútil]
agente huraño   [əxéntéurán͡ɔ]
gente indecente   [xentɛiɲdəséɲtɐ].

One may combine vowel sounds which go from less openness to more openness and vice versa provided the stress is on the most open of the vowels in combination.

THEORY

A. ANSWER THE FOLLOWING QUESTIONS BRIEFLY.
1. What is the function of utterances in human communication?
2. How does one define phonetics?
3. What is a phoneme?
4. What is a phone? an allophone?
5. What is a voiced sound? a voiceless sound?
6. What are the principal organs used in the production of sound?
7. What is a minimal pair? Give four examples in English and four in Spanish.
8. What is the difference between an open and closed syllable?
9. What is stress or accent?
10. What is prosodic stress? Give an example.

B. FILL IN THE BLANKS ACCORDING TO THE SENSE OF EACH STATEMENT.
1. In phonetic syllabication the final consonant of one word forms a(n) _____ with the following word.
2. Proparoxytones are words stressed on the _____ syllable.
3. If the tongue is flapped, a(n) _____ sound results.
4. A(n) _____ syllable is one which ends in a vowel or diphthong.
5. Allophones are sound variants of a basic _____.
6. A(n) _____ is a word stressed on the penultimate syllable.
7. _____ accent refers in general to the stress of the spoken language.
8. A _____ sound is one in which the sound is made by releasing air through the mouth.
9. A _____ sound is one in which there may be friction but no obstruction produced by the vocal cords.
10. Vibrations in Spanish are always identified with the consonants _____.
11. The frontal portion of the tongue is usually referred to as its _____.
12. Anteprepoparoxytones are words which have

their stress on the _____ syllable from the last.

13. Synaeresis and synalepha refer to the _____ of identical or similar vowels in words or breath groups.

14. Palabras llanas are words stressed on the _____ syllable.

PRACTICE

A. PRONOUNCE EACH OF THE FOLLOWING WORDS CAREFULLY AND THEN UNDERLINE THE STRESSED SYLLABLE IN EACH CASE.

CUE	RESPONSE (ORAL)	RESPONSE
MODEL: palpita	"palpita"	palpita
nene		
comunica		
Valladolid		
llamaba		
loco		
estoy		
balbucea		
perjudica		
tutear		
lunes		
bondad		
seseo		
hambre		
jugo		
Dolores		
virtud		
ventana		
apresura		
hablador		

B. PROVIDE A WORD IN WHICH EACH OF THESE SOUNDS MAY BE USED.

1. [θ] _____
2. [đ] _____
3. [k] _____
4. [s] _____
5. [z] _____
6. [b] _____
7. [f] _____

16

8. [l̩] ══════
9. [ɹ̩] ══════
10. [n̩] ══════

C. DIVIDE THE FOLLOWING WORDS INTO TRADITIONAL SYL-
   LABLES

acta	....	hallazgo	....
concepto	....	echar	....
expresar	....	precepto	....
entablar	....	expresión	....
aclarar	....	inspirar	....
generalizar	....	enredar	....
submarino	....	gitano	....
Málaga	....	desunir	....
transpirante	....	alrededor	....

D. TELL WHICH OF THE FOLLOWING WORDS ARE <u>ACUTE</u>,
   <u>GRAVE</u> OR <u>PROPAROXYTONES</u>.

llamar	....	luciérnaga	....
comedor	....	inyección	....
libertad	....	estoy	....
cavidad	....	hablan	....
decir	....	estricto	....
sátira	....	repitiéndole	....
todo	....	apóstol	....
vendiéndolo	....	tomad	....
Zúñiga	....	albóndiga	....
relámpago	....	alcázar	....

E. ARTICULATE THE FOLLOWING GROUPS OF WORDS AC-
   CORDING TO NORMAL HISPANIC SPEECH HABITS (SYNA-
   LEPHA).

	CUE	RESPONSE	RESPONSE
MODEL	tus	tus	
		...	
	arreglos	arreglos	
		....	
			tus⌢arreglos
			....
	mis	....	
	hijos	....	
			....
	con	....	
	ésta	....	
			....

17

sus   . . . .
árboles   . . . .
                              . . . .

con   . . . .
el   . . . .
ojo   . . . .
                              . . . .

el   . . . .
acta   . . . .
                              . . . .

el   . . . .
atrio   . . . .
                              . . . .

las   . . . .
últimas   . . . .
épocas   . . . .
                              . . . .

los   . . . .
abrigos   . . . .
                              . . . .

tus   . . . .
ensueños   . . . .
                              . . . .

las   . . . .
aves   . . . .
                              . . . .

tus   . . . .
abuelos   . . . .
                              . . . .

los   . . . .
últimos   . . . .
                              . . . .

el   . . . .
ante   . . . .
                              . . . .

con   . . . .
un   . . . .
enano   . . . .
                              . . . .

mis   . . . .
artículos . . . .
                              . . . .

el   . . . .
hacha   . . . .
                              . . . .

18

F. PRACTICE OPENING THE O'S IN THE FOLLOWING WORDS
   BY GIVING THE SINGULAR FORM IN EACH CASE.
                    CUE   RESPONSE
MODEL
                    [o]   [ɔ]
                  actores   actor
conductores   ....   profesores ....
pecadores   ....   pescadores ....
reflectores   ....   traductores ....
constructores ....   cantores   ....
bailadores   ....   resplandores..........
fumadores   ....   oradores   ....
trabajadores   ....   inspectores ....
luchadores   ....   confesores ....

G. PRACTICE CLOSING THE O'S IN THE FOLLOWING WORDS
   BY GIVING THE PLURAL FORM IN EACH CASE.
                    CUE   RESPONSE
MODEL   [ɔ]   [o]
                  infanzón   infanzones
dormilón   ....   bodegón   ....
oración   ....   hombrón   ....
cerrazón   ....   peatón   ....
colchón   ....   don   ....
apretón   ....   guión   ....
llorón   ....   nación   ....
cabrón   ....   facción   ....
mesón   ....   halcón   ....
Sansón   ....   malecón   ....

ASI SE DICE
     It is advisable to associate sound with
meaning. Spanish is rich in riddles, tongue
twisters, proverbs, and idioms which reflect the
culture and civilization of the many peoples that
speak it. Repeat carefully each segment and finally the complete statement as given.[4]
Al pan   ....
pan   ....
al pan pan   ....
y al   ....
Al pan pan y al   ....
vino   ....
vino   ....
y al vino vino   ....
Al pan pan y al vino vino.   ....

19

```
A lo                    ..........
A lo hecho              ..........
pecho                   ..........
hecho pecho             ..........
A lo hecho pecho.       ...............................

En un                   ..........
en un plato             ..........
plato de trigo          ..........
en un plato de trigo               ..........
comen                   ..........
comen tres              ..........
comen tres tigres       ..........
En un plato de trigo comen tres tigres. ...........

El dar                  ..........
El dar es               ..........
dar es honor            ..........
El dar es honor         ..........
y el                    ..........
y el pedir              ..........
pedir dolor             ..........
y el pedir dolor        ..........
El dar es honor, y el pedir dolor. ................

Cada                    ..........
cabeza                  ..........
cabeza es               ..........
es un                   ..........
es un mundo             ..........
Cada cabeza es un mundo.        ....................
```

FOOTNOTES

[1] See pages 10-12 and 110-116 for stress.

[2] This sound is the relaxed aspiration of the speech of certain southern Spaniards and most Latin Americans. The more typically Castilian aspiration is more pronounced and in some cases harsher [x]. This sound in either version occurs with j before any vowel, g before e and i, and, in sporadic cases with x before vowels in certain family names and place names; i. e., Ximénez, Jiménez; México, Méjico.

[3] Rule One: when a word ends in a vowel or -n or -s, the stress is on the penultimate syllable as in comunica, traduce, hablan, comen, Dolores, flores; Rule Two: when a word ends in a consonant except -n or -s, the stress is on the final syllable as in hablar, trabajar, conocer, atender, partir, lucir, Muñoz, Valladolid, Madrid, farol.

[4] For the meaning of all rhymes, sayings, proverbs, riddles, tongue twisters, and related material, see Appendix II.

CHAPTER TWO

VOWEL SOUNDS

INTRODUCTION. One often thinks of any conventional
alphabet in terms of vowels and consonants. Traditionally, we think of the Spanish vowels as being a,
e, i, o, u, and all the other letters of the alphabet as consonants. Diphthongs are combinations of
strong vowels and the semi-consonants i (y) and u
which form one syllable as in viaje, bien, socio,
cuando, cuero, cuota. When i (y) or u follows a
strong vowel, it functions as a semi-vowel as in
baile, caimán, boina, aun, deuda, bou, causa, cauce. Diphthongs are also formed by the coming together of two weak vowels--diurno, diurético, muy,
gratuito, buitre, viuda, cuita. Triphthongs (los
triptongos) are a combination of three vowels with
a strong vowel in the middle flanked by weak vowels
as in Paraguay, miau, escorpioide, Guaira, Vieytes,
apaciguáis, continuéis. Diphthongs and triphthongs
are an important part of the Spanish sound system
since they have a considerably high frequency.

What exactly is a vowel? A vowel is a voiced
sound whose basic quality is determined by the
shape of the mouth and lips, but more goes on in-
side the oral cavity. The quality of the vowel is
determined to some extent by the opening between
the jaws, the shape which the tongue assumes, and
the position of the soft palate. If the tongue
gradually moves forward and is raised toward the
front palate, the result is a front vowel (la vocal anterior). In Spanish, e and i are considered
front vowels as in deber, verter, jira, pila. If
the tongue gradually rises toward the back of the
oral cavity, the result is the back vowels (las vocales posteriores) o and u as in motor, voto, choclo, fuma, puma. The vowel a has a medial articulation in most cases.

Openness or closeness of vowels is determined
by the relative distance between the tongue and the

23

roof of the oral cavity. When the lips are relaxed
and lowered, an open vowel is produced. Think of
the English lost sheep and their "bah, bah, bah."
On the other hand, a close vowel is produced when
there is greater tension and elevation of the tongue
toward the palate. The ee, ea sound in beet, bleat
is a good example of this phoneme. An age-old
treatment of vowels is to view them in a triangle of
openness and closeness. Traditionally, this focus
is called a vocalic triangle (el triángulo vocáli-
co). According to this view, a is the most open
vowel, i, the most close of the front vowels, and u,
the most close of the back vowels.

Spanish vowels have a clarity and precision
which distinguish them from the more diphthongal
quality of English vowels. The glides in the English vowels e and o in tea, she, and toe, row are
never heard in Spanish. Vowels should be viewed as
separate entities at first, this being the most important stage of their perception and production.
Then they should be assimilated as parts of other
sounds, frequently diphthongs and triphthongs, or
in conjunction with consonants. Although the articulatory thrust is upon the stressed vowel in a
word or breath group, initial and final unaccented
vowels are given the same degree of precise pronunciation. While unstressed vowels are produced with
less emphasis, their degree of laxity is never so
great as it is in normally produced English vowels.

THE VOWELS VIEWED INDIVIDUALLY.

    1. Medial a (a media) $\lceil \alpha \rceil$
      In producing the sound of the vowel a, the
tongue lies almost flat against the lower ridge
of the teeth and gums. The posterior portion
of the tongue is elevated slightly toward the
soft palate. Of all the vowels, a is produced
with the greatest degree of openness of the
buccal cavity. The most general Spanish a,
especially in accented syllables, is medial a.
      dama [dáme]⁵   paso [páso]

24

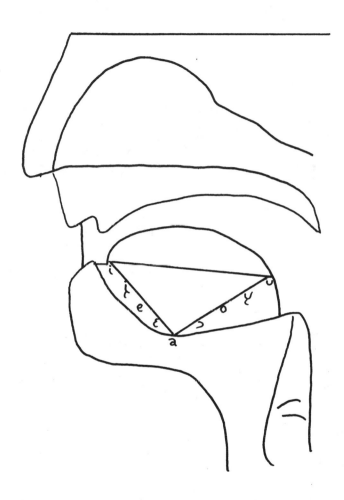

FIGURE 2   VOCALIC TRIANGLE

25

hallar [pǎár]　　　rana [ráne]
When a comes before a palatal sound such as ch [ĉ],
ll [ĺ], ñ [ņ], and y [ɏ], it is generally considered a palatal a. Often this distinction is omitted in the actual transcription of sounds.

2. Velar a (a velar) $\lceil$ a $\rceil$
　　　The position in the mouth is more toward
the back of the buccal cavity if compared with
medial a. It always occurs in the diphthong
au--stressed or unstressed. It also takes
place before o Bilbao, Mindanao, cortaos. It
is also found in syllables followed by l, any
aspiration, or intervocalic g--manantial, agua,
bagual, ultraje. Observe the velar quality of
a in the following words:

ajo	[áxː]	pausa	[páuse]
cautela	[kautéle]	quitaos	[kitáɔs]
federal	[faðarál]	pago	[páɡː]
hago	[áɡː]	comunal	[kɔmʌnál]

3. Lax a (a relajada) $\lceil$ɐ$\rceil$
　　　Lax or relaxed a is always encountered in
any unstressed syllable. (See fig. 9).

We have seen that the basic phoneme /A/ has
three allophonic variants medial a [a], velar a
[a], and lax a [ɐ] (and palatal a, which we have
chosen to disregard). While these distinctions are
less important in Spanish speech than they are in
some other languages, the basic distinguishing features of each allophonic variant should be kept in
mind (see fig. 3).

4. Close e (e cerrada) $\lceil$ e $\rceil$
　　　The middle of the tongue is raised somewhat toward the palate with the tip of the
tongue touching the lower teeth. The opening
of the mouth is somewhat more reduced than for
the articulation of a but somewhat greater than
for the articulation of i. The English
speaker should avoid lapsing into glide sounds

26

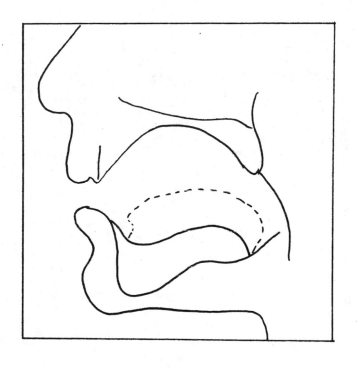

FIGURE 3   VOWEL <u>A</u> AND ITS ARTICULATION

27

as they are very unpleasing to the Hispanic
ear, especially in the production of e̲ and o̲.

The openness and closeness of vowels depend upon their immediate linguistic ambience
(el ambiente lingüístico); that is to say, a
vowel is open or close according to the contact
which it makes with other sounds. For example,
e̲ is open in contact with rr, yielding perro
and cerro, whereas e̲ is close in open syllables
as in pero and cero. The phoneme /E/ is an important one in Spanish since many contrastive
pairs depend upon the difference between the
open allophone [ɛ] and the·close one [e].
While some degree of openness and closeness
varies considerably from one Hispanic speech
zone to the next, it remains a contrastive feature which is important not only from the point
of view of correct articulation, but meaning as
well.

Where exactly does close e̲ occur? It appears in all open syllables (syllables which
end in the vowel). It also appears in all syllables closed by d̲, m̲, n̲, and x̲, s̲, z̲, whether
voiced or voiceless. Syllables closed by final d̲ are not really absolutely closed since
this sound tends to be barely perceptible in
spoken Spanish. Sibilants (las sibilantes) or
ssss/zzzz sounds do not open the preceding e̲
either. The same may be said of the effect of
nasals (m̲, n̲) upon the vowel e̲. The sound of
x̲ presents a more complex picture. Frequently,
in Spain and in some parts of Latin America it
has a voiced sound when between vowels [ɸz],
as in the word exacto [əɸzáktɔ], whereas elsewhere it remains voiceless [ks]. In some
variants of peninsular Spanish x̲ is heard as a
simple s̲ [s] before consonants, while in other
areas it may be heard either as the voiced or
voiceless variant. In Castile the x̲ of a few
words is an automatic s̲--taxi [tásı], Xiquena
[sıkénɐ]. Observe the sound e̲ in the following words:

aldea [ɐ̨ldée̞]   peso [pésɔ]

28

```
este  [ésta]              sed    [séd]
hablé [eblé]              veces  [bésəs]
harén [erén]              vez    [bés]
```

5. Open e (e abierta) $\left[\varepsilon\right]$ or $\left[\epsilon\right]$

In pronouncing open e, the aperture in the
buccal cavity is enlarged since the tongue-pal-
ate distance is greater than in the case of
close e and lesser than in a. In other words,
the degree of openness in open e is midway between the two sounds. This vowel is the one
which most closely resembles close e although
there is greater aperture in the oral cavity.
In addition, the place of articulation is farther back along the hard palate. This sound
is much closer to the -er in leather and fea-
ther than it is to much of American-English articulation in words like rate, fate, pay, say,
although the -er is frequently a schwa.

Open e is heard first of all in all closed
syllables or syllables which end in a consonant
with the exception of those closed by d, m, n,
s, z, and x. It also takes place before any
aspiration, which in the written language is
either a j or a g (phonetically [x] or [h]).
E is also open in the diphthongs ei (ey) [ɛi]
and eu [éy]. Open e also occurs in cases of
contact, the latter referring to the fact that
the sound affects the openness and closeness
whether it precedes or follows the vowel (in
this case e). The vowel e is open whenever it
comes in contact with strong r or rr, both multiple vibrants (las vibrantes múltiples),
whether the vibrant is first or last.6 Observe
the sound e in the following words:

```
barrer  [beřér]          enreda [ənřédɐ]
deleite [dəlɛitə]        deudo  [déydː]
eje     [éxa]            res    [řés]
erre    [éřə]            vender [bəndér]
```

6. Lax e (e relajada) $\left[\partial\right]$

Lax e is heard in all unstressed syllables

29

(see fig. 9).

Phoneme /**E**/ has three allophonic variants
close e [e], open e [ɛ], and lax e [ə].

7. Close i (i cerrada) [i]
In producing this vowel sound accurately,
the tip of the tongue rests lightly upon the
inner ridge of the lower teeth. At the same
time, the frontal portion of the tongue is elevated in the direction of the hard palate while
the sides of the tongue make a kind of contact
with the palate. The sound produced is one
which is analogous to ea and ee in teeth, meet,
sea, beat. Again one should avoid glide sounds
as in canteen, Aberdeen, glean. Spanish close
i is close in all syllables which are open
(those not closed by a consonant). Observe
close i in the following cases:

lima	[límɐ]	Potosí	[pɔtɔsí]
mira	[mírɐ]	tío	[tíɔ]
partí	[pɐrtí]	tina	[tínɐ]
fino	[fínɔ]	cima	[símɐ]

8. Open i (i abierta) [ɨ]
In the production of this sound the tongue
assumes basically the same position as in the
case of its close variant. However, the
opening of the buccal cavity is somewhat
greater, the lip tightness slightly reduced,
and the distance between the tongue and the
palate is greater. This sound is analogous to
i and ee in thin, sin, been. The more open
variant typical of bliss, kiss, tryst should
be strenuously avoided.

Open i is used basically in closed syllables, and especially in syllables closed by
the laterals (las laterales) l and r and by the
sibilant s (z). Notice the open i's in the
following cases:

alfil	[ɐlfɨl]	listo	[lɨstɔ]
abril	[ɐbrɨl]	mismo	[mɨzmɔ]
emir	[ɐmɨr]	vivir	[bɨbɨr]

30

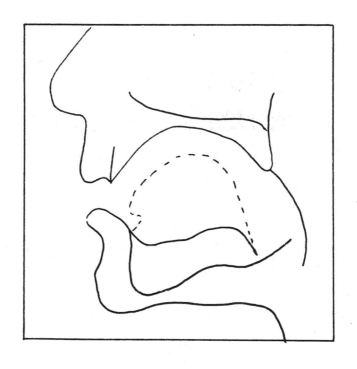

FIGURE 4   VOWEL E̲ AND ITS ARTICULATION

31

perejil ⌈parəxíl⌉ quisiste ⌈kisísta⌉[7]
The sound i opens in contact with the multiple
vibrant r ⌈r̄⌉; that is, after initial r or before or after the digraph rr. Compare the effects of r in the following cases:

barril ⌈bariíl⌉   mirra ⌈mír̄ɛ⌉
Rita   ⌈ríte⌉   río   ⌈r̄íɔ⌉
rizo   ⌈r̄íso⌉   risa ⌈r̄ísɛ⌉
rico   ⌈r̄íkɔ⌉   rima ⌈r̄ímɛ⌉

The same type of open i occurs before any aspiration (⌈x⌉ or ⌈h⌉) since this aperture actually facilitates the harsher sound that follows
it.

revoltijo ⌈r̄əbɔ́ltíxɔ⌉   desdije ⌈dəzdɟíxə⌉
baratija ⌈bɐretɟíxɛ⌉   hijo   ⌈íxɔ⌉
sortija   ⌈sɔrtɟíxɛ⌉   dije   ⌈dɟíxə⌉
clavija   ⌈klɛbɟíxɛ⌉   elijo   ⌈əlɟíxɔ⌉

9. Lax i (i relajada) ⌈ ị ⌉
The most relaxed form of i, lax or relaxed
i. is any i which is not stressed and to which
none of the aforementioned rules applies. Its
sound is reminiscent of the sound -in- in in-
stigate, institute, thin, but the excessively
relaxed quality of the English equivalent
should be avoided.

10. Semivocalic i (i semivocálica) ⌈ i̯ ⌉
This sound is found in all diphthongs and
triphthongs in which i is the final element.
In this type of vowel combination only one element is heard as the essential sound; that is
to say, only one vowel receives the principal
stress while the other vowel or vowels are articulated more weakly. Observe the following
semivowels:

avaluéis   ⌈ɐbɛlwéi̯s⌉   caray ⌈kɐrái̯⌉
amortiguáis ⌈ɐmɔrtiɣwái̯s⌉ peine ⌈péi̯nə⌉
Monterrey   ⌈mɔntərréi̯⌉   hoy   ⌈ɔ́i̯⌉
rey   ⌈r̄éi̯⌉   muy   ⌈múi̯⌉

32

11. Semiconsonantal i (i semiconsonantal) [j]
     The frontal portion of the tongue is ele-
vated toward the hard palate in the production
of this sound. There is heard a barely perceptible friction (la fricción or el roce) made
by the sides of the tongue as they make contact
with the palate. This sound is vaguely similar to y in such words as yankee, yen, yesterday, but the Spanish sound is more close. I in
Spanish is semiconsonantal when it appears before a vowel with which it forms one syllable.
Since it is semiconsonantal in these cases,
the following vowel is the principal vocalic
sound. Observe the semiconsonantal i in the
following cases:

abulia	[ɐβúlja]	pie	[pjé]
clemencia	[klɐménsja]	piojo	[pjóxɔ]
familia	[femílja]	quien	[kjén]
piensa	[pjénsɐ]	quiero	[kjérɔ]

     The basic phoneme /I/ has five allophones in
Spanish: close i [i], open i [i̯], lax i [ı], semiconsonantal i [j], and semivocalic i [i̯] (see fig.
5).

12. Close o (o cerrada) [O]
     In producing this sound, the tongue is
elevated sufficiently in the direction of the
soft palate. The tip of the tongue makes contact with the lower alveolar ridge. Unlike o
in English words like anon, cow, drone, fodder, fold, and on, a single phoneme must be
maintained. The Spanish sound only vaguely approximates o in the words bone, tone, alone,
atone. In order to produce the very distinct
quality of close o, a somewhat tense buccal
aperture is desirable. Close o occurs only in
open syllables. Observe close o in the following cases:

enfoque	[ɐmfókɐ]	loco	[lókɔ]
cosa	[kósɐ]	Lola	[lólɐ]
decoro	[dɐkórɔ]	mozo	[mósɔ]
fogoso	[fɔɣósɔ]	todo	[tóðɔ]

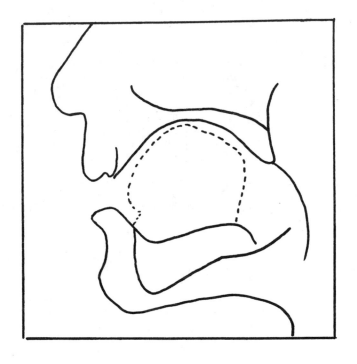

FIGURE 5   VOWEL I̲ AND ITS ARTICULATION

34

13. Open o (o abierta) $\begin{bmatrix} \mathbf{\mathfrak{I}} \end{bmatrix}$ or $\begin{bmatrix} \mathbf{Q} \end{bmatrix}$

In pronouncing open o the position of the
tongue is essentially the same as for close o.
There is, however, a wider opening between the
tongue and the soft palate. The aperture of
the buccal cavity is more pronounced, the lips
being slightly more relaxed. The sound of
Spanish open o is similar to a taut English o
without the typical glide. It is found in the
following cases:

    a) in closed syllables

        coliflor [kɔliflɔr]   ardor [ɐrdɔr]

        candor [kɐndɔr]   flor [flɔr]

        señor [sɐnɔr]   col [kɔl]

    b) in contact with rr (including initial r
      [r̄])

        horror [ɔr̄ɔr]   roto [r̄ɔtɔ]

        corro [kɔr̄ɔ]   rosa [r̄ɔsɐ]

        ronco [r̄ɔŋkɔ]   rojo [r̄ɔxɔ]

    c) when stressed between a and l and a and
      r

        bailaora [bailɐɔrɐ]   la hora [lɐ ɔrɐ]

        cantaora [kɐntɐɔrɐ] la ola [lɐ ɔlɐ]

        ella ora [ɐlɐ ɔrɐ]   ahora [ɐɔrɐ]

    d) when before an aspiration

        escojo [ɐskɔxɔ]   piojo [pjɔhɔ]

        hoja [ɔhɐ]   Rioja [r̄jɔhɐ]

        ojo [ɔxɔ]   flojo [flɔxɔ]

    e) in the diphthongs -oi (-oy), -ou

        boina [bɔinɐ]   Sousa [sɔusɐ]

        bou [bɔu]   oiga [ɔiɡɐ]

        soy [sɔi]   Mou [mɔu]

14. Lax o (o relajada) $\begin{bmatrix} \mathbf{\mathcal{O}} \end{bmatrix}$

Lax o occurs in all syllables which are
not stressed (see fig. 9).

The phoneme /O/ has three allophonic
variants close o [o], open o [ɔ], and lax o
[ɔ].

35

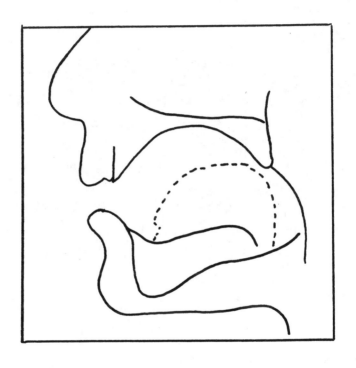

FIGURE 6   VOWEL <u>O</u> AND ITS ARTICULATION

15. Close u (u cerrada) $\lceil \mathsf{U} \rceil$

There is an elevation toward the back of the tongue when articulating this sound. The tip of the tongue is kept on a level with the lower alveolar ridge. There is clearly a more tautly rounded effect here than in the case of close o. The sound of close u remotely approximates the sound of oo in the words spoon, moon, and noon.

pulula	[pʌlúℓɐ]	puño	[púnɔ]
luna	[lúnɐ]	tuna	[túnɐ]
pluma	[plúmɐ]	uva	[úbɐ]
puma	[púmɐ]	una	[únɐ]

16. Open u (u abierta) $\lceil \mathsf{ʋ} \rceil$

This sound is produced exactly in the same manner as described for close u except that there is a greater opening between the elevated back portion of the tongue and there is slightly less tension in the buccal aperture. The sound is midway between the close u in Spanish and the u in pudding, hood, and stood, but the relaxation is never excessive. Open u is found in all closed syllables, in syllables in contact with [f], and before aspirations ([x], [h]). Observe open u in the following words:

Catalayud	[kɐtɐlɐɣʋ́ᵈ]	atún	[ɐtʋ́n]
virtud	[bɪrtʋ́ᵈ]	lujo	[lʋ́xɔ]
bruja	[brʋ́xɐ]	burro	[bʋ́fɔ]
luzco	[lʋ́skɔ]	común	[kɔmʋ́n]

17. Lax u (u relajada) $\lceil \mathsf{ʌ} \rceil$

Lax u occurs in any unstressed position (see fig. 9).

18. Semivocalic u (u semivocálica) $\lceil \mathsf{ʋ} \rceil$

This sound is produced when u is the weak element in a combination of vowels; that is, whenever u occurs after the strong vowels a, e, and o or after the weak vowel i, it becomes

37

the secondary vowel heard as part of the strong
vowel. One should remember that the first element is a strong ah when combined in the au
combination. One should avoid the combination
which sounds like ow as in cow or ouch uttered
in parts of the United States. Observe carefully the semivocalic sounds in the following
combinations:

neuralgia	[nɛurálxja]	cauce	[káusə]
aplauso	[ɛpláusː]	causa	[káusɐ]
deuda	[déuɐ̯ɛ]	pauta	[páu̯tɛ]
sauce	[sáu̯ɵə]	aun	[áu̯n]

19. Semiconsonantal u (u semiconsonantal) [W]
    This sound is similar in articulation to
close o produced with a greater degree of
brevity. There is also the slightest, almost
imperceptible friction since the vowel assumes
a partially consonantal function. This sound
is found when u occurs initially with a vowel
with which it forms one syllable. Observe the
semi-consonant u in the following cases:

acueducto	[ɛkwedúktː]	bueno	[bwénː]
puerto	[pwértː]	suelo	[swélː]
abuelo	[ɛbwélː]	cuando	[kwándː]
duende	[dwéndɐ]	puente	[pwéntɐ]

The phoneme /ʊ/ is very important in
Spanish. For English speakers the main
carry-overs seem to be pronouncing au as in
ouch! and gliding the u in general, both of
which should be avoided. U has five allophones: close u [u], open u [ʊ], lax u [ʌ],
semivocalic u [u̯], and semiconsonantal u [w].
(See fig. 7).

38

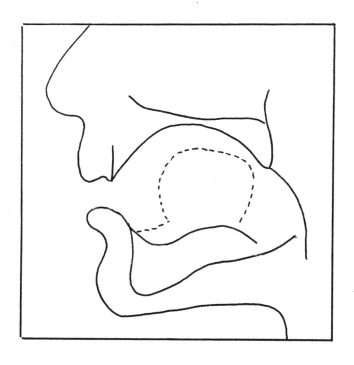

FIGURE 7   VOWEL U̲ AND ITS ARTICULATION

39

FIGURE 8 VOWELS

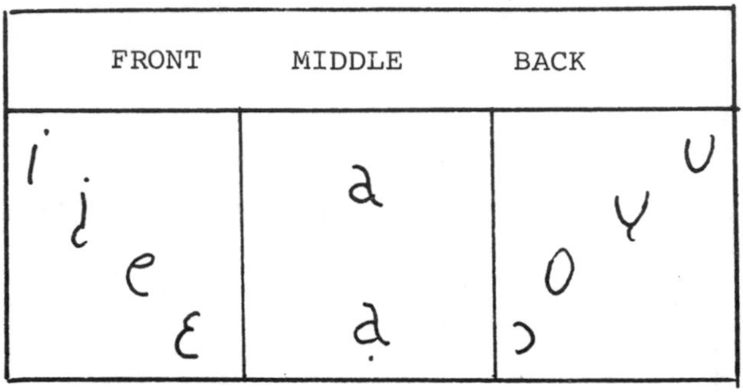

FRONT	MIDDLE	BACK
i ɪ e ɛ	ə ɑ	ɔ o ʊ ᵁ

FIGURE 9 LAX VOWELS

FRONT	MIDDLE	BACK
ɪ ə	ɐ	ᵁ ᶜ

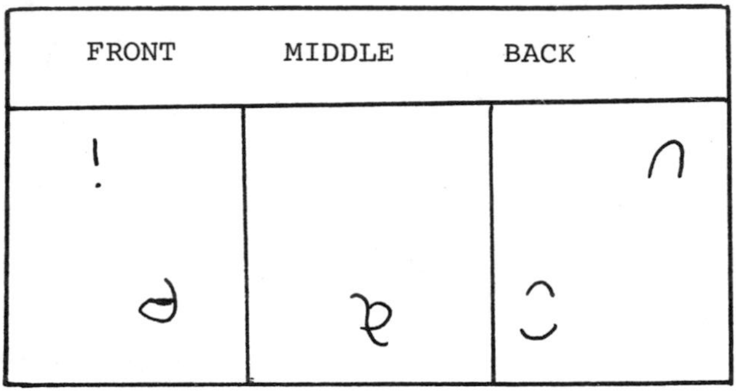

ANOTHER LOOK AT VOWELS IN COMBINATION. We have already mentioned diphthongs and triphthongs--combinations in each case of a strong vowel plus a weak vowel, two weak vowels, or, in the case of triphthongs, a strong vowel flanked by two weak vowels. Let us review that a, e, and o are strong vowels (las vocales fuertes), while i and u are weak vowels (las vocales débiles). Diphthongs may be combinations of strong plus weak vowels

paulatino	[áu̯]		Europa	[έu̯]
neutro	[έu̯]		caray	[ái̯]
Sousa	[óu̯]		reina	[έi̯]

or weak plus strong vowels

monopolio	[jó]		familia	[já]
cuando	[wá]		cuero	[wé]
duomo	[wó]		hierro	[jέ]

or any combination of the two weak vowels

diurético	[jú]		gratuito	[wí]
cuita	[wi̯]		cuidar	[wi̯]
yugo	[jú]		yunque	[jú]

Triphthongs normally have a strong vowel at the core with a weak vowel preceding and following

continuáis	[wái̯]	Camagüey	[wέi̯]	riais	[jái̯]
perpetuáis	[wái̯]	avaluéis	[wέi̯]	miau	[jáu̯]
acentuéis	[wέi̯]	actuáis	[wái̯]	buey	[wέi̯]

In combinations of three vowels one may proceed according to the degree of perceptibility--from the more open to the less open vowel as follows:

a e i, a e u, a o i, a a e, a a u

or from less open to more open vowel

i e a, u e a, i o a, u o a, i a a, u a a

Should there occur a vowel in the middle that is more close than either vowel on each side, the sound system requires a separation into two distinct syllables. This does away with the triphthong entirely. For purposes of clarity, we have chosen not to relax vowels in these combinations in the transcriptions although they are relaxed in actual articulation. When the weak vowels occur as the final element, they are considered semi-vowels ([i̯], [u̯]). When they are the initial element, they are semi-consonants ([w], [j]). The combination of two weak vowels presents somewhat of a problem in Spanish. Normally, in these combinations the second element is considered the main vowel while the first is con-

41

sidered a semi-consonant. This is the normal focus
of a strong vowel plus a weak one and vice versa.
Spanish does, however, have some inconsistencies in
the combinations -uɨ and -iu. For instance, in the
infinitive form huɨr, which would be considered one
syllable according to the traditional rules of pronunciation, the principal stress falls on the i as
in ⌈wέr⌉. However this verb and many others ending
in -uir are generally pronounced with a rather clear
hiatus huir ⌈ʌ-ίr⌉, concluir ⌈kɔŋklʌ-ίr⌉, argüir
⌈ɛrɥʌ-ίr⌉. It is difficult in these cases to be
very arbitrary since one hears both types of articulation in Spain from north to south, not to mention
the rest of the Spanish-speaking world. Other words
like brioso, diario, dieta, and diurno tend to preserve the hiatus, possibly for reasons of etymology.

NORTHERN	SPAIN	ELSEWHERE
buitre	⌈bwítra⌉	⌈búįtra⌉
cuida	⌈kwíðe⌉	⌈kúįðe⌉
descuida	⌈daskwíðe⌉	⌈daskúįðe⌉
gratuito	⌈qrɛtwítɔ⌉	⌈qrɛtúįtɔ⌉
muy	⌈mwí⌉	⌈múį⌉

These divisions are somewhat arbitrary since both in
Spain and Latin America exceptions are heard for a
variety of reasons. Some features of language are
putatively "southern," others "eastern," and still
others, "northern." In many cases these designations
are inaccurate but are used frequently by the layman to characterize the general articulation of one
area as contrasted with that of another area, or,
more importantly, with the articulation of his own
native area. Frequently, these oversimplifications
do serve a purpose. More often than not, they are
used to separate or even attack speech patterns and
forms of pronunciation which are different from
one's own. The fact remains that forms of language
do not fit so neatly into patterns of geographical,
political, or socioeconomic distributions. The division into regions or zones is used often by students of language merely to indicate general trends
and developments indigenous to certain areas.
These divisions may serve to point out how certain
speech zones incline in one direction or another

42

with reference to articulation, intonation, or other features of speech. Frequently, a more helpful approach is to think in terms of features of language which are primary and those which are secondary in one region as contrasted with another zone. One should bear in mind, however, that frequently geographical distribution in terms of language practice is only a guide--often arbitrary--and that there is considerable overlapping from region to region and zone to zone.

SPECIAL LINKAGE PROBLEMS. Linkage words like y, e, o, and u are special cases of articulation depending upon the ambience in which they occur. They normally take place in order to facilitate the uninterrupted flow of speech characteristic of natives. An analogous situation in English is found in the difference in pronunciation of the articles--the ⌐ɣi⌐ apple and the ⌐ðə⌐ beginning and a ⌐ə⌐ book and an ⌐ən⌐ angel.

The conjunction y is generally linked with a preceding or following sound according to the rules which follow:
1. When between consonants, it functions as a lax i:
   van y vienen   ⌐bá ni bjénən⌐
   luz y sombra   ⌐lú si sɔ́mbrɐ⌐
   papel y sobre   ⌐pɐpé li sóbrə⌐
   mujer y marido   ⌐mʌxé ri mɐrídɔ⌐
2. When initial in a breath group before a consonant, it is also lax i:
   y lo dijo   ⌐i lɔ díxɔ⌐
   y no lo quiso   ⌐i nɔ lɔ kísɔ⌐
   y vendrá   ⌐i bəndrá⌐
   y trabaja mucho ⌐i trɐbáxɐ múĉɔ⌐
3. When preceded by the consonants -s, -z, or -d, y is articulated as the voiced palatal fricative ⌐y⌐, frequently sonorizing the previous consonant:
   lapiz y hoja   ⌐lápiᶻ yɔ́xɐ ⌐
   duermes y oras   ⌐dwɛ́rməz yɔ́rɐs⌐
   Muñoz y Orozco   ⌐mʌnɔ́z yɔrɔ́skɔ⌐

43

libertad
y hermandad ⌈l!ɓərtáᵈ yərmɐɳdaᵈ⌉
In certain types of articulation the sound ⌈y⌉ acquires an affricate quality ⌈ŷ⌉-una y otras veces
⌈únɐ ŷótrɐʐ ɓésəs⌉.

4. When following all other consonants and preceding a vowel, it is articulated as the semiconsonant ⌈j⌉:
   gritan y hablan   ⌈qritɐn jáɓlɐn⌉
   altar y adorno   ⌈ɐltár jaɖórnᴐ⌉
   Juan y Elisa   ⌈xwán jelísɐ⌉
   difícil
   y exigente   ⌈dif ís!l jeɐz!xéɳtə⌉

5. Between a vowel and a consonant, y becomes the semivowel ⌈i⌉:
   cuarto y ventana   ⌈kwártᴐi ɓəɳtánɐ⌉
   gata y perra   ⌈qátai péɼɐ⌉
   digo y repito   ⌈díɐᴐi ɼəpítᴐ⌉
   orgulloso
   y patriota   ⌈ᴐrɐnlósᴐi pɐtrjótɐ⌉

6. Between vowels y takes on the features of the voiced palatal fricative ⌈y⌉:
   vinagre y aceite   ⌈bináɐrə Yɐsɛ́itə⌉
   verde y anaranjado   ⌈bɛ́rɖə Yɐnɐrɐ ɳxáɖᴐ⌉
   lea y escriba   ⌈léɐ Yəskríɓɐ⌉
   Ernesto y Elena   ⌈ɐrnéstᴐ Yəléne⌉

The linkage of final y between words frequently depends on the pronunciation typical of a given speech community or region. For example, an utterance like el rey ora is articulated either ⌈əl ɼɛ́ Yórɐ⌉ or ⌈əl ɼɛ́i órɐ⌉. Thus the following two versions are possible throughout the Spanish-speaking world:

voy allá   ⌈bó Yɐyá⌉   ⌈bói ɐyá⌉
el buey
estaba   ⌈əl bwɛ́ Yəstáɓɐ⌉   ⌈əl bwɛ́i əstáɓɐ⌉
le doy a él   ⌈lə ɖó Yɐ ɛ́l ⌉   ⌈lə ɖói ɛ ɛ́l ⌉
es muy
ordinario   ⌈éz mú Yᴐrɖ!nárjo⌉ ⌈éz múi ᴐrɖ!nárjo⌉

In daily speech the conjunction y becomes e before i- or hi- --oportuno e inesperado, padre e hijo, molestar e irritar. In cases in which the i- is unstressed, the e forms a diphthong with the ini-

44

tial vowel of the following word:
    hermoso e inteligente   [ɔrmósɔ εiɲtɔlixéɲtɔ]
    Pablo e Ignacio   [páblɔ εiǥnásjɔ]
    nerviosa e irritable   [nɑrbjósε εiɾitáblɔ]
    inútil e incierto   [inútiɭεinsjértɔ]
When **i** is stressed, the sound **e** is handled variously.
If **e** is preceded by an identical vowel, it tends to
blend with the latter:
    madre e hija   [mádrə íxɐ]
    agente e ídolo   [ɐxéɲtə ídɔlɔ]
even though in some types of speech the linkage
tends to lengthen the final **e**. When preceded by a
consonant, **e** is linked with it and is relaxed:
    gris e índigo   [qrísə íɲdiɣɔ]
    mujer e hija   [mɔxérə íxɐ]
    español e indio   [ɐspɐɲólə íɲdjɔ]
Words beginning with the diphthong hie-- are exceptions in that **y** is retained as the conjunction--hie-
rro, hiena, hielo, hiato, hiedra.

    Similar linkage takes place with the conjunc-
tion **o**. When preceded by a consonant, it is linked
with the latter and is normally relaxed:
    cantor o pianista   [kɐɲtórɔ pjanístɐ]
    amor o desprecio   [ɐmórɔ dɐsprésjɔ]
    cantan o bailan   [káɲtɐnɔ báilɐn]
When preceded by a vowel, **o** is relaxed and linked--
veinte o treinta [béiɲtəɔtréiɲtɐ], grata o triste
[qrátɐɔtrístɐ]. When the preceding vowel is an -**o**,
both vowels blend to form one sound--alto o bajo
[áltɔ báxɔ], rápido o lento [fápidɔ léɲtɔ]--even
though in certain variants the final -**ó** of the preceding word is lengthened--amado o rechazado [ɐmá-
dɔ̃ɔ faĉɐsádɔ].

    Traditionally, the conjunction **o** becomes **u**
when followed by an o- --piano u órgano, humilde u
orgulloso. Thus whether a consonant or a vowel
precedes, the conjunction **u** becomes the semiconsonant [w]:
    verdura u hortaliza   [bɐrdúrɐ wɔrtɐlísɐ]
    arreglo u orden   [ɐféɣlɔ wórdɐn]
    agua u horchata   [áɣwa wɔrĉátɐ]

The problems of linkage are actually few in

number since the language normally flows according to basic rules of pronunciation and liaison. These exceptions and possible variants are quite helpful, however, in making for smooth-flowing, near-native articulation.

EXERCISES

THEORY
A. ANSWER THE FOLLOWING QUESTIONS BRIEFLY.
1. What is a vowel?
2. Which are the front vowels and which are the back vowels?
3. What are the allophones of the phoneme /E/? Of the phoneme /O/?
4. What is the difference between medial and velar a in Spanish?
5. What is a lax vowel and when does it generally occur?
6. When does close e occur in Spanish?
7. What are the chief characteristics of semiconsonants?
8. When does Spanish close o occur?
9. What is a diphthong? A triphthong? Give several examples of each.
10. What are the essential characteristics of semivowels?
11. How do we distinguish between close and open i?
12. What are the various kinds of u in Spanish?

B. FILL IN THE BLANKS ACCORDING TO YOUR UNDERSTANDING OF BASIC PHONETICS.
1. Spanish vowels have a clarity and precision of pronunciation which distinguish them from the more _____ of English vowels.
2. There is no significant difference in Spanish between _____ and short vowels as such.
3. A(n) _____ vowel generally occurs in a final unstressed position or in any unstressed syllable.
4. The three basic groups of sounds--weak d, nasals, and s/z sounds--close syllables after _____ but do not open the vowel.
5. Open i is used in _____ syllables, especially in syllables closed by l, r, and s.
6. Semivocalic i is found in diphthongs and triphthongs in which i is the _____ element.
7. In pronouncing open o, the position of the tongue is basically the same as in _____ o.

47

8. The correct position of the tongue in articulating close e̱ is _____.

9. The _____ generally shows the relative openness and closeness of Spanish vowels.

10. The allophonic variants of the phoneme /o/ are _____.

C. PROVIDE EXAMPLES FOR EACH OF THE FOLLOWING:
1. a vowel glide
2. linguistic ambience
3. contact
4. friction
5. relaxation

D. ANSWER THE QUESTIONS BRIEFLY.
1. What does the o̱ in the words dot, cot, bother, mop, top have in common with Spanish a̱ ?
2. In which English words can one find an approximation of the Spanish open e̱ ?
3. Which English phoneme does the Spanish close i̱ ⌈i⌉ most closely resemble? Give some English examples.
4. What additional feature does the English o̱ have in such words as bone, shone, tone, tow, and below?
5. Which sounds in English most closely approximate the Spanish close u̱ ⌈u⌉ ?
6. Are the u̱ in the English words could, should, and would and the Spanish open u̱ identical? Give examples.
7. Are the Spanish au̱ in cauce and sauce identical to the English ou̱ in couch and slouch?
8. Why should the English glide sound be avoided in most forms of Spanish articulation?
9. What is the basic difference in English between the stressed vowels in the following pairs: fetter/fate, nether/Nate?
10. Which group of English sounds does the Spanish close i̱ more closely resemble--feet, reed, seat, or sixteen, Charlene, Aberdeen?

48

PRACTICE

A. ANALYZE EACH OF THE VOCALIC PHONEMES.

MODEL:
roño   open o in contact with r
       lax o in unstressed syllable

1. bajo _____ _____
2. relampaguea _____ .
3. general _____ _____
4. hablado _____ _____
5. hablé _____ _____
6. veces _____ _____
7. sartén _____ _____
8. sentaos _____ _____
9. reja _____ _____
10. Saltillo _____ _____
11. pipa _____ _____
12. averiguáis _____ _____
13. choclo _____ _____
14. comáis _____ _____
15. abulia _____ _____
16. rosario _____ _____
17. oiga _____ _____
18. decoro _____ _____
19. ahora _____ _____
20. humo _____ _____

B. TRANSCRIBE EACH UNDERLINED VOCALIC PHONEME.
1. Ellos tardan en hacerlo.
2. La alabanza nos encanta a todos.
3. Nos envían una amena carta.
4. ¿Ud. quiere ir a la hacienda de los señores?
5. Me lo queréis comunicar sin decir ni pito ni
   flauta.
6. El estilo del libro no es lindo en ningún sentido.
7. Las nubes se juntan con el humo.
8. La pintura es algo lúgubre.
9. Pidió una sopa de cebolla.
10. La nena no le tiene miedo al duende.
11. Al general no le agrada viajar por ese barco.
12. El esposo de Dolores Redondo no volvió.
13. Delibes no tiene los seis pesos que le debe.
14. Los mozos lloraron con tono melancólico.
15. Ellos hicieron cuanto pudieron.
16. El ahijado de Pepita no quiso aceptar lo dicho.

49

C. IDENTIFY THE SOUNDS WHICH APPEAR IN PHONETIC
TRANSCRIPTION.
1. [e] _____   6. [ɔ] _____
2. [ə] _____   7. [i̯] _____
3. [ʌ] _____   8. [a̯] _____
4. [j̯] _____   9. [ɛ] _____
5. [w] _____   10. [o̯] _____

D. TRANSCRIBE PHONETICALLY THE LINKAGE WORDS IN THE
FOLLOWING PAIRS:
1. carne o̱ pescado   _____
2. comprender y̱ entender _____
3. único y̱ especial   _____
4. acuarela u̱ óleo   _____
5. leones u̱ o̱sos   _____
6. pista e̱ hipódromo   _____
7. crítica e̱ historia   _____
8. flor y̱ hi̱erba   _____
9. entero e̱ ileso   _____
10. perverso e̱ idólatra _____
11. plaza e̱ iglesia   _____
12. plata u̱ oro   _____
13. lobo y̱ hiena   _____
14. trepadora y̱ hiena   _____
15. vista u̱ oído   _____
16. barato y̱ horrible   _____
17. fruta y̱ ensalada   _____
18. macho o̱ hembra   _____
19. rápida e̱ inesperada _____
20. cobre y̱ hierro   _____

ASI SE DICE
REPEAT CAREFULLY EACH SEGMENT AS GIVEN AND FINALLY
THE COMPLETE UTTERANCE.
Cada   ....
loco   ....
con   ....
Cada loco con   ....
su   ....
tema   ....
con su tema   ....
Cada loco con su tema. ....

50

```
Tres                    . . . . . . . . . .
grandes                 . . . . . . . . . .
tigres                  . . . . . . . . . .
tragantones             . . . . . . . . . .
Tres grandes tigres tragantones
                        . . . . . . . . . . . . . .
tragan                  . . . . . . . . . .
trigo                   . . . . . . . . . .
y se                    . . . . . . . . . .
atragantan              . . . . . . . . . .
tragan trigo y se atragantan
                        . . . . . . . . . . . . . .
tragantones tragan trigo y se atragantan
                        . . . . . . . . . . . . . . . . . .
tigres tragantones tragan trigo y
se atragantan           . . . . . . . . . . . . . . . . . .
Tres grandes tigres tragantones tragan trigo y se
atragantan.             . . . . . . . . . . . . . . . . . . . . . . . . . . .

A perro                 . . . . . . . . . .
viejo                   . . . . . . . . . .
A perro viejo           . . . . . . . . . .
no                      . . . . . . . . . .
no hay                  . . . . . . . . . .
tus tus                 . . . . . . . . . .
no hay tus tus          . . . . . . . . . .
A perro viejo no hay tus tus.  . . . . . . . . . . . . . . . . . .

A Dios                  . . . . . . . . . .
rogando                 . . . . . . . . . .
A Dios rogando          . . . . . . . . . . . . . .
y con                   . . . . . . . . . .
y con el                . . . . . . . . . .
y con el mazo dando     . . . . . . . . . . . . . .
A Dios rogando y con el mazo dando.  . . . . . . . . . . . . . .

Haz                     . . . . . . . . . .
bien                    . . . . . . . . . .
Haz bien                . . . . . . . . . . . . . .
y no                    . . . . . . . . . .
y no mires              . . . . . . . . . .
y no mires a            . . . . . . . . . .
y no mires a quien      . . . . . . . . . . . . . .
Haz bien y no mires a quien.  . . . . . . . . . . . . . . . . . .
```

51

FOOTNOTES

[5] All vowels which appear as though upside down are lax or relaxed vowels--those upon which a primary stress does not fall.

[6] In Spanish all initial r's and r after l or n are pronounced exactly like rr [r̃].

[7] Note that vowels retain their basic quality even though they may be relaxed.

CHAPTER THREE

THE SPANISH CONSONANTS

PRELIMINARY NOTIONS OF ARTICULATION. A consonant
is properly defined as a voiced or voiceless sound
affected in one way or another by the speech organs
above the larynx and with a degree of audible friction. Vowels, instead, are characterized by the
absence of friction and by relatively free passage
of air. An additional feature of consonants is
that they are pronounced with a stricture in the
air passage. They may be voiced or voiceless depending upon whether or not the vocal cords vibrate
during their production. Aside from the aspect of
being voiced or voiceless, consonants are categorized according to their place of articulation
(el punto de articulación), that depends upon which
organs come into play and where in the production
of the sound, and manner of articulation (la manera de articulación), which points out whether there
is some stoppage, partial stoppage, or a combination of these.

PLACE OF ARTICULATION. The organs involved in producing consonants provide the names of this classification. The consonants are classified as follows:
   1. Bilabials (bilabiales)--both lips are used
      as the organs of articulation [b], [b], [m],
      [p].
   2. Labiodentals (labiodentales)--the lower lip
      and the edges of the upper teeth are the
      organs of articulation [f], [m].
   3. Interdentals (interdentales)--the tip of
      the tongue and the edges of the upper teeth
      function as organs [θ], [d], [z].
   4. Dentals (dentales)--the tip of the tongue
      and the inner surface of the upper teeth
      come into play [d], [t].
   5. Alveolars (alveolares)--the tip of the
      tongue and the alveolar ridge of the upper
      teeth are the functional organs [l], [n],

[r], [r̃], [s], [z].
6. Palatals (palatales)--the front part of the tongue and the hard palate are the organs of articulation [c̆], [ʎ], [ɲ], [ɟ], [ʸ].
7. Velars (velares)--the back of the tongue and the soft palate function in this case as the organs of articulation [g], [ɣ], [k], [ŋ], [x], [h].

It is important to remember that the place of articulation is generally according to the passive organ in the production of sounds. Most often the tongue itself is the active organ.[8] It is helpful to think of the relationship between the active and the passive organs when analyzing accurate articulation.

MANNER OF ARTICULATION. Spanish consonants are classified according to this point of view as follows:

1. Explosives (oclusivos or explosivos)--these sounds are formed by a complete stoppage (la cerrazón) resulting from a momentary blocking of the passage of air followed by a sudden opening of the blockage, allowing free passage of air [b], [d], [g], [k], [p], [t]. These sounds are also referred to as stops or oclusives.

2. Semi-explosives or affricates (semiexplosivos or africados)--these sounds are produced by a complete but momentary stoppage followed by a rather slow and very gentle removal of the obstacle [c̆], [ɟ].

3. Continuants or fricatives (fricativos)-- these sounds are produced by a stoppage which is partial, allowing the air to pass through a relatively narrow passage. This yields a sound characterized by continuous friction [b̞], [f], [θ], [ð], [z], [s], [ʎ], [ʝ], [ʸ], [ɟ], [ɣ], [x], [w]. The fricatives which result from the passage of air through the sides of the mouth are known as laterals (laterales); those which are essentially continuants or ssss/zzzz sounds

54

are known as sibilants (sibilantes) [s̺],
[z̺].
4. Nasals (nasales)--this sound is formed by
   lowering the soft palate so that the
   uvula--the fleshy part in the back of the
   throat--shuts off the passage of the breath
   through the mouth and forces it to pass
   through the nose or the nostrils (las narices) [m], [n], [ɲ], [ŋ].
5. Vibrants (vibrantes)--these sounds are
   formed by a vibration or a series of rapid
   vibrations of the tongue against the alveolar ridge [r], [r̃].

IN-DEPTH ANALYSIS OF SPANISH CONSONANTS.
  1. Bilabial consonants
     a. b, v voiced explosive (bilabial oclu-
        siva sonora)

        phonetic symbol ⌊ b ⌋.[9]
        These occur in
          (1) an initial position in a breath
              group
          basta [bás̺t̪ɐ]   valle [báʲə]
          voy [bɔ́ i]   varían [bɐríɐn]
          (2) after m or n (always pronounced
              [m] whether within a word or be-
              tween words)
          hombre   [ɔ́mbrə]
          invierno [ımbʲérnɔ]
          sin vida [s̺ımbíɖɐ]
          en balde [əmbáʲɖə][10]
        The English counterpart of this sound
        is similar but is articulated as more
        of an explosive and with the aspira-
        tion which is typical of English ex-
        plosives--boy [ˈbɔy], boat [ˈbot],
        bubble [ˈbubl], big [ˈbɪq].

     b. b voiced continuant or fricative (bi-
        labial fricativa sonora)

        phonetic symbol ⌊ ƀ ⌋.

In all other positions, that is, when
not initial in a phonic or breath group
as in (1) above or after m̲ or n̲ as in
(2) above, b̲ ⌈ɓ⌉ is a bilabial continuant or fricative. In the production
of this sound the lips are not closed
completely, allowing breath to pass
through a very narrow aperture in the
buccal cavity. It is pronounced as
though one were pronouncing a soft
English b̲ with some form of obstruction. There is no real equivalent of
this phoneme in English. It occurs
in:
   (1) any intervocalic position (l̲a̲
      posición intervocálica),
  abierto ⌈ɐ̟bjértc⌉   Cuba ⌈kúbɐ⌉
  renovar ⌈Fɘnɔɓár⌉   lobo ⌈lóɓɔ⌉
   (2) any semi-open position (l̲a̲ p̲o̲s̲i̲-
      ción entreabierta)
  por bailar ⌈pɔr baiɫɐ̆r⌉
  cubre   ⌈kúbrɘ⌉
  sobre   ⌈sóɓrɘ⌉
  pobre   ⌈póɓrɘ⌉

c. m̲, n̲ voiced bilabial nasal (b̲i̲l̲a̲b̲i̲a̲l̲
n̲a̲s̲a̲l̲ s̲o̲n̲o̲r̲a̲)

phonetic symbol ⌊ m ⌋.
The bilabial nasal ⌈m⌉ is quite similar
to the m̲ in m̲o̲u̲t̲h̲, m̲a̲d̲e̲, m̲u̲t̲t̲e̲r̲. The
velum i̲s̲ open and the breath passes
through both the mouth and the nose.
It is heard in the following cases:
  (1) the sound of the letter m
  ambiguo ⌈ɐmbíqwo⌉   cama ⌈kãmɛ⌉
  tiempo ⌈tjémpɔ⌉   madre ⌈mádrɘ⌉
  (2) the letter n before the bilabial
    consonants b̲, v̲, and p̲ is also
    pronounced like this m̲
  envejecer ⌈ɘmbaxɘsɛ́r⌉
  en blanco ⌈ɘm blánkɔ⌉
  en balde ⌈ɘm báldɘ⌉
  en papel ⌈ɘm pɛ̝pél⌉

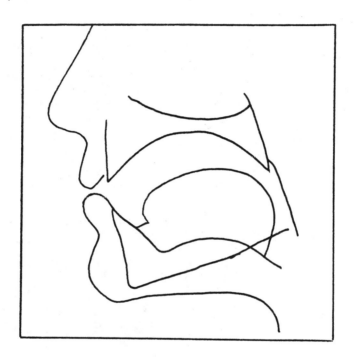

FIGURE 10   CONSONANT B AND ITS ARTICULATION

57

(3) whenever the letter m appears as
a final consonant in a relatively
small number of words, it is pronounced like an n
vademécum [beɗəmékʌn] Abraham [ɛ́brán]
ultimátum [ʌ́ʔtimátʌn] álbum [ắlbʌn]

d. p voiceless explosive (bilabial oclusiva sorda)

phonetic symbol [p].
This sound is bilabial and explosive
just like the English p but weaker and
without the aspiration typical of English pronunciation in such cases as
pitter [ˈpɪtʳ], Peter [ˈpiˈtʳ], pope
[ˈpop], pat [ˈpæt]. The Spanish [p]
occurs
(1) in almost every case of the letter p
culpa [kṹlpɐ]   papa [pápɐ]
papel [pɐpél]   parte [pártə]
(2) this consonant in contact with t
becomes implosive (implosivo),
characterized by a type of closure or stop but without any
truly explosive quality
aptitud [ɛᵇtitṹᵈ]   raptar [rɛᵇtár]
captar [kɐᵇtár]   apto [áᵇtɔ]

2. Labiodental consonants
a. f voiceless labiodental continuant or
fricative (labiodental fricativa sorda)

phonetic symbol [f].
In this case the lower lip is the active organ while the edge of the upper
front teeth is the passive organ. It
is very similar to f in French, foot,
and feel. The Spanish phoneme is encountered whenever the f sound is
heard
esfuerzo [əsfwérθɔ] afecto [ɛféᵏtɔ]
perfecto [pərféᵏtɔ] flaco [flákɔ]

58

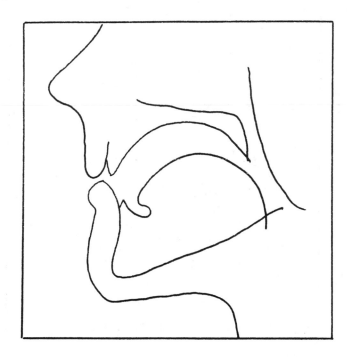

FIGURE 11   CONSONANT M̲ AND ITS ARTICULATION

59

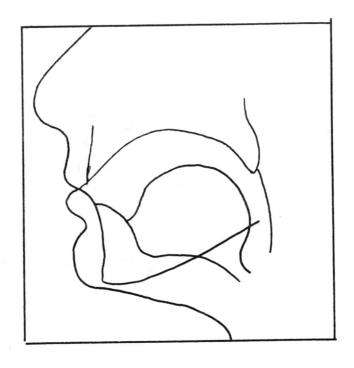

FIGURE 12   CONSONANT P̲ AND ITS ARTICULATION

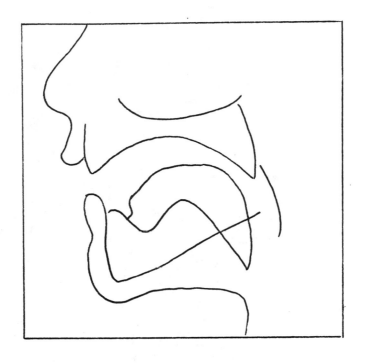

FIGURE 13   CONSONANT F AND ITS ARTICULATION

61

b. ṇ voiced labiodental nasal (<u>labioden-</u>
   <u>tal</u> <u>nasal</u> <u>sonora</u>)

   phonetic symbol ⌊ ɱ ⌋.
   The sound of this phoneme is that of m
   immediately before f, but since the
   breath passes through the nose the manner of articulation is like that of m.
   In less clearly articulated Spanish,
   this sound often disappears, leaving a
   nasalized vowel such as ⌈ ẽ ⌉, ⌈ õ ⌉, and
   ⌈ ʊ̃ ⌉. This nasal sound is heard as
   follows:
   confiesa ⌈ kɔɱfjésɛ ⌉ enfadar ⌈ əɱfɛdár⌉
   un favor ⌈ʌɱ fɛɓɔ́r ⌉ un fiel ⌈ʌɱ fjél⌉
   There is no equivalent sound in English.

3. <u>Dental</u> <u>consonants</u>
   The place of articulation for the dentals t and d is fairly similar, but the manner of articulation is different. This
   sound is somewhat more apico-alveolar in English (the tip or apex of the tongue against
   the alveolar ridge) accompanied by the characteristic aspiration--<u>dodo</u> ⌈ 'dodo⌉, <u>dad</u>
   ⌈ 'dad ⌉, <u>done</u> ⌈ 'dʌn⌉. Characteristically, the
   Spanish articulation is quite soft and without aspiration.
   a. ḍ voiced dental explosive (<u>dental</u>
      <u>oclusiva</u> <u>sonora</u>

      phonetic symbol ⌊ d ⌋.
      This sound is encountered
      (1) in the initial position of a
          breath group
      durante ⌈dʌránta⌉   don ⌈dón⌉
      decir ⌈dəsír⌉   dama ⌈dámɛ⌉
      (2) after n or l
      un duende ⌈ʌŋ dwénda⌉
      aldea   ⌈ɛldéɛ⌉
      con dos ⌈kɔn dɔ́s⌉
      el dolor ⌈əl 'dɔlɔ́r⌉

   b. ṭ voiceless dental explosive (<u>dental</u>
      <u>oclusiva</u> <u>sorda</u>)
                    62

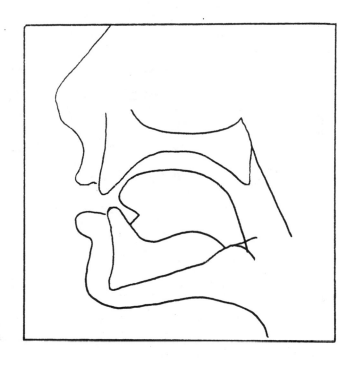

FIGURE 14   CONSONANT D̲ AND ITS ARTICULATION

63

phonetic symbol ⎣t̪⎦.
The tip of the tongue touches the inner surface of the upper front teeth.
The sides of the tongue touch the upper molars. It is very similar to the
English t, which is an aspirated al-
veolar--too [ˈtʰu], time [ˈtʰaɪm], tea
[ˈtʰi]. Instead, Spanish t is purely
dental and unaspirated. It occurs in
almost every case of t in Spanish as
follows:
   (1) cuatro [kwát̪r̥] pintar [pint̪ár]
       tutear [t̪nt̪aár] tigre [t̪í4rə]
   (2) in an internal final position
       (not the same as a final syl-
       lable since it can be followed by
       one or more syllables), it be-
       comes voiced and takes on the
       quality of a voiced interdental
       ⎣d⎦
   atmósfera [ɐdmósfarə]
   atlántico [ɐdlántiks]
   atleta   [ɐdlétɐ]
   atlas   [ádlɐs]

4. Interdental consonants
       These sounds are produced with the tip
   of the tongue against the upper teeth. The
   interdental quality is subtle but quite important. This phoneme occurs with c before
   e and i and z before any vowel or in final
   position as follows:
       a. z, c voiceless interdental continuant
          or fricative (interdental fricativa
          sorda)

          phonetic symbol ⎣θ⎦:
          Its English equivalent is a voiceless
          interdental fricative as in thin
          [ˈθɪn], thick [ˈθɪk], and thud [ˈθʌd].
          In Spanish this sound occurs initially,
          intervocalically, and in absolute final
          position and is strictly limited to the
          ceceo version of Spanish.

64

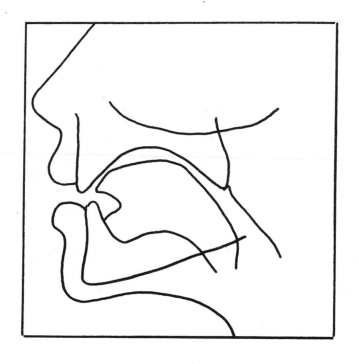

FIGURE 15   CONSONANT T̲ AND ITS ARTICULATION

65

(1) voz [bɔ́θ]   haz [áb]
    cruz [krýθ]   hacer [æθér][11]
(2) it becomes voiced in contact with
    a voiced consonant, yielding the
    voiced interdental continuant
    (<u>interdental</u> <u>fricativa</u> <u>sonora</u>)

[ẓ] as in <u>these</u> ['ðɪz],
<u>those</u> ['ðoz], and <u>bother</u> ['baðr].
Thus the Spanish <u>avestruz</u> [æbæṣ-
trýθ] becomes avestruz maldito
[æbæṣtrýẓ mæ̧ldítː]. Similarly,
one encounters
en vez de   [æm béẓ ðə]
hallazgo   [æláẓɑ̧ː]
complazgo   [kɔmpláẓɑ̧ː]
cruz buena   [krýẓ bwénæ]
        In other words, one goes from [θ]
        to its voiced counterpart [ẓ],
        or, in purely English terms, one
        goes from the <u>th</u> in <u>thin</u> to the
        <u>th</u> in <u>those</u>.
(3) the <u>seseo</u> variant of [ẓ] is [z]
    since <u>seseo</u> has no interdental
    sounds in these positions
avestruz maldito [æbæṣtrýz mæ̧ldítː]
en vez de   [æm béz ðə]
complazgo   [kɔmpláẓɑ̧ː]
cruz buena   [krýz bwénæ]

b. <u>d</u> voiced interdental continuant or
   fricative (<u>interdental</u> <u>fricativa</u> <u>so-</u>
   <u>nora</u>)

phonetic symbol [ð].
Unlike <u>ceceo</u> z/c above, this sound is
absolutely universal throughout the
Spanish-speaking world. The place of
articulation is basically the same as
[d] except that the sound is interdental. It is used in
   (1) intervocalic positions
   vendido [bændíðː]   su día [sɴ díæ]
   dado   [dáðː]   dedo   [déðː]
   (2) in all other cases of Spanish <u>d</u>

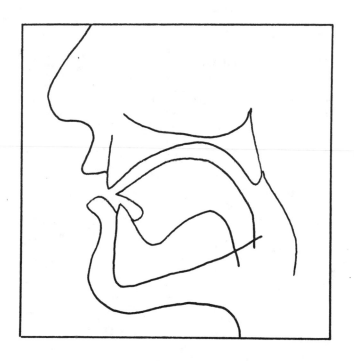

FIGURE 16   CONSONANTS $\underline{z}$, $\underline{C+e}$, $\underline{C+i}$ AND THEIR ARTICU-
LATION

67

except initial d of a breath group
or after n or l
en donde [an dónda] el día [al díe]
un día [ʌn díe] un don [ʌn dón]
This particular d has several other
features. The d in the ending -ado
has several variants. Usually, this d
is pronounced as a voiced interdental
fricative [d].

(3) condado [kɔndádɔ] arado [ɐrádɔ]
    danzado [dɐnsádɔ] atado [ɐtádɔ]
In ordinary daily speech and relaxed
conversation, this phoneme d is articulated rather weakly.[12] Final -d in
Spanish may be considered rather weak
inasmuch as it is heard in varying degrees of perceptibility according to
the speech community. If this sound
is immediately followed by another word
in the same breath group, it takes on
the phonetic qualities of a voiced interdental fricative [d]. Observe the
sound in the following examples:

(4) la edad media [le ɐdáᵈ médja]
    lavadlos [lɐbáᵈlɔs]
    su bondad es [sʌ bɔndáᵈ é-
    infinita sɪmfɪnítɐ]
    vendedlos [bɐndéᵈlɔs]
When d is absolutely final before a
pause, it is pronounced very weakly, at
times virtually imperceptibly and becomes partially unvoiced. In rapidly
spoken Spanish this sound becomes completely voiceless; that is to say, one
goes from [d] to [ᵈ] to [ɸ]. In the
majority of words ending in -dad like
bondad, caridad, mitad, verdad, comunidad, whether within a phonic group or
in absolute final position before a
pause, d often becomes completely silent. Thus the following variants are
heard:
caridad [kɐrɪdáᵈ], [kɐrɪdáᵈ], [kɐrɪdá]
bondad [bɔndáᵈ], [bɔndáᵈ], [bɔndá]
mitad [mɪtáᵈ], [mɪtáᵈ], [mɪtá]

68

verdad [bərðáɗ], [bərðáᵈ], [bərðá]

Some consonants tend to be influenced by
their ambience since they anticipate the quality of those that follow. For instance, the liquid consonants have a tendency to acquire the
interdental nuances of the interdentals which
follow them. For example, the alveolar consonants n and l and the dental consonant t assume an interdental quality if they precede an
interdental and therefore become [n̪], [l̪], and
[t̪]. Thus we have
    etcétera [ət̪θétərɛ̃]
    onza   [ón̪θə]
    alzar   [ɛl̪θár]
The same phenomenon occurs with consonants
which precede a dental, thus assuming themselves the qualities of dentals. In other
words, the alveolar phonemes [s], [n], and [l]
become dentalized before dental phonemes [s̪],
[n̪], and [l̪]: (bés̪tja], [án̪trə], [bul̪t̪ɔ]).

5. Alveolar consonants

In the production of these consonants the
tip of the tongue is the active organ once
again. The passive organ is the alveolar ridge
of the upper teeth. The blades of the tongue
rest on the sides of the mouth against the inner surface of the upper molars. The central
portion of the tongue assumes a somewhat concave form. The alveolar consonants are
    a. l voiced alveolar lateral fricative or
    continuant (alveolar lateral fricativa
    sonora)

    phonetic symbol [l].
This sound is made with the tip of the
tongue against the alveoles of the upper teeth with breath passing around
the sides of the tongue producing a
slight friction. Its English equivalent is found in words like live
['lɪv], lose ['luz], let ['lɛt]. The
lateral fricative l is found in most

69

cases of l in Spanish
clavo ⌈klát:⌉   habla ⌈áblɛ⌉
lana ⌈láne⌉   papel ⌈pɛpél⌉

b. n voiced alveolar nasal (alveolar nasal sonora)

   phonetic symbol ⌊n⌋.
   When producing this sound, the tip of
   the tongue touches the upper alveolar
   ridge while the sides of the tongue
   touch the inner surface of the upper
   teeth. In all nasals there is a passage of air, to one extent or another,
   through the nasal passage. The English counterpart of this sound is identical, especially when initial--note
   ⌈'not⌉, never ⌈'nɛvr⌉, need ⌈'nid⌉,
   not ⌈'nat⌉. This nasal sound is heard
      (1) in an initial position
            nada ⌈náðɛ⌉   nudo ⌈nuð: ⌉
            no ⌈nó⌉   nao ⌈náɔ⌉
      (2) intervocalically
            anudar ⌈ɛnnðár⌉ enano ⌈ɘnánː⌉
            nene ⌈néna⌉   suena ⌈swénɛ⌉
      (3) before any consonant except a bi-
          labial, a velar, a dental, an
          interdental, or an f
            carne ⌈kárna⌉   piensa ⌈pjénsɛ⌉
            himno ⌈ímnː⌉   junio ⌈xúnjo⌉
   Frequently, in prefixes such as ins-,
   cons-, trans-, and others, this phoneme
   is pronounced in a fairly weak manner
   or even disappears.

c. r voiced alveolar single vibrant (alveolar vibrante simple sonora)

   phonetic symbol ⌊r⌋.
   The term single is an allusion to the
   fact that in this type of r there is
   theoretically only one vibration,
   whereas the multiple vibrant is thought
   of as having two or more vibrations.
   In the production of this sound the

70

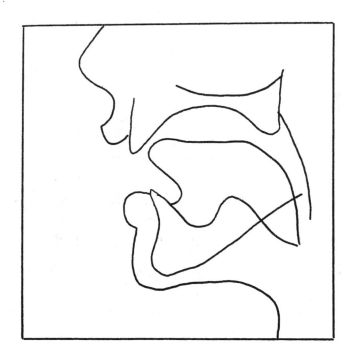

FIGURE 17   CONSONANT L̲ AND ITS ARTICULATION

71

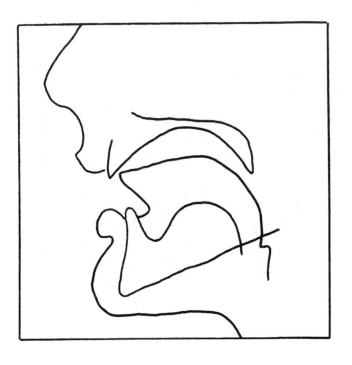

FIGURE 18   CONSONANT N̲ AND ITS ARTICULATION

72

sides of the tongue rest on the gums
and the inner surface of the upper
teeth, thus obstructing the passage of
air through the sides of the mouth.
The tip of the tongue is raised rather
quickly to touch the upper alveolar
ridge in a single vibration. At the
same time, the tongue is drawn back,
assuming a concave shape in the middle.
This type of sound is also commonly referred to as a <u>trill</u> or <u>tap</u>. The
single vibrant occurs

  (1) when not preceded by <u>l</u>, <u>n</u>, or <u>s</u>
     breve [bréba]   creo [kré:]
     dar   [dár]   por [pór]
  (2) when not initial
     corto [kórt:]   puerto [pwért:]
     era [éɾɐ]   daré [daɾé]

d. <u>r</u> (<u>rr</u>) voiced alveolar multiple vibrant
  (<u>alveolar vibrante múltiple sonora</u>)

phonetic symbol [r̄].
The place and manner of articulation of
this multiple vibrant are in general
the same as those of the single vibrant
except that there are additional vibrations. The muscular tension here is
greater and the tongue contact, more
pronounced. Frequently the single and
multiple variants are contrastive.
The multiple vibrant occurs in

  (1) all initial <u>r</u>'s
     rosa [r̄ósɐ]   rey [r̄éi]
     roe [r̄óɐ]   ron [r̄ón]
  (2) any orthographic <u>rr</u>
     tierra [tiér̄ɐ] carro [kár̄:]
     perro [pér̄:]   zurro [súr̄:]
  (3) after <u>l</u> or <u>n</u>
     alrededor [el̄r̄adadór]
     el río [əl r̄í:]
     Ulrico [ɑlr̄ík:]
     Enrique [ənr̄íkɐ]

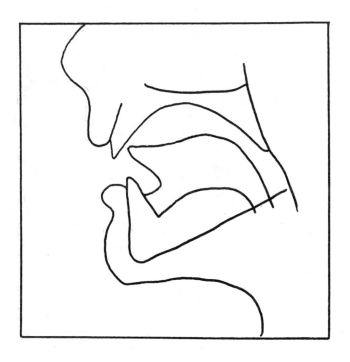

FIGURE 19   CONSONANT R AND ITS ARTICULATION

74

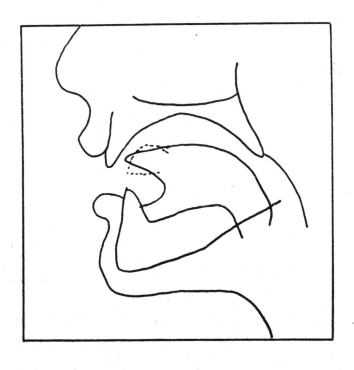

FIGURE 20   CONSONANT <u>RR</u> AND ITS ARTICULATION

75

e. s voiceless alveolar fricative (alveolar fricativa sorda)

phonetic symbol $\lfloor S \rfloor$.
The s sound in erase and center ($\lceil$s-
'reys$\rceil$ and $\lceil$'sentr$\rceil$ and asar and asir
are quite similar. There is, however,
a slight difference in the articulation
of the Spanish sibilant since the central portion of the tongue assumes a
concave position, the tongue touching
the alveolar ridge. In addition, the
blades of the tongue make contact with
the inner surface of the upper molars.
The Spanish sibilant is heard in
  (1) all instances of s which do not
    occur before a voiced consonant
    soso $\lceil$sós:$\rceil$ esa $\lceil$ésɛ$\rceil$
    saber $\lceil$sɛbér$\rceil$ ser $\lceil$sér$\rceil$
  (2) all cases of seseo pronunciation
    of c before e and i and z before
    any vowel
    despacio $\lceil$dəspásjo$\rceil$ hacer $\lceil$ɛsér$\rceil$
    zaguán $\lceil$sɛɣwán$\rceil$ hacia $\lceil$ásja$\rceil$

f. s voiced alveolar fricative (alveolar
fricativa sonora)

phonetic symbol $\lfloor Z \rfloor$.
This sound is articulated in the same
way as the voiceless variant except
that the vocal cords come into play.
In English this sound occurs frequently
in a final position as the indicator of
plurals as well as elsewhere--Jews,
$\lceil$'dzuz$\rceil$, blues $\lceil$'bluz$\rceil$, ooze $\lceil$'uz$\rceil$,
twos $\lceil$'tuz$\rceil$. The Spanish s is voiced
when it occurs immediately before a
voiced consonant
es verdad $\lceil$éz bərdáⁿ$\rceil$ jazmín $\lceil$xɛzmín$\rceil$
las matas $\lceil$lɛz mátɛs$\rceil$ desde $\lceil$dézdə$\rceil$
This phoneme, like its voiceless coun-
terpart, tends to be somewhat weak in
Spanish. In fact, in phonic groups in
which the sounded sibilant appears be-

fore a voiced alveolar multiple vibrant ⌈r̄⌉, as in <u>las ramas</u> or <u>los reyes</u>, the voiced sibilant tends to disappear in normal speech.

6. <u>Palatal consonants</u>
 a. <u>ch</u> voiceless palatal affricate (<u>palatal africada sorda</u>)

 phonetic symbol ⌊ Ĉ ⌋
 The Spanish digraph <u>ch</u> represents a single sound in actu<u>al</u> pronunciation. The tip of the tongue is raised against the alveolar ridge of the front teeth while the frontal portion of the palate makes an instantaneous but complete stoppage. When the tongue is removed from the alveolar ridge and the front palate, breath escapes through a narrow passage and produces a slight friction. It is similar to the <u>ch</u> in the English words <u>cheer</u> ⌈'ĉi:r⌉, <u>cheese</u> ⌈'ĉi:z⌉, and <u>chattle</u> ⌈'ĉæ+l⌉. It occurs in all cases of orthographic <u>ch</u>
 chicano ⌈ĉɪkánɔ⌉   leche ⌈léĉə⌉
 chico ⌈ĉʲkɔ⌉   hacha ⌈áĉɐ⌉

 b. <u>ll</u> voiced palatal lateral fricative (<u>palatal fricativa lateral sonora</u>)

 phonetic symbol ⌊ ʎ ⌋
 The middle of the tongue is raised as with the other palatals, but the blades of the tongue form two narrow passages through which the stream of air flows. This produces a kind of lateral friction, which is the reason for the name of this phoneme. The sound occurs in all cases of <u>ll</u> pronounced as a palatal lateral
  (1) caballo ⌈kɐbáʎɔ⌉ llave ⌈ʎábə⌉,
    llorar ⌈ʎɔrár⌉ olla ⌈óʎɐ⌉[13]
 In many parts of Spain and in much of Latin America, ⌈ʎ⌉ usually becomes ⌈Y⌉. The latter sound has its equivalent in

77

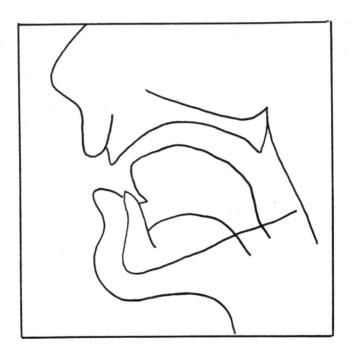

FIGURE 21   CONSONANT S̲ AND ITS ARTICULATION

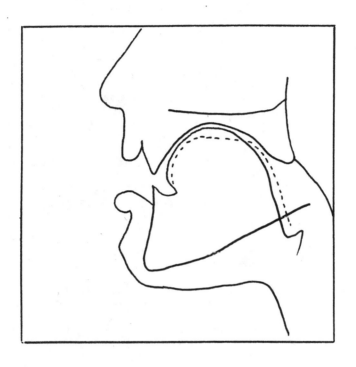

FIGURE 22   CONSONANT <u>CH</u> AND ITS ARTICULATION

79

words like ma<u>yor</u> [ˈmæyr̩], la<u>yer</u>
[ˈlæyr̩], <u>yes</u> [ˈyɛs], and yo<u>yo</u> [ˈyoyo].
In Latin America the palatal lateral in
(1) above is most often articulated as
a non-lateral
  (2) estrella [əstréYɛ] pillo [píY̥ə]
      caballo [kə̣báY̥ə] olla [óY̥ɛ]

c. ñ voiced palatal nasal (<u>palatal</u> <u>nasal</u>
   <u>sonora</u>)

   phonetic symbol [ɲ].
   The middle of the tongue is raised
   against the hard palate, making a complete stoppage. The tip of the tongue
   rests on the lower front teeth. In the
   production of this sound, the tongue is
   elevated, the soft palate is lowered,
   and most of the air is passed through
   the nostrils. The Spanish [ɲ] is a
   single uniform sound, and it occurs
   whenever ñ is encountered
   enseñar [ənsəɲár]   isleño [izléɲə]
   año   [áɲə]   roña   [r̃óɲɛ]
   While this sound is described as the
   <u>ny</u> in <u>canyon</u> and <u>Kenya</u>, the Spanish one
   is more definitely a single phoneme.

d. y (hi) voiced palatal affricate (<u>pala-</u>
   <u>tal</u> <u>africada</u> <u>sonora</u>)

   phonetic symbol [Ŷ].
   The tongue is elevated so as to form
   complete contact with the hard palate
   over a wide area. The sound is similar
   to the <u>j</u> in the word <u>jam</u> but articulated more softly. It occurs
     (1) whenever y (<u>hi</u>) is found in an
         emphatic accented position
     ¡YERBA MALA eres! [Ŷérbə málɛ érəs!]
     ¡mi YERNO!   [imı Ŷérnə!]
     ¡YO!   [iŶó!]
     ¡su YUGO!   [isʌ Ŷúɣə!]
     (2) when immediately after <u>l</u> or <u>n</u>

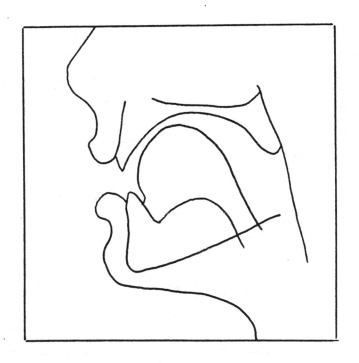

FIGURE 23   CONSONANT <u>LL</u> AND ITS ARTICULATION

81

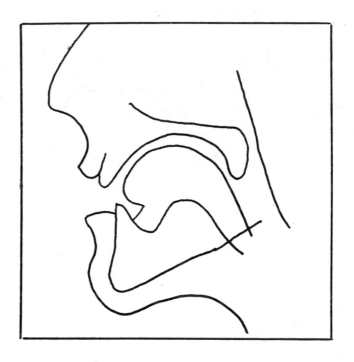

FIGURE 24   CONSONANT Ñ̲ AND ITS ARTICULATION

inyectar [ɪnŷəktár]
cónyuge [kɔ́nŷ ʌxə]
el yunque [əl ŷ ṷŋkə]
el hielo [əl ŷél:]
In daily speech many speakers of Spanish extend this phoneme to all cases of y and hi--technically an error but one which is heard often. This is the reason for which we hear untrained hispano speakers of English refer to jour, joung, and jankee.

e. y (hi) voiced palatal fricative or continuant (palatal fricativa sonora)

phonetic symbol ⌊ Y ⌋.
In the production of this sound the tip of the tongue rests on the lower teeth, and the front and middle of the tongue are raised in a convex shape very close to the hard palate. The breath passes through a narrow opening in the middle of the mouth, producing strong friction. This sound [Y] is stronger in palatal friction than the y in yes and yodel. A very clear distinction must be made between the palatal fricative y and the palatal affricate. This affricate version is frequently extended to all cases of Spanish y and hi. The fricative occurs whenever y or hi appears in normal articulation and not after l or n
se hiere [sə ɣéra]   leyes [léɣəs]
arroyo   [ɐ̈rɔ́ɣ:]   ya   [ɣá]

7. Velar consonants
    a. c, k, q(ue), q(ui) voiceless velar oclusive (velar oclusiva sorda)

phonetic symbol ⌊ K ⌋.
The back of the tongue is elevated against the soft palate, creating a complete stoppage and then suddenly removing it. It is similar to [k] as in

83

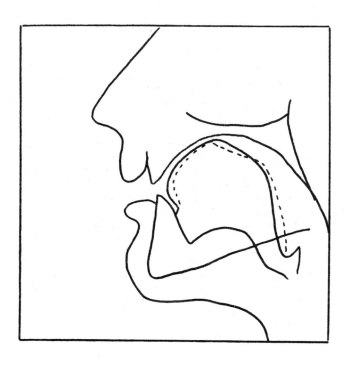

FIGURE 25   CONSONANT Ŷ AND ITS ARTICULATION

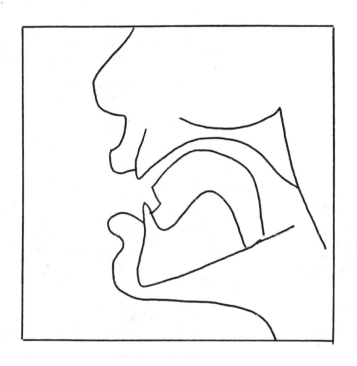

FIGURE 26   CONSONANT Y̲ AND ITS ARTICULATION

85

cop ['kap], cater ['kɛytr], Capri [kɐ-'pri]; however, the Spanish sound has no aspiration. It is found

(1) whenever c appears before a, o, and u

capa [kápɐ]   como [kómɒ]
cuna [kúnɐ]   caldo [káɫdɒ]

(2) whenever qu appears before e or aquí [ɐkí]   porque [pɔ́rkɐ]
quepo [képɒ]   quien [kjén]

(3) in those rare instances in which k is used orthographically in Spanish

keroseno   [kɐrɒsénɒ]
kilogramo [kilɒɣrámɒ]
kilate   [kilátɐ]
Kirie   [kírje]

b. g (gu) voiced velar oclusive (velar oclusiva sonora)

phonetic symbol [g].

The place and manner of articulation are exactly the same as in the voiceless [k], but this is its softer voiced equivalent. The English phoneme is similar but harsher and aspirated giggle ['gɪgl], goggle ['gagl], begat [bi'gæt]. The Spanish [g] is encountered

(1) whenever initial

gana [gánɐ]   gorra [gɔ́Fɐ]
grande [grándə]   gris [grís]

(2) immediately after n

pongo [pɔ́ŋgɒ]   engaño [əŋgáɲɒ]
tengo [téŋgɒ]   sangre [sáŋgrə]

(3) in the orthographic combinations gue, gui when initial or after n

guión [gjśn]   guerra [gɛ́Fɐ]
guiño [gíɲɒ]   guitarra [gitáFɐ]

c. g (gu) voiced velar fricative (velar fricativa sonora)

phonetic symbol [ɣ].

86

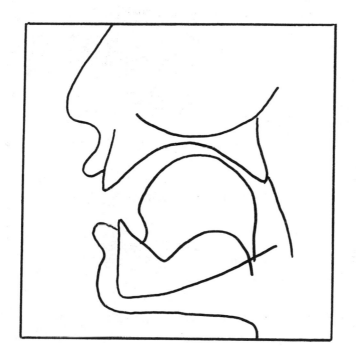

FIGURE 27   CONSONANT K̲ AND ITS ARTICULATION

The place and manner of articulation
are the same as the oclusive variant
[g]. There is usually no equivalent of
this sound in English. The Spanish
phoneme [q] occurs
   (1) in all intervocalic positions,
   aguardiente [ɐqwardjéņtə] agua [áqwa]
   llaga   [láqz]   lago [láqːɔ]
   (2) rarely in an absolutely final
     position
   Calambuig [kɐlɐmbwíꜜ] Puig [pwíq]
   ilang   [ìláŋꜜ]   Roig [fɔíq]
One should bear in mind that in the
orthographic groups <u>cc</u> and <u>cn</u> the ordinary pronunciation of the first <u>c</u> is
as a velar explosive [k] lección [lək-
sjɔ́n], acción [ɐksjɔ́n], técnica [tɛ́k-
nikɐ]. In familiar conversation, however, the same phoneme may take on the
characteristics of the fricative [q]
[ləqsjɔ́n], [ɐqsjɔ́n], [tɛ́qnikɐ].

d. <u>n</u> voiced velar nasal (<u>velar nasal so-
   nora</u>)
   phonetic symbol [ŋ].
   This particular nasal is used only before a velar consonant, the former being somewhat more reduced. Velar n is
   similar to the <u>n</u> in <u>ping pong</u> and <u>King
   Kong</u>, occurring only before a velar
   consonant.
   lengua [léŋqwa]   en casa [əŋ kász]
   ángel [áŋxəl]   cinco   [sìŋkɔ]

e. <u>x</u> voiceless velar fricative (<u>velar fricativa sorda</u>)
   phonetic symbol [ks], [s],
   [qz].
   In standard spoken Spanish this sound
   admits of a number of variants. This
   sound
   (1) before a consonant often takes on

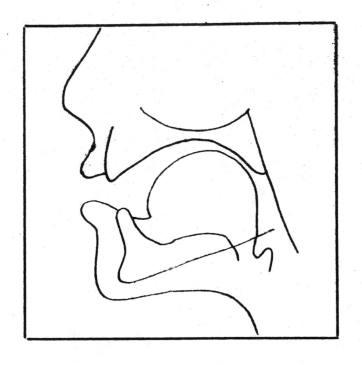

FIGURE 28   CONSONANT G̲ AND ITS ARTICULATION

89

the qualities of a sibilant
exponer [əspɔnér] exclamar [əsklɛmár]
extra [éstrɛ] explicar [əsplikár]
(2) between vowels is often pronounced [qz]
exhibición [əqzibisjɔn]
examen [əqzámən]
existe [əqzístə]
exagero [əqzɛxér:]
(3) in popular speech is often heard
as a sibilant even between vowels
exacto [əsákt:] auxiliar [aʊsiljár]
examen [əsámən] auxilio [aʊsíljo][14]
In English the [s] version of this letter does not occur. Most renderings
of English x are either [ks] before
consonants (expect [6ks'pɛkt]) or [qz]
before vowels (example [6qz'ampl]).

f. j, g (before e and i)   voiceless velar
fricative (velar fricativa sorda)

phonetic symbol [X].
Spanish j in all positions and g before
e and i produce this articulation. The
back of the tongue is raised toward the
end of the soft palate, and air produces
a strong friction on passing through
the narrow passage. Before a, o, and u
it takes on a uvular quality since the
friction is produced between the back
of the tongue and the uvula. Spanish
[x] is somewhat different from English
h, the latter being a weak pharyngeal
aspiration. The aspiration tends to be
greater in peninsular articulations than
in most parts of Latin America, where
it generally tends to be a medial aspiration [h]. Spanish aspiration occurs
(1) whenever j occurs in any position[15]
ajo [áx:]   hijo [íh:]
Juan [hwán]   rojo [r̄óx:]
(2) in the case of g (j) before e or
i

90

perejil [pərahíl]   ajeno [əxénə]
gesto [xéstə]   jira [híre]

SILENT CONSONANTS. Silent consonants are rare since
Spanish orthography is basically very close to the
spoken sounds of the language. As things now stand
b is a letter which is not often pronounced when it
occurs in a prefix or in what was originally a prefix. For example it is never pronounced in words
like obscuro and obstáculo (written also oscuro and
ostáculo). While b is still written in most cases
of the prefix sub-, it is not heard unless it is
followed by a vowel or the liquids r and l. Therefore one does not pronounce b in the prefix of
subclase, subcolector, subcomendador, subcomisión,
subconsciencia, subcontinente, subcontratar. However, in words in which a liquid follows the b of
the prefix, the letter is heard--sublevar, sublime,
sublevado, subrayado, sublimación. If a vowel follows, it is always heard--subalterno, subarrendar,
subantártico, subestimar, subestructura, subexposi-
ción.

   A similar type of omission takes place with p
in the prefixes psico- and pseudo- and their deri-
vatives. All of these forms may be spelled, in
fact, with or without the initial p since they are
pronounced in the same way in either case--(p)sico-
análisis, (p)sicoanalizar, (p)sicópata, (p)sicolin-
güística, (p)seudónimo, (p)seudoprofeta, (p)seudo-
morfo.

   The only really consistently silent consonant
in Spanish is h. It appears rather infrequently as
the initial consonant of verbs: hallar, henchir,
hinchar, holgar, hundir, helar, hartar, hendir, hervir; nouns: huerta, hinojo, hueso, hoz, haz, hada,
helado, horchata, horquilla, humo, huelga, hurí,
hormiga, harén; and adjectives: hirviente, helado,
holgazán, hablador, higiénico, histérico, himalayo,
hindú, hípico, hipnótico, hiriente, hirviendo, hispánico, holandés, hondureño. Occasionally, silent
h is encountered intervocalically almohada, al-

91

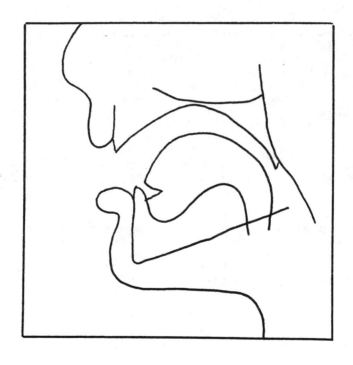

FIGURE 29 CONSONANTS J̱, G̱+e̱, G̱+i̱ AND THEIR
ARTICULATION̄S

cohol, ahorro, alhaja, ahijado, ahuyentar, aprehender, ahí, ahinco, Alahambra. Many names, surnames,
and geographical place names begin with silent h--
Henríquez, Hoyos, Hurtado, Huerta, Henares, Haití,
(la) Haya, (el) Havre, Horacio, Hortensio(a), Hér-
cules, Herodes, Herminio(a), Hebe. H also appears
in all forms of the auxiliary haber in all tenses
and moods, including all impersonal forms deriving
from haber (hay, habrá, había, habría, haya, hu-
biera, hubiese, and others).

CONCLUDING WITH THE CONSONANTS. In Spanish consonants are an indispensable segment of the basic
syllabic pattern which normally consists of a nucleus of an independent vowel (ea, ah, eh, oh), a
consonant-vowel (pelota, camarero), a vowel-consonant (aún, ay, uf), and a consonant-consonant-
vowel (producto, trigo). Unlike English, Spanish
does not favor consonantal clusters. Needless to
say, in English they are very frequent: thrash,
squeal, giggle, clothes, clutch, wedge, wretch,
contusion, butter, Venetian, jogging, Polynesian,
battle. In the relatively few consonantal clusters
possible in Spanish, those combinations of highest
frequency are those which contain a C (consonant)
plus [w] (cuando, cuero, cuan), C plus [j] (familia, Amalia, folio), C plus [r] (frente, entre,
mientras), and C plus [l] (pleno, clave, plegaria,
doblar, tabla). Aside from these combinations and
some few others, consonantal clusters do not have
the frequency in Spanish found in some other languages.

     A reduction of the number of consonants in cer-
tain clusters is typical of careless or uneducated
speakers. Thus instead of innumerable, innecesario,
innato, ómnibus, doctor, actor, rector, one hears
fairly frequently reduced consonantal groups,
yielding such forms as inumerable, inecesario, ina-
to, ónibus, dotor, ator, retor.

93

Similarly, in popular speech there is the tendency to aspirate sibilant sounds when they are the final element in an internal syllable, this being a linguistic trait typical of certain areas of southern Spain, parts of Latin America, and much of the Caribbean. In this particular articulation words like fresco, Taxco, asco, bosque, tasca, este, esta, esto, estos, estas tend to be articulated frehco, Tahco, ahco, bohque, tahca, ehte, ehta, ehto, ehtos, ehtas. While sibilants in this position are often weak and dentalized, the total nasalization should be avoided. An even more serious linguistic aberration is the omission of -s as an indicator of the plural form, which is a very Caribbean characteristic but which occurs habitually throughout the Spanish-speaking world. One hears with considerable frequency such versions as lo padre, la madre, lo chico, son la do, son la tre, lo panecillo, ma o meno, todo lo bueno, toda la chica. An even more serious deviation from the norm is the aspiration of all unarticulated sibilants as in loh padreh, lah madreh, loh chicoh, son lah doh, son lah treh, loh panecilloh, mah o menoh, todoh loh buenoh, todah lah chicah. One might argue that all dialect constitutes communication and there is much that might be said pro and contra. For the non-native, at least, all three tendencies should be avoided; that is, sibilants in internal syllables should be pronounced as such, final sibilants should be articulated, even if only weakly, and the nasalization of final unarticulated sibilants is to be avoided.

FIGURE 30   CHART OF SPANISH CONSONANTS

POINT OF ARTICULATION	explosive VOICED	explosive VOICELESS	fricative VOICED	fricative VOICELESS	affricate VOICED	affricate VOICELESS	nasal VOICED	lateral VOICED	vibrant SINGLE	vibrant MULTIPLE
BILABIAL	b	p	b̄				m			
LABIODENTAL				f			m̧			
DENTAL	d	t								
INTERDENTAL			d̄	θ						
ALVEOLAR			z	s			n	l	r	r̄
PALATAL			y	ŝ	ŷ	ĉ	ñ	ḷ		
VELAR	g	k	ǥ	x			ŋ			

95

EXERCISES

THEORY

A. ANSWER THE FOLLOWING QUESTIONS BRIEFLY.
1. What is a consonant?
2. What is a voiced consonant? A voiceless consonant?
3. What is the function of the vocal cords in the production of consonants?
4. How do semi-explosive consonants differ from explosive consonants?
5. What is an affricate?
6. How are nasals produced?
7. What are the bilabial consonants?
8. What are the essential characteristics of a palatal sound?
9. What is the definition of a velar sound?
10. Which sounds are included in the alveolar group?
11. What happens to the aspiration of j in absolute final position?
12. What are the principal characteristics of interdental consonants?
13. What are the dental sounds in Spanish?
14. What are the two cases of labiodental sounds in Spanish?
15. How do fricatives and affricates differ?

B. COMPLETE THE STATEMENTS.
1. _____ phonemes are never aspirated in Spanish.
2. A voiceless consonant differs from a voiced consonant in that _____.
3. A sound which is characteristically made by a complete stoppage followed by immediate release of air is known as a(n) _____.
4. The tip of the tongue and the inner surface of the upper teeth are used in producing a(n) _____ consonant.
5. When there is partial stoppage accompanied by air, the sound produced is known as a(n) _____.
6. Labiodentals are produced by using the lower _____ and the upper _____.
7. In very popular conversation the interdental in a(n) _____ position is articulated very

96

weakly.

8. _____ in phonetics refers to the phenomenon whereby certain consonants acquire the qualities of consonants which follow.

9. Orthographic b and v always share the same _____ characteristics in Spanish without any differentiation.

10. It is essential to differentiate between _____ and _____ vibrants in Spanish since they are often contrastive.

C. ANSWER BRIEFLY.

1. How does one explain the initial consonants of such words as boot and bubble, voy and batalla?

2. What are the characteristics of the sound [p] in words like peat, putt, and pull?

3. How does one explain the initial sound in such words as titter, tote? What about tarde and toro?

4. What are the essential characteristics of the interdental sound in thrift, thrust? What about dice and zozobra?

5. What are the essential characteristics of the initial nasal in words like knead, Nat? What about nada and noche?

6. What do the sibilants in the following English words share in common--lose, news, booze? What about Circe and circle?

7. How do the sibilants in rosa, este, and diezmar differ?

8. How does one describe the ch sound in chow, chisel, chatter?

9. What do the following words have in common--Armenia, Kenya, Tasmania, familia, noria?

10. What is typical of English velar consonants as in cap, cover, and covert? Does the initial phoneme of cada and caro differ in any way?

11. The oclusives in words like go, put, cot, and tide differ from those in ganga, pata, cola, and taro. Why is this so?

12. How many ways may one pronounce the letter x in English? What about Spanish?

13. What are the essential features of Spanish aspiration?

14. What are the main silent consonants in Spanish?

PRACTICE
A. REVIEW THE CONSONANTS THOROUGHLY. ANALYZE EACH
   OF THE CONSONANTAL PHONEMES ACCORDING TO PLACE
   AND MANNER OF ARTICULATION.

	place: RESPONSE	manner: RESPONSE	voiced/voiceless RESPONSE
CUE			
gana	velar	oclusiva	sonora
1. perejil	....	....	....
2. técnica	....	....	....
3. exacto	....	....	....
4. ajo	....	....	....
5. las manos	....	....	....
6. año	....	....	....
7. ángel	....	....	....
8. estanque	....	....	....
9. guerrero	....	....	....
10. inyectar	....	....	....
11. lengua	....	....	....
12. capa	....	....	....
13. llamar	....	....	....
14. quiosco	....	....	....
15. kilate	....	....	....
16. caballo	....	....	....
17. olla	....	....	....
18. nao	....	....	....
19. admito	....	....	....
20. cuatro	....	....	....
21. confesar	....	....	....
22. voz baja	....	....	....
23. Aruba	....	....	....
24. norteño	....	....	....
25. duende	....	....	....
26. total	....	....	....
27. papa	....	....	....
28. capacidad	....	....	....
29. chicharrón	....	....	....
30. portugueses	....	....	....

ASI SE DICE
REPEAT CAREFULLY EACH SEGMENT AS GIVEN AND FINALLY
THE COMPLETE UTTERANCE.

No   ....

```
No decir                    ..........
No decir uno                ..........
uno esta                    ..........
uno esta boca               ..........
esta boca es                ........
esta boca es mía            ..............
No decir uno esta boca es mía
                    ...........................

Volver                      ..........
Volver uno                  ..........
pie                         ..........
pie atrás                   ..........
Volver uno pie atrás.       ...........................

Menester                    ..........
Menester es                 ..........
no meterse                  ..........
entre marido                ..........
marido y mujer              ..........
Menester es no meterse entre marido y mujer.
                    ...........................

Más                         ..........
Más vale                    ..........
Más vale tarde              ..........
que                         ..........
tarde que                   ..........
tarde que nunca             ..........
Más vale tarde que nunca.
                    ...........................

Perro                       ..........
Perro que                   ..........
Perro que ladra             ..........
que ladra no                ..........
ladra no muerde             ..........
Perro que ladra no muerde.
                    ...........................

Por                         ..........
Por la boca                 ..........
boca muere                  ..........
muere el                    ..........
muere el pez                ..........
```

Por la boca muere el pez.
....

A cada ....
A cada puerco ....
puerco le llega ....
llega su San ....
San Martín ....
A cada puerco le llega su San Martín.
....

Hombre ....
Hombre prevenido ....
prevenido vale ....
vale por dos ....
Hombre prevenido vale por dos.
....

*Erre con erre guitarra . ...
Erre con erre carril ....
¡Qué rápido ruedan ....
las ruedas del ferrocarril! ....

*El perro de San Roque ....
no tiene rabo ....
porque Ramón Ramírez ....
se lo ha robado. ....

*El perro de San Roque ....
no tiene rabo ....
porque el carretero, Ramón ....
Ramiro Ramírez, con la rara rueda ....
de su carro ....
se lo ha arrancado. ....

* (These exercises do not appear in Appendix
Two.)

100

FOOTNOTES

8 For a more detailed analysis of Spanish consonants from a traditional point of view, see Tomás Navarro Tomás, _Manual de pronunciación española_, 5th ed. (New York: Hafner, 1957), pp. 72-145.

9 b and v are pronounced in the same manner in Spanish. The fact that there is no difference in practice is attested by the fact that children are often taught to refer to b grande and v pequeña or b de burro and v de vaca. Some peninsular dialects like valenciano and the regionalistic speech of certain areas of Latin America have retained the difference in varying degrees.

10 Note that in the transcription of words like envío, en vano, and en balde, e plus any nasal may be transcribed [em], [e̜], or [e̜]; this applies to all vowels.

11 For further details on this ceceo versus seseo question, see pp. 9; 180-183; 199-200.

12 The pronunciation of the d in -ado is an interesting case in the Spanish of Castile and elsewhere. The -d is omitted about fifty percent of the time--considered by many a permissible linguistic variant.

13 In Latin America, especially in certain regions like Argentina, Paraguay, and Uruguay, the palatal lateral [l] becomes the palatal [ž], for which see the section on yeísmo, pp. 183-185; in much of Spain and Latin America it is articulated as the voiced palatal [y], for which see pp. 185, 234, 236.

101

[14] For a detailed analysis of the sounds represented by x, see John B. Dalbor, Spanish Pronunciation: theory and practice, 2nd ed. (New York:
Holt, Rinehart & Winston, 1980), pp. 98-103; for an
excellent contrastive treatment of all Spanish consonantal phonemes, see Dalbor, pp. 48-140.

[15] Note that j in the final position as in reloj, boj, and troj is never articulated, but such
instances of final j are extremely rare. In the
plural of these nouns the aspiration returns.

CHAPTER FOUR

GROUPING SOUNDS

MORPHOLOGY. Morphology (la morfología) is the study
of the internal composition of words and the interrelationships of word segments. Just as a minimal
unit of sound is referred to as a phoneme, a minimal
unit of sound linked with perceivable meaning is
known as a morpheme (el morfema),[16] customarily
written between braces (las llaves) { }. While the
morpheme refers to minimally perceivable units as
categories of sound-meaning, the isolated sounds per
se are most frequently referred to as morphs. For
example, in English the words childishness, motherhood, and advisement are easily segmented into re-
cognizable morphemes which are automatically accepted by speakers of English as minimal units with
a meaning-function even though the latter may at
first seem artificial. Any English speaker will re-
cognize the following divisions of words as units
with a meaning:
>   child   ish   ness
>   mother   hood
>   advise   ment
In other words, the first morpheme {child} provides
the image or content segment; the morpheme {ish}
adds the element of similarity or likeness; the morpheme {ness} contributes an element of abstract
category or quality. The morphemes in motherhood
and advisement are equally analyzable on this level.
In Spanish a similar type of segmentation is observable callejoncito (callej(a)/on/cito), ferrocarril (ferro/carril), libresco (libr(o)/esco).

The morphological aspects of word-formations
are not limited to internal segments as morphology
also concerns itself with the interrelationships of
words as these occur in different environments. For
example, a non-speaker of English would not take
very long to observe that [s], [z], and [ɪz] are
markers of plurality bat bats [s], pod pods [z],

103

smudge>smudges [ɪz]. Therefore, we see that the
basic morpheme {s} is the marker of the plural in
English. Due to the environment in which the plural occurs, however, the three basic variant morphemes or allomorphs are [s], [z], and [ɪz]. The
same occurs in Spanish, in which the basic marker
of the plural is {s} potro>potros, cuerda>cuerdas,
agente>agentes. The variant morpheme {es} occurs
in other environments (-l, -n, -d, -r, -s, -z)

delantal	delantales
harén	harenes
red	redes
color	colores
anís	anises
perdiz	perdices

     In such words as tío/tía, chico/chica, espo-
so/esposa, the morpheme {o} is a clear marker of
masculinity while the variant morpheme {a} indicates
femininity. Since in such cases the morpheme is attached to the stem, the morpheme is considered a
bound morpheme (el morfema ligado); that is to say,
the morpheme is the gender-marking element for
either the masculine or the feminine form. This
type of morpheme varies according to traditional
Spanish word-formation perro/perra, actor/actriz,
conde/condesa, chillón/chillona, inglés/inglesa,
doctor/doctora, alemán/alemana, chiquitín/chiquiti-
na, príncipe/princesa. Free or unbound morphemes
(los morfemas libres) are completely independent,
dissimilar forms macho/hembra, carnero/oveja, ma-
rido/mujer, yerno/nuera, padre/madre, hombre/mujer,
caballo/yegua, varón/hembra, toro/vaca, tiburón/tin-
torera.

     In the case of what is known traditionally as
the conjugation of verbs, the sounds that are generally thought of as basic verb-endings are in fact a
string of variant morphemes. The age-old subject in
each case might be thought of as the environment of
the morpheme.

	MORPHEME:			INFLEXIONAL MORPHEMES:

AMAR	AM-			-o -as -a -amos -áis -an

BEBER	BEB-			-o -es -e -emos -éis -en

PULIR	PUL-			-o -es -e -imos -ís -en

While all these morphemic variations are fairly
simple in the regular verbal pattern, there is a
slight complication when stem-changing verbs (los
verbos de cambio radical) and irregular verbs come
into the picture. There are many verbs in which
the vowel changes from the infinitive form with
final stress and the root-stressed conjugated form.
Thus there is a shift in morpheme from $\{e\} > \{ié\}$

alentar   aliento   ascender   asciendo   sentar   siento
apretar   aprieto   entender   entiendo   mentir   miento
cegar   ciego   querer   quiero   invertir invierto

from $\{o\} > \{ué\}$

almorzar   almuerza   volcar   vuelca   mover   mueve
contar   cuenta   doler   duele   soler   suele
rogar   ruega   moler   muele   dormir   duerme
sonar   suena   morder   muerde   morir   muere

from $\{e\} > \{i\}$

pedir   pido   corregir   corrijo
medir   mido   regir   rijo
despedir   despido   henchir   hincho
impedir   impido   elegir   elijo
ceñir   ciño   gemir   gimo
concebir   concibo   freír   frío
teñir   tiño   reír   río
engreír   engrío   sonreír   sonrío

The opposite shift in morpheme also takes place
continuar   continúo   guiar   guío
graduar   gradúo   liar   lío
avaluar   avalúo   fiar   fío
actuar   actúo   criar   crío
evaluar   evalúo   piar   pío
acentuar   acentúo   desafiar desafío
perpetuar   perpetúo   confiar confío [17]

Verb-forms which do not follow the normative
pattern are a bit more complex in that the morpheme
is often a completely different form but not always.
Ir and ser are two such verbs whose morphemes are
completely different.

106

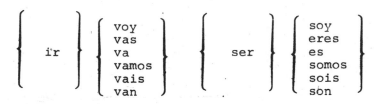

$$\left\{ i\cdot r \right\} \left\{ \begin{matrix} voy \\ vas \\ va \\ vamos \\ vais \\ van \end{matrix} \right\} \left\{ ser \right\} \left\{ \begin{matrix} soy \\ eres \\ es \\ somos \\ sois \\ son \end{matrix} \right\}$$

Thus far we have dealt primarily with <u>inflex-ional morphology</u> (<u>la morfología inflexional</u>). <u>Derivational morphology</u> (<u>la morfología derivacional</u>) differs somewhat in that it deals with base-forms to which endings must be attached according to the internal logic of a given language. It examines the different parts of words and determines acceptable patterns within their combinations. Derivational morphology is basically lexical in nature since it concerns itself with image-words and segment formations. Thus the speaker is able to control, not only the production of words as such, but can also use the basic stems such as <u>cant-</u>, <u>orient-</u>, <u>enferm-</u>, and <u>comun-</u>, in combination with suffixes like <u>-or</u>, <u>-al</u>, <u>-izo</u>, and -ismo, and with prefixes like <u>des-</u>, <u>in-</u>, <u>bis-</u>, and <u>tri-</u>. In other words, careful observation of stems and their relationship to other segments (traditionally prefixes and suffixes) provides a valuable step toward fluency in the language learning process. Note carefully the following combinations of observable morphemes:

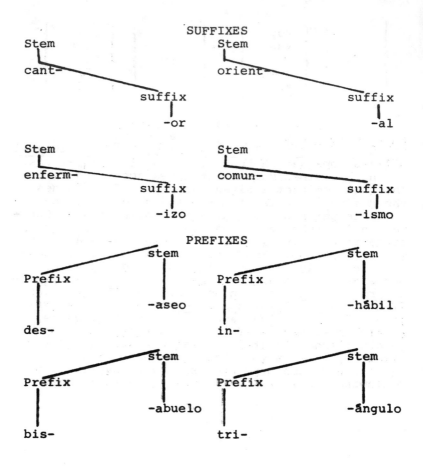

SUFFIXES

Stem   Stem

cant-   orient-

            suffix   suffix

             -or   -al

Stem   Stem

enferm-   comun-

            suffix   suffix

             -izo   -ismo

PREFIXES

            stem   stem

Prefix   Prefix

            -aseo   -hábil

des-   in-

            stem   stem

Prefix   Prefix

            -abuelo   -ángulo

bis-   tri-

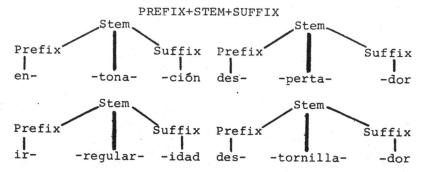

PREFIX+STEM+SUFFIX

Prefix	Stem	Suffix	Prefix	Stem	Suffix
en-	-tona-	-ción	des-	-perta-	-dor
Prefix	Stem	Suffix	Prefix	Stem	Suffix
ir-	-regular-	-idad	des-	-tornilla-	-dor

Stem-morphemes may also combine with other morphemes to form the characteristically Spanish compounds which are found in great proliferation throughout the language.

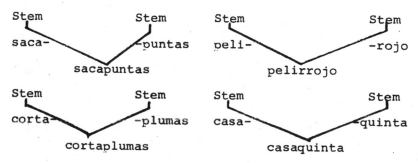

Stem	Stem	Stem	Stem
saca-	-puntas	peli-	-rojo
sacapuntas		pelirrojo	
Stem	Stem	Stem	Stem
corta-	-plumas	casa-	-quinta
cortaplumas		casaquinta	

SUPRASEGMENTALS. In the analysis of any language there are many factors involved which go far beyond the basic elements of efficient vocalic and consonantal production, linkage, sound grouping, and related matters. It is, in fact, quite possible to articulate all vowels, vowel combinations, and consonant-vowel segments in a given language with great precision and clarity and still remain a virtual stranger to that idiom. Moreover, it is precisely on this level of mastery that many students of language ultimately remain despite a lifetime of effort to the contrary. One might even go so far as to say that perhaps so much formal emphasis is placed on the accurate production of sound segments and grammatical forms per se that the more comprehensive features essential to near-native expression are ultimately neglected or perhaps never even touched upon meaningfully. In short, fluency in a language comprises much more than drill in sounds, sound groupings, grammar, syntax, and related features. Instead, mastery of a language requires a gradual but thorough sensitization to its rhythm and flow, its pacing, its high points and low points, its accompanying facial gestures and hand signs, and many other features of its native production. For the average native, all these aspects of language are learned long before formal training of any kind commences since it is really a process which is begun in infancy and continues, consciously or otherwise, throughout one's life.

As one analyzes a language from without, it becomes progressively more apparent that there is an almost unending series of elements to be observed and mastered which make up the whole gamut of tonal patterns characteristic of one language and which differ considerably from other languages. In a very technical sense there are physiological and acoustical aspects. In addition, there are characteristic rises and falls in pitch closely linked with features of stress and intonation. There is also a characteristic cadence which may seem rapid or slow, monotonous or replete with highness and lowness. Finally, all of these aspects of a language, as well as many others, reflect not only its normative oral production, but the entire spectrum of intentions, emotions, and attitudes on the part of its speakers.

While one might delve into each of the aspects mentioned, we shall limit ourselves to five additional features of language which are often referred to as suprasegmentals (los suprasegmentos): stress, pitch, intonation, duration, and timbre.

STRESS. Stress (la acentuación) is very important in most of the world's languages. It refers to the

greater articulatory thrust which is placed on one
syllable more than on all others. Stress may occur on a vowel, vowel-consonant, or consonant-vowel
combination in any series of segments. Observe the
following basic patterns of stress:

STRESS ON A VOWEL	amo	[ámᴐ]
STRESS ON A VOWEL-CONSONANT	árbol	[árbᴐl]
STRESS ON A CONSONANT-VOWEL	casa	[kásᴇ]

Whereas in Spanish stress occurs at fixed
points (see pages 10-12), in English it often varies
from one word to another according to a number of
factors. Normally, stress placement is on the first
syllable in English, but there are as many exceptions as there are cases which follow the general
rule. For example, words like PERcolator, Imitator,
CARpet, SENsible, Arid, and INsulate all follow this
stress pattern. Nonetheless, there are as many words
in which the stress will appear on any one of a number of syllables--from the second to the final. Observe the following randomly selected possibilities
of stress:

STRESS ON THE SECOND SYLLABLE dependency
[dɪ'pɛndɘnsi]
redundancy
[rɘ'dʌndɘnsi]
STRESS ON THE THIRD SYLLABLE apperception
[apr'sɛpʃn]
appreciation
[ɘpriʃyæʃn]
STRESS ON THE FINAL SYLLABLE pioneer
[pʌyo'nɪr]
veneer
[vɘ'nɪr]
chandelier
[ʃændɘ'lɪr]

In addition, there are identical and near-identical
words which are distinguished on the basis of
stress placement. For example, the word dessert is
distinguished from desert merely by stress--[dɘ-
zɘrt], ['dɛzɘrt]. The same might be said of combinations like billow ['bɪlou] and below [bɪ'lou],
expert ['ɛksprt] and expert [ɘks'pɛrt], address
['adrɘs] and address [ɘ'drɛs].

111

In longer English words there are often primary and secondary stresses. The former may be indicated by ['] and the latter by [ˌ].

complementary	[ˌkɑmplɪˈmɛntɛri]
parliamentary	[ˌpɑrlɪˈmɛntɛri]
penitential	[ˌpɛnɪˈtɛnʃl̩]
usually	[ˈjuˌʒwɑli]
inattentiveness	[ˌɪnəˈtɛntɪvnɛs]
hospitable	[ˈhɑsˌpɪtɑbl̩]

Stress in Spanish is distinctive, but it does not have an important effect on the quantity of the vowels since quantity is not contrastive as such. In such words as <u>taco/barco</u>, <u>pecho/peste</u>, <u>coche/corso</u>, <u>puna/purga</u>, we can observe whether the vowel is in an open or closed syllable; nonetheless, the length or quantity of each of them is the same. The force of the production of sound or stress gives prominence to the vowel in the utterance. This is particularly distinctive in the case of diphthongs whether they are combinations of strong plus weak, weak plus strong, or weak plus weak vowels.

For natives there are many clues in utterances with varying patterns of intonation which point to the exact meaning of a word or utterance. Their hearing has been conditioned, consciously or otherwise, to the many subtleties of the language, and in matters of correct stress they generally react positively. Moreover, they react with automaticity of response, which is an essential feature of native fluency. The <u>hispanohablante</u> never says [pɛˈpá] pop when [ˈpɑpɛ] pope is intended. Likewise he does not say [ˈbɑila] dance! when [baiˈlé] I danced is meant. The context also provides all sorts of phonemic clues, and the speaker distinguishes immediately between <u>el</u> <u>Papa</u> <u>es</u> <u>viejo</u> (the <u>Pope</u> <u>is</u> <u>old</u>) and <u>el</u> <u>papá</u> <u>es</u> <u>viejo</u> (the <u>daddy</u> <u>is</u> <u>old</u>). For the non-native these matters are not so simple and are by no means automatic. Hence awareness of changes in morphology and phonemic aspects is essential in order to be able to understand what is being said.

In addition to its phonemic value, stress always

112

touches upon the morphemic level as well, particularly in verb conjugations since it is often a regu-
lator of tense and mood.

INDICATIVE PRESENT	INDICATIVE PRETERITE	SUBJUNCTIVE PRESENT
(yo) canto	(yo) canté..........	(yo) cante
(él) canta·.........(él)	cantó ·.....(él)	cante
(yo) tomo	(yo) tomé..........	(yo) tome
(él) toma·.........(él)	tomó ·.....(él)	tome

It should be apparent by now that stress is far from
being regular and that there are many inconsistencies. Even in monosyllabic segments in which a
written accent is used to differentiate otherwise
identical pairs, there is also a noticeable difference in oral production. Some good examples of
this are sé (I know) and se (oneself), tú (you) and
tu (your), te (you) and té (tea), sí (yes) and si
(if, whether), dé (give) and de (of, from). When
these words occur together in an utterance, the
stress used differs ever so slightly according to
meaning and point of emphasis. In an utterance
like yo sé que se la dio, there is clearly greater
stress on the first sé. In one like te digo que
siempre toma té, the greater stress is on the
second té. It should be obvious, then, that stress
in such cases is also regulated by context.

In distinguishing verb-tenses stress is morphologically very basic, frequently indicating shifts
not only in tense, but mood as well. These matters
are distinctive to the native's ear, however, without having to resort to something as elemental as a
written accent. Compare the stress in each of the
following minimal pairs: hay/ahí, aire/aíre, ha-
lla/allá, anden/andén, paro/paró, hábito/habito,
mama/mamá, fábrica/fabrica, paso/pasó, río/rió,
máscara/mascara, cante/canté, pague/pagué, quite/
quité.

Frequently in English a shift in stress is contrastive, one stress placement providing a substan-
tive form, the other, a verb-form. For instance
EXtract is the noun while exTRACT is the verb-form,

and this is a fairly recurrent pattern. Notice in the following words how the difference in stress placement makes for a different part of speech:

CONtract	[ˈkɑntrɑkt]	conTRACT	[kʌnˈtrɑkt]
CONvert	[ˈkɑnvrt]	conVERT	[kʌnˈvɛrt]
ABstract	[ˈɑbstrɑkt]	abSTRACT	[ɛbˈstrɑkt]
ADdress	[ˈɑdrɛs]	adDRESS	[ɛˈdrɛs]
TORment	[ˈtɔrmɛnt]	torMENT	[tɔrˈmɛnt]
PERmit	[ˈpɛrmɪt]	perMIT	[pɛrˈmɪt]
PROduce	[ˈprodus]	proDUCE	[proˈdus]
TRANSfer	[ˈtrɑnsfɛr]	transFER	[trɑnsˈfɛr]

Many words which are near-cognates in Spanish and English are distinguishable on the basis of stress placement since in the latter the stress is always on the first syllable and in the former it is on the last.

AGitator	agitaDOR
ORator	oraDOR
REGulator	regulaDOR
PALpitator	palpitaDOR
DEmonstrator	demostraDOR
INnovator	innovaDOR
REnovator	renovaDOR
IMmolator	inmolaDOR
CARburetor	carburaDOR

A similar group of English-Spanish contrastively stressed words is found in those which end in -ista (pianista/pianist, comunista/Communist). Normally speaking, in this type of word the stress in English is upon the first syllable or upon the originally stressed syllable in the root word. In Spanish the matter is simplified in that the stress placement is automatically on -ista.

flautist	flautista
nihilist	nihilista
absurdist	absurdista
violinist	violinista
harpist	arpista
Marxist	marxista
violoncellist	violoncelista
Baptist	bautista
anarchist	anarquista

Methodist   metodista
monarchist   monarquista[18]

Each word has a prominent stress, but in an utterance when many sounds follow each other a primary
stress is prevalent over the whole sequence. Often,
though not always, the primary stress is on the verbal element:
                 Paco vende periódicos.
                 Compra siempre aquí.
Even when the utterance is lengthy, although a secondary stress is added, the latter never has the
prominence of the primary one.
            El lector, a quien tú miras, es el pro-
            tagonista de la obra.
            El tabajo le resulta muy pesado desde que
            se mudó a las afueras de la ciudad.
It is understood that individual words have their
own stress according to the basic rules of articulation
            la casa [læ kásæ]
            tiene   [tjéna]
            cinco   [síŋkɔ]
            cuartos [kwárt:s].
But when one articulates in a sequence, the individual
stress is diluted. The part of the utterance that
has more importance for the speaker becomes prominent enough to carry the primary stress, thus reflecting the attitudinal or intentional aspect of
stress. If one groups the words which appear above
in one utterance, the result in most cases will be
four slightly differing meanings according to the
particular element which is stressed in each case.
            La casa tiene cinco cuartos.
            La casa tiene cinco cuartos.
            La casa tiene cinco cuartos.
            La casa tiene cinco cuartos.
By giving the primary stress to each underlined word,
we in effect give importance to different concepts
through a subtle use of stress. In the first case
the verbal element is stressed and is probably the
most frequently encountered type of Spanish utterance. In the second case we are stressing the fact
that the house has five rooms and not the bungalow

115

or the palace. In the third case we are emphasizing the fact that there are five and not four or six rooms. In the final version the emphasis is upon the fact that we are dealing with rooms and not bathrooms or dining rooms. Thus stress may go from one element to the next, depending upon the desired emphasis.

In English, when stress functions on the utterance level, it does not change the meaning of lexical items per se but increases the relative importance of the lexical item being emphasized or contrasted. For example, in an utterance like I have to go home, stress placement varies according to the segment of the utterance being stressed in any given case. Thus, the following four possibilities result:

I have to go home.
I have to go home.
I have to go home.
I have to go home.

While this is also done in Spanish, the latter also admits of word rearrangement without altering the meaning in any way. Thus, the above-mentioned utterance might be expressed Tengo que ir a casa yo or A casa tengo que ir yo as well as Yo tengo que ir a casa.

PITCH. Pitch (el tono) refers to the relative rise and fall of a sound. Together with stress, it often provides various patterns of intonation. Since it colors an utterance to the extent that it affects its meaning, it is phonemic in nature. For example, any speaker of English will quickly perceive the difference between Bill is here and Is Bill here? I think she is pretty differs considerably from Do you think she is pretty? We could take this utterance a step farther by asking Don't you think she is pretty? Since the native speaker is conditioned to the basic sound system, his or her voice will automatically descend at the end of the affirmative statement, it will rise when asking a question, and

116

will rise when asking the second type of question
but less so.

In Spanish there are similar patterns of intonation as in Escribe bien. ¿Escribe bien? ¿No
escribe bien? On the level of basic speech patterns,
intonation is really a matter of the voice going up
or down or being sustained in order to express a
variety of meanings and nuances. The ascendencies
(los ascensos) and descendencies (los descensos) of
the Spanish speaker are similar in these basic patterns to those of the three English ones. However,
this is not always the case. In fact, one of the
sources of beauty and dimension of expression in
Spanish lies precisely in the area of pitch and intonation.

The problem of these two aspects of speech is a
very complex one. With reference to pitch, we are
not speaking of the narrowly acoustical sense of
frequency of vibrations or the various acoustical
aspects of the musical flow of the voice. In this
sense the melody of the human voice is associated
with the acoustics of pitch as well as matters of
duration, timbre, and individual modulation. While
interesting and useful, these are not the aspects
of pitch with which we are concerned at this point.
Instead, it is a matter of pitch being inextricably
bound with intonation patterns--the tonal quality
of the voice, its rising and falling, its sustaining
aspects, and its modulation according to meaning.

INTONATION. Intonation (la entonación) refers to
the musical rhythm or flow of a language. There are
many accepted ways of marking patterns of intona-
tion--musical notes, arrow-indicators, numbers, and
graphic lines. The latter have been arbitrarily
chosen for the purposes of this text. In marking
intonation patterns, it is helpful to think in terms
of one's normal tone of voice (el tono normal de
voz) as a straight line, hereafter indicated by
T. N. and dotted lines: T. N. ....

117

Some utterances begin on the same level of pitch as the basic normal tone of voice while others begin considerably above or below. Others end fairly high above the normal tone of voice while still others end somewhat below or on the same level. What occurs between the beginning and end of an utterance is what gives language its assertive, emotional, interrogative, and exclamatory range of possibilities.

In English contours of intonation can be specified in terms of pitch levels--high (ascendant), low (descendant), and sustained; however, there are shades and gradations according to the individual speaker, the speech community, and the area of the world where the language is spoken.

In American English the basic pattern for affirmative and negative utterances is similar to the Spanish one. One begins on the level of the normal tone of voice and descends progressively.

He is going to the theatre.

She is buying coffee.

In simple questions, that is, the yes-no type, there is sustained intonation in the beginning, followed by a fairly ascendant rise in intonation which is never so high as the equivalent Spanish interrogative intonation pattern.

Are you a retired employee?

Is she the professor's aunt?

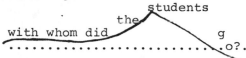

    In questions which begin with an interrogative pronoun or some form of adverb, the intonation pattern changes somewhat. It goes from a middle tone to an ascendant tone and then falls beneath the normal tone of voice. Consequently, the basic interrogation pattern is there but shortened, followed by a fairly significant drop.

When did you go home?

With whom did the students go?

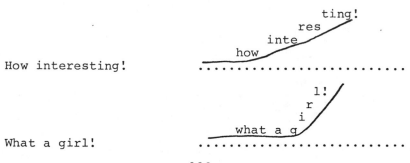

    In brief exclamatory utterances the pattern begins at the normal tone of voice and rises considerably at the end. In an exclamation like How nice!, the initial segment begins at the normal tone and ascends rapidly on the second segment

This pattern is fairly recurrent in brief exclamatory utterances in English.

How interesting!

What a girl!

In longer exclamatory utterances, the pattern
changes. The speaker starts at the normal tone,
descends below, and ultimately ascends far above.
Thus, in an utterance like I wish I knew that story!,
the first segment (I) is uttered at the normal
level, the second (wish) descends, the third returns
to the normal tone (I), and the rest ascends (knew)
and may be sustained (that story). These slightly
more complex patterns are fairly recurrent.

If only I were there with you!

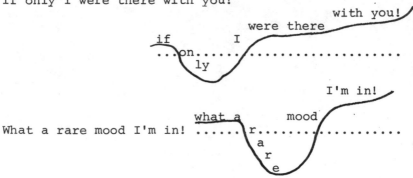

What a rare mood I'm in!

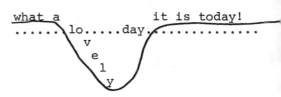

What a lovely day it is today!

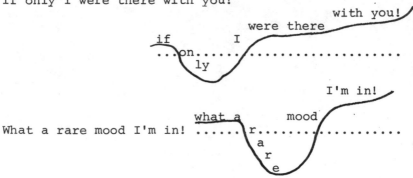

Needless to say, there are many other patterns of
intonation in English, many of which are expansions
of the basic patterns outlined above.[19]

   There are three basic patterns of intonation
in Spanish. The affirmative utterance (la frase
enunciativa) starts rather slowly and gradually
rises to the normal level, and eventually descends
again.

```
Estudias el asunto.   T. N./...tudia.sel.asun.......
                          /  Es              to.
```

In the <u>interrogative</u> utterance (la <u>frase</u> interroga-tiva) there is a definitely altered pattern. It begins somewhat low, then rises above the normal level, comes down to the normal level again, and ultimately rises.

```
                                        /to?
                                      /sun
                              dia \ / a
¿Estudias el asunto?  T. N. /..tu...sel.............
                           /¿Es
```

The <u>exclamatory</u> <u>utterance</u> (la <u>frase</u> <u>exclamatoria</u>) be-gins rather low, goes up steadily and then drops off abruptly.

```
                                  /lasun
                                 /  se     to!
¡Estudias el asunto!  T. N. ./....dia.............\...
                            /      tu
                           /¡Es
```

In more complex utterances there is frequently an added clause between the subject and the final clause. In this type the voice lingers along the horizontal line before the interruption of the breath group, then it comes down again, is held normal and is somewhat suspended before the following pause, then it comes down for a third time, goes up for just a bit, and finally falls.

El hombre que lee el periódico es el jefe de la ofi-cina.

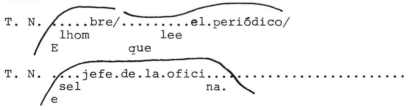

```
T. N. /.....bre/.........el.periódico/
      /  lhom            lee
     /  E          que

T. N. /...jefe.de.la.ofici...\............
      /  sel              na.  \
     / e
```

121

In this same type of utterance, if one or two more
clauses or phrases are added, the basic pattern remains the same although it is of necessity somewhat
extended.

En los meses del verano trabaja en el campo con los
obreros de mi padre.

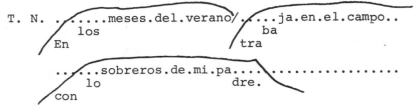

T. N. ....meses.del.verano/.....ja.en.el.campo..
      los   ba
    En   tra

..,...sobreros.de.mi.pa.....................
    lo   dre.
  con

El que sepa la verdad es mejor que la diga.

T. N. ......sepa.la.verdad/.....jor.que.la.di.....
      que   me   ga.
    El   es

     The most frequently employed interrogative
utterance is the <u>absolute</u> type or yes-no type since
in asking the question nothing is supplied except
the inquiry. The voice begins below the normal tone
of voice, remains at the normal level, and finally
ends by going up.

¿Es Ud. el dueño?   T. N. /...Ud...el.due....
                                  ¿Es   ño?

A <u>relative</u> question--one in which the person asking
the question supplies a type of summing up--begins
at the normal tone of voice, rises only briefly, and
ends on the normal level.

¿Con que hace lo que puede?

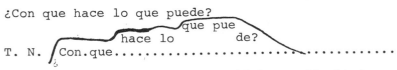

T. N. /Con.que................................

An <u>information</u> question--one which usually begins

with a pronoun, a preposition and a pronoun, or other
parts of speech--starts rather low, then rises to
the normal tone of voice, and then goes down again.

¿Qué desean Uds.?   T. N.

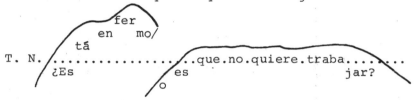

A choice question--a this-or-that kind of question--
begins rather low, rises quickly, comes down a bit
and levels, goes down again, rises once more, remains on the normal level, and finally descends.

¿Está enfermo o es que no quiere trabajar?

T. N.

While there are other types of interrogative utterances, those analyzed thus far are the basic ones.

     Exclamatory statements are somewhat more com-
plex. Probably the simplest type of exclamatory
utterance is the simple basic command, which begins
below the normal tone of voice, rises very sharply,
and comes down again just as quickly.

¡Afuera!   T. N.

Any kind of begging or supplication starts rather
low, goes up, and comes down again before a brief
pause. Following the pause, it begins again below
the normal tone of voice, rises quickly, and descends at a point a little lower than normal.

Una limosnita, por favor.

123

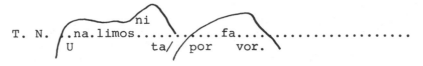

```
                      ni
T. N. /.na.limos.....\./...fa....\...............
      /U         ta//por    vor.   \
```

Admiration begins rather low and maintains the normal level, lowering just a bit at the very end.

¡Qué hermoso sol hace!

```
                                moso sol ha
                  T. N./....her..............\
                      /¡Qué                ce!\
```

Statements expressing quantity or intensity start rather low, go up to the normal tone and rise slightly more at the very end.

Hace tanto calor.

```
                                      lor.
              T. N.../...tanto.ca........
                    /  ce
                   /Ha
```

Statements of approval begin below the normal tone of voice, rise somewhat, and go down at the end.

Con mucho gusto.

```
              T. N../...mucho.gus....\...
                    /Con           to. \
```

Answers to yes-no questions have essentially the same pattern as those found in statements of approval. The question begins low and ends by ascending. The answer starts at the normal tone of voice, pauses, descends, rises to the normal level, and descends at the end.

¿Lo quieres?

```
                              res?
              T. N. /....quie............
                    /¿Lo
```

Sí, lo quiero.

```
              T. N. Sí/./..quie...\.......
                     /lo        ro. \
```

¿Está aquí?

```
                              quí?
              T. N. /...tá.a............
                    /¿Es
```

124

No, no está aquí.   T. N.

Patterns of intonation are difficult to limit in
type and number. Even within the framework of the
basic patterns included in each type, there are
circumstances in which the regular pattern may be
altered for the sake of emphasis or contrast. In
contrastive or emphatic statements stress and pitch
may fall on any unit of the utterance, regardless
of place. In these cases the entire meaning of the
utterance is changed. For instance,the intonation
pattern for an utterance like He comes only at one
would be

T. N.   ......solo.a.la.u..............................
           ne   na.
       Vie

For the utterance He comes alone at one, the pattern
of intonation is somewhat different.

T. N.   solo a la ....u.........................
           ne   na.
       Vie

     One of the salient features of unfinished ut-
terances is that the voice is held at the same
level for a period of time, affecting the pitch and
intonation pattern. Traditionally this is shown
orthographically by a series of dots (los puntos
suspensivos) .... The voice is held at the
same level above the normal tone in this type of
incomplete utterance.

T. N. ...tó.que.vivía.................................
     Con

T. N. ....pre.habla..................................
     Siem

T. N. /....re.café.leche.huevos.....................
      /Quie

It is possible to express oneself in a single
utterance, and it occurs frequently in daily speech.
Quite often there is more than one statement involved, and they are logically interrelated. In
this type of grouping a new element enters the pic-
ture--one known as juncture (el enlace). The latter on the orthographic level is usually indicated
by the use of blanks between words, colons,
semi-colons, commas, and other forms of punctuation.
In the spoken language, juncture refers simply to
any kind of pause--long or short.

When one refers to pauses on a larger scale, as
in the case of pauses between utterances, one refers
to terminal junctures (las terminaciones).[20] Again
in this area there are conventional ways of marking
these pauses. We have chosen to give preference to
the single slash to separate phonemic or breath
groups (/) and double slashes (//) to refer to the
equivalents of the orthographic period.

//El muchacho les dijo todo lo que sabía/ pero
no pudieron averiguar la verdad//

//Mira como brilla/ aunque es tan pequeño //

Junctures are not so simple to detect or inter-
pret in certain cases. Even a native cannot tell
them apart unless the phonemic group is heard in
context or is aided by intonation. Junctures are
indications of pauses, and the latter are often
intimately linked with meaning. In other words, it
is not simply a matter of traditional punctuation.
The following statements contain varying types of
juncture according to meaning:
        Visitaron la Casa Blanca.
        La casa blanca es de mi hermano.
        ¿Está seguro de que la sabes bien?
        Prefiere observar las aves desde el balcón.
        Está barriendo el patio.

126

Va _riendo_ mientras piensa en lo que dijo.
¿Le llamaste a _Montenegro_?
Ese _monte negro_ es el más grande de la región.
If these utterances were presented completely out of
context, even natives would encounter a certain de-
gree of difficulty in knowing which is which.

DURATION. Duration (_la duración_) or _quantity_ (_la_
cantidad) refers to the length that a vowel may
have in any given segment or utterance. The same
may apply to consonants depending upon the manner
of articulation. In many languages like English
there are long and short vowels. For instance, the
vowels in the words _mean_ and _car_ are long while
those in _mint_ and _cut_ are short. Phonetically,
length of vowel is usually indicated by the diacrit-
ical sign ⌈:⌉ following it. Thus we have long
vowels in ⌈'mi:n⌉ and ⌈'ka:r⌉ and short vowels in
⌈'mɪnt⌉ and ⌈'kʌt⌉. Although one encounters variants for a variety of reasons, normally speaking, the
long vowels in English tend to be ⌈ɑ:⌉ _far_, _father_,
bother; ⌈i:⌉ _beet_, _sea_, _need_; ⌈ɔ:⌉ _bought_, _saw_,
naught; ⌈u:⌉ _food_, _tool_, _rule_. Most other vocalic
phonemes tend to be short ⌈ɪ⌉ _sit_, _split_, _pit_; ⌈ɛ⌉
pet, _red_, _get_; ⌈æ⌉ _grass_, _ask_, _flask_; ⌈o⌉ _produce_,
tote, _moat_; ⌈u⌉ _hood_, _should_, _took_; ⌈ʌ⌉ _mutter_, _stut-_
ter, _thunder_. The schwa sound ⌈ə⌉ in current practice often symbolizes any unstressed vowels in English _enable_ ⌈ə'neybḷ⌉, _enough_ ⌈ə'nʌf⌉, _annoy_ ⌈ə'nɔɪ⌉.[21]

In Spanish all vowels have the very same length,
so that this particular sound feature is not distinctive. The length of vowels was a main distinctive
feature in Classical Latin and continues to be so
in languages like Italian, English, and German. In
Spanish, however, vowel length is never of primary
consideration. In fact, Spanish should be thought
of as a syllable-timed language; that is, every syllable in the language is articulated with nearly
equal articulatory thrust even though there are syllables of primary and secondary stress. This does
not mean to imply that the language is phonated in
a monotonous stress-value after stress-value pattern

127

without varying degrees of prominence. Instead, all
syllables are enunciated with nearly equal clarity
and stress while some syllables carry an additional
articulatory thrust.

As has been alluded to, consonants are also
characterized by duration even though this aspect is
less important in Spanish than it is in some other
languages. For example, an explosive [t] or [d]
tends to have less duration than a multiple vibrant
[r̄]. Likewise, sibilants and fricatives tend to
have more duration than explosives or stops.

TIMBRE. Timbre (el timbre) is closely related to
the production of a given sound and cannot really
be detached from it. On a very elementary level,
timbre refers to the relative clearness or fuzziness
with which a sound is produced. It is a relatively
important aspect of speech, particularly for actors,
singers, public speakers, speech pathologists, pho-
neticians, and people involved in general with the
technical production of sound. To the average layman, it is significant only when judging the different types of voices that may or may not violate
what one considers the normal standard of speech.
Thus people tend to classify voices as thin, husky,
grave, hoarse, shrill, and shrieking, or they may
use terms of their own invention if they react negatively to a voice. In many cases it is merely a
matter of taste, yielding one type of reaction in
one case to a certain type of voice and still
another to another type of voice. There is no question that the relative importance of timbre figures
in such matters as clear speech, normal as opposed
to pathologically abnormal speech, speech in the
field of communication, television, movies, and the
theatre. Nevertheless, it does not usually create
serious variations in phonemes and their production
and consequently does not really function on a phonemic level. Timbre does not essentially alter the
efficaciousness of daily speech or interfere with
basic communication in any way. Thus, its importance

is secondary in a study of this type.

   Stress and pitch become basic when one wishes
to analyze the suprasegmentals of a spoken language.
On various occasions we have observed bilingual individuals whose pitch is altered considerably when
shifting from one language to another. From the
layman's point of view, a male speaker may sound
more "masculine" in one language and less "masculine" in another. Such observations are related to
pitch as the individual speaker has mastered the notion of pitch and related suprasegmentals in connection with language. Fortunately, speech is never
objectively bound up with notions of sex on the
level of pitch except for the slight differences encountered in the oral production of males versus fe-
males and children. On a practical level, the notion
of pitch becomes very important when one progresses
to near-native status in the acquisition of a language.[22] This does not mean to imply that the notion should be discarded completely. Instead, one
should have a basic awareness of pitch and its
function on many levels of communication since both
pitch and stress provide us with different intonation patterns with significant phonemic and morphological effects.

STRESS AND ASSIMILATION ACROSS CULTURES. A very
interesting aspect of stress is found in rather
curious examples provided by borrowings from English
into Spanish. Very often brand names of English or
American origin enter the language in a matter-of-
fact manner and are adapted very quickly to the prevailing sound system. It is interesting to observe
what occurs in a short period of time to names which
are virtually household items in our country. Notice in the following random examples how the stress
and phonetic features of Spanish take over and create a sound grouping which would be virtually foreign
to the originators of these products:
Cadillac   [kɐ́ɗɪyák]   Anacin   [ʔɐnɐs̩ín]
Kaopectate   [kɐːpɐktátə]   Bayer   [bɐyɛr]

129

Bufferin	[bʌfərín]	Buick	[bwík],
Ultraban	[n̩ltreban]	Aerosol	[earːsɔ́l]
Palmolive	[pélmːlítə]	Colgate	[kːlqátə]
Ban Roll-On	[benrːlśn],	Entoral	[əntːrál]
Vicks Vapor Rub	[bıkzteepːrỵ]	Kodak	[kódeᵏ]

Frequently, words are borrowed but undergo the process of the addition of the characteristic Spanish epenthetic e̲--the vowel sound always heard before s̲ plus a consonant.

Sprite	[əsprítə]	smoking	[əzmókın]
spray	[əsprái]	spaghetti	[əspeeéti]
Spry	[əsprái]	Spam	[əspán]

Some words have become popular like club̲--[klú]̲, singular, and [klútə̲s], plural. All languages force words quite naturally into this same process. This is done frequently in English in adopting foreign words. The following are some examples:

au gratin	[oʹqrǽtɛn]
chantilly	[ʃæn'tili]
champagne	[ʃam'peyn]
Cordova	[kor'dovɛ]
egret	[ʹi:qrɛt]
matador	[ʹmatɛdɔr]
volaré	[voʹlarɛy]

The strength of the system and its influence upon word formation can be appreciated in onomatopeic renderings of sounds. In English a dog barks bow wow while a Spanish one howls ¡gua-gua! In the Hispanic world cats cry miau-miau; cows, mu-mu; birds, pi-pi-pi; sheep, ba-ba-ba; goats, be-be-be; roosters, qui-qui-ri-quí; chickens, clo-clo, clo-clo. One need hardly mention that animal sounds are identical throughout the world. It is the manner in which humans hear them that makes them significant from the point of view of sound production. In other words, humans provide a rendition of animal sounds, not according to acoustical animal sound production, but in relation to their human perception of those sounds as a result of native conditioning to a given sound system. Verbs which develop in a language to express the sounds made by animals may or may not have an onomatopeic origin since the concept involved may derive either from an imitation of the sounds as perceived or may be

130

simply a philologically derived image-word based on a description of animal behavior or sounds. Regardless of their origin, the following verbs are a random sampling of some of the verbs used in modern Spanish to describe animal sounds:

animal(s):	verb:
lobo, perro	aullar
oso, toro, caballo	bramar
rana	croar
loro	charlar
conejo, liebre, zorra, loro	chillar
ruiseñor, canario, golondrina	gorjear
gorrión, grillo	chirriar
gallina	cloquear
oveja, ciervo, cabra	balar
cuervo, gaviota	graznar
puerco, jabalí, zorra	gruñir
gato	maullar
buey, vaca	mugir
caballo, burro	relinchar
loro, serpiente	silbar
lobo, perro	ulular
canario, ruiseñor	trinar
gorrión, polluelo	piar
abeja, mosca, mosquito	zumbar
canario	gargantear
burro, asno	rebuznar
perro	ladrar

Thus, it is easy to see how languages frequently reflect, not only the imitation of animal sounds as they are perceived, but descriptions of these sounds which develop variously from language to language. Whatever their source may be, the cries of animals in any language can tell us a great deal about the phonetic and phonemic approaches of the particular speech community in question.[23]

EXERCISES

THEORY
A. ANSWER THESE QUESTIONS BRIEFLY.
1. What are the main suprasegmentals in Spanish?
2. What is a bound morpheme?
3. What is a free morpheme?
4. How significant is duration in Spanish?
5. What does the study of morphology focus upon?
6. What is meant by inflexional morphology?
7. How does derivational differ from inflexional · morphology?
8. What is meant by stress?
9. What do the pairs macho/hembra and caballo/yegua exemplify?
10. What are some examples of stem-morphemes in Spanish?

B. FILL IN THE BLANKS IN THESE STATEMENTS.
1. Primary and _____ stress both have a function with reference to pitch and stress.
2. Ascendencies and _____ are basic to Spanish patterns of intonation.
3. In the study of stress one should always depart from the point of view of the original normal _____ of voice.
4. Intonation patterns help the learner to master the various features of _____, interrogation, and exclamation.
5. _____ refers, on the level of spoken Spanish, to the various pauses and their significance within the sound system.
6. When one refers to pauses on a larger scale, as in complete or complex utterances, one refers to _____.
7. Stress is a very important feature of spoken Spanish, but it does not affect the _____.
8. _____ deals with word segments and word interrelationships.
9. _____ morphology deals with the various endings that words or utterances take in different syntactical positions.
10. A(n) _____ morpheme is one which is attached to the root of a stem.

132

C. DEFINE BRIEFLY.
1. a syllable-timed   4. a morpheme
   language
2. intonation   5. pitch
3. a relative question   6. terminal juncture

D. ANSWER BRIEFLY.
1. Where are English words generally stressed?
2. What kind of stress do words like dependency,
   appreciation, and pioneer carry?
3. What is the only distinction in pronunciation in
   words like dessert/desert, address/address?
4. What are some cases of distinguishing stress
   placement in English and Spanish?
5. What can you say about the English ending -ist
   versus the Spanish -ista?
6. If you want to give relative importance to one
   segment of an utterance, what do you do?
7. What is the difference between duration in English and Spanish?
8. Generally what happens when a foreign word is
   borrowed either in Spanish or in English?
9. Do onomatopeic renderings of sounds reflect the
   strength of the system? Show how.
10. What do words like sheet and fool have in common?

PRACTICE
A. REPEAT THESE WORDS CAREFULLY AND WRITE OUT THE
   STRESSED SYLLABLE.
mientras   ....   gratuito   ....
criado   ....   luciérnaga ....
cuota   ....   pleito   ....
deuda   ....   murciélago ....
guapa   ....   Camagüey   ....
escorpioide ....   suficiente ....
argüir   ....   veinte   ....
Europa   ....   incluir   ....
real   ....   puente   ....
reina   ....   neutro   ....

133

B. DO A PHONETIC TRANSCRIPTION OF THE MORPHEME
   MARKER IN THE PRESENT INDICATIVE IN THE ENVIRON-
   MENT OF YO.

acostar	....	nevar	....
arrendar	....	perder	....
apostar	....	poder	....
comenzar	....	referir	....
convertir	....	rogar	....
dormir	....	querer	....
empezar	....	requerir	....
volver	....	discernir	....

C. HOW WOULD YOU CHANGE THE MEANING OF THESE UT-
   TERANCES BY MOVING THE PRINCIPAL STRESS? GIVE
   TWO POSSIBILITIES IN EACH CASE.
1. Sebastián Elcano fue el primer marino español que
   dio la vuelta al mundo.

_____

2. Las buenas intenciones no son nada si no son se-
   guidas de buenas acciones.

_____

3. Tres son los elementos que constituyen la indus-
   tria: idea, dinero, y trabajo.

_____

4. Al enterarse de la noticia, un sudor frío le ba-
   ñaba la cara.

_____

5. Estaba muy impaciente porque el avión no partiría
   en hora.

_____

D. READ THESE UTTERANCES CAREFULLY AND THEN WRITE
   OUT THE PATTERN OF INTONATION IN EACH CASE.
   (For the meaning see Appendix II).
1. Ud. sabe que no tiene pelos en la lengua.

T. N. ....

2. Siempre le pagará con la misma moneda de la ingra-
   titud.

134

T. N. ....

3. Cada vez que toco el tema se anda por las ramas.

T. N. ....

4. La policía registró todo pero era como buscar una aguja en el pajar.

T. N. ....

5. Sus ideas no son claras y siempre va con la corriente.

T. N. ....

6. Ese asunto déjemelo a mí que irá viento en popa.

T. N. ....

7. Al perder su juguete el niño comenzó a hacer pucheros.

T. N. ....

8. No le convencerá; siempre se está en sus treces.

T. N. ....

9. José es el brazo derecho de su jefe.

T. N. ....

10. Nestor es la piel de Judas (el diablo).

T. N. ....

11. El se cree la octava maravilla del mundo.

T. N. ....

12. El pobre marido es un cero a la izquierda.

T. N. ....

13. Perdió el concurso por dormirse sobre los laureles.

T. N. ....

14. Cuando puede siempre hace de las suyas.

T. N. ....

15. Antes de contestarme, consulta con la almohada.

T. N. ....

16. La miraba y la miraba y se le hacía agua en la boca.

T. N. ....

17. Se hizo un ovillo cuando oyó los gritos.

T. N. ....

18. Cuando lo interrogaron se hizo el zorro.

T. N. ....

19. El padre le sugirió que encontrara trabajo pues ya era bastante grande para seguir calentando la silla.

T. N. ....

20. Todo lo tomaba a pecho.

T. N. ....

21. Aunque no viene al caso, ¿sabe lo que le pasó a María?

T. N. ....

22. No necesitaba presentación pues era más conocida que la ruda.

T. N. ....

E. REVIEW THE VOWELS AND CONSONANTS IN CHAPTERS TWO
AND THREE. THEN GIVE AN ACCURATE PHONETIC TRAN-
SCRIPTION OF THE FOLLOWING UTTERANCES.
1. Los perros y los lobos aúllan.
....
2. Por lo visto los osos y los toros braman bastante.
....
3. La rana croa.
....
4. Las ovejas balan a menudo.
....
5. Los puercos gruñen a cada paso.
....
6. Este caballo relincha de vez en cuando.
....
7. Los loros y los serpientes no silban continuamente.
....
8. El gorrión pía con frecuencia.
....
9. Las moscas y los mosquitos zumban por naturaleza.
....
10. Los canarios gargantean a veces sin cesar.
....

ASI SE DICE
REPEAT CAREFULLY EACH SEGMENT AS GIVEN AND FINALLY
THE COMPLETE UTTERANCE.
Estar   ....
Estar uno   ....
Estar uno en   ....
Estar uno en ascuas.   ....

Estar   ....
Estar uno   ....
Estar uno sobre   ....
uno sobre ascuas   ....
Estar uno sobre ascuas.   ....

Tomar   ....
Tomar a   ....
Tomar a mal.   ....

137

```
Llevar                  ..........
Llevar a                ..........
Llevar a mal.           ...........................

No                      ..........
No digas                ..........
No digas nunca          ...............
de esta                 ..........
de esta agua            ...............
no beberé               ...............
de esta agua no beberé  ...................           .
No digas nunca de esta agua no beberé.
                        ...........................

Genio                   ..........
Genio y                 ..........
Genio y figura          ...............
hasta la                ..........
hasta la sepultura      ...............
Genio y figura hasta la sepultura.
                        ...........................

Con                     ..........
Con las                 ..........
Con las glorias         ...............
se olvidan              ..........
se olvidan las          ...............
se olvidan las memorias. ...................
Con las glorias se olvidan las memorias.
                        ...........................

Poco                    ..........
Poco a                  ..........
Poco a poco             ..........
se anda                 ..........
se anda lejos           ...............
poco se anda lejos      ...............
Poco a poco se anda lejos.
                        ...........................
```

138

FOOTNOTES

¹⁶ For further information on the concept of morphemes and morphology, see Emilio Alarcos Llorach, Gramática estructural (Madrid: Editorial Gredos, 1951), pp. 59-73; Simon Belasco, ed. Manual and Anthology of Applied Linguistics (Washington, D. C.: U. S. Dept. of Health, Education, and Welfare, 1960); Robert A. Hall, Jr., Introductory Linguistics (Philadelphia: Chilton Books, 1965), pp. 130-137.

¹⁷ Many of the infinitives ending in -iar present a case of inconsistency since, according to the basic rules of pronunciation, this syllable should be completely diphthongized; yet, in the spoken language this syllable is often heard as two; i. e., li-ar, cri-ar, and many other cases.

¹⁸ For further elucidation of the IPA applied to the English language and notions of stress, see Donald Decker, Mastering the International Phonetic Alphabet (New York: Simon & Schuster, 1970); Dalbor, pp. 209-220; Cynthia D. Buchanan, A Programmed Introduction to Linguistics (Lexington, Mass.: D. C. Heath & Co., 1963), pp. 872-874; 1074-1076; William A. Smalley, Manual of Articulatory Phonetics (Tarrytown, New York: Practical Anthropology, 1963), pp. 453-466; T. Donald Bowen and Robert P. Stockwell, Patterns of Spanish Pronunciation. A Drillbook (Chicago: University of Chicago Press, 1960), pp. 8-26.

¹⁹ For patterns of intonation in English, see Buchanan, pp. 255-259; Smalley, pp. 89-101.

²⁰ Dalbor, pp. 221-240; 250-254.

²¹ For a complete discussion of English vowels, glides, and their corresponding phonetic symbols, see Daniel Jones, An English Pronouncing Dictionary

(London: J. M. Dent & Sons, Ltd., 1937), pp. xiii-xxv; Albert C. Baugh, History of the English Language (New York: D. Appleton-Century Co., 1935), pp. 424-469; Bertil Malmberg, Phonetics (New York: Dover Publications, Inc., 1963), pp. 33-39.

22 For detailed analyses of quantity and related aspects of speech, see Ilsa Lehiste, Suprasegmentals (Cambridge: the M. I. T. Press, 1970), chapter II; William J. Moulton, A Linguistic Guide to Language Learning, 2nd ed. (New York: Modern Language Association, 1970), pp. 59-64.

23 Noel Perrin, "Old Macberlitz Had a Farm," New Yorker, 27 January, 1962, pp. 28-29.

CHAPTER FIVE

SPEECH AND ITS LEVELS

INTRODUCTION. Forms of language and social class,
family background, and formal education are intimately related. Most speakers reflect some or all of
these aspects of community and upbringing through
their use of language whether the latter is viewed
strictly on an individual basis (idiolect), a com-
munal level (dialect), or in the broadest sense of
formal and informal speech (language). Consciously or unconsciously, speakers adopt certain expressions and choose certain words while avoiding or re-
jecting others. This subtle linguistic process is
practiced in order to interact effectively within
different social groups. In other words, one reacts
to language as a valuable means of communication reflecting socio-economic background, professional-vo-
cational associations, family and personal ties,
formal education or lack of same, and other factors
of background. Since individual use of structure
and semantics is often the direct result of environment, meanings are adjusted or altered according to
new interests and experiences, shifts in status,
changes in cultural environment, and even relocation.
All of these aspects of language, speech levels, address and local peculiarities are often considered
the main purview of sociolinguistics (la sociolin-
güística).[24]

    While the United States does not have speech
communities which are mutually unintelligible as
are found in areas of Italy, Spain, Germany, and .
many other places in the world, Americans are by
and large aware of the vast differences which exist
in this country from east to west and north to
south. Many Americans acknowledge "Texas pronunciation," "New England accents," "western and southern
drawls," "coal cracker talk," even "white English"
and "black English." Residents of certain cities
are thought to have a certain "twang" or an "odd-

141

sounding" lilt or intonation. From a technical
point of view these labels are purely subjective or
even non-existent since dialect and language have
come to be synonymous with any satisfactory means of
verbal exchange within given speech communities.
Even in this country, where national communication
has been more sophisticated than elsewhere, there
are definite regional differences. Moreover, in a
pluralistic society typical of the United States regional variations are often complicated by overlays
of distinctly ethnic influences of one variety or
another and their resulting hypercorrections.

Americans traditionally think in terms of a
so-called "standard English," which has never to our
knowledge been clearly and definitively described.
Even if merely on a theoretical level, this brand of
English is an ideally deregionalized version exem-
plified by the speech heard on radio, television, in
the movies, and in the theatre. Despite many attempts at "learned deregionalization," locally
throughout the country informal and vulgar speech
continues to be a more natural reflection of the unfettered development of the language. What is more,
what applies to American English is basically true
of all forms of English since the language has such
wide geographic distribution and is used by millions
of speakers the world over. Thus, despite claims of
"superiority" by speakers of "Oxford English" and
other versions in the British tradition, there are
innumerable types of English touted as perfectly acceptable means of communication.

Hispanically speaking, the question of speech
levels is somewhat more complex in that Spain and
Latin America have by and large continued to preserve more conservative, tradition-bound societies
with relatively stagnant socio-economic levels and
rigidly fixed social classes. So the concept of
levels of language tends to be more pronounced and
more consciously cultivated as a definite reflection
of one's status in life.

142

LEVELS OF LANGUAGE. In addition to factors of class and social background, languages are affected by scientific breakthroughs, artistic achievements, commercial growth, social revolution, and even war. Events, discoveries, and international conflicts are all transmitted via the channel of human communication--language--which grows and changes endlessly. Languages peculiar to ancient civilizations in which social levels are of paramount importance and are rigidly fixed actually have honorific, polite, and normal levels of speech patterns.[25] Levels of this type do not exist in English or Spanish although the two idioms make similar distinctions to one extent or another. Both languages have what may be considered formal, familiar, and vulgar levels.[26] Thus in English one may convey the same message on three basically distinct levels:

FORMAL	Please don't speak!
	Please refrain from speaking!
FAMILIAR	Quiet!
	Shut up!
VULGAR	Shut your damn trap!
	Shut the hell up!

Parallel levels are present in Spanish as well:

FORMAL	¡Por favor no hable!
	¡Tenga la bondad de callarse!
	¡Cállese por favor!
FAMILIAR	¡Cállate!
	¡Chitón!
VULGAR	¡Cierra esa bocona!
	¡Cierra ese pico!

Like English, Spanish is rich in such shifts according to social background, sensitivity to language, or sarcastic use of speech. In a statement like "The millionaire died," each version shows less respect or more contempt for the deceased in the following order:

> Pasó a mejor vida.
> Se murió el ricachón.
> Estiró la pata el platudo.

Likewise, an utterance like "What a miserable life!" becomes progressively stronger as one descends the social scale:

> ¡Qué vida tan pobre!
> ¡Qué vida tan perra!

143

¡Qué vida tan jodida!
In the same way, in an utterance like "He gave him
a punch" ("He struck him"), the blow becomes more
graphic as one progresses along lines of informality
or baseness:
Le dio un golpe.
Le zumbó una bofetada.
Le encajó una torta.
Matters concerning sex, pregnancy, the human body,
and relations between the sexes are often couched
in euphemistic terms, and speakers once again react
according to their background and awareness of
speech in general. The examples which follow express "She is pregnant" with considerable variety--
from a highly indirect, euphemistic level to a
rather base one:
Ella está en estado interesante.
Ella está embarazada.
Ella está encinta.
Ella está gruesa.
Ella está preñada.

Spanish probably has a greater range of levels
than English in either the direction of elaborate
structure and euphemism or popular, vulgar, or even
taboo language (for the latter see Chapter Eight).
The broad range of possibilities of language choice
is enhanced by the traditionally accepted patterns
of politeness and the variety afforded by levels of
address. Unlike the American social set-up, which
tends to be fairly permissive in terms of speech
and social class, the Hispanic world clings more
tenaciously to the obvious social implications of
speech patterns and levels of language set by the
various social classes.

In current usage the concept of language comprises much more than the formal, familiar, and
vulgar levels. In a theoretical sense there is the
classical language--a form of expression which
exists essentially in abstraction. It is a carefully regulated form of language reflected in the
traditional literature and theatre of the Hispanic
world. The term contemporary language includes
popular language, current language, and the literary

144

language of present-day writers. Speech broadly
conceived as correct comprises current language,
which includes both written and spoken forms, as
well as familiar and formal language. In most
modern societies, and the Hispanic social scene is
no exception in this sense, there are two linguistic
forces which converge--popular language and literary
language. Thus, the parlance of most cultivated
natives touches upon both extremes but normally
functions within a middle range in daily use. The
following graphic view of current spoken Spanish
shows clearly the interrelationships among the
levels of the language and their cross-currents.[27]

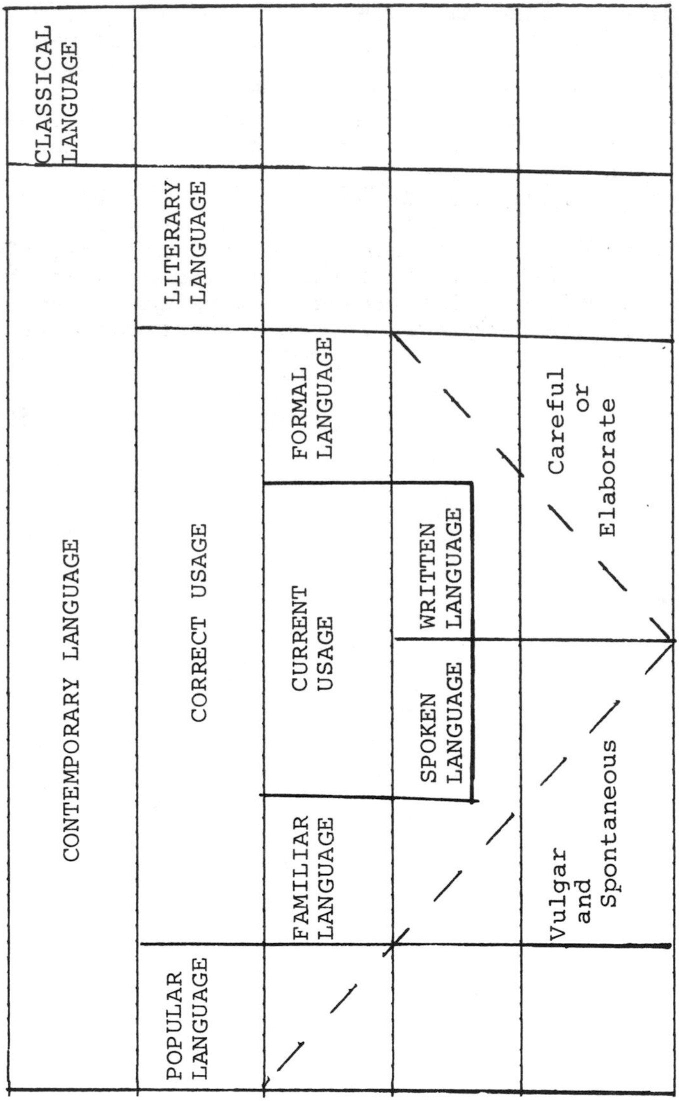

CLASSICAL LANGUAGE

LITERARY LANGUAGE

CONTEMPORARY LANGUAGE

CORRECT USAGE

FORMAL LANGUAGE

CURRENT USAGE

WRITTEN LANGUAGE

SPOKEN LANGUAGE

FAMILIAR LANGUAGE

POPULAR LANGUAGE

Careful or Elaborate

Vulgar and Spontaneous

FIGURE 31

FORMS OF ADDRESS IN SPANISH. In Spanish there is an
area of differentiation of persons known as address
(el trato), which includes familiar and polite and
singular and plural forms. English no longer distinguishes between polite and familiar address in
any formal way. One might argue, however, that
some Americans do make a distinction of sorts by
using patterns which differentiate between the two
forms in a subtle way. Many Southerners do this by
using "ya" on the familiar level and "ya'll" on the
polite. Other speakers may use "you" for both
forms of address but reserve "yourself" for purposes
of deference. Although English originally did make
use of two forms, "you" has long since replaced
both. It is understandable that in a country like
the United States with its equalitarian emphases
one form should develop, thereby doing away with the
polarities of relationship between "subordinates"
and "insubordinates." Nonetheless, while subordi-
nation is not expressed formally, there are definite
signs of the same psycholinguistic factors which
have undoubtedly kept alive the familiar-polite
forms in other languages. In the United States sub-
ordination is usually expressed more indirectly but
is definitely present in such gestures as a false
cough, a condescending grin, the scratching of one's
head in feigned bewilderment, and other forms of
deprecatory body language.[28]

In Spanish familiar and polite address are important since there is a multiplicity of social relationships and personal attitudes implied in
either form. There are two distinct forms--familiar
tú and polite usted (abbreviated Ud., Vd., and V.).
In addition within each form of address one distinguishes between one person--tú and Ud.--and more
than one person--vosotros(as) and ustedes (abbreviated Uds. or Vds.).[29] The forms of address, then,
are as follows:

	SINGULAR	PLURAL
FAMILIAR	tú	vosotros, vosotras
POLITE	usted	ustedes

The whole concept of address in Spanish is a fairly
complex one since its appropriate use depends not

simply on correct grammatical usage but on a basic familiarity with Hispanic sociolinguistic sensitivities. When the forms of address and their basic corresponding verb-forms have been mastered, there remains the task of becoming accustomed to the subtle nuances typical of social and personal ties as well as specific traditional requirements. Knowledge of the various types of Hispanic societies helps immeasurably in developing an awareness of the rich variety which this aspect of the language provides.

The verb <u>tutear</u> means <u>to address in the tú form</u>, but a verb as such for the polite equivalent does not exist. Instead, the latter is usually expressed <u>hablar de usted</u> or <u>tratar de usted</u>. In the utterance <u>(tú) dime la verdad</u> there is a much greater bond of intimacy expressed between the speaker and the person spoken to than in the more formal <u>dígame Ud. la verdad</u>. Matters of address, whether polite or familiar, are not necessarily permanent or fixed in any way. If a person wishes a relationship to take on less formal overtones, he or she simply states <u>no me hable (trate) de usted</u>; <u>tutéeme</u>. The latter provides an invitation to shift immediately to a less formal basis of exchange. On the other hand, friends who have used the familiar for decades may shift into the polite after a serious misunderstanding or disagreement. In sum, matters of address are a reflection of human relations which are subject to change or which assume new dimensions, and in this sense familiarity and formality can become rather a delicate matter. For the non-native it is best to allow native speakers to establish the tone through the desired form of address since many factors enter the picture. The single most important element is native conditioning to the language; in addition, social class, degree of education, professional and personal relationships, age, and sex all play an important role. The following chart provides a random sampling of the countless possibilities of polite versus familiar address and singular versus plural:

148

SPEAKER	PERSON SPOKEN TO	SINGULAR		PLURAL	
		FORMAL	FAMILIAR	FORMAL	FAMILIAR
Individual	God		tú		vosotros[30]
Bishop	Congregation			ustedes	vosotros
Priest	Congregation			ustedes	vosotros
Priest	Individual	usted	tú	ustedes	vosotros
People	Bishop/Priest	usted		ustedes	vosotros
Gentleman	Gentleman	usted	tú	ustedes	vosotros
Gentleman	Ladies	usted	tú	ustedes	vosotros
Ladies	Gentlemen	usted	tú	ustedes	vosotros
Ladies	Ladies	usted	tú	ustedes	vosotros
Husband	Wife		tú		
Wife	Husband		tú		
Father/Mother	Son/Daughter	usted	tú	ustedes	vosotros
Son/Daughter	Father/Mother	usted	tú	ustedes	vosotros
Brother/Sister	Brother/Sister	(usted)	tú	(ustedes)	vosotros
Uncle/Aunt	Nephew/Niece		tú	ustedes	vosotros
Nephew/Niece	Uncle/Aunt	usted	tú	ustedes	vosotros
Cousins	Cousins		tú	ustedes	vosotros
Grandparents	Grandchildren		tú	ustedes	vosotros
Grandchildren	Grandparents	usted	tú	ustedes	vosotros

FIGURE 32

SPEAKER	PERSON SPOKEN TO	SINGULAR		PLURAL	
		FORMAL	FAMILIAR	FORMAL	FAMILIAR
Professor	Student	usted		ustedes	
Teacher	Student	usted	tú	ustedes	vosotros
Student	Student	(usted)	tú	ustedes	vosotros
Student	Professor/Teacher	usted		ustedes	
Employer	Employes	usted	tú	ustedes	vosotros
Employes	Employer	usted		ustedes	
Housewife	Servant	usted	tú	ustedes	vosotros
Servant	Housewife	usted		ustedes	
Merchant	Customer	usted		ustedes	
Customer	Merchant	usted		ustedes	

FIGURE 32, continued

150

In the chart certain relationships between the speaker and the person spoken to allow them considerable latitude. It may seem strange at first to note that God is addressed in the familiar form; yet, it is the intimacy of the Creator-creature relationship which is emphasized. Thus, in the most common prayers like the Lord's Prayer and the Hail Mary, tú is always used.

Padre nuestro, (tú) que estás en los cielos, santificado sea tu nombre...

or

Dios te salve, María, llena eres de Gracia, el Señor es contigo...

The liturgical invocation of saints follows the same pattern since the familiar imperative form is traditionally used. The Litany of Saints is interesting in that it provides an example of a linguistic levelling process. Here one finds in Latin America one of the few instances of the imperative of vosotros as it is used in much of Spain.

....

San Gabriel	ruega (tú) por nosotros
San Rafael	ruega por nosotros
Todos los Santos Angeles y Arcángeles	rogad (vosotros) por nosotros
Todos los Santos Coros de los Bienaventurados	rogad por nosotros
San Juan Bautista	ruega por nosotros
San José	ruega por nosotros
Todos los Santos Patriarcas y Profetas	rogad por nosotros.31

Young people are more apt to use familiar forms among themselves--friends, co-workers, classmates, siblings, and peers. On the other hand, when addressing a person from another age group, they normally opt for usted. Only if the person addressed encourages more familiar terms, does the younger person proceed to be more informal. As has been stated, one's family background conditions one to react to these matters with varying degrees of sensitivity. A person's careful or careless use of tuteo often provides clues as to background and upbringing. Frequently people who are bright and ambitious may attempt to improve their lot by devel-

151

oping a skillful handling of forms of address. In fact, in the Hispanic world it is safe to say that the lower the social class, the less tendency there is to know exactly how to shift gracefully and adroitly from familiar to polite and vice versa.[32]

Whether children address their parents in the polite or the familiar depends largely upon family background. Some upper-class families prefer usted under normal circumstances while others tend to make greater use of tú. Parents who habitually use tú in addressing their children may switch upon occasion to a sarcastic use of the polite form to make a scolding more effective. The American-English equivalent used in prefacing reproaches is "look here, young man/lady!"

Frequently matters of address are a direct result of one's station in life in relation to others. Normally speaking, employers use usted(es) in speaking to their employees, but there are exceptions. For instance, office boys, apprentices, and unskilled laborers are usually addressed as tú since they normally perform more menial tasks. Conversely, a beginner at a job who happens to come from a wealthy or well-known family is addressed as usted regardless of the task performed within the work force.

Housewives fairly high on the social scale tend to use either form of address depending on the age and relative status of their domestic help. In formal settings the lady of the house uses the polite form with most of them. On the other hand, she may lapse into tú with younger, more inexperienced help. It is not uncommon to hear both forms of address within the same household. By way of example, an older established cook, Mercedes, might be addressed consistently in the polite form whereas her younger assistant, Juana, might be spoken to in the familiar. The familiar-polite shifts are rather subtle but tend to be reflective of the mistress's view of and attitude toward her domestic help. The following dialogue is typical:

SEÑORA:	Mercedes, <u>tráigame</u> la toalla de baño. Y Juana, ¡que no se <u>te</u> olvide el jabón! Y <u>tráelo</u> en seguidita.
LAS CRIADAS:	Ahorita, señora.
SEÑORA:	Juana, <u>hazme</u> el favor de llevar <u>las</u> flores a Mercedes para que las ponga en la sala. ¡Apresúrate! Mercedes, <u>trate</u> de hacerme un buen <u>arreglo</u> para esta noche, <u>se</u> lo ruego, que usted <u>se</u> entiende de esas cosas.

When addressing animals and pets, speakers usually make use of the familiar <u>tú</u>. Calls to animals such as " ¡arre, burro!" " ¡qué flojo estás!" are by no means uncommon. With pet owners both negative and positive utterances are normally made in the familiar form: "ven acá," "siéntate," "cómete esto," "¡no seas tan bobo!" "¡estás hecho una fiera!" On the other hand, if dog or cat owners are angry or annoyed, a sarcastic overtone is achieved by shifting momentarily to the polite form: "venga para acá," "usted se siente muy viva hoy." As has been mentioned in the case of children, the shift to the polite adds a twinge of sarcasm and makes reproaches stronger.

What should be derived from these notions of address? First, that these patterns vary considerably from individual to individual and speech community to speech community. Secondly, the best and safest form of address in general and whenever in doubt is <u>usted/ustedes</u>. Thirdly, the practice of well-spoken natives is often a valuable barometer of correctness and good taste in these elusive matters. This does not mean to imply that one never resorts to <u>tú</u> and its corresponding forms, but the uninitiated should employ familiar forms with caution. In Spain, it is understood, knowledge of <u>vosotros</u> and its forms is indeed very useful.

153

COMMONLY USED TITLES. The terms señor, señora, señorita are heard much more frequently than their
counterparts in English. They are found both before
family names and first names--señor Fernández, señora López, señorita Redondo, señorita Dolores, señora Julia, señor Reynaldo. These titles are not only
used with great frequency with or without first or
last names, but their use is extended to professional
titles as well. Thus one hears with regularity combinations such as señor capitán, señora dentista,
señorita profesora, señor doctor.³³ A curious instance of usage is found with elderly maiden ladies
who are addressed as señorita by friends, servants,
and local merchants but who are conventionally
called señora out of respect in less familiar settings unless the ladies themselves indicate otherwise.

        Spanish has a unique form in the titles don/do-
ña. Although originally intended for nobility and
high church officials, their use was later extended
to professionals, functionaries, lawyers, and others
as in don Martínez, don Peñalosa, doña Montáñez.
The elderly who enjoy some degree of status by virtue of background or money are frequently addressed
in the same way. Persons of high social rank and
professional or intellectual attainment are also
given this title. Probably the best known don outside of the Hispanic world is don Juan, the legend-
ary embodiment of virility and seduction. In Spain
doña and the Castilian señá are often applied to
married women.

        There are other titles which have considerable
frequency in modern Spanish. The terms hombre/mujer
are, more frequently than not, used to connote more
familiar or more informal types of relationships.
Hombre is heard a great deal; in fact, one might
venture to say that it is overused, especially in
informal or careless speech. English has no real
equivalent even though man, boy, fellow, buddy, hon,
girl are heard in similar contexts. More recently
hombre has come to be used with persons of either
sex. The term is also applied to animals of both

                            154

sexes as in " ¡anda, hombre!," said to a donkey or a
horse. While familiarity is the keynote here, the
use of these titles does not normally have offensive
overtones although the latter is possible. Doctor
as a title of respect is quite universal, and it
very often has no reference to persons of the medical profession. In normal parlance it is understood
that persons so addressed are university graduates,
professionals, or academics even though it is applied indiscriminately in many instances. Maestro
is generally reserved for persons of distinction in
music and the arts. The titles caballero and dama
are the Spanish equivalents of lady and gentleman
although the former is a fairly ubiquitous title
with the force of sir and in many instances is heard
simply out of deference or respect.

A major difference between Spanish and American-
English usage is the frequent occurrence in the former of last names as a form of address. It is rare
in professional settings to refer to one's colleagues
by their first names as is the normal practice in
the United States. The custom in Spanish is to mention the last name without a preceding title, thereby creating a type of address which is midway between the highly formal and the excessively familiar.
So a statement like "Hey, Joe, bring me the tele-
gram" is characteristically expressed "Fernández,
tráigame el telegrama."

When approaching a stranger to ask for directions or to initiate conversation, there are many
formularios de cortesía in general use. The normal
procedure is to initiate conversation by excusing
oneself--perdón, perdone Ud., dispense Ud. This is
customarily followed by any general title of re-
spect--caballero, señor, señorita, señora; in pro-
vincial settings or in small towns, buen hombre/bue-
na mujer; with the very elderly, abuelo/abuela. In
addressing children, chico/chica, muchacho/muchacha,
nene/nena, mozo/moza may be used with equal effect.
When speaking to children for the first time, hispanos automatically use the familiar form of address.

155

CLIMBING THE LADDER OF ACCEPTABILITY. The three
levels of speech--formal, familiar, and vulgar--have
been identified as present and functional in both
English and Spanish. Since language as a means of
communication is an ever-evolving system, the various levels at times overlap and often change. Forms
or lexical choices which were at one time considered
unacceptable, offensive, or even vulgar in certain
circles may eventually ascend the ladder of acceptability. In other words, what is unacceptable today
may, for a variety of reasons, become completely ·
permissible tomorrow. More often than not, even
what was considered taboo in proper speech a decade
or so ago eventually achieves respectability.

All levels of speech contribute in different
ways to the enrichment of the language of which they
constitute important aspects. The lower levels tend
to provide all sorts of colorful nouns and verb-forms,
not to mention interesting idiomatic expressions and
turns of phrase. It is understood that lower forms
of speech exist in all languages of the world. In
America they are referred to as slang, gutter talk,
thieves' jargon, hip talk, and the like, and people
who speak in this fashion normally exist on the
fringe of society. The French call this type of
speech argot; the Italians, gergo; the Spaniards,
jerga or jerigonza--the language of the germanía
(underworld)--and caló (calé)--the speech of gyp-
sies. In Latin America, the terms coa, replana,
lunfardo, and others are employed to indicate speech
on this level. Generally speaking, this type of
parlance developed as a result of the illegal enter-
prises in which its speakers were engaged. Within
these subgroups the primary aim was to keep from
being understood or otherwise detected by more conventional members of society. What is more, this
form of spontaneous communication was used primarily
as a means of identifying those who belonged from
those who did not. Eventually unique lexical items,
characteristic constructions, and turns of phrase
became fixed--at least on the local level.

The underworld has contributed to popular

Spanish quite a number of interesting expressions
and unique extensions of signification. Some typical verbs are afufar (escaparse), birlar (robar),
sornar (dormir), and many others. The term cuatrero
means petty thief; chirlo, a wound or blow; a tas-
quera, a fight or quarrel; a trena, a prison. The
image of good-looking or attractive is usually expressed by chulo. These forms are merely a random
sampling of originally rejected modes of expression
which have gained popular acceptance in a variety of
ways.

Many words originally limited exclusively to
caló speech are now considered part of common par-
lance--babián (beautiful, arrogant), cate (blow),
carda (scolding), jindan (fear), gachó/gachí (man/
woman not a gypsy), lacha (shame), sandunga (grace,
elegance). The verb camelar means to deceive with
false adulation, and chalarse, to fall in love.

As has been mentioned, much of this lexicon
originated as part of the code language of secret
societies and social outcasts and was eventually extended to popular or substandard language. Oftimes
this level of language is fundamentally metaphorical
or figurative but passes over to more extended pe-
destrian use as time goes on. It is important to
keep in mind that this type of expression is by no
means limited to the modern world since it has been
in evidence as a linguistic phenomenon over the centuries. Its origins may differ from place to place,
but a good deal of it reaches the general public
through songs, popular poetry, theatrical perfor-
mances, jokes, banter, and bawdy tales. A current
possible source of popular and vulgar language in
the United States is the speech patterns and lexicon
of rock music and "acid culture." Another example
of the same linguistic process is the lunfardo of
Argentina.

The word lunfardo derives from lunfa meaning
thief (Augusto Malaret, Diccionario de americanismos),
and it contains many words deriving from the underworld and crime in general. As time went on, many
of the words and expressions found popular acceptance

in the speech of porteños (natives of Buenos Aires).
The assimilation of these terms over a period of
time added a characteristic flavor to the rather
colorful speech of that city.[34] Most of the verbs
which entered the language via the port city belong,
characteristically, to the first conjugation--abom-
bar (aturdir), aceitar (sobornar), estrilar (rabiar), macanear (mentir), morfar (comer), picárselas
(salir corriendo). By way of example, anyone who is
easily confused or bewildered is described as "el
primero que se abomba." If one must be bribed for
whatever reason, "hay que aceitarle un poco." Anyone given to mendacity, "macanea que da miedo."
¡Cómo morfa!" is a typical reaction to any glutton.
A person who is not courageous is described as "se
las pica ni bien hay peligro." Other terms which
originated in the same fashion are: batidor (dela-
tor), informer; cana (cárcel), jail; cantar (confesar), to confess; pequero (delincuente que estafa),
young operator or swindler; raje (huída), flight;
ratero (carterista), pickpocket.

    Terms associated with various currents of im-
migration in Argentina that had contact with lower
elements are also part of lunfardo. Thus boleto, a
bastardization of the popular bola (hoax), takes on
the meaning of mentira. Camorra, from the same Nea-
politan word, is extended to mean pelea. Chucho,
from the Quechua chucchu (tremor), has taken on the
meaning of miedo. The Portuguese verb escangalhar
has yielded the adjective descangayado (viejo, de-
teriorado). The verb esgunfiar is of Piedmontese
origin (gofié) and has assumed the meaning of molestar, irritar. Fané, a rather archaic form, has the
force of out of date, out of fashion. The word
fiaca, from the Italian noun and adjective (fiac-
chezza, fiacco), has come to mean cansancio. A
large nose is popularly referred to as a napia from
the Genoese nappia. The term gil, of caló derivation meaning stupid, provides a dimension of the
words tonto, bobo in popular Spanish.[35]

    Some other developments gradually emerged from
the popularity of bawdy sketches in the theatre and

plays on words in various forms of nightclub enter-
tainment. In some instances the comic element was
achieved by inverting the normal order of syllables
within words, thereby creating what eventually became known as el vesrre (from al revés). In a sense
this form of language play is similar to Pig Latin
even though Spanish does have its own equivalent of
the latter. However, while Pig Latin is normally
used by or for children, vesrre is handled by adults
and teenagers for purposes of humor, sarcasm, or
even bawdiness. For instance, café con leche is rendered feca con chele; tango, gotán; trabaja derecho,
jatraba chorede. Even though teachers and parents
attempt to suppress its use, this language game remains quite popular. In fact, it is considered so
appealing to certain segments of the population that
its attraction seems to be increasing. Even though
a full coverage of vesrre is of necessity limited in
a work of this type, some additional popular examples
are as follows: cobana (abanico), yeca (calle),
chochamu (muchacho), cambasa (bacana), ajoba (abajo),
cocín (cinco), colo (loco), daví (vida), dorapa (pa-
rado), mionca (camión), naca (cana), nami (mina),
novi (vino), ronga (garrón), sabeca (cabeza), same
(mesa), somo (mozo), sova (vaso), tacorba (corbata),
talope (pelota), tapuer (puerta), tordo (do(c)tor),
troli (litro), yobaca (caballo), pruga (uruguayo),
yoyega (gallego, español), and many others.

HIGHER LEVEL JARGON. When substandard forms achieve
a degree of acceptability, they become permissible
forms of jargon. "Jargon" in this sense refers to
the characteristic language of professional groups
such as professors, social workers, physicians,
lawyers, and the like. On this level of use, it is
understood to be relatively high-level speech with
emphases, abbreviations, and peculiarities of its
own. Frequently there are semantic shifts and
oblique references, and specialized terms are shortened or reduced to their initials. For example, all
medical personnel know that the O R is an operating
room; D O A, dead upon arrival; shrink, psychiatrist

159

or psychologist; G P, general practitioner; GI man, gastrointestinal specialist; RN, registered nurse. In the same way all policemen and detectives are familiar with terms like APB (all points bulletin), a positive ID (positive identification), a John Doe (unidentified person), a DA (district attorney). Similarly, college students and academics make considerable use of terms like snap course, cram, gut course, streak, cut, panty raid, Ivy League, drop-add, withdraw-passing, auditor, credit-by-examination, credit for life experience, challenged courses, practicum, required courses, electives, and many others.

Spanish-speaking students also develop similar types of jargon. The verb joder--the equivalent of the four-letter Anglo-Saxon verb--is heard often with the meaning of annoy, vex, irritate. When used as an adjective, it usually has the force of extremely annoying, downright irritating, or much worse. Typically, a boring course is called materia jodida; a very demanding, officious professor, profesor jodido; a tedious lecture, conferencia jodida. Reactions to annoyance or interruption are often expressed by means of the same verb as in déjate de joder, no jodas, no seas jodón.37 Like their English-speaking counterparts, Hispanic students are quite familiar with terms like sobresaliente, distinguido, aprobado, suspendido, aplazado, pasar raspando, sacar dos bolillas, asistente, profesor titular, catedrático, and others.

Students young and old often resort to the popular device of dropping a syllable or lopping off the last part of words. It is not uncommon to hear voy al cole (colegio); se le rompió la bici (bicicleta); cuidado que viene la poli (policía); en ese café no tienes que dejar mucha propi (propina);38 ¿me das un bolo (bolígrafo)?; ellos están en la mili (milicia). First names are often shortened or changed in informal or affective language by dropping one or more syllables or by shifting to a different root--Fede (Federico), Guille (Guillermo), Lola, Lolita (Dolores), Bastián (Sebastián), Tere

(Teresa), Merce (Mercedes), Teo (Teófilo), Paco, Paquito (Francisco), Pepe, Pepito (José), Rafa (Rafael), Charo (Rosario), Lupe, Lupita (Guadalupe), Nina (Benina), Mari (María), Pepa, Pepita (Josefina), Paca, Paquita, Frasquita (Francisca), Lolo (Manolo), Chabe (Isabel), Nuni (Nuncio), and many others. Certain first names have taken on vulgar connotations in different parts of the world. For instance marica, an archaic form of María, is universally used to refer to male homosexuals. By extension maricón--the augmentative of the same name--is more offensive and is applied to weak or effeminate males or to male homosexuals in general.[39] In the River Plate area a name like Cornelio, elsewhere accepted as perfectly normal, is identified with the word cornudo--cuckold--to be avoided whenever possible. The same may be said of Concha/Conchita since it is perceived in the same area as a substitute word for the female organ.

LOCAL COLOR. Since Spanish is spoken as the first language in so many countries of the world, changes in semantic force and extended significations are bound to occur. By way of example, a basic word like head is expressed on a popular level from country to country in a variety of ways. So an utterance like "he fell and broke his head" may have the following versions among others:

SPAIN   Se cayó y se rompió la cabeza.
               Se cayó y se rompió la crisma.
               Se cayó y se rompió el cráneo.
               Se cayó y se rompió el bautismo.

MEXICO   Se cayó y se rompió el ayote.

COLOMBIA   Se cayó y se rompió la cocorota.

ARGENTINA   Se cayó y se rompió la chirimoya.
               Se cayó y se rompió el mate.

CARIBBEAN   Se cayó y se rompió la tutuna.

CHILE   Se cayó y se rompió el zapallo.[40]

161

In Argentina, Uruguay, and contiguous areas, the verb coger is understood to be synonymous with intercourse and is usually replaced by agarrar or asir. The word pato, duck, is a universally harmless word except in Puerto Rico, where it is used as a synonym of maricón. In short, each area develops sensitivities to certain lexical items while these retain perfectly normal connotations elsewhere, and such shifts in nuance are often attributable to immigration currents, local historical events, or unknown factors.

Throughout the Hispanic world certain words take on vulgar connotations when applied personally which they really do not have on a denotative level. For instance, one normally speaks of marido and mujer, husband and wife, in general; however, when speaking to a husband about his wife, one is expected to shift automatically to señora or esposa. The basic image-words for male and female are macho and hembra. And yet, a mother conventionally refers to herself as having cuatro hijos--dos varones and dos hijas.

As has already been pointed out, the complexities of language levels and word signification are countless, and within the Hispanic world they are even more complex and varied. Spain remains the mother country, and her essential language patterns and age-old traditions have been carried over to the New World. Nonetheless, the various linguistic and folk traditions in Spanish America have developed from within their own geographical limits, often greatly modifying the Spanish substratum as such. The picture is further complicated by the fact that the peninsular element was eventually fused with Indian, African, and other cultures--all of which makes for an even more complex approach to language levels within each society. For instance, certain customs and fruit and vegetable names are found only in Mexico and surrounding areas--the well-known Christmas piñata; the equally well-known hat dance, jarabe tapatío; the miniature walnut-sized tableau, chinches vestidas; the alcoholic beverages, pulque and tequila; the food names such as maíz, aguacate, guacamole, cuajolote, enchilada, tamal, jalapeños, and countless others. In Argentina words related to the pampas and gaucho culture have proliferated over the centuries, especially with reference to horses--macarrón (old nag), pingo (young powerful horse), alazán (sorrel horse), pintado (appaloosa). Terms describing beef and dishes containing meat and corn are numerous--matambre (flank steak), matambre relleno (rolled, stuffed flank steak), choclo (corn on the cob), humita (crushed corn in cream), asado con cuero (beef roasted in its own hide), puchero (stew with greens). Caña, a pulque type, sugar-based liquor, is also very common while mate and cimarrón (sweetened mate) are the national drinks of Argentina. The interesting term menjunje is used to refer popularly to any kind of liquid or solid mixture which has turned out badly. Mandinga, in this part of the world at least, is the fairly recurrent name for the devil.[41]

In many parts of the Latin-American world, the convergence of traditional Spanish values and the various Indian substrata made for a new mestizo society in which the age-old traditions were assimilated, rejected, or characteristically modified to meet the needs and aspirations of struggling peoples in a New World. Language as the chief means of human communication ultimately reflects on all levels the slow process of acculturation. Much of Latin America has retained traditional Spanish mores and values; nonetheless, history has demonstrated that the struggle has been bitter and all-pervasive. One of the chief sources of pride of Hispanics the world over is the fact that the Spanish language has remained their universal means of communication despite conflicting differences in ideology and way of life. Since their language is used so widely and the ethnic and national identities so varied, it is reassuring to Hispanics to view their tongue as the binding force of LA RAZA regardless of race, creed, color, or socioeconomic background. The wise student of language strives to be ever-vigilant with reference to the entire gamut of sociolinguistic phenomena to which every native speaker is sensitive--traditional social conventions, linguistic patterns, language

levels, forms of address, titles, patterns of cour-
tesy, and related aspects of language which characterize the multi-faceted speakers of Spanish throughout the globe.

EXERCISES

THEORY

A. ANSWER THESE QUESTIONS BRIEFLY.
1. What is the relationship between language and social background?
2. What is meant by language levels?
3. What exactly is meant by "standard English"?
4. How many types of address are there in peninsular and Latin-American Spanish?
5. What is meant by tutear and what is its formal equivalent?
6. What is the sarcastic use of the polite form on a familiar level of exchange?
7. How are pets and children normally addressed in Spanish?
8. How are don/doña and hombre used in the Hispanic world?
9. What is the difference between jerga and germanía?
10. What is meant by lunfardo?

B. EXPLAIN THESE TOPICS BRIEFLY.
1. el vesrre
2. the social impact of maricón
3. current language
4. polite address
5. porteño speech
6. vosotros in Spain
7. the use of the title doctor
8. professional jargon
9. last names in addressing people
10. caló

C. WRITE A BRIEF PARAGRAPH ON EACH OF THE TOPICS BELOW
1. non-linguistic factors which affect language levels
2. student language in the Hispanic world
3. the notion of contemporary language
4. how words climb "the ladder of acceptability"
5. non-Hispanic elements in lunfardo
6. class consciousness in the Spanish world

D. MATCH THE UTTERANCES IN COLUMN A WITH THOSE IN
   COLUMN B. THEN ATTEMPT TO IDENTIFY THE LANGUAGE
   LEVEL IN EACH CASE.

COLUMN A

1. No lo invites porque es un plomo. ___
2. Acuso recibo de su amena carta del 22 del mes
   actual.
3. Al oír el himno nacional, el caballero se descubrió. ___
4. Al oír el disparo, aguce los oídos. ___
5. Los dos se pelean como perros y gatos. ___
6. A él le tratan con mucha consideración y delica-
   deza. ___
7. Ella pertenecía a la gente de alta sociedad.
8. La señorita se destripaba de risa al verlos.
9. Al recibir la noticia, nos quedamos blancos como
   un papel. ___
10. A mí me da asco porque es muy gallina para de-
    fenderse. ___
11. Al saberlo, se quedó fresco como una lechuga.
12. ¡Estoy completamente mojado! ___
13. ¡Están molidos por trabajar tan duro! ___
14. Esa pobre vieja siempre parece una bolsa de pa-
    pas. ___
15. Ese condenado se mueve como un ratón. ___
16. ¡Chitón! ¡Cierra esa bocona! ___

COLUMN B

a. ¡Estoy hecho una sopa!
b. A mí no me gusta por nada porque es un hombre bastante cobarde.
c. Ese maldito se mueve hábil y surrepticiamente.
d. Ambos discuten constantemente.
e. Hágame el favor de guardar silencio.
f. Más vale no convidarlo ya que es tan aburrido.
g. Paré la oreja cuando se oyeron aquellos disparos.
h. Esa anciana tiene muy poca gracia al vestirse.
i. Suelen tratarlo con guante blanco.
j. Recibí su correspondencia firmada el 22 del mes.
k. Al oír la canción, el señor se quitó el sombrero.
l. La chica se moría de risa cuando los vio.
m. Cuando se lo dijeron, se quedó impávido ante la noticia.
n. Al saber las nuevas, nos quedamos extremadamente pálidos.
o. Se ve que era del grupo de gente copetuda.
p. Están bien cansados por trabajar excesivamente.

PRACTICE

A. GIVE THE STANDARD SPANISH EQUIVALENT OF EACH
   WORD.
   1. el cole   _____
   2. la bici   _____
   3. la mili   _____
   4. camelar   _____
   5. yobaca   _____
   6. yeca   _____
   7. tacorba   _____
   8. aceitar   _____
   9. afufar   _____
   10. yoyega   _____
   11. cantar   _____
   12. chorede   _____
   13. davĩ   _____
   14. el batidor _____
   15. macanear   _____
   16. gotán   _____

B. TRANSCRIBE THESE PROVERBS IN CONVENTIONAL
   SPANISH.

   1. //sóꞵrə ꝗʸṣtːs/nː ái̯ dɪspútɐ//

   2. //nː é sórː/tódː lː kə Fəlúθə//

   3. //qátː kə dwɛ́rmə no kásɐ Fɐtónəs//

   4. //də pjɛ́dɾɐ/no sə sákɐ xúꝗː//

   5. //sóꞵrə ꝗʸṣtːs/nː ái̯ nádɐ əskɾítː//

   6. //dɪnɛ́rɔi̯ sáɲtː sáθən mɪláꝗrːs//

   7. //ái̯ kə ꞵai̯lá rɐ̀l sɔ́ŋ kə sə tókɐ//

   8. //mjɛ́ɲtrɐ sai̯ álmɐ/ái̯ əspəránsɐ//

168

C. GIVE THE STANDARD SPANISH FOR EACH OF THE AB-
BREVIATED NAMES LISTED BELOW.
1. Merce   _____
2. Lola   _____
3. Nuni   _____
4. Tere   _____
5. Chabe   _____
6. Teo   _____
7. Paquita   _____
8. Lolo   _____
9. Bastián   _____
10. Lupita   _____

D. IDENTIFY THE AREA OF THE HISPANIC WORLD IN WHICH
THE ITEMS WHICH FOLLOW ARE HEARD.
1. el mate   _____   6. chulo   _____
2. el pulque   _____   7. vosotros decís _____
3. la chirimoya   _____   8. chalarse   _____
4. picárselas   _____   9. el guacamole   _____
5. la camorra   _____   10. el matambre   _____

ASI SE DICE
REPEAT CAREFULLY EACH SEGMENT AS GIVEN AND FINALLY
THE COMPLETE UTTERANCE.

Aunque   . . . .
Aunque la mona   . . . .
la mona se vista   . . . .
se vista de seda   . . . .
Aunque la mona se vista de seda
                                . . . .
mona   . . . .
mona se queda   . . . .
Aunque la móna se vista de seda mona se queda
                      . . . .

El ojo   . . . .
El ojo del   . . . .
ojo del amo   . . . .
amo engorda   . . . .
engorda al   . . . .
engorda al caballo   . . . .
El ojo del amo engorda al caballo.

169

```
                        . . . . . . . . . . . . . . . . . . . . . .
Quien                   . . . . . . . . . .
Quien siembra           . . . . . . . . . .
Quien siembra vientos   . . . . . . . . . . . . . .
recoge                  . . . . . . . . . .
recoge tempestades      . . . . . . . . . . . . . .
Quien siembra vientos recoge tempestades.
                        . . . . . . . . . . . . . . . . . . . . . .

A                       . . . . . . . . . .
A quien                 . . . . . . . . . .
A quien madruga         . . . . . . . . . . . . . .
madruga Dios            . . . . . . . . . .
Dios le                 . . . . . . . . . .
Dios le ayuda           . . . . . . . . . . . . . .
A quien madruga Dios le ayuda.
                        . . . . . . . . . . . . . . . . . . . . . .

Agua                    . . . . . . . . . .
Agua pasada             . . . . . . . . . .
pasada no               . . . . . . . . . .
no muele                . . . . . . . . . .
no muele molinos        . . . . . . . . . .
Agua pasada no muele molinos.
                        . . . . . . . . . . . . . . . . . . . . . .

Quien                   . . . . . . . . . .
Quien mal               . . . . . . . . . .
Quien mal anda          . . . . . . . . . . . . . .
anda mal                . . . . . . . . . .
mal acaba               . . . . . . . . . .
Quien mal anda mal acaba.
                        . . . . . . . . . . . . . . . . . . . . . .

No                      . . . . . . . . . .
No se                   . . . . . . . . . .
No se ganó              . . . . . . . . . .
se ganó Zamorra         . . . . . . . . . . . . . .
ganó Zamorra en         . . . . . . . . . .
Zamorra en una          . . . . . . . . . .
en una hora             . . . . . . . . . .
No se ganó Zamorra en una hora.
                        . . . . . . . . . . . . . . . . . . . . . .
```

```
No                        . . . . . . . . . .
No hay                    . . . . . . . . . .
No hay mal                . . . . . . . . . .
hay mal que               . . . . . . . . . .
mal que por               . . . . . . . . . .
que por bien              . . . . . . . . . .
por bien no               . . . . . . . . . .
bien no venga             . . . . . . . . . .
No hay mal que por bien no venga.
                          . . . . . . . . . . . . . . . . . . . . . . . .

Por                       . . . . . . . . . .
Por todas                 . . . . . . . . . .
Por todas partes          . . . . . . . . . . . . . .  '
todas partes se           . . . . . . . . . .
partes se va              . . . . . . . . . .
se va a Roma              . . . . . . . . . . . . . .
Por todas partes se va a Roma.
                          . . . . . . . . . . . . . . . . . . . . . . . .
```

FOOTNOTES

24 William Labov, Sociolinguistic Patterns
(Philadelphia: University of Pennsylvania Press,
1972), pp. 110-121.

25 Robbins Burling, Man's Many Voices: Language
in Its Cultural Contact (New York: Holt, Rinehart, &
Winston, Inc., 1970), pp. 82-88.

26 F. R. Palmer, Semantics (Cambridge: University Press, 1976); Charles E. Kany, Semántica hispanoamericana, trans. Luis Escolar Barreño (Madrid:
Aguilar, 1969), pp. 70-84.

27 The above chart is based on a similar classification by Leonor Tejada, Hablar bien no cuesta
nada (Mexico: Organización Editorial Novaro, 1974),
p. 60.

28 Roger Brown and Albert Gilman, "The Pronouns
of Power and Solidarity," in Style in Language, ed.
Thomas A. Sebeok (Cambridge: The M. I. T. Press,
1960), pp. 253-276.

29 The plural of tú is traditionally vosotros
(-as)--a form used widely in much of Spain and in
variant forms in some parts of Latin America. All
Spanish speakers have some familiarity with this
type of address and its derivational forms, but
usage in Spanish America shifts automatically to Uds.
for the plural of both tú and Ud. (although the pronoun Uds. per se is frequently omitted when it functions as the plural of tú); also see Vos, Chapter
Six.

30 Most of the vosotros forms, with few exceptions, apply to linguistic usage in peninsular

172

Spanish only.

[31] Andrés Azcárate, ed., Misal diario para América (Buenos Aires: Guadalupe, 1946), p. 603.

[32] Magnus Morner, Race and Class in Latin America (New York: Columbia University Press, 1970), pp. 1-8; Julio Mafud, Psicología de la viveza criolla (Buenos Aires: Américaleer, 1971), pp. 75-78.

[33] Robbins Burling, pp. 88-91; Peter Trudjill, Sociolinguistics (Middlesex, England: Penguin Books, Ltd., 1974), pp. 105-107.

[34] Federico Cammarota, Vocabulario familiar y del lunfardo (Buenos Aires: Peña Lillo, 1970), pp. 1-16.

[35] See Cammarota; also José Gobello and Luciano Payet, Breve diccionario lunfardo (Buenos Aires: Peña Lillo, 1959).

[36] See Cammarota and Gobello and Payet.

[37] Charles E. Kany, Semántica hispanoamericana, pp. 233-235; Werner Beinhauer, El español coloquial, trans. Fernando Huarte Morton (Madrid: Editorial Gredos, 1963), p. 216.

[38] See Rafael Lapesa, Historia de la lengua española, 7th ed. (Madrid: Escelicer, 1968), p. 306.

[39] Beinhauer, p. 44.

[40] Kany, Semántica, pp. 26-30.

173

[41] See Tito Saubidet, Vocabulario y refranero criollo (Buenos Aires: Editorial G. Kraft, 1952).

CHAPTER SIX

SPECIAL FEATURES OF SPANISH
AND PENINSULAR LANGUAGE/DIALECTS

WHERE SPANISH IS SPOKEN. Aside from its official status in Spain and most of Latin America, Spanish might be used on a continent like Africa, where it is a valuable means of communication in such places as the Rio de Oro Region, Spanish Sahara, Spanish Guinea, and Spanish Morocco. On nearby Canary Islands Spanish is the official language. In the Philippines the language shares its status with English and Tagalog (an Indonesian group of languages which is part of the Malayo-Polynesian family). Spanish is also heard in "Cerdeña catalana," mainly Alghero, a Sardinian seaport city, where the dominant dialect is Catalonian. In many parts of Europe, Central and South Americas, and the United States, Sephardic Jews still speak a semi-stagnant form of the language of their ancestors with local semantic modifications. Moreover, many thousands of native Americans speak Spanish either as their dominant or second language.

One may wonder if, in fact, a language spoken by so many millions of peoples in different parts of the globe is essentially the same. Curiously enough, despite minimal variations in structure, local peculiarities in syntax, and regional semantic modifications, all Spanish-speaking areas are intimately bound by the same phonology, morphology, and syntax which provide a consistent structure that makes for communication and exchange of ideas in a very precise manner.

The Hispanic linguistic picture is such that communication is not only automatic but provides a definite bond whether one is in Spain, many parts of Europe, North Africa, the Philippines, the Caribbean, many parts of the United States, and most places south of the border. Equipped with a solid foundation in the spoken language, one may embark on a fascinating odyssey which is virtually boundless in territorial expanse and very rich in varieties of peoples, customs, and mores (see statistics p. 179).

(see statistics p. 179)

CASTELLANO VS. ESPAÑOL. Standard Spanish is derived from Castilian with significant influences from other regional dialects. In a limited sense, the word castellano refers to the language spoken in New and Old Castiles. In a broader sense, the term castellano has come to mean the language of Spain which has spread throughout the world and is known as general standard Spanish of either peninsular or Latin-American variety. Over the centuries, the term español has also been applied to describe the same language. In other words, both español and castellano are now used to signify both variant forms of the language as well as the universal Hispanic model.

Many of the reasons for differing degrees of assimilation of the national "Castilian model" (castellano) go back in time to the epoch in which the "Reyes Católicos" attempted to impose many of their own ideals--linguistic, religious, sociological, and political--on much of Spain. As Castilian eventually spread throughout the peninsula, it was assimilated on the local level according to pre-existing patterns of phonation. As frequently occurs in matters of language assimilation, the phonological and morphological features indigenous to the various speech zones made an indelible imprint upon the brand of Castilian spoken from region to region. As the language continued to evolve, linguistic habits native to given speech communities (the substrata) and the more prestigious Castilian (the adstratum) made for the countless regional varieties of the language. As a matter of fact, what was spoken in many areas was not predominantly Castilian at all but modifications of local dialects which were perceived as castellano. While this explanation is by no means sufficient to provide a sound philological overview of the origins of regional variations and dialectal differences,[42] in essence it may be considered one

SPANISH AROUND THE GLOBE

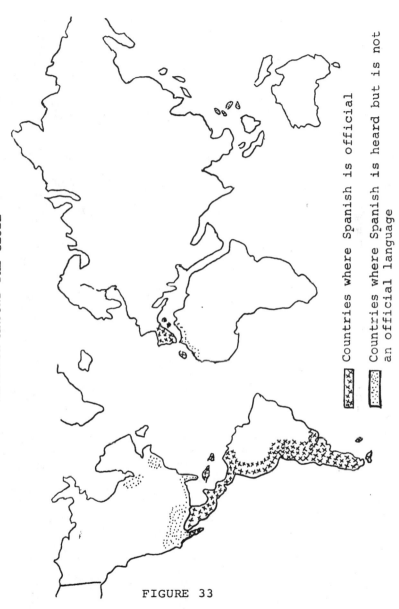

Countries where Spanish is official

Countries where Spanish is heard but is not
an official language

FIGURE 33

of the fundamentally accepted explanations of linguistic variations within the Iberian Peninsula.
Contrary to popular opinion concerning the type of
Spanish transplanted to the New World, the colonizers
brought with them a truly polylingual heritage rather
than one national ideal language. This fact provides
one of the best insights into the innumerable variations of Spanish which exist in the Americas and
elsewhere outside of Spain.[43]

In current usage, the terms español and castellano are by and large synonymous. Both signify
the standard language spoken by Hispanics the world
over. While it is true that Castilian retained its
appeal as the language of the cultural and linguistic élite, the fact remains that the significations
of castellano have been extended over the years.
Thus to some, the term signifies the ideal form of
the dialect of the Castiles. To others, it simply
means the national language of Spain in whatever
form it exists locally. To others, its meaning is
fundamentally identical to español without reference
to the place where it is spoken. Outside of Spain
some speakers opt for castellano since the term español has taken on somewhat distasteful nuances due
to frequently inflamed political separatist movements and anti-Spanish sentiments. In fact, many
Spanish Americans use the term "gallego" to refer to
the version of the language thought of as castellano
castizo--the dialectal variant characterized by interdental articulation in certain positions.

Aside from the terms castellano and español,
hispano has a great deal of diffusion. It refers to
all people of Hispanic origin and speech regardless
of nationality, race, religion, or political loyal-
ties. A good example of this type of Hispanic solidarity is found in the celebration of Columbus Day
(October 11), known universally as el DIA DE LA RA-
ZA. Understood in the word raza is the adjective
hispana since it unites Spaniards, Latin Americans,
Caribbean Islanders, Chicanos, Puerto Ricans, and
all who feel emotional and historical ties with the
Hispanic world. The term hispánico, while often

178

STATISTICS OF SPANISH SPEAKERS

Total number of Spanish speakers in the world	219.000.000
Argentina	26.730.000
Bolivia	4.886.700
Chile	10.917.500
Colombia	26.587.000
Costa Rica	2.224.000
Cuba	9.648.900
Dominican Republic	5.275.400
Ecuador	8.047.000
El Salvador	4.663.000
Guatemala	6.835.900
Honduras	3.691.000
Mexico	66.944.000
Nicaragua	2.395.000
Panama	1.891.000
Paraguay	2.974.000
Peru	17.291.000
Philippines	2.108.000
Puerto Rico	3.378.000
Spain (with Balearic and Canary Islands)	37.551.000
Spanish Sahara	108.000
Trinidad and Tobago	1.133.000
Uruguay	2.864.000
Venezuela	13.515.000
U. S. A.	9.800.000
	(10.000.000 aliens)

(These statistics are based upon the 1980 Britannica Book of the Year.)

used as a synonym, is best applied with broader sociological and cultural connotations.[44]

CECEO AND SESEO. One of the characteristic features of a major variety of peninsular Spanish is ceceo, by which is meant the articulation in which c before e and i and z before all vowels are pronounced as interdental fricatives--⌈θ⌉ voiceless and ⌈z̧⌉ voiced. This pronunciation is typical of a good deal of Spain--Old Castile, New Castile, and the southwestern third of Andalusia; in addition, it occurs as a variant articulation elsewhere. In some instances, the use of ceceo is a result of social level and educational background, but the interdental articulation is indigenous to the speech zones mentioned. Observe the interdental quality of c before e and i as the fricative ⌈θ⌉ in the following examples:

cero	⌈θérʊ⌉	cine	⌈θínə⌉
centauro	⌈θəntáʋr̩⌉	ceniza	⌈θəníθʊ⌉
cenicero	⌈θəniθér̩⌉	cinc	⌈θíŋk⌉
encima	⌈ənθímʊ⌉	pronunciar	⌈pr̩nʌŋθjár⌉
circo	⌈θírkʊ⌉	cima	⌈θímʊ⌉

When c occurs before other vowels, it is produced as the velar oclusive ⌈k⌉, casa ⌈kásʊ⌉, cura ⌈kúrʊ⌉, Cuzco ⌈kúskʊ⌉, Coca ⌈kókʊ⌉, corral ⌈k̩rál⌉. In ceceante pronunciation, z is always interdental--⌈θ⌉ voiceless before all vowels and ⌈z̧⌉ voiced in most other instances. Observe both sounds in the following examples:

zapatilla	⌈θʊpʊtíłʊ⌉	Zeus	⌈θéʊs⌉
zaga	⌈θáɣʊ⌉	zambullida	⌈θʊmbʌłídʊ⌉
ensalzar	⌈ənsʊ̧łʊár⌉	zorro	⌈θór̩⌉
diezmar	⌈djez̧már⌉	juzgar	⌈xʌz̧ɣár⌉
zueco	⌈θwékʊ⌉	zus	⌈θús⌉
aplazar	⌈ʊplʊ̧θár⌉	gozar	⌈q̇θár⌉
luz maldita	⌈lúz̧ mʊ̧łdítʊ⌉	cruz beata	⌈krúz̧ ᵬʊátʊ⌉

The combination of the voiceless sibilant ⌈s⌉ followed by the voiceless interdental fricative ⌈θ⌉ as in discípulo, ascensor, ascender, and descender allows two possible articulations. In one variant,

180

a very weak, barely perceptible sibilant followed by
the interdental is heard. The other is characterized
by the elimination of the sibilant. Thus one hears
[dɪsɵ́(pʌĺː] and [dɪɵ́(pʌĺː], [ɐ́sɵənsɔ́r] and [ɐ́ɵənsɔ́r],
[ɐ́sɵəɴdέr] and [ɐ́ɵəɴdέr], [daˢɵəɴdέr] and [daɵəɴdέr].
Although the second variant is frequently considered
substandard, it is heard with regularity in relaxed
conversation and familiar speech.

An extension of the interdental articulation to
all or most sibilants is heard in Andalusia <u>soso</u>
[ɵóɵː], <u>tos</u> [tʲɵ], <u>sentir</u> [ɵəɴtʲr], <u>queso</u> [ĸéɵː],
<u>persona</u> [pərɵóɴɐ]. Although frequent enough in this
area, such articulation is an undesirable rendering
of a recurrent phoneme.

Outside of Spain <u>ceceo</u> is not heard, with the
exception of immigrant families and their children,
professional speakers, actors, and some <u>españoles
fingidos</u> .

In the <u>seseo</u> variety of Spanish, <u>c</u> before <u>e</u> and
<u>i</u> and <u>z</u> before all vowels and in all other positions
are articulated as sibilants. Orthographically, of
course, there is no change, and an apico-alveolar
sound--[s] voiceless and [z] voiced--replaces the <u>ce-
ceo</u> interdentals. This articulation is characteristic of a large part of Andalusia, other sections of
the south, much of the eastern coast, and is in competition elsewhere. Moreover, it is one of the essential phonetic features of all non-peninsular
Spanish. While <u>seseo</u> has not enjoyed the traditional prestige of <u>ceceo</u> within certain Spanish circles, it is used by most of the world's speakers of
the language. In southern Spain plays and novels
often use <u>ceceo</u> articulation as a form of comical
satire since it is usually focused as a rather low-
class form of speech or dialect with rustic overtones.[45] The situation in Latin America tends to be
similar. In fact, the average <u>latino</u> reacts to <u>ce-
ceo</u> articulation with some degree of discomfort.
These basic differences should not influence non-
native speakers since both pronunciations are equal
in function, and matters of "preferred forms" simply

do not enter the picture. Suffice it to say that
the ceceo variety is normally associated with the
Old World and the language spoken on the central meseta, and seseo is identified with the rest of the
Hispanic world. The non-native often feels put upon
to make a kind of choice, but this may be more a matter of personal preference or original exposure.

All matters of preference aside, the one aspect
to be avoided is a mixture of both varieties. Even
though this does take place sporadically in the oral
production of natives from overlapping speech zones
in Spain and in the children of immigrant parents
elsewhere, this substandard version should be
avoided. By way of example, an Argentinian or Colombian whose parents emigrated from Castile might
be heard to say //él ma dísa ka ní prafjera ʁθérlɔ
ní dɑséɹ dɑsírlɔ: dése menérɹ tɑ̃m faθiɹ//. Such instances of variant phonemes within the same oral
production are indeed rare and should not be emu-
lated.

Observe the differences between the interdental
and sibilant articulations in the following words:

	ceceo	seseo
decir	[daθír]	[dasír]
hacer	[ʁθér]	[ʁsér]
rezar	[ʁaθár]	[ʁasár]
zigzaguear	[θiʁθeʁɡaár]	[siʁseʁɡaár]
a las once	[ʁ lɛ sɔ́nθɑ]	[ʁ lɛ sɔ́nsɑ]
la pronunciación	[lɛ prɔnɔnθjajɔ́n]	[lɛ prɔnɔnsjasjɔ́n]
la nación	[lɛ naθjɔ́n]	[lɛ nasjɔ́n]
mucha zozobra	[múʧɛ θɔθóbrɛ]	[múʧɛ sɔsóbrɛ]
Badajoz	[baðɛxɔ́θ]	[baðɛxɔ́s]
diezmo	[djézmɔ]	[djézmɔ]

In spite of the fact that ceceante speakers
clearly distinguish between minimal pairs in which
the sibilant and interdental are contrastive, this
is not significant to seseo speakers since their
handling of the language is not linked to that particular focus. Minimal pairs in the ceceo setup are
in no way contrastive to seseantes, and the following

182

are differentiated by the latter merely contextually: casa/caza, casar/cazar, vos/voz, coser/cocer, sien/cien, serrar/cerrar, asar/azar. In conclusion, seseo articulation makes use only of the sibilant version as meaningful, and the interdentals in these positions are totally rejected.[46]

LLEISMO, YEISMO, AND OTHER VARIANTS. By lleísmo is meant the traditional rendering of the digraph ll as a lateral palatal ⌈ʎ⌉--usually associated with certain varieties of peninsular articulation. The phoneme is produced as a clear liquid as follows:

ella	⌈éʎɐ⌉	hallazgo	⌈ɐʎáʐɣɔ⌉
olla	⌈óʎɐ⌉	llama	⌈ʎámɐ⌉
ello	⌈éʎɔ⌉	llaga	⌈ʎáɣɐ⌉
hallar	⌈ɐʎár⌉	llanto	⌈ʎántɔ⌉
calle	⌈káʎɐ⌉	llanura	⌈ʎɐnúrɐ⌉

The lleísta ⌈ʎ⌉ is generally associated with more conservative types of oral production found in much of Murcia, Castilla la Nueva, Castilla la Vieja, parts of León, Navarra, Aragón, and elsewhere.

   Yeísmo is used to describe the variant pronunciation of the same sound produced in a less liquid fashion, yielding in its place the phoneme ⌈y⌉. This variant is met frequently in southern Spain and is often identified with Andalusia, where it is in competition with ⌈ʎ⌉. Yeísmo is the variant which predominates outside of Spain and is heard in all forms of Judaeo-Spanish, in the Balkans, Asia Minor, and North Africa. In addition, it is typical of the articulation of the Canary Islands, the Philippines, and most of the Americas.[47] While there is a slight difference in the production of the sound, both the lleísta and yeísta variants are in free variation. Thus ll is articulated most frequently either as ⌈ʎ⌉ or ⌈y⌉.

	lleísta	yeísta
calle	⌈káʎɐ⌉	⌈káyɐ⌉
valle	⌈báʎɐ⌉	⌈báyɐ⌉

183

taller	[teḽér]	[teɣér],
callejuela	[keḽəxwéle]	[keɣəxwéle]
callado	[keḽáðː]	[keɣáðː]
velludo	[baḽúðː]	[baɣúðː]

Aside from the two basic [ḽ] and [ɣ], yeísmo admits
other free variants as well. One is a voiced palatal affricate [ẑ], produced with the apico-dorsal
portion of the tongue in an elevated position.
Another is a voiced palatal affricate [dz], articulated with the dorsal portion of the tongue in the
same position. A third variant of [ɣ] is [ø]; that
is to say, the phoneme normally disappears after
stressed i and e and sporadically in other positions
in certain forms of articulation.

Generally speaking, a rather clear distinction
is made between [ḽ] and [ɣ] in southern Peru, central Colombia, much of Bolivia, northern and southern Chile, and the northernmost tip of Argentina.
The articulation of [ɣ] as a clear voiced palatal
fricative is associated with those parts of Mexico
where the [ø] sound is not in competition, much of
Panama, Venezuela, Ecuador, Peru, central Chile, and
most of Colombia. The voiced palatal affricate [dz]
is typical of the interior of Puerto Rico and most
of the Caribbean, where the [ɣ] variant is in competition. The other voiced palatal affricate [ẑ] is
associated with Argentina, much of Paraguay, Uruguay,
and a small area of Colombia. The phoneme [ø] occurs
in certain versions of Judaeo-Spanish speech, North
Africa, a good deal of Mexico, and sporadically in
Central America. In the latter articulation, forms
like aquello, anillo, mujercilla, hebilla, amorcillo
are rendered aqueo, anío, mujercía, hebía, amorcío.
While all of these variants have their roots in different parts of Spain, they have been assimilated in
different ways outside of the peninsula.

If one were to travel from the southwestern
section of the United States to the tip of Argentina,
the following phonetic renderings would be encountered:

	[ļ]	[ʸ]	[dž]	[ž]	[ø]
muralla	[mʌráļɐ]	[mʌráʸɐ]	[mʌrádzɐ]	[mʌrážɐ]	-------
ardilla	[ɛrðíļɐ]	[ɛrðíʸɐ]	[ɛrðídzɐ]	[ɛrðížɐ]	[ɛrðíɐ]
olla	[óļɐ]	[óʸɐ]	[ódzɐ]	[óžɐ]	-------
toalla	[tːáļɐ]	[tːáʸɐ]	[tːádzɐ]	[tːážɐ]	-------
Coello	[kːéļː]	[kːéʸː]	[kːédzː]	[kːéžː]	[kːéː]
caballo	[kɐɓáļː]	[kɐɓáʸː]	[kɐɓádzː]	[kɐɓážː]	-------

Despite the variations and the vast geographical territory over which they are spread, yeísmo in one
form or another remains characteristic of southern
Spain, other Spanish-speaking areas of Europe, and
most of the New World. All five variant phonemes are
in free variation, having no effect whatsoever upon
meaning.48

TU, VOSOTROS, AND VOS. Vosotros as the second-person
plural form of address is identified traditionally
with Spain. Normally, one shifts from the singular
tú to the plural vosotros and vice versa with regularity

tú eres ⟵⟶	vosotros sois
vosotros hablasteis ⟵⟶	tú hablaste
tú venías ⟵⟶	vosotros veníais
vosotros estudiaréis ⟵⟶	tú estudiarás
tú tendrías ⟵⟶	vosotros tendríais
vosotros salgáis ⟵⟶	tú salgas
tú vivieras ⟵⟶	vosotros vivierais

In most of Spain, with the exception of Andalusia and
isolated pockets, vosotros and its corresponding
verb-forms (-áis, -éis, -ís; -abais, -íais; -asteis,
-isteis; -aréis, -eréis, -iréis; -aríais, -eríais,
-iríais; -éis, -áis; -arais, -ierais; -ad, -ed, -id)
and pronoun-forms (os, vuestro(a), vuestros(as)) are

185

a natural part of everyday speech. To complicate
matters further, variant forms have been in competition with vosotros in Andalusia and other
places. Throughout the centuries many changes occurred in connection with this pronoun and its corresponding forms, not only in Spain but the New
World as well.

Voseo--the use of the pronoun vos as a familiar
singular form of address--has had a vivid history
since its more limited beginnings in its country of
origin. Two important shifts in common usage in
Andalusia took root in connection with forms of address early in their history. Tú as a pronoun of
familiar address was replaced by vos in many speech
zones. Similarly, vosotros disappeared in all of
Latin America and was replaced by ustedes both for
familiar and polite plural forms of address.[49] In
many areas of Spanish America tuteo--the traditional
use of tú and corresponding forms for familiar ad-
dress--is in competition with voseo, and in many
areas there is a kind of hybrid usage in which both
forms are mixed. A good example of this is found in
Uruguay, where tuteo and voseo seem to vie for first
place, resulting in a variety of mixed forms. In
other words, one hears voseo--vos as the familiar
singular pronoun-form--accompanied by tuteo verb-
forms, producing combinations like vos tienes, vos
hablas, vos dices. The opposite phenomenon also occurs in which tuteo pronoun-forms are used with voseo verb-forms tú tenés, tú hablás, tú decís.[50]

Voseo, tuteo, or combinations of the two are met
throughout Spanish America. In the River Plate Re-
gion--Argentina, Paraguay, and Uruguay--voseo usage
is fairly universal. Here the second person plural
of the modified verb-form is used together with vos
functioning as the second person singular. Typical
of this area are combinations like vos hablás, vos
tenés, vos estás, vos ves, vos reís. There are
speech communities as well in which tuteo and voseo
are in competition, so that forms like vos tomas,
vos tienes, vos sales compete with vos tomás, vos
tenés, vos salís. The utterances cited in this con-

186

nection by Zamora Vicente are fine exemplifications
of this rather interesting linguistic phenomenon--
"Vos te gastáis tu vida con vos solo" (Chile) and
"vos te has guardado esa platita para vos solo" (Argentina).[51] Such combined variants are normally
heard among rural voseante or tuteante speakers.
Aside from its use in the River Plate Region, voseo
is characteristic of the Yucatan Peninsula, southern
Mexico, and most of Central America. The areas in
which tuteo and voseo are in definite competition include much of Chile, northern and southern Peru,
southwestern Bolivia, all of Ecuador, the southern
half of Colombia, the western portion of Venezuela,
and the eastern part of Cuba.

Morphologically speaking, there are basically
three types of voseante verbal setups, even though
different emphases are found in some areas and not
in others and forms in competition abound. Despite
the obvious complexities, the verb-endings for the
present indicative may be reduced to the following
three basic patterns:

TYPE ONE	TYPE TWO	TYPE THREE
habláis	hablás	habláis
coméis	comés	comís
salís	salís	salís

The endings are reversed according to the traditional
pattern to express the subjunctive mood in the same
tense.

TYPE ONE	TYPE TWO	TYPE THREE
habléis	hablés	hablís
comáis	comás	comáis
partáis	partás	partáis

Type one is typical of the speech of Cuba and Venezuela. Type two is the recurrent pattern in the
River Plate area, the entire northern coast of South
America, and virtually all of Central America with
sporadic occurrences of type one. Type three is
characteristic of the usage in Chile and surrounding
border areas.[52]

Voseo future forms are based on the development

187

of four distinct patterns tomarás, tomarés, toma-
rís, and tomaréis. In the formation of this tense,
aside from the predominant pattern tomarás, habla-
rás, comerás, the use of the other endings is often
a matter of social class, family background, and
education.[53]

Although more than a third of the Spanish-
speaking population in Latin America does not use
voseo in any form whatsoever, this phenomenon has
come to be identified with speech in this part of the
world. It is understood that voseo variants are
really archaic peninsular forms of which many examples have been documented over the centuries. Originally, vos was used together with tú, the former
being applied to one's peers and with one's superi-
ors. In other words, what was originally an alternate possibility of address eventually lost hold in
large areas of Spain. When these variants were
transplanted to new soil, they were assimilated in
different ways. Thus new forms evolved and old ones
were somehow extended to meet the needs of communication in newly structured societies. Nevertheless,
while two-thirds of the speakers in Spanish America
make use of voseo or tuteo to one extent or another,
cultured speakers persist in their use of tú, usted/
ustedes when speaking formally. The traditional use
of vosotros is the only form which fell into disuse,
even though the verb-forms employed with vos clearly
derive from the traditional second-person plural
forms.

The so-called "vos of diplomacy" should be considered a phenomenon apart from the practice of
using vos for daily familiar address. Since the vos
form antedates the development of polite usted (from
vuestra merced, vuesarcé), it has been used over the
centuries for both familiar and polite address in the
singular. This older use is extended in contemporary
society in order to effect very formal address under
extraordinary circumstances. For instance, in Franco's welcoming speech to Haile Selassie, vos is used
as a form of respect, deference, and diplomatic cour-
tesy: "Vos habéis sido, Majestad, un modernizador...

188

Etiopía y Vuestra Merced han aportado algo esencial a Africa actual."[54] Several observations are in order with reference to the quotation: <u>vos</u> is followed by the traditional second-person verb-form (habéis); there is an automatic shift from <u>vos</u> to <u>Vuestra Merced</u> in addressing the same person; archaic forms are used for purposes of creating an oratorical style. Although this particular use of <u>vos</u> is generally ignored by traditional grammarians and structuralists alike, it is used extensively in affairs of state and on similar occasions throughout the Spanish-speaking world.

OTHER LANGUAGES IN SPAIN. Two of the unofficial languages used in the peninsula are, in fact, directly related to its official tongue. These are Catalonian or Catalan (<u>el catalán</u>) and Galician (<u>el gallego</u>). They developed more or less concomitantly with the official dialect and have influenced each other mutually for centuries. Consequently, many Spaniards are for all practical purposes bilingual since they speak either of these languages natively, as well as the official language. One need hardly mention that since the death of Franco and the upsurge of "independentista" movements, these languages are gaining ground and are verging on near-equal status with the official language.

CATALAN, spoken along the Mediterranean border from Barcelona to Valencia, has many features in common with French. As might be expected, it normally keeps intact the Latin initial consonantal clusters <u>pl-</u>, <u>fl-</u>, <u>cl-</u> clau (llave), flama (llama), plorar (llorar), pleno (lleno). Postonic a is closed to e or is lost haba>fabe, oveja>ubelle, cresta>creste; the same occurs with final -o todo>tot, vallado>vall, caballo>caball. Original initial f-, normally h in Castilian, is retained fum (humo), fill (hijo), fava (haba). The original -ct- cluster produced -ch- in Castilian in most positions, but in Catalan, like French, c is vocalized to i, yielding forms like treit (trecho), leit (leche), lleituga (lechuga),

189

pet (pecho).

Catalan is somewhat more conservative morphologically than Castilian. The singular articles are
lo, l, el, la; the plural los, ls, els, les. The
personal pronouns are yo, tú, él, nosaltres, vosaltres, ells, elles. Unlike Spanish, infinitives
are frequently root-stressed--caure (caer), viure
(vivir), respondre (responder), escriure (escribir).⁵⁵
Past participles end in -t and -da--amat, amada; descabalgat, descabalgada; tomat, tomada. Final -n of
Castilian -ción disappears: corporació, suspensió,
infracció, situació, participació, presentació, projecció, puntalizació. As one might observe, one of
the most striking aspects of Catalan is its rather
strident consonants.

GALICIAN, originally part of the Galician-Portuguese linguistic zone and spoken in the northwestern province of Galicia, has a good deal in common
with Portuguese. One of the chief characteristics of
both languages is a very heavy nasal quality. In addition, postonic vowels are articulated weakly and
rapidly whereas final vowels often disappear. Galician has four types of e and o--open, close, very
close, and normal. All atonal vowels are reduced or
close e>i : piligro, cipillo, ripitir, pipita, esi
niño. Similarly, vowels in hiatus are often reduced
to diphthongs real>rial, peor>pior.⁵⁶ In this sound
system, z often replaces d (Madriz), and l is sporadically substituted for internal d (melecina). Yeísmo [Y] is also characteristic of this speech zone.
Seseo, on the other hand, is the normal pattern in
Pontevedra, La Coruña, the Atlantic side of Galicia,
but not elsewhere. One of its outstanding features
is the so-called geada del gallego, in which voiced
velars [q] and [ɋ] become a voiceless fricative velar
aspiration [x]: jaita (gaita), jrilo (grillo), ajua
(agua), luejo (luego), jordo (gordo), lujat (lugar).⁵⁷

One of the characteristic features of gallego
and even español agallegado (standard Spanish with
highly regionalistic overtones) is the ubiquitous
Galician-Portuguese suffix -iño, -iña, of which exam-

ples abound as in Carmiña, prontiño, hijiña, encan-
tiño, pobriño, galiña, piño, camiño, anduriña, sero-
diño, tiña.[58]

Tense structure is simplified with less use of
compound tenses. By way of example, the preterite
often replaces the present perfect as in the following contrastive statement: Spanish usage: "El
año pasado llovió mucho pero este año no ha llovido
nada;" Galician usage: "El año pasado llovió mucho
pero este año no llovió nada."[59] Similarly, the imperfect subjunctive (-ra forms) normally functions
as the pluperfect as in fuera (había ido), caminara
(había caminado), dijéramos (habíamos dicho). The
present indicative is similar to Castilian formation
but admits several variant forms:

FALAR: falo, falas, fala,
        falamos, falades (falás), falan.

BATER: bato, bates, bate,
        batemos, batedes (batés), baten.

PARTIR: parto, partes, parte,
        partimos, partides (partís), parten.

The preterite contains a number of alternate forms:

FALAR: falei (falín), falaste (falache,
        falaches), falou,

        falamos, falastes (falástedes,
        faláchedes), falaron (falano).

BATER: batín (batei), bateste (bateche,
        bateches), bateu (batío, batíu),

        batimos, batestes (batéstedes,
        batéchedes), bateron (bateno).

PARTIR: partín, partiste (partiche,
        partiches), partíu (partío, parteu),

191

partimos, partistes (partístides, partíchedes), partiron (partino).

The future and conditional tenses are interesting since they preserve the Romance verb of obligation as a sign of futurity. In other words, gallego has the normally developed tenses (partirei and partiría), as well as some form of haber used to express either the future or the conditional (hei partir and había partir) as in the original Romance formation hablar he, hablar has, hablar ha.[60]

Galician is rich in semantic choices and lexical items peculiar to the area. Amoado is kneaded dough; berrar means to scold; billa is faucet; cascuda, cockroach; patacón, coin of little value; cirolas, underpants; empetar, to save; lambón, lover of sweets; latar, to cut glass. A túzaro is a term used to refer to any socially undesirable male. The Spanish día suelto is usually día laborable, and a voltereta (somersault) may be expressed pinchagato or pinchalagarto. While these examples are by no means sufficiently representative, they show to some degree the typical Galician wealth of imagery and local color.[61]

For native speakers of Spanish, Catalan or Galician is not totally unintelligible since it is relatively easy for them to grasp the gist of what is being said, but details of syntax and complexities of semantics do create insurmountable barriers in more cases than not.

BASQUE (el vascuence) is spoken along the northeastern border of Spain and the southwestern coast of France. Of all the language/dialects spoken in the Iberian Peninsula, Basque is the only non-Romance tongue. Although it has been used in this area for centuries, its origins have never been completely explained, and it remains unintelligible to both the Spanish and the French. To further complicate matters, there is little documentation available of either the spoken or the written language. Even though there are sporadic Spanish and

French influences, Basque or Eskuara, as it is known
to its native speakers, contains morphological and
syntactical features which are non-existent in Romance languages.

PORTUGUESE (el portugués) is the other official
Iberian language. While it has many features in
common with Spanish, in its morphology it has a
greater number of similarities with Galician and Catalan in that many of the stressed vowels are not
diphthongized:

SPANISH/PORTUGUESE	SPANISH/PORTUGUESE
puerta/porta	cuerpo/corpo
siesta/sesta	fuero/foro
muerte/morte	tiempo/tempo
puerco/porco	fuerza/força

The characteristically Portuguese phonemes are close
a [ɐ], cama [ké̃mɐ]; "mute" e [ə], pedir [pədír]; final o [u], mudo [múðu]; posterior l [ł], mal [mał];
the voiceless palatal sibilant ch [ʃ], chuva [ʃúvɐ];
z/s [z], fazer [fəzér], casa [kázɐ]; s/g, a voiced
palatal sibilant [ʒ], José [ʒuzé], reger [rriʒér].
The signs [ã], [ẽ], [ĩ], [õ], and [ũ] are indicators
of nasalized vowels; in addition, final -m also indicates nasalization--am, em, om, um, fogão, conju-
gação, ocasião, cento, bom, cinco, num, fim, bem,
com. There are also four nasalized diphthongs: ãe
(mãe), õe (sabaões), ũi (muito, mũi), ão (estão).
A unique vowel quality exhibits an alteration known
as metaphony--a vowel shift from close to open in
the root of radical syllables--porco [pórkʌ] porcos
[pórkʌs]. This alteration takes place not only in
plural forms but in most derivational words as well.

From the view of morphology and syntax, Portuguese has some variations of its own. In familiar
address tu is the singular form in Portugal. In
Brazil tu is normally replaced by Voçe--a form with
more intimacy than the rigidly formal o senhor, a
senhora but less familiarity than tu. The older
plural pronoun vos is used like the Spanish diplomatic vos in public speeches, sermons, and public

193

functions. The verbal structure in general is similar to the Castilian setup

	I	II	III
	FALAR	ESCREVER	PARTIR
eu	falo	escrevo	parto
tu	falas	escreves	partes
o senhor, a senhora	fala	escreve	parte
nós	falamos	escrevemos	partimos
vós	falais	escreveis	partis
os senhores, as senhoras, êles, elas	falam	escrevem	partem

Unlike Spanish, the auxiliary for compound tenses is ter (tener) eu tenho falado (he hablado), eu tenho escrito (he escrito). A characteristically Portuguese development is the use of two infinitive forms-- the impersonal (falar, escrever, partir, ter) and the personal, which takes the following endings for all verbs--regular and irregular ---, -es, ---, -mos, -des, -em. The personal form is used when a subject is strongly implied or clearly understood and when there is a definite change in subject as in Ao irem, pago (Upon their going (irem and not ir), I shall pay). While the Spanish verb system forms most compounds with haber, Portuguese forms its pluperfect as an additional simple past--falar: falara, falaras, falara, faláramos, faláreis, falaram. Speakers of Spanish have little difficulty in reading Portuguese for basic comprehension, and there is some degree of mutual understanding when conversation is attempted. On the other hand, details are lost, and speakers of either language do not fare very well when attempting to pronounce the other tongue with any degree of precision.

THE SPANISH DIALECTS. Language analysts currently

tend to view the intelligible speech of a community or an individual as "dialect." The term has also been used to describe languages which have met with political, social, or economic catastrophe. Consequently, many dialects are touted as "superior" while others are held rather low on the social scale. In the course of history, some dialects like the koine of Greece and the Malay of Indonesia actually acquired the dignity and status of national languages.[62] Whatever one's notion of "dialect" may happen to be, it seems fairly clear that the linguistic picture in Spain tends to favor a more historical approach.

Aside from castellano, the representative dialects are leonés, aragonés, and andaluz--major forms of communication in a large part of the peninsula. Minor dialects are extremeño, riojano, murciano, and canario, which developed semantic and phonological aspects on a local level but which share the same broad historical developments as the others.

It is difficult if not impossible to delimit the geographical areas in which Spanish dialects are spoken as there is a great deal of overlapping. Moreover, there are border areas where a major dialect is spoken with pronounced influences from nearby speech communities. There are even transitional areas in which two or more forms of parlance actually vie for first place. In any case, any statements concerning boundaries in a linguistic sense are at best approximate since languages and dialects are as difficult to pin down as the people who speak them.

LEONESE is spoken in Asturias, Santander, Leon, Zamora, Caceres, Badajoz, and Salamanca, but its influence is felt far beyond these boundaries.

Leonese vowels contain diphthongizations not found in standard Spanish. For instance, as a general rule, $[o] > [u\acute{o}]$ or $[u\acute{e}]$--puobru (pobre), nueche (noche), ueyo (ojo). The non-diphthongized variant is also encountered--fonte (fuente), ponte (puente). The reduction of final vowels ($[o] > [u]$ and $[e] > [i]$) is also typical, rendering maridu,

195

otru, conventu, mediu, pescadu, esti, padri, madri.
The ending -ino is generally articulated -ín molín,
camín, padrín, focín.

Leonese consonants are by and large quite conservative. Latin initial f- is normally retained
fijo, farina, fumo, formiga, filar, figo, fuella,
forno. Palatalized initial ñ- is also frequent
ñube, ño, ñoramala, ñariz. A similar type of pala-
talization also takes place with initial l- llobo,
llengua, llinaza, lluna, llombu, llagaña, Valle de
Llamiellas.63

An interesting syntactical feature is the use
of the prefix per- as an adverbial intensifier--per-
blancu (muy blanco), perlimpio (muy limpio). Frequent shifts in gender are also common. For example, Spanish la sal, el peral, el nojal are said el
sal, la peral, la nojal, and such examples abound.

Castilian verb-forms like conozco and merezco
lose the velar oclusive conozo, merezo. In addition, many Castilian diphthongizations are not so
handled in Leonese, and the opposite phenomenon occurs even more frequently. For example, forms like
viendo (vendo), cueso (coso), cuentar, piescar, a-
prietar, enmiendar are encountered with regularity.64

Because of the vast territory in which the dialect is spoken, multiple forms are prevalent. As one
might expect, many of the double and triple forms
have much more in common with each other than they
do with standard Spanish.

ARAGONESE is spoken primarily in Huescas, Cata-
layud, Zaragoza, Teruel, Benasque, Espadilla, Cue-
vas de Cañart, Castelnovo, Soneja, and Segorbe.
While Leonese and Aragonese have a good deal in common vocalically, the latter tends to reduce to one
syllable vowel clusters which are in hiatus in standard Spanish. For example, acarrear is said carriar,
and this type of reduction is typical. Aragonese
tends to reject proparoxytonic articulation, preferring paroxytonic stress such as cantáro, medíco, ma-

quína. Initial f- is normally retained ferrar, es-
follinar, fuesa, faba, finojera, farineta. Initial
pl- and cl- are frequently retained as well plover,
plegar, plorar, clamar, clau. Initial s- plus a
consonant is kept intact without the typically Castilian epenthetic e- scudero, speciería, statuto,
striperas, spalda. Finally, there is little sonori-
zation of intervocalic consonants liapre, presepe,
capeza, espata.[65]

From the point of view of morphology and syntax, certain major differences are worthy of note.
Standard adjectives ending in -e have an Aragonese
feminine variant granda, verda. The first- and
second-person plural pronouns are nusotros and vuso-
tros (gusotros), respectively. The masculine articles are lo and o; the feminine, la and a.

Like Leonese, infinitives often have diphthongized roots not found in standard Spanish cuentar, juegar, aprietar. The standard strong preterite is often regularized, but not always; that is,
tuve, dije, supe, quise, vine are often said tenié,
dicié, sabié, querié, venié.[66] What is more, there
are sporadic shifts in stress as in habiá (había).
The present indicative has a number of alternate
forms in some persons as follows:

VER	CREER	SER	FACER
veigo	creigo	so (soy)	fago (fo, foi)
ves (ve-yes, vei)	creyes	yes (yas)	fas (faces)
ve (vey)	crey	ye	fa (face)
veyemos	creyemos	semos	femos (facemos)
véis (viyéis)	creyes	sez (soz)	feis (feiz)
veyen	creyen	son	fan (facen)[67]

197

LANGUAGES-DIALECTS IN SPAIN

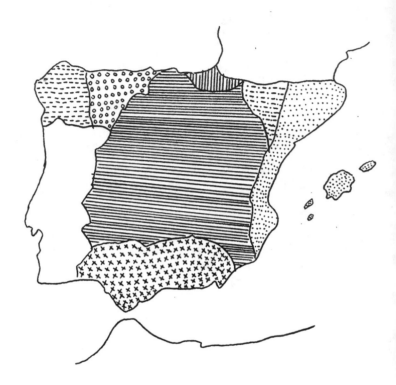

≡≡≡ CASTELLANO   ▦ CATALAN

▦ LEONES   ▦ GALLEGO

▦ ARAGONES   ▦ ANDALUZ

▦ VASCUENCE

FIGURE 34

198

Intervocalic -b- in the imperfect tense is retained
in the second and third conjugations--creyeba, ri-
yeba, comeba, rompeba, meteba, pleveba--and ser is
diphthongized in all persons yera, yeras, yera,
yéramos, yeraz, yeran.

ANDALUSIAN, an offshoot of Castilian, is spoken
principally in Seville, Cadiz, Algeciras, Malaga,
Cordova, Granada, and Nerja. It is, in fact, the
form of communication employed by the greatest number of people in Spain. The vocalic system is not
so precise as the Castilian variety. This is especially true of a, which often becomes [ä] in the
plural, though not always. A typical feature is the
characteristic aspiration of final -s as in voh, loh,
toh, noh, lah, ehto, doh. Also typical is the dropping of the intervocalic consonants -d- and -g-
deo, fluo, esnuo, peír, miaja, mijita (migajita).
The articulation of r is somewhat more complex than
in Castilian. In internal final position it loses
its vibration and is assimilated by the following
phoneme carne>canne, pierna>pienna, virgen>vihen,
arte>atte, tierno>tienno, parte>patte. In absolute
final position it is often lost or assimilated
traerlo>traelo, pedirlo>peílo, llevarla>llevala, su-
birlos>subilloh, bajarlas>bajallah, escucharme>escu-
chame.68

Probably the most significant aspect of the Andalusian consonantal system is seseo articulation,
even though the latter is not universal and variants
are heard. This particular form of sibilant production gives Andalusian a sharp timbre, contrasting
with the more grave version typical of Castile. This
is due to the fact that the tip of the tongue is
placed against the lower teeth while the rest of the
tongue is in a convex position in producing this sibilant. Observe the differences between the sibilant
and interdental articulations in the following examples:

	CASTILIAN	ANDALUSIAN
zapato	[θɐpátɔ]	[sɐpátɔ]

cerro	[θέr̄ɔ]	[sér̄ɔ]
cine	[θínə]	[sínə]
zozobra	[θɔθóbrə]	[sɔsóbrə]
zumo	[θúm̩]	[súm̩]
acertar	[æθərtár]	[æsərtár]
cenizas	[θəníθɐs]	[sənísɐs]

The seseo articulation in Andalusia is important not only as a feature of the local dialect but also as the chief source of español seseante the world over.

In addition to the dominant fricative sibilants [s] and [z], an interdental sibilant [θ] is heard in Cadiz and surrounding areas. As a result, such unappealing forms as zozo, perzona, azar (for asar), zingular, acir, azquerozo are heard a good deal.

Aspiration of initial h-, always silent in Castilian, is encountered with some regularity [húm̩], [hiǫérə], [hɔ́mbrə], [hártɔ], [hɐɣár], [hímnɔ], [hɐstíɔ], [hɔ́s]. The dropping of final consonants, with or without aspiration, is not uncommon, creating alternate forms like [pɐré] or [pɐréh], [ʌʂté] or [ʌʂtéh], [ɐrðí] or [ɐrðíh], [marsé] or [marséh]. Although standard Castilian permits dropping of intervocalic -d- (especially in the ending -ado) about fifty percent of the time in normal relaxed speech, Andalusian eliminates this phoneme fairly consistently. This dropping of -d- occurs in this speech zone regardless of social class, education, or background.

Yeísmo is virtually universal throughout Andalusia. It is heard in both the [ʝ] and [dz] variants [éʝɐ] and [édzɐ], [ɐʝár] and [ɐdzár], [ʝér̄ɔ] and [dzér̄ɔ].

Substitution, or transposition of the order of sounds within words, is also characteristic of this area. This phenomenon is encountered most often with the liquids r and l barcón, mardito, argún, arguien, saltén, polque, picaldía, puelta.

In the general morphological setup, changes in gender are quite frequent la sartén>er sartén, la costumbre>er costumbre. There are also some of the

archaic vacilations as in <u>la</u> <u>color</u>/<u>el</u> <u>color</u>, <u>el</u> <u>ca-</u>
<u>lor</u>/<u>la</u> <u>calor</u>.

A peculiarity of the western part of Andalusia
is the replacement of the second-person plural form,
<u>vosotros</u>, with the third-person plural, <u>ustedes</u>. In
this practice, <u>ustedes</u> and its corresponding forms
function both as the plural of the familiar as well
as the polite. This brings about a weakening of the
second-person plural verb-forms, which compete with
those of the third-person. For example, one nor-
mally hears both <u>ustedes</u> hacen/<u>ustedes</u> hacéis; <u>uste-</u>
<u>des</u> dicen/<u>ustedes</u> <u>decís</u>, <u>ustedes</u> hablan/<u>ustedes</u> ha-
<u>bláis</u>. This particular development is important not
only as a feature of Andalusian, but it provides one
of the explanations of the shift from second-person
singular to the third-person plural universal throughout Latin America.

Verbs of the second and third conjugations retain
intervocalic -b- in the imperfect indicative caer,
<u>caíba</u>; <u>creer</u>, <u>creíba</u>; <u>oír</u>, <u>oíba</u>; <u>traer</u>, <u>traíba</u>. This
retention is peculiar to other dialects as well.

The lexicon in this area reflects its cultural
and historical ties over the centuries. Many forms
are clearly of Arabic derivation <u>marjal</u> (medida a-
graria), almatriche (reguera), <u>almud</u> <u>(celemín)</u>, al-
<u>carcil</u> <u>(alcachofa silvestre)</u>, <u>cauchil</u> <u>(registre de</u>
<u>aguas)</u>. Others derive from archaic Castilian forms
<u>más</u> <u>que</u> (aunque), atacarse (abotonar), desatacarse
<u>(desabotonar)</u>, <u>ansias</u> <u>(náuseas)</u>, <u>babero</u> <u>(bata que</u>
<u>usan los niños)</u>, <u>barfolla</u> <u>(hoja que recubre la ma-</u>
<u>zorca del maíz)</u>, <u>empreñar</u> <u>(mortificar, fastidiar)</u>,
<u>fiemo</u> <u>(estiércol)</u>, <u>malacotón</u> <u>(melocotón)</u>.[69]

This dialect has performed a valuable function
by virtue of its interesting localisms, characteristic turns of phrase, and amusing barbarisms.
Since it has been associated traditionally with comical elements and witty puns, the dialect has been a
great asset to the Hispanic theatre with its abun-
dance of jargon, gypsy patois, local slang, witti-
cisms, and folk expressions. The comical touches
and amusing circumlocutions on the Spanish stage

201

have depended, to one extent or another, on what is affectionately known as "gracia andaluza."

CONCLUSION. What has been mentioned about Spanish dialects is merely an overview. The major peninsular dialects are leonés, aragonés, and andaluz; the minor dialects, murciano, riojano, extremeño, and canario. The latter have a great deal in common with the major dialects on the phonological, morphological, and syntactical levels. The lesser known forms of local speech are characterized by sporadic differences in their vocalic and consonantal systems and by innumerable local semantic developments, but, by and large, they are rather similar. The area of semantics presents a far more complex picture since each dialect reflects the history and mores of the people who use it as their chief means of communication. In this sense, dialect reflects the natural, unfettered development of the language of a given speech community without refinement of education. Thus, in a very fundamental sense, it is the first or native language of a given region. Spanish, when all is said and done, remains the official language of all educated Hispanics throughout the world. More often than not, what remains of dialectal speech is a type of regional inflection, characteristic patterns of intonation, local pronunciation, amusing, time-tested turns of phrase, colorful idioms, or uniquely quaint semantic choices.

EXERCISES

THEORY

A. ANSWER THESE QUESTIONS BRIEFLY.
1. In how many places in the world is Spanish the official language?
2. In which countries is Spanish unofficial?
3. Where is Spanish spoken in North Africa?
4. What is the difference between español and castellano in modern Spanish?
5. What are the main features of ceceo? Where is it used?
6. How does seseo differ from ceceo?
7. Where is vosotros used as a familiar plural form of address?
8. How is vos used on a diplomatic level?
9. What is the difference in usage between tuteo and voseo?
10. What forms of the verb are used with voseo?
11. How is the word hispano used?
12. What kind of voseo is typical of the River Plate region?
13. What is meant by lleísmo?
14. How many variants of yeísmo are there?

B. FILL IN THE BLANKS ACCORDING TO THE SENSE OF THE STATEMENT.
1. _____ is the version of Spanish in which z before all vowels and c before e and i are pronounced as sibilants.
2. The minimal pairs casa/caza, vos/voz, os/hoz may be easily distinguished only in the _____ form of Spanish.
3. _____ and _____ are variants in free distribution of the more basic yeísmo.
4. The language/dialect _____ has many features in common with the French language.
5. The only official languages of the Iberian Peninsula are _____ and _____ .
6. _____ is the dialect which derives from Castilian.
7. _____ refers to the transposition of the order of sounds within a word.
8. A(n) _____ may be known as the intelligible

203

collective idiolect or speech of individuals.

9. Ceceo Spanish is totally rejected in _____.
10. _____ is the only non-Romance language spoken on the Iberian Peninsula.

C. DEFINE THESE ITEMS BRIEFLY.

1. Castilian   5. español tuteante
   (in the narrow sense)
2. hispano (hispánico)   6. español seseante
3. español voseante   7. metaphony
4. Basque   8. español ceceante

D. TRUE OR FALSE.

1. In some of the smaller islands of the West Indies and nearby islands, Spanish is very widespread.

2. In the Philippine Islands Spanish is used together with Tagalog and English. _____
3. Español and castellano usually have identical meanings. _____
4. Ceceo is the dominant form of Spanish the world over. _____
5. Seseo is associated only with southern Spain. _____

6. In a certain sense lleísmo and yeísmo are parallel to ceceo and seseo. _____
7. Vosotros or any derived form is absolutely never heard in Latin America. _____
8. Portuguese is a language in which few nasals are heard. _____
9. O senhor and a senhora are the traditional polite forms in Portuguese. _____
10. Leonese, Andalusian, and Aragonese are the principal dialects spoken in Spain. _____
11. The Leonese vowel system contains diphthongs which are not found in standard Spanish. _____
12. Leonese tends to retain the original Latin f- as an initial consonant. _____
13. Aragonese tends to reject proparoxytone articulation in general. _____
14. Aragonese has four definite articles lo, o, la, and a. _____
15. Final and initial aspirations are typical of Leonese. _____
16. Verb-forms like veigo, creigo, fago are typical

of Catalonian. _____
17. Portuguese has a personal and an impersonal in-
    finitive. _____
18. Catalan keeps intact the Latin initial consonants
    pl-, fl-, and cl-, unlike modern Spanish. _____
19. Galician shares many features in common with
    Portuguese. _____
20. The verb-forms used with voseo are fairly uni-
    form throughout Latin America. _____

E. IDENTIFY THE FOLLOWING TERMS EITHER BY LANGUAGE/
   DIALECT OR REGION.
    1. flama   ....
    2. piligro   ....,......
    3. ajua   ....
    4. luejo   ....
    5. força   ....
    6. porco   ....
    7. clau   ....
    8. pobriño   ....
    9. jaita   ....
   10. camiño   ....
   11. molín   ....
   12. camín   ....
   13. maquína   ....
   14. cantáro   ....
   15. babero   ....
   16. empreñar   ....
   17. ansias   ....
   18. plorar   ....
   19. pleno   ....
   20. meniño   ....

ASI SE DICE·
REPEAT EACH SEGMENT AS GIVEN AND FINALLY THE COM-
PLETE UTTERANCE.

A la   ....
A la tierra   ....
tierra que   ....
tierra que fueres ....
haz   ....

205

```
haz lo                   . . . . . . . . . .
haz lo que               . . . . . . . . . .
lo que vieres            . . . . . . . . . .
A la tierra que fueres, haz lo que vieres.
                         . . . . . . . . . . . . . . . . . . . . . .

Cuando                   . . . . . . . . . .
Cuando a Roma            . . . . . . . . . .
Roma fueres              . . . . . . . . . .
haz                      . . . . . . . . . .
haz lo                   . . . . . . . . . .
haz lo que               . . . . . . . . . .
lo que vieres            . . . . . . . . . .
Cuando a Roma fueres, haz lo que vieres.
                         . . . . . . . . . . . . . . . . . . . . . .

Haz                      . . . . . . . . . .
Haz como                 . . . . . . . . . .
Haz como Blas            . . . . . . . . . . . . . .
Blas, come               . . . . . . . . . .
come y te                . . . . . . . . . .
y te vas                 . . . . . . . . . .
come y te vas            . . . . . . . . . . . . . .
Haz como Blas, come y te vas.
                         . . . . . . . . . . . . . . . . . . . . . .

Donde                    . . . . . . . . . .
Donde una                . . . . . . . . . .
Donde una puerta         . . . . . . . . . .
una puerta se            . . . . . . . . . .
puerta se cierra         . . . . . . . . . .
otra                     . . . . . . . . . .
otra se                  . . . . . . . . . .
otra se abre             . . . . . . . . . .
Donde una puerta se cierra, otra se abre.
                         . . . . . . . . . . . . . . . . . . . . . .

El amor                  . . . . . . . . . .
el amor es               . . . . . . . . . .
amor es ciego            . . . . . . . . . .
El amor es ciego.        . . . . . . . . . . . . . .

Matrimonio               . . . . . . . . . .
matrimonio y             . . . . . . . . . .
matrimonio y mortaja     . . . . . . . . . .
```

mortaja del   . . . .
del cielo   . . . .
del cielo baja   . . . .
Matrimonio y mortaja del cielo baja.
                     . . . .

Saber   . . . .
Saber es   . . . .
es poder   . . . .
Saber es poder.   . . . .

Quien   . . . .
Quien poco   . . . .
poco lee   . . . .
poco   . . . .
poco aprende   . . . .
Quien poco lee poco aprende.
                     . . . .

Un   . . . .
Un hoy   . . . .
Un hoy vale   . . . .
vale más   . . . .
vale más que   . . . .
más que dos .   . . .
más que dos mañanas . . . .
Un hoy vale más que dos mañanas.
                     . . . .

Dios   . . . .
Dios cura   . . . .
Dios cura y el   . . . .
y el médico se   . . . .
médico se lleva   . . . .
se lleva el   . . . .
lleva el dinero   . . . .
Dios cura y el médico se lleva el dinero.
                     . . . .

Cría   . . . .
Cría cuervos   . . . .
cuervos y   . . . .
y te   . . . .
y te sacarán   . . . .
sacarán los   . . . .

```
sacarán los ojos          ..............
Cría cuervos y te sacarán los ojos.
                          .......................

La                        ..........
La experiencia            ..........
La experiencia es         ..............
es madre                  ..........
es madre de               ..........
madre de la               ..........
de la ciencia             ..........
La experiencia es madre de la ciencia.
                          .......................

Lo                        ..........
Lo barato                 ..........
Lo barato cuesta          ..............
cuesta caro               ..........
Lo barato cuesta caro.    .......................
```

FOOTNOTES

42 For further details concerning the development of the language, see Lapesa, Historia, pp. 348-356; also, Amado Alonso, Estudios lingüísticos: temas españoles (Madrid: Editorial Gredos, 1951), pp. 314-330; also, Gloria Toranzo, Un elemento de interés en la fonética española (Pamplona: Ediciones Universidad de Navarra, 1974), pp. 125-133.

43 Pedro Henríquez Ureña, Sobre el problema del andalucismo dialectal de América (Buenos Aires: Instituto de Filología, 1932), pp. 1-14.

44 For additional historical information on castellano/español, see Amado Alonso, Estudios lingüísticos: temas hispanoamericanos (Madrid: Editorial Gredos, 1953), pp. 341-342.

45 See Navarro Tomás, p. 109.

46 See Lapesa, pp. 325-328.

47 See yeísmo in Alonso, Temas hispanoamericanos, pp. 184-200.

48 Alonso, Temas hispanoamericanos, pp. 159-212.

49 José Pedro Rona, Geografía y morfología del "voseo" (Porto Alegre: Pontifícia Universidade Católica do Rio Grande do Sul, 1967), p. 9.

50 See Rona, pp. 56-60.

[51] Zamora Vicente, Dialectología española (Madrid: Editorial Gredos, 1960), p. 401.

[52] This geographical distribution is based on the investigations of Rona, pp. 71-90.

[53] Rona, p. 110.

[54] Alexey Almusov, "Vos and Vosotros as Formal Address in Modern Spanish," Hispania 57 (1974), 305.

[55] For further details on Catalan, see Vicente García de Diego, Manual de dialectología española (Madrid: Instituto de Cultura Hispánica, 1946), pp. 269-286.

[56] See Manuel Rabanal, Hablas hispánicas. Temas gallegos y leoneses (Madrid: Ediciones Alcalá, 1967), pp. 22-23.

[57] Rabanal, pp. 31-32.

[58] See Rabanal, p. 35; García de Diego, pp. 58-59.

[59] Rabanal, pp. 36-39.

[60] For a full discussion of the Galician verbal setup, see García de Diego, pp. 99-124.

[61] See Rabanal, pp. 48-51.

[62] Mario Pei, The Story of Language (New York:

The New American Library, Inc., 1966), pp. 415-417.

[63] Rabanal, pp. 130-133.

[64] For a detailed treatment of the Leonese dialect, see Zamora Vicente, pp. 84-210; also, Vicente García de Diego, "Dialectismos castellanos," Revista de filología española, III (1916), 305-308.

[65] For further details on aragonés, see Manuel Alvar, El dialecto aragonés (Madrid: Editorial Gredos, 1953), pp. 157-195.

[66] Zamora Vicente, pp. 258-275.

[67] Alvar, pp. 225-232.

[68] For an interesting discussion of these points, see Américo Castro, Lengua, enseñanza y literatura (Madrid: Victoriano Suárez, 1924), pp. 62-68.

[69] Castro, pp. 66-75.

CHAPTER SEVEN

SPANISH IN THE NEW WORLD

INTRODUCTION. The colonizers brought to the New
World, among countless other things, their native
language with as many levels and types as there were
representative groups that embarked upon the adven-
ture. The well educated spoke the standard language
of the period with many variations: regionalisms,
local accents, dissimilar inflections, different
lexical forms. Nonetheless, the language transplanted to the Americas was essentially the same.
Typically, when natives of a given language communicate in a new ambience on foreign soil, their speech
patterns are somewhat altered for purposes of facility in linguistic exchange. This is precisely what
happened in Latin America, where speakers from Andalusia, Aragon, Leon, Castile, and other regions
probably made conscious or subconscious attempts to
communicate in a meaningful, less local manner.
Thus, more often than not without total awareness,
they eventually made use of a more standard level of
communication than they would have utilized had they
never left their native regions. In this way there
developed more emphasis upon general usage as the
localisms and regionalisms began to wane. What they
spoke in the New World eventually became the linguistic adstrata imposed upon the different regional
Indian substrata encountered by the Spaniards.

    What precise forms of Spanish were brought to
the Americas? This question has been a source of
controversy for a number of decades. Henríquez Ureña has provided valuable insight into the problem of
whether or not the dialect of Andalusia was the primary basis of speech in the colonies.[70] The important fact is that most groups of Spanish speakers
were represented to one extent or another throughout
the colonial period--Andalusians, Castilians, Leonese, Estremenians, and others. While some aspects
of phonology and morphology may be traced with pre-

cision to one area or another, basically they all
contributed a great deal. Amado Alonso sees the entire linguistic setup as a levelling process:

> Cada expedicionario, como todo hablante,
> hacía oscilar su lenguaje entre el uso lo-
> cal y el uso general. El uso local lleva
> a la fragmentación indefinida, al dialec-
> to, al patois, y, si no tuviera el contra-
> peso del otro, a la lengua del barrio, de
> la familia, del individuo, a la destruc-
> ción del lenguaje en su esencia de instru-
> mento social de comunicación. El uso ge-
> neral lleva a las lenguas nacionales, y se
> va cumpliendo e imponiendo por nivelacio-
> nes y compromisos, cada vez más extensos y
> más profundos, orientados generalmente
> desde el hablar de una región directriz.[71]

The main differences which developed are in the area
of phonetics and semantics. Today many phonemic
variations are observable from daily speech in Mexico to very plain talk in Tierra del Fuego, some
areas preferring certain types and others favoring
different forms. The factor of historical development to be kept in mind is that all aspects of dialect, regional speech, and phonemic variations are
clearly rooted in the country of origin. Other differences are attributable to the native speech encountered by the colonizers. In the course of time,
various forms of spoken Spanish were imposed upon
the native Indian speech zones which eventually became the linguistic substrata of the language introduced. At first, the Indian languages existed side
by side with Spanish, influencing each other mutually. Since Spanish was the language of the con-
quering people, it gradually supplanted most of the
Indian tongues. Nevertheless, the latter did have
a lasting influence upon the phonemics and lexicon
which evolved variously under Spanish domination.

THE INDIAN SUBSTRATA. What was the linguistic picture found by the Spanish in the New World? Basi-

214

cally, there were five major language zones. The form of communication in what is now the southern and southeastern portions of the United States, all of Mexico, and much of Central America was Nahuatl (el náhuatl). What was spoken in the area now known as Cuba, Puerto Rico, the Dominican Republic, much of Venezuela, and northern Colombia was Arawakan (el arauaco). The populations of the Andes zone of Venezuela, western Colombia, Ecuador, Peru, northern Chile, and most of Bolivia communicated in Quechuan (el quechua). Most of the people in the territory that is now Chile used Araucanian (el arauco). The speech in present-day Argentina, Uruguay, and Paraguay was originally Guarani (el guaraní).72 While there still remain areas in which Indian dialects and languages are spoken exclusively, Hispanic-American countries consider their official language Spanish.

ELEMENTS OF GENERAL LATIN-AMERICAN SPANISH. It is generally conceded that the various Indian languages had little or no influence upon Spanish syntax. Instead, considerable pressure was exerted upon the phonological and lexical levels since interference was introduced unavoidably in the areas of sounds, and the lexicon was affected by new concepts and discoveries. While the language heard in Spanish America is by no means uniform, there are characteristic features shared by the majority of speakers, even if not by all. From the point of view of phonetics, certain characteristic traits have evolved.73 The loss of pretonic vowels is typical in much of Mexico, Ecuador, Peru, and Bolivia, so words like ahorita are pronounced orita and viejecito, viejsito. Final d normally disappears throughout this area: verdad>verdá, usted>usté, virtud>virtú, ardid>ardí. Orthographic v, most often a bilabial fricative or oclusive in much of Spain, is occasionally articulated as a labiodental as in [vɔ́iˌ], [vɛ́ṣtə], [vwéˈ lːˌ]. Another nearly universal characteristic is the weakening of the aspiration [x]>[h].

A kind of lallation, or equalization of the liquids l and r, typical of Andalusia, is encountered

215

sporadically from Mexico to Argentina. This equalization is especially characteristic of Puerto Rico ⌐pwέrtə⌐>⌐pwέ¦tə⌐; ⌐ɑ́rtːɔ>⌐ɑ́ltːɔ; ⌐wέrtə⌐>⌐wέ¦tə⌐.

Another interesting phenomenon occurs with the multiple vibrant ⌐r̄⌐, frequently velarized in popular speech ⌐r̃⌐. Similar vibrants have also been recorded in Cuba ⌐xɑ́r̄ːɔ>⌐hɑ́r̃ːɔ; ⌐pːtɔ́r̄ːɔ>⌐pːtɔ́r̃ːɔ; ⌐sέr̄ːɔ>⌐sέr̃ːɔ.

The velarization of final -n ⌐ŋ⌐, typical of normative Spanish only before a velar consonant, is a recurrent feature in this area. It is especially common to hear this n in the third-person plural of verbs ⌐tjénəŋ⌐, ⌐dísəŋ⌐, ⌐ásəŋ⌐; more sporadically, in internal final syllables ⌐kːŋprəŋdέr⌐.

The loss of the final sibilants ⌐s⌐ and ⌐z⌐ is typical of all South American speech, particularly among the less educated and in informal parlance. Versions such as son la do (las dos), la mano (las manos), lo chico (los chicos) are met with regularity. In the Caribbean and sporadically elsewhere, internal-final and final -s are aspirated--another carry-over from Andalusia: son lah doh, lah manoh, loh chicoh, ehto, puehto, loh otroh.[74]

Among less polished speakers, there are fairly consistent phonemic variations. A common shift vocalically is e to i in unstressed syllables vecino>visino; lección>lisión; seguro>siguro; según>sigún; peor>pior; real>rial; teatro>tiatro. The opposite phenomenon also occurs cevil (civil), vesita (visita), prencepal (principal). Similar to the closing of e to i is the reduction o to u, rendering forms like cuete for cohete, gurrión for gorrión, tuavía for todavía. Equally typical is the reduction to a single consonant of combinations such as -pc-, -gn-, and -ct-, as in corrución, interrución, indino, Inasio, inoble, inorante, Benina, dotor, retor. The loss of intervocalic -d- and -g- is not atypical either piaso (pedazo), cuidao (cuidado), jorobao (jorobado), ilesia (iglesia). The opposite is also encountered owing to hypercorrection

216

FIGURE 35

MEXICO-CENTRAL AMERICA

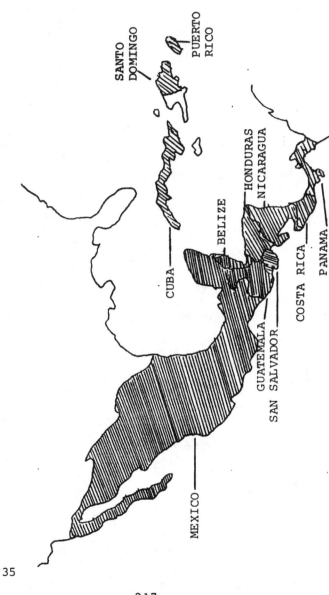

MEXICO

CUBA

BELIZE

GUATEMALA
SAN SALVADOR

HONDURAS
NICARAGUA

COSTA RICA

PANAMA

SANTO
DOMINGO

PUERTO
RICO

AREAS OF SPANISH SPEECH

(la ultracorrección)--vacido (vacío), tardido (tardío), bacalado (bacalao). Sporadically, stressed
syllables are diphthongized where they are not so
treated in the standard language and vice versa--
priesa, dientista, quebra, apreta. Shifts in stress
are frequent as well--caido for caído, baul for baúl.

HISPANIC-AMERICAN VARIETIES OF SPANISH. Although
most phonological, morphological, and syntactical
features are shared by Hispanic countries, there are
some linguistic peculiarities which are more in evidence in some areas than in others. Since the
countries involved are so varied and the scope of the
material quite broad, we have chosen to focus upon
those few traits which are uniquely characteristic of
the speech habits of individual nations.

MEXICO. This area is important as a Hispanic country
since it is the home of the largest segment of Spanish speakers in the world. Aside from the general
tendencies already identified, this speech zone has
well developed, distinct patterns of its own.

From the point of view of sound production, a
tensely articulated sibilant is probably the most
outstanding trait. This s is a very tense, sharp
sibilant, which we have chosen to identify as [S].
When compared with Castilian or even Andalusian sibilants, this phoneme sounds a bit exaggerated to
the ear. Observe this particular s in Mexican articulation as follows:

estanque [əstáŋkə]   especial [əSpəsjál]
estudio [əstúdjo]   estar   [əStár]
The phoneme is actually quite pronounced and tends
to disappear only before other sibilants, before
multiple vibrants, and before the lateral l.

las señas   [lɛ sénɛs]
las rosas   [lɛ r̃ósɛs]
más lento   [málént:]
las sendas   [lɛ séŋdɛs]
dos ricos   [d: r̃íkːs]
menos limpio   [mén: límpjo][75]
The aspiration of final -s is sporadic, but this is

218

recurrent throughout much of Latin America. Aspiration in general (g(e), g(i), j) tends to be much softer in Mexican Spanish than in the Castilian variety ([hɛlískɔ] instead of [xɛlískɔ]). The aspirated sibilant in medial and final positions so characteristic of Caribbean speech and elsewhere is not typical of Mexican Spanish.[76]

An even more typically Mexican phoneme is found in the sibilant x, articulated [ʃ], an example of the widespread Indian influence in the pronunciation of toponimics and other words. This sibilant is similar to but not identical with the sh sound in wash, fish, clash. Observe this sound in the following examples:

Xochimilco	[ʃɔĉimílkɔ]	Xitle	[ʃítlə]
xola	[ʃólɛ]	Xuco	[ʃúkɔ]
Xocomil	[ʃɔkɔmíl]	maxocote	[meʃɔkótə]
puxchaua	[pʌʃĉáwa]	xoxoco	[ʃɔʃókɔ]

Another outstanding aspect of Mexican articulation is the weakening or eliminating of unstressed vowels--pretonic and postonic. Thus mexicano becomes [ma-kánɔ], gracias>[qrásəs], [qrásɪs], vamos>[báms], todos>[tɔds], francés>[ɸránsɪs], [ɸráns].[77]

Mexican Spanish follows no normative patterns in syntax and usage, but there are certain features which might be viewed as representative. This area has retained the use of tú as the second-person singular pronoun, making much of Mexican tuteante in nature. Rarely is there confusion with the form vos, even though the latter is encountered in the Yucatan Peninsula and surrounding areas. There are several unique tense shifts and substitutions. For instance, whereas in Spanish the present perfect tense is used in the negative under certain conditions, Mexicans replace it with the simple present tense. By way of example, "ya es tarde, ¿por qué no te has acostado?" is rendered "¿por qué no te acuestas?" Similarly, "ya se fueron y tú no los has acompañado" is expressed "y tú no los acompañas." Frequently the imperfect tense replaces the pluperfect used negatively, so an utterance like "se lo dijo aunque no había sabido la verdad" is often said "se lo dijo aunque no sabía la verdad."[78]

Approximately thirty percent of all Mexican
lexicon is Aztec in origin, about seven percent being place names. These semantic items include names
of vegetables like aguacate, jitomate, pulque, chi-
cle, quelite, ejote, puerro, nopal, chile, camote;
fruits and nuts, plátano, mango, papaya, cacahuete;
spices, chile molido, estafiate, ajonjolí, epazote;
liquors, tequila, pulque, mescal; breads and similar
staples, tortilla, enchilada, taco, tamal. Hundreds
of place names are of Indian derivation as well--
Oxajaca, Querétaro, Xochimilco, Tonanztintla, Ameca-
meca, Teotihuacán, Coahuila, Zacatecas, Chilapa, Jalapa, Tecali.79

GUATEMALA. The most noteworthy feature in this area
is the oclusive articulation of ⟦b⟧, ⟦d⟧, and ⟦g⟧
following ⟦r⟧, contrary to standard usage
              jerga ⟦hérga⟧ jardín ⟦hɐrdín⟧
              argot ⟦ɐrgó⟧ árbol ⟦árbɔl⟧
Another unique feature of Guatemalan Spanish is the
articulation of r either voiced ⟦r̃⟧ or voiceless
⟦r̈⟧.
     rata ⟦r̈átɐ⟧   reja ⟦r̈éhɐ⟧   rana ⟦r̈ánɐ⟧
     rojo ⟦r̃óhɔ⟧   rito ⟦r̃ítɔ⟧   rural ⟦r̃ɐrál⟧
In certain instances r actually takes on the quality
of the sibilant ⟦s⟧ ropa ⟦sópɐ⟧.80

     A typical morphological trait is the elimination
of the definite article in exclamatory utterances.
For example, "felices ojos que la miraron" is more
common than standard "felices los ojos que la miraron." In subordinate clauses the conditional often
replaces the imperfect subjunctive. In other words,
"su padre esperó entregarle el dinero hasta que se
lo pediría" is encountered more regularly than standard "su padre esperó entregarle el dinero hasta que
se lo pidiera."81

     Indian lexicon is typical of this area as well.
An azacuán is a water carrier; caite, sandal; izca-
co, fading tan; patojo, little boy; patoja, good-
looking young lady; patoja canche, pretty young
blonde.82

HONDURAS, NICARAGUA, AND EL SALVADOR. These coun-

220

tries share much of the above described articulation
except for [b], [d], and [g] after [r]. In Honduras
and Nicaragua the articulation is oclusive, whereas
in El Salvador it is a very relaxed intervocalic
phoneme.

	Honduras/Nicaragua	El Salvador
bergamota	[bɔrgᵊmótᵊ]	[barᵠᵊmótᵊ]
cargar	[kᵊrgár]	[kᵊrᵠár]
discorde	[dɪskɔ́rda]	[dɪskɔ́rᵈᵃ]
tardar	[terdár]	[terᵈár]
escorbuto	[ᵊskɔrbútᵊ]	[ɔskɔrᵇútᵊ]
arbusto	[ᵊrbýstɔ]	[ᵊrᵇýstᵊ]

Despite the great geographical expanse of this territory, there is a surprising degree of uniformity
in vocalization and articulation in general.[83]

Morphologically speaking, the three countries
have very little that is dissimilar. There is, on
the other hand, an interesting subjunctive use of
the verb ver in Nicaragua and Honduras. A normal
utterance like "espero que vea cuánto me preocupo por
su hermano" is normally said "viera cuánto me preocupo por su hermano." In El Salvador the subjunctive
form pueda is used in the idiomatic expression pueda
ser que in lieu of standard puede ser que, so an utterance like "pueda ser que venga" is part of everyday speech.[84]

All three countries depend a good deal on derivations from Pipil (a sublanguage of Nahuatl) as in
chele (blond), cipote (boy), pushco (dirty), peche
(slender).[85]

COSTA RICA. This country has virtually the same articulatory characteristics as her neighbors--Nicara-
gua, Honduras, and El Salvador. Perhaps the only
exception is found in the articulation of r, which
has retroflex qualities [ř]--perro [péřɔ], río
[říɔ], rana [řánᵊ].

Morphologically, Costa Rican patterns follow
the development of general Hispanic American. There
is, however, the custom of using the imperfect in-

221

dicative in place of the pluperfect, especially in negative statements. By way of example, standard "había pasado una hora y la muchacha no había aparecido" is expressed as a rule "había pasado una hora y la muchacha no aparecía."

The Costa Ricans are often referred to popularly as ticos due to their frequent use of the diminutive ending -(t)ico as in chiquitico, calientico.[86] In their lexicon there are words which also derive from non-Hispanic sources like chingo, corrongo, noriero, aguaitar, chiverre, and jalado.[87]

PANAMA. If the Spanish of Panama were compared with the speech patterns in the rest of Central America, one would realize that the major difference lies in the implosive r, which is confused with the other liquid, l. Words like puerta, pardo, and corto are generally produced [pwéʰte], [páʰdɔ], [kɔʰtɔ].[88]

Morphologically, one of the peculiarities of the Panamanians is the use of the verb regresar as a reflexive verb. In other words, a typical utterance like "al llegar a España, regresó pronto sin dar explicación" is expressed identically with the exception of the use of regresarse. What is more, the same verb is used as a transitive substitute for the more commonly accepted devolver, restituir. Thus, instead of "devuélveme el libro," one hears "regrésame el libro." Occasionally, verbs of physical sensation constructed with tener (tener frío, calor, hambre, sed) are often formed by making use of the verb hacer as in "es medio día y hace hambre."[89] Such constructions are typical of children, even though they are heard in the speech patterns of both children and adults here and there throughout Latin America.

THE DOMINICAN REPUBLIC, CUBA, AND PUERTO RICO. The Dominican Republic clings to a series of archaisms not heard in other areas. The vocalization of r is typical, producing forms like comei, vendei, poique, paique. Occasionally the same linguistic phenomenon takes place with l (sueldo > sueido).[90] A more

222

modern development is the elimination of the sibilant s preceding a consonant hopital, comunita,
pianita, guitarrita, flamenquita, San Critóbal, es-
pecialita.⁹¹ Expressions like ir EN casa de--an obviously old Castilian form--are used in place of the
more modern ir A casa de. The pseudo-reflexive forms
have been retained as well, as in "me se fue" and "le
se olvidó" with the characteristic inversion of pronouns no longer accepted in standard usage.⁹²

The influence of the indigenous language is
enormous, most of which is Taino (a sublanguage of
Arawakan) origin, contributing vocabulary like abey,
ajay, amate, bera, cacheo, canistel, cumaní, guara,
jina, malva. Most of this lexicon has reference to
animals, vegetables, and fruits of the region. Henríquez Ureña suggests that some of the derivation is
Carib (another sublanguage of Arawakan) as in colibrí, mico, totumo, piragena, piragua, huracán, even
though this source is hard to prove.⁹³

In Cuba the outstanding variation, particularly
in the west, is the complete assimilation of r in
many cases as in the characteristic Andalusian as-
similation--cueppo, puetta, refomma.

The characteristically Cuban diminutive is -ico,
frequently replacing Castilian -illo and -ito. In
fact, whenever possible according to the sound system, this form is the prevalent one here. Words like
zapatico, momentico, chiquitico, bajico, gordico,
bonitico, calentico, chatico, and many others of
similar formation are part of daily speech.

In all of the Antilles and much of Central
America, vocabulary exhibiting African background is
strong. This is especially true in Cuba, where
Afro-Cuban influence is of long standing and where
it tends to be related to Negro dance forms like cu-
cutamos, mariandá, and calinga. There are also some
typically Black-related instruments like the marimba
and bongó. Terms having to do with Black-Cuban
meals, like ecó, ecrú, and fufú, are also heard.
Special cults and superstitions yield forms like ma-
candá (brujería), and bilongo is the Afro-Cuban term

223

for the age-old practice of the mal de ojo or evil eye.[94]

Puerto Rico shares with the rest of the Antilles the same linguistic variants. The shift r>l in medial and final positions is completely accepted with the exception of educators and purists. It is quite common to hear words like daldo, puelta, taldo, cantal, maltes, miélcoles, huelta. Perhaps one of its most unique features is the articulation of the multiple vibrant rr (r). It tends to have three possible renderings: the apico-alveolar multiple vibrant [r̄]; the dorsal velar fricative [ṛ]; the retroflex [r̃]. What is more, there is a strong tendency in the second type to add a voiceless aspiration similar to a weak Castilian jota.[95] In any case, it is not uncommon to hear one version or another of r in this speech zone. The words which follow exemplify the three variants:

	/r̄/	/ṙ/	/r̃/
tarro	[tár̄ɔ]	[tárɔ]	[tár̃ɔ]
carro	[kár̄ɔ]	[kárɔ]	[kár̃ɔ]
rana	[r̄ánɐ]	[ṙánɐ]	[r̃ánɐ]
rosa	[r̄ósɐ]	[ṙósɐ]	[r̃ósɐ]

Although a kind of medial pronunciation of open and close e and o is typical of much of the Caribbean, it is especially pronounced in Puerto Rican articulation. Another feature of this island is the retention of the ending -ado as -ao--clearly another case of Andalusian influence. In fact, many examples are found in common or even vulgar speech: achantao (person of little spirit), afrentao (saucy, impudent), agüebao (weakling), añoñao (spoiled, mama's boy), arrematao (crazy, extroverted homosexual), caricortao (scar-faced), escrachao (in bad condition; sloppily dressed), ñangotao (servile), sancochao (very sweaty), seis charreao (dance with improvised poetry), soberao (floor of a house).[96]

One practice which is deliberate on the part of Puerto Ricans is the attempt to maintain the form -ito as a diminutive: casita, arbolito, muchachito,

224

chiquita, cuadrito, cuadernito, carita, loquito,
pastelito.

The lexicon has been affected by local indigenous parlance, often producing forms of little frequency elsewhere. For example, guagua is the word
for bus; guineo, banana as a fruit; plátano, banana
for cooking purposes. Many other terms for vegetables, seafood, and cooking styles are primarily localisms. Other forms of the native lexicon derive
either directly from Taino or general Afro-Caribbean
sources. It is in the convergence of Taino and Afro
influences that the speech of Puerto Rico coincides
with that of Cuba and Santo Domingo. Moreover, in
Puerto Rico more than elsewhere, English interference
is quite strong: guafe (wharf), timba (timber), flo-
rimbó (flooring-board), chucho (switch), meple (ma-
ple), tiperrita (typist), bordín (boarding house).[97]
English influence is strong in much of Central America and Mexico, but the protectorate status of Puerto
Rico makes for greater population mobility and more
linguistic exchange and interaction.

COLOMBIA. The one striking feature of Colombian
Spanish is the double substitution r>l and l>r
    alfil>arfil   armatoste>almatoste
    alquiler>arquiler   esperma>espelma
    calcular>carcular   parietario>palietario
    colmillo>cormillo   pertrechos>peltrechos[98]
Although this trait is by no means limited to Colombian Spanish or even representative of it, there is
a strong inclination in this direction on a popular
level.

Although Old Spanish used the future as a substitute for imperative forms, the practice has diminished significantly over the centuries but remains an
integral part of the standard language. Colombian
usage, on the other hand, seems to favor the future
in this function, so imperatives like "tendrás cuidado," "mirarás lo que haces," "irás por aquí" are
used characteristically.[99] Another archaic aspect is
found in the use of the future subjunctive--on the
whole rejected in standard Spanish with few excep-

225

tions--as in "y si asina no fuere, ¿no haberá con qué pagar?"[100]

Colombia also has a number of lexical items attributed to native substrata as in chabanabasqua (burnt), zisa (worm eaten by Indians), chuza (harm), chupara (place to fish), chusquy (reed), quimba (sandal), vijua (salt). Today most of the words in this category tend to be considered extremely popular or even vulgar.[101]

ECUADOR. The appreciable differences in the speech of this country are those connected with Quechua influence. This applies particularly to final vowels e and o reduced to i and u. Thus, leche>lechi, coche>cuchi, calle>calli, bochinche>bochinchi, buche> buchi. The change from o>u is actually more recurrent than Ecuadorians wish to acknowledge lindo> lindu, vayo>vayu, tranquilo>tranquilu, ocupado>ocupadu. Within the production of consonants, there is a relatively unique phoneme resulting from the reduction of the cluster -str-. The first part is a kind of sh [š] produced with a groove in the tongue with the sides of the tongue touching the palate and with the apex remaining free, the lips being quite rounded. The second part is a kind of r, articulated [ř]. Phonetically the cluster is represented as [šř]. This sound cannot be directly linked to Quechua influence, nor can it be traced to any other Spanish-speaking country. Nonetheless, the phenomenon occurs in words like maestro [mɑišřɔ], instrucción [inšřnsjɔ́n], nuestro [nwéšřɔ], monstruo [mɔ́nšřɔ], mostrar [mɔšřár].[102]

In popular speech the imperative is softened by a construction modeled on Quechua. In addition to being used by peasants and illiterates, this imperative form has reached the familiar level even with educated people. The construction is unusual in that it makes use of the imperative of dar followed by the gerund of the verb normally in the imperative. Therefore, constructions like "déme escribiendo esta carta" are more frequent than the authoritative "escríbame esta carta."[103]

A characteristic of the lexicon which has been
extended to other Hispanic-American countries with
strong Quechua influence is the formation of compounds based on Quechua roots. While Spanish normally rejects noun-noun and noun-adjective compounds, the compounding of nouns in Quechua is frequent, especially in toponimics--Rumichaca: rumi
(piedra) and chaca (puente); Huairapungo: huaira
(viento) and pungo (puerta); Alcuquiru: alcu (perro) and quiru (diente).104

VENEZUELA. The habit of nasalizing vowels has been
observed in a number of Latin-American countries, but
in Venezuela the practice seems more in evidence.
Nasalization per se is merely a phonetic change as it
has no phonemic implications. For example, the words
mentira, libertad, mano, mina, monte, anda, and humo
are generally articulated [mə̃ntírɐ], [lìbərtǽ], [mǽ-
nɔ], [mĩ́nɐ], [mɔ̃ŋtə], [ǽɳdɐ], [ú̃mɔ].105

    Venezuela shares with Colombia and Cuba the ten-
dency to use the diminutive form -ico as in jardini-
co, pobrecico, tranquilico. In modern speech recor-
dar is not used reflexively, but the construction
persists in this area: "de vez en cuando se recuer-
da de su importancia."106 The reflexive form with
its attendant syntactical changes takes place rather
recurrently in Venezuela and in much of the New
World.

    Vocabulary, aside from names of plants, fruits,
and animals indigenous to the area, has in some
cases developed characteristics of its own. For instance, misiú, misiá (French monsieur) is the name
given to all foreigners. The bolívar is the unit of
money comparable to a dollar, its origin being quite
clear. On the other hand, silver coins worth about
five dollars are known by different names such as
cachetes, carones, lajas, tostones, ojos de buey, and
fuertes. In the same way, accelerator of a car is
referred to as a chancleta or chola; flux is a suit
of clothing; escaparate, closet; coroto, the designation for any insignificant object--a thing. The
verb guindar in common parlance has the meaning of

227

<u>to</u> <u>hang</u> (clothing, etc.).[107]

PERU AND BOLIVIA. From the phonological point of view, speech in this area is by and large representative of general Hispanic American.

Morphologically there are a few observable differences. The present perfect frequently replaces the preterite, this being fairly normal practice in other countries, too. It is typical to hear "ese chico ha tenido un mal sueño" or "ayer has solicitado audiencia" instead of "ese chico tuvo" and "ayer solicitaste."[108] The preterite is also used but with much less frequency. Both countries have a great deal of Quechua derivation in their lexicon, which has extended far beyond their geographical boundaries. Words like <u>poncho</u>, <u>cóndor</u>, <u>pampa</u>, <u>puma</u>, <u>quinina</u>, <u>llama</u>, <u>alpaca</u>, and <u>gaucho</u> are excellent examples of non-Hispanic influence.[109]

CHILE. Pronunciation in Chile, like that of many neighboring countries, is deeply rooted in Andalusian articulation. A typical trait is the opening of vowels when there is aspiration of a consonant. Thus, in a word like <u>verdad</u>, <u>a</u> is opened slightly as a result of dropping <u>the final d</u>. The reduction of two identical vowels is the normal practice--<u>nada⟩ na</u>, <u>leer⟩ler</u>, <u>creer⟩crer</u>, <u>loor⟩lor</u>.

A unique feature of this consonantal articulation is the transformation of -sb- into -f- <u>resbalar⟩refalar</u>, <u>desbaratar⟩defaratar</u>, <u>esbelto⟩efelto</u>.[110] An aspect of popular and rustic Chilean Spanish is the use of <u>los</u>, nasalized, to replace <u>nos--los fuimos</u> [l⟩ʰ fwĩmːs] in place of standard <u>nos fuimos</u>.

Typical Indian influence abounds in the lexicon--in this case Arawakan; in addition, elements of Nahuatl, Carib, and Quechua are present. Some words of Arawakan origin are <u>cahuín</u>, <u>drinkers' meeting</u>; <u>chepica</u>, <u>grass</u>; <u>guata</u>, <u>belly</u>; <u>machi</u>, <u>quack</u>; <u>mingo</u>, <u>party for harvesters</u>; <u>pichitún</u>, <u>very small portion</u>. There are expressions as well which have developed their own semantic force: <u>roto</u> means <u>poor man</u>; <u>to-</u>

228

mar el once, to have high tea; voy al tiro, I am
coming in a jiffy.[111]

ARGENTINA, PARAGUAY, AND URUGUAY. One of the outstanding speech habits in this area is the almost
universally diffuse [ž] variant of yeísmo. In fact,
this particular variant is normally identified with
River Plate speech throughout the Spanish-speaking
world.

Argentina has the reputation of speaking the
worst and the most distorted forms of the language.[112] This is due to a number of factors: the
strong foreign influence (Italian, French, Dutch,
German, and others); the deeply-rooted use of voseo;
sporadic semi-Italianate vocalization and intonation;
native Quechua and Guarani influences.

A distinctive trait is the typically Argentinian
displacement of stress in certain verb-forms. By way
of example, standard dígame, hágase, siéntese, vámo-
nos are commonly pronounced digamé, hagasé, sientesé,
vamonós.[113] A similar shift in stress occurs in the
vos imperative forms--sentáte, miráte, levantáte--
and more sporadically in the first-person plural of
the subjunctive--váyamos, dígamos, cuéntemos.

An equally interesting aspect is the idioms and
typical expressions used by porteños, often of lunfardo derivation or influence, as in atorrante (vaga-
bond), cachada (joke), canillita (young newspaper
vendor), conventillo (low-income housing), colectivo
(small bus), macanudo (excellent), chau--from Italian ciao--(so long, goodbye). Frequently, adjectives
are intensified by repetition as in Italian (ragazza
bella bella, bambino biondo biondo, uomo alto alto),
so one hears combinations like nieve blanca blanca,
chico alto alto, muchacha linda linda in place of the
normal pattern.

The vocative che, of unclear origin, has become
identified with speech in this area, and it is almost
universally recognized as a synonym of this country's
brand of Spanish.[114] It is used to initiate conversation, to get a person's attention, to begin one's

229

SOUTH AMERICA

FIGURE 36

utterance, or as a weak salutation. The form che may even have a link with the peninsular ce used throughout the Middle Ages and the early part of the Golden Age. In any case, today it is considered one of the earmarks of Argentinian Spanish.

Although there are many instances of Quechua and Guarani influence in the vocabulary of this area, the Indian substratum has never been so important as Taino, for example, in the Caribbean. Nonetheless, Indian-derived words are heard sporadically--china, woman; choclo, corn; yuyo, weed; cancha, field; ananá, pineapple; ñandú, American ostrich. The other source of non-Hispanic lexicon is foreign influence, particularly in the international port of Buenos Aires, where words and expressions are introduced by tourists, immigrants, businessmen, travel experts, and the like.

URUGUAY. The language here is similar to the Argentinian version. Nonetheless, owing to geographical location, words of Brazilian derivation enter the picture (mucama, maid; bondi, trolley), which eventually find their way into Argentina as well. Like their neighbors to the west, Uruguayans utilize gaucho terminology since both countries have relatively similar economic structures.

In popular speech there are several idiomatic uses worthy of note. The verb meter followed by an infinitive replaces the more standard dale que dale. In other words, the expression is used to conclude a narration as in "and he kept on eating candy." The peninsular version is normally "y dale que dale comer dulces," whereas in this area the same idea is conveyed by "y meta comer dulces."115 Similar examples are: "le hablaba y lo único que hacía era meta suspirar" ("she spoke to him and the only thing he did was keep on sighing"); "trataba de convencerlo y la única manera de reaccionar era meta oponerse" ("she kept trying to convince him and his only reaction was to keep on opposing it"). Frequently que replaces donde in this area to express the place in which as in "fue aquí que se cometió el crimen."116

231

PARAGUAY. Standard Spanish is the language of Paraguay used in public administration, teaching, newspapers, magazines, and business. But in family situations, among close friends and relatives, and in most informal speech, Paraguayans use Guarani. This is the one example in Latin America of the original native language and the imposed language coexisting with equal force. It is thought that, due to the native oxytonic stress pattern in Guarani, the general stress has been displaced to the last syllable in a great number of words. For instance, normally grave caballo, cebolla, morcilla are oxytonic in Paraguayan Spanish [kɐβɐɣú], [sɐβǰí], [mɔrsjá].117 While there are other local characteristics, these are few in number since Spanish in this area has remained somewhat "pure" by virtue of the fact that it is not the language used on a popular and vulgar level. Malmberg makes this point quite clear: "The popular and vulgar characteristics have never been adopted by Paraguay for the simple reason that a complete popular Spanish does not exist in this country."118

There are a few peculiarly Paraguayan syntactical features found elsewhere in the River Plate Region. An interesting one is the use of the imperfect subjunctive viera [bjére] used adverbially with the meanings unfortunately, certainly, you wouldn't believe it but,119 as in "¡viera cuánto hemos llorado!" and "¡viera se lastimó tanto el brazo!". Similarly, dar un susto and pegar un julepe120 normally replace standard asustarse as in "pegó un julepe cuando vió el animal" and "dió un susto cuando llamaron a la puerta en plena noche."

Although the Spanish in Latin America is essentially a unified language despite local variation in syntax and lexicon, the area of intonation is probably the most complex and the least universal. It is a monumental task to attempt to differentiate intonation patterns from region to region and country to country, and the far greater task lies ahead. Some work has been done in this area, primarily on standard Spanish in relation to Mexico121 and isolated areas, but a more detailed analysis by country has

232

not as yet been undertaken, to our knowledge. In the broadest terms, there is a characteristic inflection, a special rhythm, a peculiar cadence with ascendencies and descendencies that are indigenous to one speech zone and not to others. In short, patterns of intonation can and do vary appreciably from one speech community to another. On the other hand, there are unquestionably many features held in common. And yet, even in matters of intonation, the distinguishing traits receive a particular designation in one country and another elsewhere.

In general, it may be said that most of the studies done on Spanish American tend to have the same basic points of focus. Most of them agree on the following: a certain level of laxity in articulation; grammatical forms which are often simplified or have minor syntactical variations; the preservation of a goodly number of archaisms--phonetic, morphological, and lexical; a strong tendency toward the adoption of indigenous word-roots and derived forms; a readily observable trend toward the development of neologisms, often based on local availability or out of pure necessity as a result of cross-currents in social, political, and historical experiences. In any case, the Spanish of all countries in Latin America is an expedient, intelligible means of communication with all speakers of Spanish anywhere in the world.

JUDEOESPAÑOL. The Jewish people were ousted from Spain in 1492, and many of them settled in Turkey, North Africa, Italy, Portugal, and Greece. They took with them a varied linguistic heritage, including elements from both Castiles, Galicia, Portugal, Leon and Aragon, as well as other parts of Spain. Since they had lived in different parts of the peninsula, many regions had an influence upon the language spoken by the Jews in the various communities in which they settled. It followed naturally that areas where a Romance language was spoken would have a stronger influence upon their Spanish than places where non-

Latin languages predominated. In any case, the form
of communication was passed on from father to son,
from generation to generation, and most areas of Judaeo-Spanish have a number of features in common. In
the vocalization, there is the tendency to reduce
Castilian diphthongs to one vowel--preto for prieto,
ponte for puente, sorte for suerte, tútano for tuétano, pasensia for paciencia, and sensia for ciencia.122
Also, e becomes a in contact with r--pierna, piarna;
tierno, tiarno; ternero, tarnero; tierra, tiarra.
Initial f-, which becomes h- in Castilian, is retained fazer, filo, ferida, furmiga. Unlike Castilian Spanish, the bilabial ⎡b⎤ and labiodental ⎡v⎤
are differentiated. This form of Spanish also retains the medieval Castilian phonemes ⎡ž⎤ and ⎡š⎤
without developing the characteristic aspiration ⎡x⎤,
so forms like diši (dije), tišir (tejer), trušu (truje), alguža (aguja), šešo (piedra) are quite common.

    Yeísmo is universal among all Sephardics since
the liquid lateral pronunciation has completely disappeared in their system. Thus, one hears with a
fair degree of regularity forms like yavi (llave),
amariyu (amarillo), fayar (hallar), sevoya (cebolla),
cueyo (cuello), gayina (gallina). At times, ll (y)
is reduced to l--luvia (lluvia), pileyu (pellejo),
kaleza (calleja), fulí (hollín), pelisku (pellizco),
peliskar (pelliscar). Sporadically, it becomes ⎡ø⎤
bía (villa), castío (castillo), bolsío (bolsillo),
gaína (gallina), aí (allí).123 The sound of d vacil-
ates between a voiced oclusive ⎡d⎤ and a voiceless
one ⎡t⎤, a typical phenomenon of other Hispanic
areas as well. The substitution d/r is an archaic
hold-over which is fairly recurrent, especially in
imperative forms alvaldu (alabadlo), daldi (dadle),
sintildu (sentidlo). Zamora Vicente cites the ancient ballad of Jewish oral tradition which exempli-
fies this practice quite well

parildu, infanta, parildu/que ansí me parió mi
madre124

As has been pointed out in connection with voseo, voseante forms are universal among Sephardics. Hence
vos functions as the familiar singular pronoun to-

234

gether with voseo verb-forms, as well as the more
traditional verb-endings (-áis, -éis, -ís) as in pa-
rildu=paridlo.

Judaeo-Spanish is characterized by other archaisms as well. Like modern Italian and Old Spanish,
the possessives are usually preceded by the definite
article--el mi padre, la mi madre. The demonstrative
forms aqueo(a), aqueos(as) clearly reflect older
usage and constitute an aspect of [ɸ] yeísmo.

The lexicon is replete with traditional imagery
but frequently mirrors the areas to which Jews immigrated, thereby developing over the centuries alternate semantic forms. Even though more standard lexical items are encountered, the following is a random
sampling of such variants: antinada, hijastra; an-
tier, anteayer; arrinchir, relinchar; asúkir, azúcar;
atabafar, ahogar, sofocar; atorgar, consentir; baba-
žada, tontería; bidro, vidrio; enguyos, náuseas; ka-
zal, aldea; koĉo, cocido; safumare, sahumar; sayo,
traje; luito, luto; sentea, centella; ruco, riachuelo; entožos, antojos.125

Most aspects of Judaeo-Spanish reflect archaic
or unstable forms due to its widespread unofficial
use, not to mention the innumerable external pressures and types of interference from dominant languages. Sephardic Jews the world over have no difficulty communicating on a basic level although vocabulary can vary greatly from country to country.
This relatively isolated nucleus of Spanish speakers
has preserved very important poetic creations transmitted orally from father to son over the centuries.
The wealth of this very old oral tradition has remained untapped as an invaluable source of Hispanic
language and poetic development throughout the ages.

SPANISH IN THE PHILIPPINE ISLANDS. The Spanish spoken in the Philippine Islands is a good example of a
"creolized language," which is a contact language
used daily as a means of communication by a socially

235

or politically defeated people. In this case,
Spanish came in contact with Tagalog and English.
When Tagalog officially became the "national language" of the islands after centuries of competition
with the other two languages, its primacy began to
undermine the popularity of Spanish.

Hernando Magallanes first took Spanish to the
Philippine Islands in 1521. Unlike the approach in
most other colonizing attempts by the Spaniards, the
religious orders taught the various Tagalog dialects
while Spanish remained the language of the conquerors
and later of the élite of the islands. Eventually
there developed a type of creolized language known as
Tagalog-Spanish. The two languages coexisted for
centuries and eventually four main branches became
distinguishable--caviteño, ermitaño, zamboangueño,
and davaoeño. While there remain speakers of Spanish
in the Philippines, these are only a minority since
Tagalog enjoys official status and English is clearly
in competition.

Spanish in this part of the world retains a number of features common to its development in the New
World together with influences from Tagalog. Seseo
and yeísmo are universal throughout the islands.
Spanish initial h- deriving from Latin f-, is usually
heard as an aspiration jablar (hablar), jambre (hambre), jací (hacer), jaltao (hartado).126 Since the
indigenous dialects have no f sound, the latter is
often substituted by a bilabial p pondo (fondo);
puera (fuera), plores (flores), puelte (fuerte), di-
perente (diferente), suprí (sufrir), protá (frotar),
pastidiá (fastidiar), Pilipinas (Filipinas).127 The
infinitive ending -ar is articulated as a stressed
final -á pastidiá, protá, jablá, andá, ritirá. The
second and third conjugations are reduced in the infinitive form to a stressed final -í cumí (comer),
ingrandicí (engrandecer), puní (poner). The definite
article is normally invariable--el and sporadically
los--for both genders; the indefinite article--un--
follows the same pattern.

As might be expected, there are strong native

236

influences, as well as sporadic in-roads made by English. The following are some common examples: alimango (cangrejo), asuán (brujo), bago (recién llegado), bata (indio joven, criado), bichara (charla), maguinóo (señor, persona noble), matandá (persona de edad).128 While place names (San Pablo, Luzón, Cape Encanto, San Ildefonso, Rosales, San José, and many others) and surnames still provide living proof of a once predominantly Spanish society, much of this has been lost over the years. Standard Spanish is spoken today only by a very small minority, and Tagalog-Spanish and its subdivisions are fast disappearing.

PIDGINIZATION, CREOLIZATION, AND PAPIAMENTO. A "pidgin" is usually the result of the coming together of two or more languages in a contact situation which generally requires arriving at an elementary, mutually intelligible means of communication. The first examples of pidginization took place in the seventeenth century in southern China, where merchants and traders attempted to arrive at a kind of linguistic compromise between English and Chinese. This was eventually accomplished by accomodating the former in very simplified form to a rudimentary version of the speech of the natives. Essentially the means of exchange used was based upon routine articulation and simplified syntax with English as the source of vocabulary.129 English is now the world language with the greatest number of pidginized versions, which are found along the west coast of Africa, the China coast, throughout the South Sea Islands, the islands of Melanesia, Australia, Malaya, and in some parts of the West Indies.130

The terms "pidgin," "creole," "pidginized," and "creolized" are normally heard in connection with these forms of communication, which seldom have any real prestige and which often have arisen from emergency situations. Today it is best to think in terms of pidgin-creole (la lengua franca-la lengua criolla), which may encompass either or both phases of the development of these languages. Pidginization is a temporary phase of a structurally and lexically rudi-

237

mentary language functioning under unusual or pressing circumstances. Creolization refers to the development of a substandard language based on emergency contact situations but which has become the native language of most of its speakers.[131] Creole languages are spoken by about six million persons in the Caribbean, West Africa, South Africa, and South and Southeast Asia.[132]

"Cocoliche," the hybrid pidgin spoken by uneducated Italian immigrants in Argentina and falling into disuse, is a good example of languages in contact. Since Spanish and Italian have obvious similarities in phonology, morphology, and lexicon, Italian immigrants used this form of communication with little interference from the dominant language. More often than not, pseudo-Spanish and pseudo-Italian forms were used in competition with each other. By way of example, a flower vendor might be heard to say "vendo flores frescas" or "vendo flori freschi." Forms which offered little resistance were assimilated first, and more unfamiliar phonemes were borrowed only after the passage of time. The Italian morphological forms which do not exist in Spanish (i. e., the particles ci, vi, and ne and partitives) were often retained for a period of time but eventually disappeared. This hybrid pidgin never really attained the status of a full pidgin and therefore certainly not of a creolized language, but it is a good example of one language in contact with another.[133]

"Papiamento" is a creolized language deriving from Spanish and Portuguese with admixtures of Dutch, English, and African dialects. It is spoken in the Dutch Antilles--Aruba, Bonaire, and Curaçao-- although Dutch remains the official language of the government, public administration, and education. In fact, Dutch must often be accomodated to the Papiamento sound system in order to be intelligible to a greater number of natives. This creole actually derives from the speech of the Portuguese slave population which had prolonged contact with speakers of Spanish, Dutch, and later, English.

238

Because of the strong Portuguese basis, there
is a good deal of nasalization in the vowel system.
The vowel cluster ee is articulated [ɛ̃i] geel (yel-
low); ao and au are pronounced [áṷ] causa (cause)
and abao (below); uu is [i] stuurman (pilot). The
combinations ai, oe, and ui are not normally diphthongized. Like Spanish, Papiamento aspirates g before e and i. The consonantal cluster dj is articulated [dẑ] (djab, job); z is pronounced [ẑ] (zjo-
zjoli, sesame); sh is articulated [š] (shinishi,
ashes).134 There is no distinction made between b
and v, but, contrary to Spanish custom, the former
often replaces the latter in current orthography.
As a result of African influence, there is a marked
tendency to avoid vowels in initial positions. This
tendency often produces an aspiration initially as in
habri (abrir) and hancho (ancho).135 Another trait
is the reduction of polysyllabics to two syllables
tende (entender), riba (arriba), masha (demasiado),
mucha (muchacho).136

From the morphological point of view, Papiamento
is characterized by rather simplified forms. All
nouns are invariable, and there are no changes in
gender or endings. An African root, nan (they), is
appended to the singular form to create the plural
(parti, partinan). At times, gender is clarified by
adding a reinforcement noun--e yíu hómber (el hijo
hombre) and e yíu muhé (el hijo mujer)--son and
daughter. Adjectives are likewise invariable bon
(good), nobo (new), bunita (pretty, handsome). The
personal pronouns evince a number of influences mi
(Sp. mí, Port. mim), bo (Sp. and Port. vos), ele, el,
e (Sp. él, Port. ele), nos (Sp. and Port. nos), boso
(Sp. and Port. vosotros), nan (Afr. ana, ene). The
second-person plural in a more emphatic sense is rendered bos-nan, bosonan. The pronoun tu is retained
only in the vocative, and bo, boso (bosonan) are the
second-person singular and plural in all other cases.
The polite form in direct address is Shon (Señor),
Señora, Señorita. Verbs of Spanish and Portuguese
derivation come into the language with the characteristic vowel minus r bandoná (abandonar), compañá (a-
compañar), admirá (admirar), aparecé (aparecer), que-

239

ré (querer), defendé (defender), combiní (convenir), bistí (vestir), sintí (sentir), huí (huir). The verb of Dutch or other derivation do not follow this pattern zom (to hem), huur (to hire), pak (to pack), piqui (to pick), leza (to read), krimp (to shrink), zag (to saw).[137]

The Papiamento lexicon contains words of various sources, Spanish and Portuguese being principal among them. For example, comerciante, negociante, balanza, hilo, carta, stampía (sello), papel, tarjeta postal, consejo, notario, acusado, juramento, sentencia, cartero, labadera (lavandera), timón, pisca (pesca), comedia, tragedia, naturaleza, criminal, diariamente, semper (siempre) are clearly derived from the Iberian peninsula. On the other hand, there are nearly as many which derive from Dutch toonbank (mostrador), corki (corcho), boshi (ramo), paki (paquete), rol (rollo), envelop (sobre), ink (tinta), pen (pluma), hof (corte), ambtenaar (oficial), dagvaarding (citación), matroos (marinero), slagter (carnicero), kokki (cocinero), stof (polvo). According to the study done by Lenz of 2500 lexical items listed by Hoyer, 2000 of them are Spanish and Portuguese in origin, about 750 are Dutch and forty are either English or French.[138]

Papiamento numerals are generally based on the Spanish system as are concepts of time. Time-telling on the other hand, provides a good case of a combination of both Spanish and Dutch. In this formation the numeral per se is Spanish-derived, but the construction is clearly Dutch. For instance, in Dutch one o'clock is één uur, two o'clock, twee uur, and so on. Papiamento combines the Spanish numeral with the Dutch construction--un or, dos or, tres or, cuat'or, cinc'or, and so on. An interesting aspect of this language is its formation of the days of the week diadomingo, dialuna, diamars, diarazon, diahuebes, diabiernes, diasabra.[139]

In the past several decades the Dutch Antilles have had ever-increasing numbers of immigrants from near-by Spanish-speaking areas for reasons of social betterment, political unrest, and commercial enterprise. In addition, tourism has played an increasingly important role in recent times. Thus, there is a growing tendency toward the reinforcement of the Hispanic elements, on the one hand, and considerable interference from English, on the other. Papiamento is a good case in point of a means of communication which began in an emergency contact situation, developed into a pidgin, and finally achieved the status of a fully creolized language.

THEORY
A. ANSWER THESE QUESTIONS BRIEFLY.
1. What type of Spanish was originally brought to the Americas?
2. What normally occurs to the various regionalistic differences in speech when immigrants live in the same speech community?
3. How many types of speakers of Spanish were represented in the colonial period?
4. What Indian languages were already spoken in the New World when the Spaniards arrived?
5. To which aspect of language did the Indian substrata contribute most?
6. Which phoneme may be considered unique to the Spanish of Mexico?
7. What may be said about the articulation of the fricatives [ƀ], [đ], and [ǥ] in the speech of Guatemalans?
8. Why are Costa Ricans often referred to as ticos?
9. In which country does hacer frequently replace tener with expressions of physical sensations?
10. What is the typically Cuban diminutive form?
11. How many types of r are heard typically in Puerto Rico?
12. How is the consonantal cluster -str- normally handled in Ecuador?
13. In which Latin American country are misiú, misiá meaning foreigner used?
14. What are the River Plate Republics?
15. Which country in Latin America has the strongest foreign influence in its Spanish?
16. Where does Guarani actually vie for first place with Spanish?
17. Of which version of Spanish are forms like diši and trušu typical?
18. Where is initial f- often heard as p- ?

B. IDENTIFY BRIEFLY.
1. lallation
2. cocoliche
3. hypercorrection
4. pidginization
5. lunfardo
6. creolization

7. retroflex r
8. Taino

9. Tagalog-Spanish
10. substrata

C. TRUE OR FALSE.
1. The conquistadores brought a representative form of Spanish dialect with them to the New World. _____
2. Probably the greatest differences developed in the New World were in the areas of phonetics and vocabulary. _____
3. There were essentially five major Indian substrata found by the Spaniards in the Americas. _____
4. The various Indian languages exerted considerable influence upon Spanish syntax. _____
5. The loss of final -d is typical of Andalusia and all of Latin America. _____
6. Gaucho terminology is used exclusively in Mexico and Argentina. _____
7. The velarization of final -d is typical of Latin-American Spanish. _____
8. The shift from e to i in unstressed syllables is characteristic of the upper classes in Spanish America. _____
9. A hypercorrection tends to make a correct form even more correct. _____
10. Mexico competes with several other Spanish-American countries as the principal Spanish-speaking population in the New World. _____
11. The aspiration of final -s is typical only of Mexico and the Caribbean. _____
12. Words like aguacate, pulque, chile, and cacahuete are typical of the Spanish of Argentina. _____
13. The influence of African languages and dialects is most strongly felt in the Caribbean and in Aruba, Bonaire, and Curaçao. _____
14. The diminutive -ico is primarily characteristic of Cuba, Venezuela, and Costa Rica. _____
15. Santo Domingo has preserved many Spanish archaisms over the centuries. _____
16. The shift r>l is typical only of Puerto Rico.
17. The tendency to nasalize vowels is very strong in Venezuela although it exists elsewhere. _____
18. The Spanish of Argentina has long been recognized

243

as the best that Spanish America has to offer.

19. Sephardic Jews who settled in Romance-speaking countries tend to preserve Judaeo-Spanish more intact. ____
20. Spanish in the Philippine Islands still vies for first place with English. ____

PRACTICE
A. GIVE THE PHONETIC TRANSCRIPTION OF THE STANDARD SPANISH FOR THESE VARIANT RENDERINGS.

1. [pwéḷtɛ]   .... 16. [ɔpɪtá̜l]   ....
2. [wéḷtɔ]   .... 17. [kwáttɔ]   ....
3. [ká̆řɔ]   .... 18. [řářɔ]   ....
4. [tjénəŋ]   .... 19. [řɔ́sɛ]   ....
5. [lɔ hótrɔʰ]   .... 20. [ɛrkɪlér]   ....
6. [báləŋ]   .... 21. [kái̯ɪ]   ....
7. [lɛʰ tréʰ]   .... 22. [mwéšřɔ]   ....
8. [máʰ léŋtɔ]   .... 23. [lɪβərtá̜]   ....
9. [fránsɪs]   .... 24. [báyɛmɔs]   ....
10. [árdə]   .... 25. [pwéttɛ]   ....
11. [bérdə]   .... 26. [ɛlqúžɛ]   ....
12. [řɔ́hɔ]   .... 27. [dá̜ḷdɪ]   ....
13. [kɛrqár]   .... 28. [díšɪ]   ....
14. [pér̆ɔ]   .... 29. [hámbrə]   ....
15. [pá̜ḷdɔ]   .... 30. [kwéŋtəmɔs] ....

244

B. GIVE THE STANDARD SPANISH STRUCTURE IN PLACE OF
   THESE REGIONAL VARIANTS.
1. Lo hicieron todo ellos, ¿por qué no los ayudas?
....

2. ¡Benditos oídos que jamás han oído tales barbari-
   dades!
....

3. Dijo que no se iba hasta que se lo devolverían.
....

4. ¡Viera cuánto nos divertimos!
....

5. ¡Pueda ser que no lleguen mañana tampoco!
....

6. Los estudiantes se vieron obligados a regresarles
   los libros.
....

7. Estábamos delante de la casa y hacíamos frío.
....

8. Vamos a ir en casa de doña Carmen.
....

9. Y aun si así fuere, ¿no lo socorrerías?
....

10. Déme haciendo todo este trabajo.
....

11. Lo único que hacía era meta burlarse.
....

12. Dio un susto cuando tocaron el timbre.
....

C. IDENTIFY THESE ITEMS ACCORDING TO REGION, COUNTRY,
   OR VERSION OF SPANISH.
1. chile, ejote, nopal   ....
2. patojo and patoja canche   ....

245

```
3. Zacatecas, Jalapa, Coahuila        ................
4. cumaní, piragua, huracán           ................
5. marimba, bongó, macandá            ................
6. arrematao, afrentao, caricortao    ................
7. Huairapungo, Rumichaca             ................
8. poncho, puma, alpaca               ................
9. tomar el once                      ................
10. conventillo, macanudo, chau       ................
11. asúkir, bidro, entožos            ................
12. jambre, jaltao, pondo             ................
13. habri, tende                      ................
14. bos-nan, bosonan                  ................
```

ASI SE DICE
REPEAT EACH SEGMENT AS GIVEN AND FINALLY THE COMPLETE
UTTERANCE.

```
A                         ..........
A buen                    ..........
A buen hambre             ..............
hambre no                 ..........
no hay                    ..........
hay pan                   ..........
hay pan duro              ..............
no hay pan duro           ..................
A buen hambre no hay pan duro.
                          ..........................

Las                       ..........
Las flores                ..........
Las flores contentan      ..............
contentan pero            ..........
contentan pero no         ..............
pero no alimentan         ..............
Las flores contentan pero no alimentan.
                          ..........................

Pájaro                    ..........
Pájaro en                 ..........
Pájaro en mano            ..............
mano vale                 ..........
mano vale por             ..............
mano vale por cien        ..................
vale por cien volando     ..................
```

246

Pájaro en mano vale por cien volando.
....

Quien   ....
Quien supo   ....
Quien supo olvidar   ....
olvidar no   ....
olvidar no supo   ....
no supo amar   ....
Quien supo olvidar no supo amar.
....

Con   ....
Con pan   ....
Con pan y   ....
pan y vino   ....
se   ....
se anda   ....
se anda el   ....
se anda el camino   ....
Con pan y vino se anda el camino.
....

Hoy   ....
Hoy por   ....
Hoy por ti   ....
mañana   ....
mañana por   ....
mañana por mí   ....
Hoy por ti, mañana por mí.
....

247

FOOTNOTES

70 Henríquez Ureña, *Sobre el problema.*

71 Alonso, *Temas hispanoamericanos*, p. 41.

72 For further details, see Zamora Vicente, pp. 410-418.

73 Max Leopold Wagner, *Lingua e dialetti dell'A-merica spagnola* (Florence: Edizioni "Le Lingue Estere," 1949).

74 Note that this particular aspiration is not generally so strong as the traditional j sound [x]; therefore, the symbol used here is [h]; ['] may also be used for this sound.

75 For more details on Mexican articulation, see Rubén del Rosario, *El español de América* (Sharon, Conn.: Troutman Press, 1970), pp. 98-101; Juan M. Lope Blanch, *Estudios sobre el español de México* (Mexico: Universidad Nacional Autónoma de México, 1972), pp. 62-68.

76 Lope Blanch, *Estudios*, pp. 62-68.

77 del Rosario, *El español*, p. 100.

78 For further examples of this aspect of Mexican-Spanish morphology, see Charles Kany, *Sintaxis hispanoamericana*, trans. Martín Blanco Alvarez (Madrid: Editorial Gredos, 1969), pp. 193-195.

248

[79] Juan M. Lope Blanch, El léxico indígena en el español de México (Mexico: El Colegio de México, Centro de Estudios Lingüísticos y Literarios, 1969), pp. 35-56; also Juan M. Lope Blanch, El español de América (Madrid: Ediciones Alcalá, 1968).

[80] This phenomenon has been studied to great advantage by Delos Lincoln Canfield, La pronunciación del español en América (Bogotá: Instituto Caro y Cuervo, 1962), p. 8.

[81] Kany, Sintaxis, pp. 197-198.

[82] D. Lincoln Canfield, "Trends in American Castilian," Hispania, 50 (1967), 915.

[83] Canfield, Pronunciación, p. 91.

[84] Kany, Sintaxis, pp. 211-219.

[85] Canfield, "Trends," 912-918.

[86] See "Glossary" in Carlos Luis Fallas, Marco Ramírez (Costa Rica: Imprenta Lehmann, 1975), p. 298.

[87] Margarita Castro Rawson, El costumbrismo en Costa Rica (Costa Rica: Imprenta Lehmann, 1971), p. 336.

[88] Stanley Robe, The Spanish of Rural Panama (Berkeley: University of California Press, 1960), pp. 230-232.

249

[89] See Kany, _Sintaxis_, pp. 230-232; 234.

[90] See Pedro Henríquez Ureña, _El español en Santo Domingo_ (Buenos Aires: Coni, 1940), p. 38.

[91] See del Rosario, _El español_, pp. 82-83.

[92] Henríquez Ureña, _Santo Domingo_, pp. 71-73.

[93] For a thorough coverage of this area, see Henríquez Ureña, _Santo Domingo_, pp. 126-129.

[94] See Wagner, pp. 102-103; also as an item of special interest, see the dialogue and the Afro-Cuban poem, pp. 103-108.

[95] del Rosario, _El español_, p. 83.

[96] See James McDonough, _Guide to Puerto Rican Slang_ (San Juan, P. R.: Publishers Group, Inc., 1972).

[97] See Wagner, pp. 103ff.

[98] For a complete, detailed explanation, see José Cuervo, _Apuntaciones sobre el lenguaje bogotano_ (Bogotá: Instituto Caro y Cuervo, 1939), p. 452.

[99] Kany, _Sintaxis_, p. 195.

[100] Kany, _Sintaxis_, pp. 185-186.

[101] For further elucidation of this point, see Cuervo, p. 404.

[102] For an interesting description of this unique phenomenon, see Humberto Toscano Mateus, El español en el Ecuador (Madrid: Escelicer, 1953), pp. 98-99; for an in-depth treatment of the vowel and consonant systems, see pp. 52-145.

[103] See Kany, Sintaxis, p. 196.

[104] Toscano Mateus, pp. 459-461.

[105] del Rosario, El español, p. 29.

[106] Kany, Sintaxis, p. 236.

[107] Angel Rosenblat, Castellano de España y castellano de América (Montevideo: Editorial Alfa, 1968), pp. 11-12.

[108] See Kany, Sintaxis, pp. 200-201.

[109] Rodolfo Oroz, La lengua castellana en Chile (Santiago: Universidad de Chile, 1966), p. 74.

[110] For a detailed presentation of the phonological system in Chile, see Oroz, pp. 53-192.

[111] See Oroz, pp. 418-471; Rodolfo Lenz, Diccionario etimológico de las voces chilenas derivadas de lenguas indígenas americanas (Santiago de Chile: Impr. Cervantes, 1904-1910).

112 Rosenblat, p. 15.

113 See del Rosario, El español, p. 116.

114 See A. Rosenblat, pp. 15-16; del Rosario, El español, pp. 119-120.

115 See Kany, Sintaxis, p. 289.

116 Kany, Sintaxis, pp. 297-298.

117 Bertil Malmberg, La fonética del español en Paraguay (Lund: C. W. K. Gleerup, 1947), pp. 4-7.

118 Malmberg, La fonética, p. 18.

119 Kany, Sintaxis, pp. 223-224.

120 Kany, Sintaxis, p. 246.

121 See Pierre Delattre, Carroll Olsen, and Elmer Penock, "A Comparative Study of Declarative Intonation in American English and Spanish," Hispania, 45 (1912), 233-241; Harold Kuy, "Outline of Mexican Spanish Phonology," Studies in Linguistics, 10: 3 (1952), 51-62; Karen Kvavik, "An Analysis of Sentence-Initial and Final Intonational Data in Two Spanish Dialects," Journal of Phonetics, 2 (1974), 181-191; Joseph Matluck, "Entonación hispánica," Anuario de letras, 5 (1965), 5-32.

122 Zamora Vicente, p. 353.

123 See Zamora Vicente, p. 356; García de Diego, Manual, p. 323.

124 Zamora Vicente, p. 358.

125 For these and other lexical elements, see Zamora Vicente, pp. 361-376; García de Diego, Manual, p. 325.

126 Zamora Vicente, pp. 450-451.

127 Zamora Vicente, pp. 453-454.

128 Zamora Vicente, pp. 453-454.

129 Mario Pei, p. 312.

130 Pei, p. 313.

131 David Decamp, "Introduction: The Study of Pidgin and Creole Languages," in Pidginization and Creolization of Languages, ed. Dell Hymes (Cambridge: University Press, 1971), pp. 15-19.

132 Decamp, p. 17.

133 For a detailed study of cocoliche, see Keith Whinnon, "Linguistic Hybridization and the 'Special Case' of Pidgins and Creoles," in Pidginization, ed. Hymes, pp. 97-102.

134 See W. M. Hoyer, A Little Guide to English-

253

Papiamento-Netherlands. (Curaçao: Boek Handel
Bethencourt, 1958), pp. 3-5.

135 Wagner, p. 153.

136 Wagner, p. 153.

137 Hoyer, pp. 55-64.

138 Wagner, pp. 153-155.

139 Hoyer, p. 35.

CHAPTER EIGHT

SPANISH IN THE UNITED STATES

HISTORICAL BACKGROUND. The Spaniards arrived in the
area that was to become the United States in the early sixteenth century. For purposes of exploration
and conquest, there were basically two points of entry: Puerto Rico, discovered and settled by Ponce de
Leon (1508-1509); Florida, where he sought the fabled
fountain of youth (1513). During roughly the same
period, the territory that was to be Mexico was con-
quered by the Spaniards, later headed by Hernán Cortés (1519-1521). In both areas of settlement in the
New World, there logically followed a gradual movement northward. New Spain, as Mexico was known at
the time, became a viceroyalty in 1535. Various
points on the map were discovered and settled, and
the northernmost establishment was settled in Saltillo in 1586. Santa Fe was founded in 1609, only
two years after the first English settlement in the
east in the colony of Virginia. The numbers of Hispanic settlers continued to grow by leaps and bounds,
and by 1680, there were some 2500 in New Mexico
alone. A permanent settlement was established in San
Antonio in 1718, and a mission and military presidio
were founded in San Diego in 1769. The city of San
Francisco was established in 1776, and in the very
same year a military fort was built in Tucson. The
year 1776 is significant since there had been many
Spanish settlements in the New World long before independence from the British was achieved. In other
words, the area which was later to become the states
of Arizona, California, New Mexico, and Texas had
been populated by Spanish-speaking peoples long before the Declaration of Independence.

With the Louisiana Purchase in 1803, there en-
sued a first major encounter of speakers of English
and Spanish. There followed problems of different
sorts, often concerning the ownership of West Florida and the boundary lines in Texas. This was settled

255

by the purchase of the Floridas from Spain in 1819, and specific agreement as to boundaries in the southwestern portion of the United States was finally reached. During the same period, English-speaking settlers continued to move westward. Texas achieved its independence in 1836, later being admitted into the United States in 1845. Continued unrest over rights and territories persisted between Mexico, on the one hand, and Texas and the United States, on the other. This strife finally culminated in the Spanish-American War in 1846. As a result, Mexico lost a good deal of territory to the United States. Therefore, many Spanish speakers who had originally settled in the Spanish-speaking community of the American Southwest suddenly found themselves reduced to a minority in a country different in language, customs, and values.

The Treaty of Guadalupe Hidalgo (1848), by which Mexico ceded its northern territory to the United States, guaranteed the language of this Hispanic territory coequality with English. The Constitution of New Mexico included the same guarantee in more specific terms, assuring Hispanics the use of their language in trials, public education, and all state legislative matters. Both countries have made many attempts to maintain an image of goodwill and reciprocity, but problems of illegal entry, intricacies of immigration, economic difficulties, and the behavior of Americans in Mexico have all contributed to complications which have arisen fairly consistently since the time of the original agreements between the two nations.

IMMIGRATION IN THE SOUTHWEST. Accessibility to the southwestern territories of the United States is relatively easy due to insufficient vigilance of the boundary lines. The relative ease of approach, despite half-hearted attempts by border authorities in both countries, has always made for a steady flow of Spanish-speaking natives. The number of immigrants in the United States has varied according to the eco-

nomic needs of the Mexican population. There have
been periods in which the influx has dropped off considerably, as in the time of the Great Depression.
On the other hand, when conditions improved, the tendency has always been in the direction of greater
numbers of Mexicans entering into the United States,
legally or illegally, for a variety of reasons--most
often simply for purposes of survival. At the present time, the number of Mexicans has reached an all-
time high.[140] The fact that illegal aliens are often
willing to provide cheap labor makes them prey to the
unscrupulousness of certain American businessmen--a
factor which creates a good deal of resentment on the
part of legitimate citizens who feel deprived of their
legal rights as a consequence. The problems created
by this type of unaccountability are countless, particularly from the point of view of adjustment, education, and linguistic identification. To find a
solution to illegal immigration is problematical at
best. Therefore, immigration officials on both sides
of the border have been involved in just such a
search since the addition of an illegal immigrant
population to an already burgeoning one is a condition threatening both public education and welfare.
Another factor which adds to the problem of both
kinds of immigration is the frequent reluctance of
Mexicans to become American citizens. Only recently
have they begun to realize the importance of American
citizenship as a key to political clout and ethnic
power.[141] Within the past decade, many newly arrived Mexicans as well as long-standing residents
feel that citizenship in the United States will give
them, not only power at the polls, but will help them
to rise from the second-rate citizenship category in
which the majority has felt trapped to the present.

IMMIGRATION ON THE EAST COAST. Patterns of immigration and emigration have been different along the
eastern seaboard as a result of dissimilar historical
ties. The Spaniards had long had commercial contact
with New York through their possessions in the Caribbean. By 1834, one quarter of Puerto Rico's trade

was with the Rican Merchants Association in New York City.[142] The earliest Puerto Ricans came to the Mainland for business purposes, but they were soon followed by political exiles and anti-Spanish revolutionaries in the nineteenth century. The Spanish-American War changed the picture in that Puerto Rico was given the status of a United States protectorate. In 1917, by the Organic Act of Congress, Puerto Ricans became citizens of the United States. This soon increased the influx of Puerto Ricans into New York and eventually many of the major cities along the east coast. The pattern since then has fluctuated according to the economic status and employment possibilities on the overpopulated island. In 1950, with the establishment of relatively inexpensive airfares, a much greater degree of population movement began to take place. Since then there has been a good deal of movement back and forth for a number of reasons: coming to the Mainland to enjoy the "American dream;" to seek temporary employment; to establish permanent or semi-permanent residence; to work as farm workers for a predetermined period of time; simply to visit friends and relatives. The frequency of movement to and fro undoubtedly reinforces the bilingual-bicultural nature of Puerto Rican life in New York, Philadelphia, parts of New Jersey and New England, and in many other sections of the United States. As a general rule, Puerto Ricans live in substandard tenement housing and do not fare especially well on the economic scale. This is sadly true since Puerto Ricans are not technically immigrants. Unfortunately, since many of them come to the Mainland for reasons of survival with no intention to remain and since there are other linguistic and racial deterrents, they often find it extremely difficult to adjust to the ways of the land and find little of the economic land of promise about which they often dream. In a sense, the 1.3 million Puerto Ricans that live in and around Manhattan and elsewhere along the eastern seaboard are the most beleaguered of all United States Hispanics.[143]

OTHER AMERICAN HISPANICS.   The other main group is

258

the Cuban population, which now constitutes the majority of the residents of Miami. After 1880, the
southeastern portion of the United States began to
receive many Hispanic immigrants, chiefly Cubans.
The first groups settled in Tampa, on Florida's Gulf
Coast, where there was also some immigration from
Spain, mainly Asturias. In Key West a small colony
of Cuban cigar manufacturers and workers was established quite early.[144] The great influx of Cuban
population actually occurred as a result of the Castro revolution when more than 700,000 Cubans left
their native island to establish residence in the
United States. The recent exodus from the Island
makes for even more complex problems. Most Cubans
who entered the mainland originally were middle-class
workers and professionals with considerable education
and in some cases a good deal of money. The current
immigration flow leaves open many possibilities concerning the future. The first immigrants from Castro's Cuba are today a rather flourishing economic
group with independent businesses, social agencies,
newspapers, and associations. They are a fairly
close-knit group and tend to maintain the linguistic
and cultural ties of the Island and have become so
identified with Miami that the latter is often referred to as Little Havana. The recent "black revolution" is a reaction to their obvious ability to adapt
to new ways of life. Like many Mexicans and other
Hispanics, a goodly number of Cubans were originally
reluctant to become American citizens since they en-
tertained the notion of returning home one day or
perhaps out of a sense of sentimental loyalty to Cuba. Others, on the other hand, soon became citizens
out of gratitude to the United States and to make
their political and social contributions to their
host country. Since the majority has now become
firmly established and aware of the political clout
possible only with citizenship, greater numbers of
them are now actively involved in becoming American
citizens and in channeling their rights as a strong
ethnic minority. The Cubans have accomplished a good
deal since their arrival, but it should be kept in
mind that they arrived with far better background and
education than other Hispanic groups. Typically, Cu-

bans tend to retain many of their customs and social
ties, and, above all, their language. In spite of
their large numbers and considerable progress, little
has been done in the way of investigating or analyzing the linguistic problems involved in English contact or the adjustment phenomena of Cubans in their
new homeland. This area will be quite significant
in the future, especially as a result of the linguistic reinforcement resulting from the most recent exodus from Cuba.

The Sephardic Jews are a very small group established in New York City since the beginning of the
century and with obviously different cultural and
linguistic ties. Linguistically speaking, they are
a very rapidly diminishing subminority since there
has been little reinforcement to maintain the Sephardic Jewish dialect. Many of them immigrated from
Turkey with little or no knowledge of English and
thus were forced to engage in more menial types of
jobs. But with the second and third generations,
much of the New York sefardí has been lost since integration in American life took place fairly rapidly.
With some minor differences and the typical Sephardic
elements, their language is reminiscent of fifteenth-
century Castilian. Until recently, they published
their own newspaper in New York, called La Vara,
which has unfortunately disappeared from the scene.
Because of linguistic stagnation, social isolation,
and little reinforcement from the outside, much of
the language has been lost. It is sad to observe
that with the disappearance of such stagnant pockets
of Hispanic speech, a vast treasure of centuries-old
oral tradition is doomed to pass into oblivion.145

It is estimated that there are over nineteen
million Hispanics in the United States, including illegal aliens. The largest single group is the Chicanos, who number approximately 7.3 million. The
second largest group is the Puerto Ricans, who number about 1.8 million, although this number is only
approximate since there is considerable movement
back and forth from the Mainland to the Island and
vice versa. The third largest group is the Cubans,

who number about 700,000, and who will increase sub-
stantially as a result of the most recent influx.
There are, in addition, thousands of Dominicans,
Ecuadorians, Colombians, Argentinians, natives of
other Latin-American countries, some few Sephardics,
and isleños (former Canary Islanders who lived side
by side with Cajuns in Louisiana). When viewed as a
whole, the picture is quite mixed, containing both
extremes in lifestyle and language as well as education and background. For example, the affluent Cubans have little or nothing in common with lowly
Mexican migrant workers and even less with impover-
ished ghetto Puerto Ricans. The same may be said of
wealthy Mexican Americans in relation to illegal
aliens. Puerto Ricans feel no real affinity for Mexican Americans, and isleños, when there is an ethnic
pattern, have few ties in common with all the rest.
Nonetheless, in the main, they share the same "his-
panicness," culture, customs, most often religion,
and, above all, language. And yet, the linguistic
bond which unites all Hispanics the world over is the
very cause of problems with relation to integration
in the United States. Even though many "Anglos" may
feel that they were in fact in the United States
first, there is much which is documented in the an-
nals of history to teach us otherwise.

THE PRESENCE OF SPANISH IN THE UNITED STATES. Even
though the political power of Spain diminished considerably in the nineteenth century, the cultural influence has never been completely lost. There are
many aspects of American English which demonstrate
the presence, at one time or another, of a Spanish-
dominant people. For example, many words referring
to plant and animal life are either derived from Mexican Spanish or have come into the language through
the American Southwest alfalfa, marijuana, mosquito,
armadillo, bronco, burro, barracuda, bonito, coyote,
mustang, palomino, pinto, jaguar. In the same way,
many words having to do with ranch life entered English as well rodeo, lasso, stampede, corral, bar-
becue, chaparral, hacienda, lariat, peon, reata. In

261

the area of food and drink, there are many terms
which are Mexican, Mexican-American, or simply American tortilla, taco, tamal, enchilada, chili con
carne, jalapeños, eggs rancheros, frijoles, flan, pi-
miento, garbanzo, plátano, mango, papaya, ceviche,
pulque, tequila, piña colada, mescal, daiquiri. Many
terms having to do with articles of clothing are used
either throughout the country or principally in the
Southwest poncho, mantilla, guarapes, sombrero, ga-
lochas, rebozo, serape. Architectural terminology
and words related to colonial Mexican building styles
are also prevalent portal, alcove, patio, plaza,
rancho, hacienda, pueblo, corral, balcón. Mexican
and American Southwestern vocabulary also contributed
to the American lexicon such terms as fiesta, siesta,
piñata, tango, marimba, rumba, mariachi, conga, mata-
dor, caballero, doña (duenna), señorita, chica, chico, don, señor, señora. The topography of Mexico and
the American Southwest has also provided us with
words like mesa, meseta, peninsula, arroyo, barranca,
canyon, canal, vista, sierra, tornado. In addition
to these words which are either true borrowings or
Spanish words used in English, there are terms typical of the Southwest and Texas which are clearly
Mexican-derived vamoose, calaboose, desperado, cuar-
tel, hoosegow, incomunicado, critter, filibuster, loco, pronto, gusto, stevedore, marina, hombre.146
Hispanic-American toponimics are countless, particularly in the Southwest and on the West Coast. Cities, counties, states, and other places have names
of Spanish origin--Alameda, Alhambra, Arcadia, Chi-
co, Chula Vista, Corona, Costa Mesa, El Cajón, El
Centro, El Cerrito, El Monte, El Segundo, Escondido,
Los Altos, Los Angeles, Madera, Sacramento, Palo Alto, Salinas. Place names based on the names of
saints are also typical--San Anselmo, San Bernardino,
San Carlos, San Diego, San Fernando, San Francisco,
San Gabriel, San Jose, San Luis Obispo, San Marino,
San Mateo, San Pablo, San Rafael, Santa Ana, Santa
Barbara, Santa Clara, Santa Maria, Santa Monica,
Santa Paula, Santa Rosa. Most of these places are in
California, but similar instances are found through-
out the country--Amarillo, Del Rio, El Campo, El Pa-
so, San Antonio, Laredo, Pampa, Pecos, San Benito,

Colorado, New Mexico, Arizona, the Rio Grande, the Sierra Nevada, Albuquerque, Florida, Boca Raton, Gasparilla, Boca Grande, Punta Gorda, Malaga, Buena, Cape Canaveral, and others.

Even though these place names and other terms are proof of a long history of Spanish-speaking people in the United States, it is no secret that there have been problems with regard to full acceptance or integration of Hispanics, of whatever origin, into the mainstream of American culture. Those with less background and education, and in some cases, identification, who enter the United States less equipped to deal with the problems of urban life and adjustment typical of the demands of life in America, often find themselves confined to areas where only people of similar background reside. As a consequence, there emerges what has come to be known as the "Spanish ghetto" or, more popularly, the "barrio."

LIFE IN THE BARRIO. The "barrio" tends to be the focus of most immigrant groups of Mexicans and Puerto Ricans. Although in original Spanish usage the word "barrio" simply means "living quarters" or "district," in the American Hispanic sense it clearly denotes "slum." Within traditional Spanish circles, the word normally must be accompanied by an adjective to give it a specific meaning: barrio comercial (business district), barrio elegante (wealthy suburb), barrio del norte (northern suburb), and barrio pobre (slum area). Sadly enough, in the American Hispanic experience the word "barrio" does not need qualification. Barrios may be found across the country in places like East Los Angeles, San Francisco, San Antonio, El Paso, Chicago, Trenton, Boston, New York, Philadelphia, and elsewhere. Most of them form part of the inner city and are depressing areas of poverty-level income and less than substandard housing, often with three generations living under one roof. It is not unusual to find only one parent at the head of a household, usually the mother in a

263

loosely structured matriarchal setup. Though such families often create social problems and become dependent sooner or later on welfare agencies, linguistically they present no major problem except that a native Spanish-speaking mother's influence seems to be much stronger than in other social arrangements. The barrio has become a source of major concern to sociologists, anthropologists, social workers, and others of similar interests; yet, little has been done in the area of linguistic studies in connection with barrio dwellers. Fishman's work (<u>Bilingualism in the Barrio</u>) is an excellent study from a fundamentally sociolinguistic point of view, contributing a great deal to American Hispanics in general. In addition, Teschner's study (<u>Anglicisms in Spanish. A Cross-Referenced Guide to Previous Findings, Together with English</u>...) is a major breakthrough in the area of English interferences in the Spanish of the Chicago barrio. To our knowledge, no major linguistic investigation has appeared dealing with the influence of English on the Spanish of all United States Hispanics and vice versa.

Whatever the reasons, barrios in the United States have become a major social and political problem with many ramifications. Many social welfare and rehabilitation programs have been established, often without success. Close to thirty percent of Hispanic families in the United States earn under $7,000 yearly, and their unemployment rate is generally quite high--about 8.9 percent.[147] This group has clung more tenaciously to its language tradition than have other immigrant groups like Italians, Greeks, Germans, Poles, Jews, and others. There is no question that the language barrier has been a major deterrent in matters of integration, socialization, education, employment, and adjustment in general. It is only fair to point out that the patterns of immigration among <u>hispanos</u> are somewhat different from those of other <u>groups</u>. First, the early Mexican Americans were established in the United States long before the "Anglo" settlements. Secondly, many legal and illegal aliens from Mexico view their stay only as a transitory experience. Thirdly, Puerto Ricans are

American citizens and are therefore not technically
immigrants. Fourthly, many of the latter view their
stay as a temporary means of acquiring sufficient
funds to establish a permanent home back on the Island. As a consequence, the tendency has been to remain more rigidly attached to the Hispanic social
structure with its language, beliefs, and customs.
It is easy to understand in view of these facts why
they feel no need to lose their ethnic identity as
other groups have in the past and thus find themselves limited to rather insular enclaves of "His-
panicness." The social problems which plague these
people are often rooted in having to settle for menial forms of employment, poor wages, and substandard housing. A long-range plan to better their lot
has been the so-called "bilingual" movement among
American educators.

THE EMERGENCE OF BILINGUALISM IN THE UNITED STATES.
Bilingual education has been conceived variously according to the objectives of the professionals involved. One of the first groups to turn its attention to these problems was the Fourth Annual Conference of the Southwest Council of Foreign Languages
held in El Paso, Texas, in 1967. The Report of the
Conference was published under the auspices of the
United States Department of Health, Education and
Welfare (Bilingual Education: Research and Teaching).148 This conference, as well as other well-in-
tentioned educational organizations, resulted in sub-
sequent legislation which has had far-reaching con-
sequences.

The coexistence of two languages in contact often brings about a type of bilingualism varying in
kind and degree according to the particular characteristics of the speech community. At best, arriving
at an appropriate definition of "bilingualism" is not
an easy task. A basic description from a traditional
point of view might be the handling of two languages
simultaneously with relative ease in basic communication. Traditional bilingualism has usually been un-

derstood to mean the ability to express oneself with
equal facility and with the same degree of proficiency in two different languages. It is safe to
say that over the years instances of true bilingualism have been rare. Frequently those who were
nearly perfectly bilingual were children of diplo-
mats, executives, military personnel, and jet set-
ters who lived for long periods of time in two countries and who had relatively equal exposure to two
different languages and cultures. Even in the case
of dual exposure, such persons normally tended to
favor one language over the other or at least identified with one and not both. The dominant language
of the family unit often remained the dominant means
of communication of such children, even though they
had a nearly similar exposure to a second language in
the community and elsewhere outside the home.

Among experts, there seems to be considerable
disagreement concerning the conception of bilingualism and even more disagreement when the concept
is applied to educational curricula. One might begin with Fr. Casso's definition as "teaching the language of the land in the language of the home."149
The aim of most bilingual educators has come to be
the teaching of the language of the dominant society
(English) in the language of the home (in this case,
Spanish). There are, it goes without saying, a number of different emphases supported by many diver-
gent theories, but this appears to be the primary
objective of most teachers and bilingual specialists. Generally speaking, there are some few secondary acquisitions which are also stressed: reinforcement of the traditionally preferred forms of
standard Spanish; identification with and respect
for Mexican, Mexican-American, Puerto Rican, Neo-Ri-
can, and American history; a renewed sense of the
identity of the ethnic group; general Spanish and
American folklore and culture.

As a result of the Bilingual Education Act
(1968), bilingual instruction must be made available
by law to any ethnic group whose dominant language
is not English, provided there is the requisite num-

266

ber of students from a given ethnic group within any
school district. The law itself met with various
types of reactions, ranging from hearty approval to
strong opposition. Consequently, this law has been
put into effect in different ways with varying degrees of success and failure. In some school districts it has simply been disregarded, somehow obviated, or cast aside until it is "economically fea-
sible." Nonetheless, bilingual educators continue to
stress the basic aims of those who support bilingualism, however conceived. While the law has provided for bilingual instruction in languages like
Italian, German, Greek, Amerindian dialects, and
others, the major thrust has been toward the bilingual education of Hispanics.

Despite various types of legislation and conflicting points of view, basically two types of bilingual education have been provided to date. They
may be categorized either as the "assimilation
type" or the "pluralistic model," as these two plans
have been aptly called by Rolf Kjolseth.150 The
pluralistic model promotes extensive use of the ethnic language in the home, school, and community with
equal emphasis both on the ethnic and non-ethnic language. It also stresses the positive values of both
cultures to the same degree. In this program the
lessons are presented first in the non-ethnic and
then in the ethnic language while in periods of rec-
reation and study, there is complete freedom as to
which means of communication should be used.151
This program involves parents both of the ethnic and
non-ethnic students. What is more, the community
resources representative of both groups are called
into action and made use of quite extensively. A
program of this kind focuses upon the differences in
culture and history of both groups and attempts to
maintain a permanent type of diglossia. This form
of comprehensive curriculum is the most desirable and
is the one to which many bilingual educators aspire.

While the pluralistic type of curriculum seems
very sound, legislators and educators who are either opposed to diglossia or who see it only as a

267

temporary concession to solve difficult social and educational problems stress the assimilation type of program. The latter does not involve the parents of both ethnic and non-ethnic children and makes little use of the multi-faceted community resources. The tendency is to deal with concepts of relative "inferiority" and "superiority" of linguistic and cultural values. The ultimate aim of this program becomes the eventual assimilation of the ethnic group into the dominant society. Moreover, the teaching of the ethnic language is kept on a fairly idealistic level without coequal status.[152] Sadly enough, most bilingual programs in the United States tend to be of the assimilation type.

Even with the differences in conception and approach, bilingual education is growing in various parts of the country according to the patterns of ethnic speech, immigration, and socio-political exigencies. More instructional materials are available today than ever before. Textbooks which deal with Latin-American, Mexican, and Puerto Rican folktales, legends, and short stories are readily available and are frequently of excellent quality. All levels of graded readers are published covering vital aspects of history, folklore, and civilization. In addition, many cultural units are created to enhance instruction, including texts on Hispanic plays, short stories, crossword puzzles, newspaper clipping units, word puzzles, games, filmstrips, slides, and movies.

Despite the tremendous strides made in the field of bilingual education, much remains to be done. There is still a great deal of political lobbying which is engendered either by a professional interest in the needs of Spanish-dominant or other-language-dominant children or by the ethnic minorities themselves. Many Americans maintain that a bilingual emphasis will ultimately have the effect of lessening the grasp of the dominant language. Others fear a type of ethnic struggle with strong political divisiveness like the French-English conflict in Canada. Still others maintain that equal knowledge of English and the ethnic tongue will make for a linguistically and culturally enlightened population. Theorists have analyzed this problem from many points of view--bilingualism and the ethnic child's IQ, bilingualism and early cognitive development, bilingualism and interference, and other points of focus.[153] Despite the divergence of opinions and strong opposition from a number of quarters, Joshua A. Fishman, one of the chief proponents of bilingual education, views the latter as the hope of tomorrow

> The day is coming when more and more genuine bilingual education, for all those who want it, regardless of income, mother tongue, or language dominance, will be part of the variegated picture of American education... It will not be just a promissory note to the poor, nor a left-handed contribution to increasingly vocal and organized (though still exploited and dispossessed) Hispanos and Indians.[154]

In bilingual education among Hispanic children, three immigrant patterns play an important role: first, first-generation immigrants or persons of immigrant status (Puerto Ricans) whose native language is Spanish and whose grasp of English is extremely minimal; second, second-generation persons who feel comfortable with basic spoken English but who also have a minimal degree of fluency in their parents' tongue; third, the children of the second generation whose language is exclusively English but who have scanty knowledge of Spanish.[155] This basic picture is often further complicated by the fact of persistent reinforcement by the steady movement between Puerto Rico and the Mainland and the Southwest and Mexico.

LANGUAGES IN CONTACT. When languages exist in contact--in this case English and Spanish--the eventual result is interference of one sort or another. In the bilingual-bicultural situation in which United States Spanish speakers live, language contact per se is only one aspect of their living experience. As

269

ethnic individuals become progressively acculturated, an infiltration of the non-ethnic language into the ethnic one and vice versa takes place. This phenomenon is known as <u>interference</u>, which generally occurs on <u>three</u> levels: phonetic, grammatical, and lexical.[156] Phonetic interference may be thought of as sound substitutions from the primary language to the secondary and vice versa.[157] All carry-overs of Spanish and English in either direction are examples of phonetic interference. The articulation of English ⌈v⌉--clearly a labiodental phoneme--as a bilabial fricative ⌈b̞⌉ is an example of phonetic interference of high frequency. Many <u>hispanoparlantes</u> articulate words like <u>live</u>, <u>love</u>, <u>very</u>, <u>cave</u>, <u>vital</u>, <u>cover</u>, <u>gravel</u> as ⌈'li̞b⌉, ⌈'lʌb⌉, ⌈'bɛri⌉, ⌈'kɛyb⌉, ⌈'baitl⌉, ⌈'kʌbr⌉, ⌈'qræb̞l⌉. Final m is almost invariably articulated as a voiced nasal alveolar ⌈n⌉, so words like <u>room</u>, <u>broom</u>, <u>home</u>, <u>comb</u>, <u>seem</u>, <u>dream</u> are produced as ⌈'run⌉, ⌈'brun⌉, ⌈'hɔn⌉, ⌈'kɔn⌉, ⌈'sin⌉, ⌈'drin⌉. Likewise, most initial consonantal clusters are articulated with the characteristic epenthetic e, yielding forms like ⌈əs'kul⌉, ⌈əs'pun⌉, ⌈əs'tʌdi⌉, ⌈əs'tul⌉, ⌈əs'pɛ/l⌉, ⌈əs'kip⌉. The English voiced interdental ⌈ð⌉ is often rendered a voiced dental ⌈d⌉ <u>this</u> ⌈'dis⌉, <u>that</u> ⌈'dat⌉, <u>those</u> ⌈'doz⌉, <u>there</u> ⌈'dɛr⌉. Its voiceless interdental counterpart ⌈θ⌉ is often produced as merely a voiceless dental stop ⌈t⌉ <u>thin</u> ⌈'tɪn⌉, <u>thick</u> ⌈'tɪk⌉, <u>Thelma</u> ⌈'tɛlmə⌉, <u>thoroughly</u> ⌈'tɛroli⌉. The combination -ng in absolute final position presents a similar degree of interference since the sound combination does not exist in Spanish, resulting frequently in the elimination of the final consonant <u>song</u> ⌈'sɔn⌉, <u>wrong</u> ⌈'rɔn⌉, <u>singing</u> ⌈'sɪnᵍɪn⌉, <u>writing</u> ⌈'raitɪn⌉. The carry-over of the Spanish multiple vibrant in initial position is fairly universal ⌈'roz⌉, ⌈'red⌉, ⌈'ritn⌉, ⌈ri'dɪkyulʌs⌉, ⌈'raund⌉, ⌈'reqyulr⌉. A unique instance of interference is the recurrent use of the palatalized variant of <u>y</u>, ⌈ŷ⌉, which occurs in Spanish only after n- or l- and for contrast and emphasis. This palatalized variant is used more often than not by Hispanics as in <u>yes</u> ⌈'dzes⌉, <u>your</u> ⌈'dzur⌉, <u>year</u> ⌈'dzir⌉, <u>yeast</u> ⌈'dzist⌉, <u>yellow</u> ⌈'dzɛlo⌉, <u>yesterday</u> ⌈'dzɛstrde⌉, <u>young</u>

[ˈdʒʌnq], yo-yo [ˈdʒo ˈdʒo]. The reverse phenomenon occurs with many English words beginning with j since these are usually given the unpalatalized pronunciation of y junior [ˈyʊnyɔr], June [ˈyun], July [yu-ˈlai], joke [ˈyoк], Joan [ˈyon], John [ˈyan], Jack [ˈyaк]. There is also a good deal of interference with palatalized sibilants, especially in the English combination -sh- since the Spanish sound system has no real counterpart. Thus words like shout, show, shoe, shovel, shoot, and shut are said [ˈʃaut], [ˈʃou], [ˈʃu], [ˈʃʌvl], [ˈʃut], [ˈʃʌt]. This phoneme also occurs in a medial position and is altered to fit the dominant sound system insure [ɪnˈʃur], fisher [ˈfɪʃr], Aleutian [əˈluʃn], treasure [ˈtrɛʃr], illusion [iˈluʃn], pleasure [ˈplɛʃr]. In absolute final position the palatalized quality of the phoneme is often completely lost English [ˈɪnqlɪs], Spanish [əˈspanɪs], British [ˈbrɪtɪs], bluish [ˈbluɪs], Jewish [ˈdʒuɪs].

Vowels are also affected by the Spanish sound system. The main area of interference is vowel length since duration of vowels as such is not contrastive in Spanish. Spanish-dominant speakers have difficulty in differentiating English contrastive pairs since their tendency is to place the sound midway between the English long and short vowels. The following contrastive pairs are quite a challenge to the average Spanish speaker: sheep/ship, feet/fit, leap/lip, peep/pip, peat/pit, beet/bit, meet/mitt, keep/kip, sleeper/slipper, keeper/kipper, fleet/flit, seat/sit, seep/sip, tweater/twitter, deed/did, beady/biddy. For the same reasons, Hispanics frequently do not distinguish between long a [ɑː] (mar, tar, park, spark, heart, apart, bottle, fodder) and its shorter variant [æ] (task, cask, mask, class, mass, bass, brass, lap, tap, sap, map, Mac). The basic inclination is toward producing these variant a's like the broad Spanish a in batalla, padre, canalla, muralla.

Similar problems of interference are encountered in the production of English diphthongs and other vowel combinations. Sounds like [o] (flow, show, row), [au] (hour, shower, power), [ju] (pure, cure,

271

curate), [ɛY] (plain, rain, Spain), [ɔi] (boy, annoy, toy), [ai] (tire, conspire, retire) are articulated in the Spanish fashion or are simplified to the
closest single-vowel equivalent.

In matters of mutual language influence, there
is a definite correlation between immigrant status
and the prevalence of interference factors. And
yet, there are other elements which enter the picture: the family unit; the extent of orientation
toward the original language and culture; the degree
of exposure to ghetto dwelling; the relative contact
with English on various levels; educational background; positive or negative linguistic sensitivity;
level of intelligence; ethnic awareness; matters
concerning employment; identity factors; social aspects of acculturation.

Morphology is another area in which interference factors are observed. English irregular plurals are often problematical for non-native speakers
especially when there is no real equivalent in their
dominant language. English plurals like oxen, mice,
children, geese, men, gentlemen, women, alumni, cri-
teria, phenomena, alumnae are frequently regularized
(oxes, mouses, mans, womans). The marker -s (-es)
in verb-forms is also a problem area. Since English
verb-forms no longer have the inflexional development
of the Spanish verb system, the verb endings are often regularized and are made completely uniform I
speak, you speak, he speak, she speak. A similar
phenomenon occurs when the marker -es is appended
where it is not normally heard (he speakes, she
sleepes, he workes). Verbs which require double
stops as past-tense markers are often a challenge to
Spanish speakers. Forms like worked, asked, plucked,
dredged, ached, baked, remarked, barked, parked, relaxed are often articulated without the final stop
since such clusters do not exist in Spanish. The
same applies to all past participles: tired, per-
spired, bored, reared, colored, relaxed are characteristically articulated [ˈtair], [perˈspair],
[ˈbor], [ˈriər], [ˈkʌlr], [riˈlaks].

272

Syntax is another area in which carry-overs from
Spanish are numerous. Interrogative forms such as
who, whom, what, which, when, why, where, and how are
often sources of difficulty. For example, English
often uses what where Spanish utilizes its equivalent
of which and vice versa. English makes use of where
interrogatively in cases in which Spanish provides a
series of choices (¿dónde?, ¿adónde?, ¿en dónde?,
¿por dónde?). Spanish distinguishes between who and
whom essentially by dint of the personal marker a
("¿quién es?" "who is it?" "¿a quién ve?" "whom do
you see?"). All interrogative structures containing
auxiliary verbs are very perplexing for Spanish
speakers. Questions like "are you going?," "is he
coming?," "aren't they staying?," "wouldn't they a-
gree?," "shouldn't you stay?" are often simplified
according to the Spanish structure ("go you?,"
"comes he?," "stay they?") or are focused in the affirmative with the appropriate or near-appropriate
interrogative intonation ("you go?," "he comes?,"
"they stay?"). In English, auxiliaries are used in
interrogative, progressive, and emphatic forms of
most tenses ("are you going?," "isn't she coming?,"
"she is writing," "she did write," "he was going,"
"he did go"). In the speech of Hispanics these
forms are either completely simplified ("she wrote,"
"he went") or, in cases of greater Spanish dominance,
the incorrect aspect of the verb is employed ("she
did speak" for "she was speaking," "he did go" for
"he was going"). The idiom "you had better (not) go"
is frequently expressed on this level as "you better
go" and "you better don't go."

The inflexions of English strong verbs are usually a source of confusion for non-native speakers.
Traditionally there are several ways in which tense
is expressed in English--either no change at all from
the basic form, a vowel change, a consonant change,
both a vowel and consonant change, and sporadic additions of suffixes (usually -en).[158] Observe the
formation of the strong verbs in English as follows:

THE PRINCIPAL PARTS OF STRONG VERBS IN ENGLISH

	One form	Two forms	Three forms
no change	put put put set set set let let let fit fit fit spread spread spread split split split hurt hurt hurt bid bid bid burst burst burst knit knit knit spit spit spit		
vowel change		shine shone sit sat find found sting stung sit sat read read [e] run ran come came	spring sorang sprung ring rang rung shrink shrank shrunk drink drank drunk begin began begun sing sang sung sink sank sunk stink stank stunk swim swam swum

FIGURE 37

	One form	Two forms	Three forms
consonant change		have had make made pay paid build built lay laid prove proved wake waked	
vowel and consonant change			break broke broken write wrote written drive drove driven ride rode ridden forget forgot forgotten throw threw thrown arise arose arisen bite bit bitten blow blew blown choose chose chosen dive dove dived do did done go went gone draw drew drawn wear wore worn weave wove woven shrive shrove shriven

FIGURE 37, cont.

	One form	Two forms	Three forms
vowel and consonant change, cont.			get got gotten eat ate eaten fall fell fallen know knew known

FIGURE 37, cont.

Although Spanish has some preterite tense irregularities which resemble English strong verbs, basically there are few other parallelisms.

Among the Spanish-dominant, the periphrastic future ("we are going to do it," "she is going to go") has a higher frequency in English than the more traditional future ("we shall do it," "she will go"). In popular Spanish and more so in Chicano and Puerto Rican, the periphrastic future has taken greater hold than in the standard language. For instance, "voy a hacerlo" is heard more frequently than "lo haré;" "van a decirlo," more than "lo dirán;" "vas a comerlo," in place of "lo comerás."

A common source of interference is found in negation. Since double negatives are the norm in Spanish, there is a common carry-over in this area. Even when Spanish permits the elimination of the negation indicator (no) in emphatic and contrastive utterances, the inverted word order intensifies the negation and is perceived as a strong (equivalent to double) negative.

NEGATION IN SPANISH

NORMAL	EMPHATIC
No lo hago nunca.	Nunca lo hago.
No veo a nadie.	A nadie veo.
No van con nadie.	Con nadie van.
No tienes nada.	Nada tienes.
No ven ningún árbol.	Ningún árbol ven.
No vas a ninguna parte.	A ninguna parte vas.

FIGURE 38

BORROWINGS AND LOANS. Barbarisms and bastardisms of various kinds are part of everyday conversation, not

277

only in Chicano and Puerto Rican Spanish, but in
most languages and are often the result of contact,
illiteracy, or simply the retention of archaic
forms. In common parlance one encounters forms like
pior (peor), dijistes (dijiste), almuada (almohada),
cuete (cohete), golpiar (golpear), abuja (aguja), a-
güelo (abuelo), celebro (cerebro), companía (compañía). There are other forms typical of Chicano and
Puerto Rican that are clearly the result of interference due to long years of contact with English.
Borrowings from English are often referred to as
"loanwords," according to the Norwegian specialist,
Einar Haugen, who maintains that loanwords are "...
usually limited to those borrowings in which both the
phonemic shape of a word and its meaning are im-
ported."159

By "pure loan" is meant the absence of morphemic
substitution, the latter being a sound change which
implies grammatical value (i. e., to do>does). This
group may be further divided into three types of phonemic substitution (sound linked with meaning): "unassimilated pure loans," "partly assimilated pure
loans," and "wholly assimilated pure loans."160
Unassimilated pure loans are those in which there is
no phonemic substitution at all. On a purely phonetic level, there are certain barely perceptible ac-
commodations which normally take place in order to
fit non-native words into another sound system.
There are countless examples of unassimilated pure
loans from English--ambassador, motel, banana, fore-
close, lease, loan, ring (sports), set, rush, play-
boy, sexy, misdemeanor, brassiere, detrimental,
folder, boss, P. O. Box, issue, panel, coach, Kotex,
Kleenex, allowance, apprentice, assembly. Partly assimilated pure loans contain some degree of phonemic
substitution--agrimen, jey féver, hamborguesa, jam-
berga, and jambórguer (hamburger), gaselín, lanlord,
stimrola (steam roller), rocanrol, incon (income),
espelen (spelling), choc (shock), cho and chou
(show), cabói and caubói (cowboy), cartún, cade and
cadilec (Cadillac), peticout, breca (brakes), pley
suit, fodge, tibí (TV), tofe (tough), bakin (baking
powder), eslecs (slacks), yerse (jersey, sweater).

Wholly assimilated pure loans are characterized by
phonemic substitution, resulting in interesting in-
novations like áis tí, aisber (iceberg), ais crím,
aiscrin, and aiscrín (ice cream), air mail [arméil],
bloaut, bil, swiminpul, suich and suichi (switch),
fultaim (full time), erjostes (stewardess), coctel,
cóctcl, and cocteil (cocktail), cámper, lipestic, li-
pistic, and lipistique, gucnsta (gangster), pana, pa-
nito (buddy, friend), cráquer, basíquel, estraic
(strike).

While pure loans concern the phonemic environment related exclusively to the sound system, "loanblends" are partial morphemic substitutions combining sound and syntactical implications.161 Loanblends may also be divided into three subgroups. The
first is characterized by partial substitution, occurring either as a suffix or stem substitution, as
in bloque, bísquete, hangueo (hang-up), missy (miss),
ganga (gang), suera (sweater), fornitura (furniture),
hamburguesa, cadilaque, lipistique, aiscrinero (ice
cream maker or vendor), baisicle (bicycle), estrai-
que (strike), lambehuevos (apple polisher), suiche
and suichi (switch). The second group of loanblends
has suffix substitutions which are meaningful as
such, often in the form of first-conjugation verbs.
The following examples are a random sampling: cla-
pear, clepiar, and clepear (to clap), dailear, dai-
liar, dalear, and daliar (to dial), espelear and es-
peliar (to spell), estraiguear and estraiguiar (to
strike), asemblar (to assemble), blofear (to bluff),
parchar (to patch), flanquear, flanquiar, flonquear,
and flonquiar (to flunk), guachicar, guachear, waxear, and waxiar (to wax), lonchar, lonchiar, and lon-
chear (to lunch), lonchera (lunch bag), lonchería
(luncheonette), trimiar (to trim), laquiar (to lock),
taipear and taipiar (to type), taipiador(a), taipis-
ta (typist), friquear and friquiar (to freak out),
mapear, mapiar, mopear, and mopiar (to mop), dropear
(to drop), brequear and brequiar (to break). The
third group of loanblends consists of compounds--of-
ten partly from English and partly from Spanish or in
free translation.162 There are many interesting
combinations within this category pantimedia (panty-

hose), minifalda (miniskirt), maxifalda (maxiskirt),
casa de borde, casa de borderos, and casa de bordos
(boarding house), discount tienda, día de gracias,
día de dar gracias, and día de acción de gracias
(Thanksgiving Day), un buen tiempo (a good time),
chúingom, jumrón (home run), Carlos yúnier (Charles,
Jr.).

While loan words are based on phonemic and morphemic changes, loanshifts are substitutions of native morphemes. These are called "calques" by
Haugen[163] and may also be divided into three basic
groups: literal creations, approximate creations,
and extensions. These adaptations include any number of interesting or quaint renderings such as pal-
mista (palm reader), viaje redondo (round-trip ticket), lumbrero (fireman), plancha dental (dental
plate), lentodos (eyeglasses), drogadicto and adicto
a drogas (drug addict), fuerza policía (police
force), alambre eléctrico (thin, skinny), dedo chi-
quito (little finger), tener un fonazo (to have a
good deal of fun), tener un mal tiempo (to have a
bad time), campana eléctrica (electric buzzer), abanico eléctrico (electric fan). In any case, whatever
the degree of borrowing and whatever form the borrowings may take, there is considerable evidence that
in the speech of Chicanos and, to a lesser extent,
Puerto Ricans, years of contact in the form of extensive social, political, and commercial relations
in a land where English is dominant and Spanish ethnic have brought about permanent changes in the
speaking habits of United States Hispanics to which
their non-American counterparts have never been totally exposed.[164]

MEXICAN-AMERICAN SPANISH. As has already been mentioned, many Mexican Americans in the Southwest found
themselves cut off from Mexican jurisdiction and language in a short period of time and continued to live
in the United States even though they retained their
strong Hispanic identity. Although the Mexicans who
continued to live in "Anglo" territory kept the lan-

guage and customs of their forefathers, the separation from Latin America brought about a series of
changes in lifestyle and, above all, language resulting from English interference and lack of reinforcement from native Spanish. The geographical expanse of the Southwest in which the Chicanos live is
quite large, and over the years, it was only natural
that a number of Mexican-American varieties of Spanish should evolve: Texan Spanish, New Mexican and
Southern Coloradan Spanish, Arizonan Spanish, and
Californian Spanish.165 Although Chicano Spanish
might be thought of as fairly uniform, there are local variations in lexicon with some minor differences in phonology and morphology. Whatever the differences, they are never significant enough to interfere with communication. For our purposes at least,
the term "American Spanish of the Southwest" or
"Chicano" is an adequate generic term embracing all
of the main variants indigenous to the area. Over
the past century, United States Hispanics have usually
been called "Spaniards" in New Mexico; in Texas,
"Latin Americans;" in California, "Mexican Americans." It is generally believed that the term "Chicano" derives from a form of the word "mexicano" although the exact etymology is open to question. The
terms "americanos," "gringos," and "gabachos" have
usually been reserved for members of the out-group,
frequently with derogative overtones. Originally
the term "Chicano" was associated with Spanish-
speaking persons of relatively low socio-economic
standing. With the more recent ethnic revolution and
the much favored return to one's roots, "Chicano"
has taken on more positive overtones since it is
identified with newly obtained power through ethnic
cohesiveness and movements for social and political
equality. The term "pochismo," based on a term of
derogation for Chicano--"Pocho," "Pocha"--refers to
a brand of American Spanish riddled with English influence both in lexicon and morphology. The term
"Pachuco" brings to mind the "zoot-suiter" culture of
the 1940's Chicano scene in and around El Paso,
Texas, but today it is usually identified with any
American-Spanish argot low on the social scale.166
"Tex-Mex," never a very popular term in anyone's

circle, is used to describe a mixture of Spanish and
English heard in many parts of Texas. Frequently,
like the term "pochismo," "Tex-Mex" tends to have
pejorative connotations.

MEXICAN-AMERICAN PHONOLOGY. Probably the most striking difference in phonology is the characteristically slower intonation pattern which is less rapid
than standard Spanish or even the normal Mexican cadence. Another important trait is the shift in
stress to the more open vowel with contiguous vowels.
For example, standard ahí is articulated ái, and such
examples abound in Chicano caer>cáir, Heloísa>Helói-
sa, maíz>máiz, país>páis, raíz>ráiz, océano>ociáno,
maestro>máistro, leído>léido, increíble>incréible.
What is more, there is the shift from standard penultimate stress to the antepenultimate, virtually
evolving a new rhythmic pattern. Commonly, traditional paroxytones become preparoxytones méndigo,
pántano, páliza, gáveta, cómeta, and many others.[167]
A similar shift occurs fairly regularly on a morphological level--the first person plural of the present subjunctive--váyamos, háigamos, siéntemos, mué-
ramos, puédamos, hiérvamos.

    Chicano has a number of vowel changes as well.
First and very striking is the simplification of
vowel clusters--ahorrar>orrar, ahorita>orita, ahor-
car>orcar, ahogarse>ogarse, extraordinario>extrordi-
nario, obediencia>obedensia, conciencia>concensia.
In a number of instances the reverse takes place in
that a diphthongization occurs where it is not normally heard as in dijieron, trayieron, dientista,
viejez.[168] An additional feature of vocalic change
is the shift from e>i in unstressed positions ano-
che>anochi, despedírse>despidirse, decir>disir, des-
pués>dispués, león>lión, señor>siñor, dirección>di-
ricción, manejar>manijar.[169] The reverse also takes
place frequently criatura>creatura, mismo>mesmo,
privilegio>previlegio, recibir>recebir, medicina>me-
decina, policía>polecía, decidir>decedir.[170] Most of
these changes occur sporadically in other parts of

the Spanish-speaking world--often a result of linguistic stagnation causing the retention of archaic
forms which normally disappear elsewhere.

The most noteworthy consonantal variation is
found either in the blending of b and v or in the
English labiodental articulation of v. A word like
varón is said either /bɛrʃn/ or /vɛrʃn/. The same
inconsistency is encountered in intervocalic positions lavar, levantar, and ubicar--/lɛbár/, and /lɛ-
vár/, /laβɛntár/ and /lavɛntár/, and /nɓɪkár/ and
/nvɪkár/. Initial sound combinations like bue- and
vue- are often replaced by güe- and we-, so words
like bueno and vuelo are often pronounced /qwén:/
and /qwél:/, /wen:/ and /wel:/. Initial f- is
often aspirated, yielding forms like huego, hue,
huerte, huites. Consonant d is lost frequently in a
number of positions: donde>onde; para donde>pa 'on-
de; libertad>libertá; virtud>virtú; merced>mercé, and
so on. One should not conclude that standard varieties are never heard, but in Chicano these changes
are frequent enough to be considered representative.

The voiced lateral fricative [l] is usually a
voiced palatal fricative [ʸ] in most of the New
World. Chicano is no exception in this case since
all instances of ll are automatically articulated
ye. However, in some cases the [ɟ] phoneme is heard
anillo>anío, aquella>aquea, tortilla>tortiya>tortía,
rodilla>rodiya>rodía, silla>siya>sía, caballo>caba-
yo>cabao, chiquitillo>chiquitiyo>chiquitío. Sporadically an intrusive nasal is also found tropezar>
trompezar, así>asina, nadie>naiden>naindie. In the
articulation of r two tendencies are observable. The
first r is an elongated phoneme similar to the typical non-vibrant American r as in señorrr, colorrr,
ardorrr. The other is the substitution for final l
as in delantar, plantanar, dentar, alimar (animal).
Consonant g frequently replaces initial or medial k
as in godornís, garraspear, desgote, gogote, güete.
In the combination -gn- the g disappears with regularity Inasio, inorante, persinarse, dino, fide-
dino. Similar to the loss of g is the tendency to
drop the phoneme k in the -ct- combination, a substandard practice found throughout much of the His-

panic world dotor, ator, letor, retor, perfeto, aspeto, sedutor, condutor. Another feature of Chicano is the articulation of the aspiration, which normally becomes a voiced pharyngeal aspirant--xalar, xalado, xeneral, xitano, xirasol. This sound occasionally occurs where there is no aspiration in standard Spanish xedondo, xerido.

In Chicano one encounters additions of syllables similar to epenthetic vowels--probar⟩aprobar, remendar⟩arremendar, figurarse⟩afigurarse, prestar⟩emprestar, comedido⟩acomedido, mejorar⟩amejorar, bastimentar⟩abastimentar, machar⟩amachar, orillarse⟩aorillarse, patalear⟩apataliar, prevenir⟩aprevenir.

Another trait is the rather extensive use of the adverbial intensifier in prefix form reque-, rede-, requete-, reteque-, a language practice found in the Caribbean and elsewhere. In Chicano this formation is quite common and often makes use of fixed forms, especially with bueno and malo: bueno⟩redebueno; retequebueno⟩requetebueno; malo⟩redemalo⟩retequemalo⟩ requetemalo.171

Other substitutions of various kinds are frequent, which reflects the retention of archaic forms estógamo, murciégalo, Grabiel, treato, hevrido. Loss of syllables is fairly frequent as well-- está⟩'sta⟩'ta, hacer⟩'cer, voy⟩vo, muy⟩mu, solo⟩so, ve ese⟩v'ese, la edad⟩l'edad, que él⟩qu'él.172 Occasionally there are obvious examples of English interference--mainly [æ] and [š] daiæmetro, gæsolina, æksidente, estrašion, šerife.173

CHICANO MORPHOLOGY AND SYNTAX. Traditional Spanish constructions often undergo considerable English influence. For example, the omission of the definite and indefinite articles is common. In standard compra un cepillo y una escoba, the articles are essential. But in Chicano practice the same utterance is expressed without the articles. A similar example

284

is standard escribe los secretos a su amiga, which is
expressed by omission of the article. Frequently the
possessive adjectives are used with parts of the body
and articles of clothing--generally obviated in standard Spanish by means of reflexive forms. Utterances
like lavo mi cabeza, quita su chaqueta, pone su abrigo, and me lavo mis manos are clear examples of interference. Prenominal placement of adjectives is
also common as in mala consciencia, muchos tiempos,
mi tiempo vino.

Word formations which combine several roots are
not atypical. The verbs atropellar and trompillar
both mean to trample upon, but the Chicano variant is
atrompillar. Caribajo, downcast, derives from standard cariacontecido and cabizbajo. Conociencia
brings together conciencia and conocimiento. Plázamo,
mo, congratulations, is a combination of pláceme and
pésamo (pésame?). Resquisito is apparently derived
from requisito and exquisito.[174]

Many verb-forms are based on English roots which
enter the language in the first conjugation. Thus,
English to wreck>arrequiar; to average>averagear; to
leak>likear; to lick>liquiar; to loaf>lofiar; to have
lunch>lonchar; to manage>manachear; to mop>mapear; to
miss>mistar; to open>openear; to watch>guachar; to
report>reportar. The shift e>i and vice versa in
verbs ending in -ear and -iar is typical--acarrear>
acarriar, apalear>apaliar, besuquear>besuquiar, de-
sear>desiar, golpear>golpiar, copiar>copear, cam-
biar>cambear.

Verbs in Chicano exhibit some few anomalies and
preserve a number of archaisms. The infinitive forms
often have a change in an unstressed vowel or completely different stress caer>cáir, creer>crer, le-
er>ler, describir>descrebir, escribir>escrebir, reír>
rir, sonreír>sonrir. Aspirated initial sounds are
also frequent in certain infinitives jayar, jervir,
juir, juyir, jalar, jincar. Diphthongizations in infinitives are also characteristic of this speech--ca-
yer, creyer, leyer, oyir, sonreyir, trayer, huyir,
juyir. In addition, there are inconsistencies in the

285

past participle--often regularized--juvido, oyido, cayido, pidido, morido, murido, escrebido, descrebido.

The present indicative has a number of irregular forms: ser (so, eres, es, semos, son), salir (salo, sales, sale, salemos, salen), traer (trago, trais, trai, traimos, train), saber (sapo (sabo), sabes, sabe, sabemos, saben), caber (cabo (capo), cabes, cabe, cabemos, caben), poder (podo, podes, pode, puedemos, poden), oler (ole (hole), olen (holen)). There is also a marked tendency toward a shift from third- to second-conjugation verb-endings, especially first-person plural forms pidemos, escribemos, salemos, sintemos, vivemos.

The future and conditional forms often have an intrusive -d- not normally heard in the standard language. Third-person forms like traerá, querrá, caerá often become traidrá, quedrá, caidrá with the accompanying reduction of the pretonic vowel. From time to time, the intrusive consonant is heard throughout all persons. The conditional may retain the intrusive consonant as well, but not always-- quería and quedría, cairía and caedría, trairía and traedría. Frequently these forms are in competition with more standard forms.

The imperfect indicative is fairly standard except for the retention of archaic forms: ser (sía, sían), ver (vía, vían), pedir (pidía, pidían), poder (pudía, pudían), dormir (durmía, durmían), caer (cayía, cayían). Like some peninsular dialects, Chicano retains the intervocalic -b- of the imperfect sporadically--caer (caíba, caíban), traer (traíba, traíban).

The chief characteristic of the preterite is the addition of a final -s in the second person singular--often accompanied by the loss of a post-tonic sibilant--hablastes and hablates, llegastes and llegates, llamastes and llamates. Although there are inconsistencies, most verbs in this tense follow the general pattern, frequently with alternate forms,

but the main departure from the norm appears to be
in the second person singular. Occasionally, standard irregular verbs are regularized as in andar
(andé, andastes, andates, andó, andamos, andaron).
In other cases archaic verb-forms are retained as in
traer (truje, trujistes, trujites, trujo, trujimos,
trujeron, trujieron) and ver (vide, vistes, vites,
vido, vimos, vieron). Frequently the third-person
root of radical-changing forms is used throughout
dormir (durmí, durmiste(s)), pedir (pidí, pidiste(s)),
sentir (sintí, sintiste(s)). From time to time, the
opposite phenomenon also takes place venir (vení,
veniste(s)). Normally, the verb ser is articulated
with harsh or medial aspiration--juí, juiste(s), jui-
tes, jue, juimos, jueron or hui, huiste(s), huite,
hue, huimos, hueron.[175]

The present subjunctive also retains archaic
forms, in most cases by analogy with cáir, caiga,
yielding analogous forms like vaiga (ir), haiga (hacer), creiga (creer), veiga (ver).[176] Often the root
of the present subjunctive is regularized as it is in
the indicative saber (saba, sabas), caber (caba, ca-
bas), oler (hola, holan). The shift in stress to the
first syllable in all first-person plural forms is
typical, often with an alternate form in -n- hervir:
hiérvamos, hiérvanos; poder: puédamos, puédanos;
ser: séamos, séanos; oír: óigamos, óiganos; salir:
sálgamos, sálganos; traer: tráigamos, tráiganos.

The imperfect subjunctive contains regularized
forms as a general rule caber (cabiera, cabieras),
andar (andara, andaras). More often than not, the
diphthongized forms of the preterite are carried
over into this tense decir (dijiera), traer (trajie-
ra, trayera, trujiera, and truyera). Although the
-se variant is heard in rare instances, it is safe to
say that it usually disappears.

English interference is also evident in certain
aspects of syntax. For example, the use of progressive forms is closer to English usage. In an utterance like "they are working hard day and night,"
standard language uses the simple present ("trabajan

287

duro día y noche"), whereas the Chicano variant definitely favors the progressive form ("están trabajando duro día y noche"). Consequently, it is not unusual to hear utterances like "están estudiando inglés," "está comiendo demasiado," "están viviendo bien," "está bajando temprano," "están saliendo con frecuencia."

Many cases of English influence are found in the area of prepositions. English syntax is clearly echoed in statements like esperar POR el taxi, pagar PARA la escuela, pagar POR los libros, mandar PARA atrás, subir PARA arriba, hacer su mente PARA arriba. On the other hand, cases of omitted prepositions in which the standard variety requires them are also frequent. English interference is obvious in examples like "vuele TWA," "va Pan Am," "entra el cuarto," "entran el coche."

Idiomatic expressions abound in Chicano either as forms deriving from English or as modes of expressions extended from standard forms. Many times, the expressions have no real meaning for the monolingual speaker of Spanish, or, at best, they sound somewhat peculiar. The influence of English is obvious in such expressions as ir al servicio (to go into the service), mostrar el mejor lado (to show one's best side), buscarle a alguien por su lado (to approach someone from his/her good side), levantar aceite (to blow off steam), levantar el alarme/la alarma (to raise an alarm), hacer tiempo (to do time), tener una buena llorada (to have a good cry), calle de una vía (one-way street), el viaje redondo (the round-trip ticket), lo único tiempo (the only time), tomar ventaja (to take advantage of), tener lengua grande (to have a big mouth). Other types of idioms are extensions of standard forms. Standard estar constipado (constreñido) is said estar tapado. The common expression levantarle el ánimo a alguien is generally rendered darle un levantón a alguien. Ser tonto or torpe is commonly andar lencho. Tener mala suerte is rendered tocarle la de malas a alguien. The fairly universal estar enamorado is achieved by means of the play on words andar lana Morado. Mur-

murar or desacreditar is normally replaced by bullir
la lengua. No hacer caso de or dejar de lado a is
frequently rendered tirar a león a. Llevar a pleito
is most often, though not universally, expressed as
meter a la ley or en la ley.

MEXICAN-AMERICAN LEXICON. Of all the areas of interference, the one most deeply affected is the lexicon.
Since word-object relationships are the most elemental and the most easily influenced by another language, the number of possibilities is immense. An
attempt has been made to focus upon the most representative ones, not according to the linguistic type
in question, but from the point of view of areas of
daily use.[177]

Words related to household activities and routine existence are interesting since they are often
rather graphic. Many examples are found in the
eating habits of the Chicano population--arvejón
(chick pea), atole (a drink of cornmeal, water, and
sugar), planta de huevo (eggplant), birria (beer),
malamé (chicken feed), machito (a chitterling-type
dish), tatema (roast meat), tomate de fresadilla
(cherry tomato), torque and torquí (turkey), aceite
(oil of any type), tomatera (a tomato packing factory), masero (vendor of readymade dough), vanela
(vanilla), vegetables (greens). Lamprear or lampriar
is used to express standard asar, to roast, as well
as the concept of covering a roast with an egg bat-
ter. A tortilla de azúcar is a flour tortilla pre-
pared as a dessert crepe; tortillero and tortillería,
vendor and store respectively. Items of clothing
have some interesting versions as follows: tarecua,
shoe; tarlango, hat; tacuche, suit; toxido, tuxedo;
mancornía, mancornilla, and manguernía, cufflinks;
paño, handkerchief. Londre and londri refer to the
room in which clothes are washed while sinc and sinque indicate basin or tub. Pinche is an obviously
more expedient version of gancho para la ropa,
clothespin. Other household items include barredora
eléctrica (vacuum cleaner), laira (cigarette lighter),

abanico eléctrico (electric fan), puela (frying pan),
plaga (plug), alevador (elevator), pipas del agua or
del gas (water or gas pipes), tejabana (dilapidated
house). The term pelar normally conveys giving or
getting a haircut. All forms of mouthwash, regardless of origin or brand, are known as listerina.
Polvear or polviar signifies the powdering of one's
face, polvero(a) being any type of powder puff. A
peinador is a vanity table, and pintura pa' las uñas,
nail polish.

Terms for the layman's medical problems and
household remedies are quite common. For example,
anemia is said sangre débil. The expression sentir
bascas runs the gamut of feelings from nausea to gag-
ging. Any kind of tumor is generally known as a ta-
cotillo; any type of ulcer, an úrzula. Intestinal
blockage and related physical problems are expressed
as tripa ida. A torzón is sharp intestinal pain, and
riuma covers most types of rheumatic pain. The standard term for navel, ombligo, is articulated umbligo.
The curious word óvulos is a generic term for vaginal
suppositories. Words like aspirina, Buferín, Anacín,
Entoral, Kaopectate, Kleenex, Kotex, Tampón are,
needless to say, universal.

Lexicon related to social activities and community affairs is quite extensive. There is almost
universal acceptance of such non-Hispanic terms as
party, drink, cocktail, coctel, cóctel, highball, and
jaibol. Most types of parade are called parada instead of desfile. The word borlo is often understood
to mean blast or wild party. A tamalada is a social
gathering in which there is a tamale bake or in which
tamales are served. Many Chicano terms have evolved
to fill in gaps for word-images which are non-existent in Latin society--niña de las flores (flower
girl), banquetear (to banquet), trabajanta and senta-
dora (baby-sitter), alimonía (alimony), birth control.
Other terms resulting from the convergence of Hispanic and Anglo society are gabachado, aculturado,
abolillado, which describe individuals with gringo
characteristics or leanings, and marca, a person os-
tracized by his peers or by Chicano society in gene-

290

ral.

Many terms having to do with sports and similar
activities have been assimilated in different ways.
Words like ring, foul, volleyball, football, baseball, coach, bat, ball, hockey, tennis, golf, field,
diamond, game, and others are used daily with or
without phonological accomodations. A referee is
known as a réfer or a referé. Noquear, noquiar, dri-
blear, dribliar, pichar, batear, batiar are obvious
Hispano-American adaptations of basic American verbs.
A hockista is a hockey player; beisbolero, baseball
player; futbolero, football player. Jumrón, junrón,
jomrón, and jonrón are used for the all-American
homerun, whereas upper cut and opercut are in competition with each other.

Technological advances have also brought about
numerous borrowings. Standard paragolpe is discarded
in favor of bompa and búmper. Caboose is preferred
to standard furgón. Pompa and pompear have replaced
standard bomba and bombear. Traque is the term for
railroad track, replacing the less expedient vía del
ferrocarril. The Spanish gato (jack) has yielded to
yaque and yec. Aer careft is an obvious adaptation
of the American-English aircraft. Treilon (tractor
trailer) is substituted for the lengthier tractoca-
mión or semi-remolque. Similarly, the word treilona
supplants standard camión (truck). Still other lexical items are obvious cases of extensions of traditional meanings: manejera (handlebars), manejador
(manager), manea (brake), llorona (patrol car or fire
engine), llantas blancas (white wall tires), lumbrero
(fireman), tuerca (monkey wrench). The term vidriera
is used to convey windshield (standard parabrisas).

In a world dominated by drug culture, it is natural that borrowings of this type should come into
being. The word gramo is a packet of heroin; gorra
or cachuca, heroin capsule; un glufo, a "high" (from
sniffing glue); el glufo, glue sniffer; jaipo, needle; leña, marihuana; leñito or grifo, reefer; estu-
fear, to sniff; azufre, heroin; toque, puff. Based
on the latter is the curious compound buscatoques

291

(junkie in need of a fix). An equally interesting compound is maricocaimorfi (person addicted to marihuana, cocaine, and morphine), which has nearly the same degree of frequency as the more standard generic equivalents (drogadicto, adicto a drogas, morfinómano). Fremar is the jargon expression meaning to frame--an excellent example of English interference. Policemen in this ambience are known popularly as tecolotes or azules. The common expression andar tirriado has the force of going about "high" from sniffing paint.

COLORFUL CHICANO SPEECH. The layman is quick to observe that slang, vulgarisms, and taboo expressions enter one's speech early in the learning process, and Chicano is no exception in this sense. Often such language derives from extensions of significations of common lexical items and expressions. For example, the perfectly innocent word madre or madrecita often takes on the force of a shapely, sexy woman. ¡Qué padre madre! is used to connote a gorgeous hunk of a woman. The term manoseadera (manosiadera) connotes handling a woman in sexual foreplay. By extension, manoseador (manosiador) describes a male in sexual activity, and manoseada (manosiada), a woman engaged in sexual activity. Words like huega, mariposa, matriz, huila, güila, huilacha, choteada, chotiada, bofa, huiza are normally used as synonyms of puta--whore or bitch. A marrana cuina is taboo for fat, old bitch. There are many derogatory terms for male homosexuals--manflor, chupón, chupacharcos, forihuán, forito, cuarentaidós, cuarentaiuno, mamalón, jotingo, joto, pípilo. The female counterpart is manflora, chupona, jota, or mamalona. The words flor and florindo have the meaning of pansy. The term fifi usually signifies effeminate male, and all of its derivations have similar connotations fifiriche, fifirincho, fifirucho.

There are indeed countless vulgar and taboo expressions related to sex, as one might expect. The vulgar verb chingar connotes to copulate and to cheat,

292

and its meaning is frequently extended to signify to
get what one is after. The very strong appellation
hijo de la chingada (SOB) can have a good deal of
emotional impact. The popular expression mandar a la
chingada, somewhat less taboo, is generally used to
mean to go to hell in no uncertain terms. "¿Qué
chingados quieres?" is heard regularly and is vaguely
equivalent to "what the hell do you want?" The vulgar words chile, tronco, pinga, and picha all refer
on this level to the male organ. Chicago, an interesting combination of chi and cago, is used popularly
to indicate john or restroom. The verb lamer (to
suck) and its Chicano variant, lamber, are important
sources of taboo and vulgar expressions. Thus, the
words lambión, lambiona can convey the meaning of apple polisher or much worse. The compounds lambecu-
los and lambehuevos are much more graphically descriptive and are basically synonymous with strong
versions of lambión. The terms lambeache, lambiache,
lambiche, lameache, and lamache are popular variants
of the same vulgar concept. The word linda on this
level can often mean the female organ, and quitar la
linda verges on the taboo meaning to deflower. The
common term for menstruation is luna, estar mala de
la luna extending itself to mean to have one's period. The verbs sanamabichar and sanamagoniar are vulgar forms meaning to call someone a son of a gun or
much worse. Various forms of the verb levantar are
given special connotations in this type of language:
levantada, pick-up; pura levantada, real pick-up; le-
vante, making sexual contact. The verb largar is
normally used to mean to skip out on or abandon, and
a largada is a woman abandoned by her mate.

PACHUCO. As has already been stated, "pachuco" is an
argot which derived from popular Chicano Spanish in
the area of El Paso and Juarez. A person from El Paso is popularly called a Del pachuco, a term originated among grifos or marihuana smokers and peddlers in
the Texas underworld. Eventually this code language
spread throughout the Southwest and became popular
among Filipinos, Negroes, and young Chicanos of the

293

"zoot-suiter" culture of the 1940's, which eventually spread as far as Los Angeles.[178]

Pachuco slang is probably based upon the dialect
of Southern Arizona with considerable interference
from American slang and underworld expressions. Many
of its lexical elements are good examples of borrowings on the most popular of levels.[179] Compare the
following Pachuco versions of the more standard Spanish or English:

PACHUCO	ENGLISH	SPANISH
birria	beer	cerveza
bonque	bunk	camita
bonquiar	to sleep (bunk)	dormir
buri	very	muy, mucho
fila	file, blade	navaja, cuchillo
guachar	to watch	mirar
ganga	gang	pandilla
controlar	to control	dominar
sanga	song	canción[180]

As is typical of speakers of jargons or code languages, many of the lexical forms and idiomatic expressions either fall into oblivion or become accepted local speech. Many speakers of Pachuco are
young people who do not identify with American, Mexican, or Chicano society as such and who in many cases
have identity problems. Moreover, in many cases they
are opposed to maintaining Mexican-American social,
cultural, and personal values and thus remain a rejected subgroup within an ethnic minority.

PUERTO RICAN SPANISH. Puerto Ricans living in the
United States run the gamut from successful professionals to large numbers of functional illiterates.
Those who enjoy a more elevated socioeconomic status
tend to be absorbed more easily into the American social setting while those who are on the lower end of
the social scale usually live together in very poor
barrios. Approximately 1.3 million Puerto Ricans

live in greater New York City--most often in East
Harlem, the Lower East Side, Brooklyn's Williams-
burg ghetto or in the South Bronx--and about a half
million live in the northeastern section of the
United States and in Florida, Chicago, and California.[181] Many were born on the Island while others
were born in any one of the ghettos to which they
seem fated. A goodly number have established permanent residence on the Mainland, and almost as many
travel to Puerto Rico and back regularly. Needless
to say, of all American Hispanics the Puerto Ricans
tend to be lowest on the socioeconomic scale and seem
to be plagued by the greatest number of social and
economic problems. Among dwellers in the various
barrios, family life is often extremely unstable--
generally in dismal dwellings headed by a single parent.[182] Many important studies have been done on
life in the barrio, most often from a sociological
point of view.[183] However, with the notable exception of the praiseworthy study on bilingualism by
Joshua Fishman,[184] little has been done to date on
the Puerto Rican use of Spanish in the United States
from a linguistic vantage point. As a result of increased ethnic awareness and social consciousness on
the part of some Puerto Ricans, a number of writers
are attempting either in fiction or in fictionalized
autobiographies to give first-hand accounts of the
grim existence of people forced to dwell in the barrio.[185] While it is true that linguistic developments are often a reflection of social and economic
change, many aspects of Puerto Rican Spanish have
been treated only superficially and much remains to
be done in this area of investigation. On the other
hand, it would be naive to expect the growth and development of the speech of Chicanos from the Puerto
Ricans since the latter have been on the Mainland in
any significant way for only about four decades.
Moreover, while Puerto Rican Spanish has been analyzed as an aspect of the growth and development of
the language in the Caribbean, the speech of Mainland Puerto Ricans has not had the centuries of
contact with English in the United States enjoyed by
their Mexican-American counterparts. The Puerto Rican situation should be viewed linguistically from

the following points of focus: relative linguistic proficiency in general; prevalent attitudes toward both languages or either; the native, non-native, or immigrant status of the speakers. All of these aspects are important factors in the analysis of bilingualism.[186]

THE SPANISH LANGUAGE AND PUERTO RICANS. Due to the obvious pressure of the Anglo-dominant educational curricula on the Island and the almost total immersion in American English in the United States, there is a gray zone in this version of the language in which Americanisms are frequent. This group is not alone in this experience since much of Latin America shares the same linguistic plight to one extent or another. For example, words like gringo (yanqui), plomero (fontanero), blofero (fanfarrón), criollo (natural de América) are not merely the result of English interference. Instead, they reflect the need to express certain concepts which are either absent in traditional Spanish or which have little frequency. Other developments are a result of the need to express new word-image relationships as in batata (bulbo comestible de la batata), turpial (pájaro americano), tusa (zuro de maíz), ardilla (clase de castaño), to mention only a few. In addition, there are newly coined verbs reflecting English influence--auspiciar (patrocinar), batear (fusilar), programar (proyectar), responsabilizar (hacer responsable), sesionar (reunirse oficialmente), antipatizar (sentir o causar antipatía), ultimar (matar), vivar (aclamar), desmanchar (limpiar).[187] There are also interesting compounds whose use is not limited to Puerto Rico--codo duro (tacaño), matasanos, matavivos, and sangrías (medicastro, medicucho), comemierda (pendejo, esnob), aguafiestas (persona que turba los regocijos ajenos), salsipuedes (callejón sin salida, barrio bajo), trotaconventos (alcahueta).

Whatever the social class, level of education, and type of background, the boricuas or boricanos (Taino for inhabitant of Puerto Rico) retain a basic-

ally Latin view of life with an essentially positive
mode of vision in which most people are accepted as
buena gente. When they falter, with or without dignity, they exclaim "¡ay bendito!" (or even "¡ay maldito!") and hasten to provide themselves with the
reasons for their difficulties--por esto, por eso,
por aquello or qué sé yo, qué sé yo cuánto (for
Heaven knows what reason), seeking always a plausible
explanation for their frequent dilemmas. Many are
torn between deeply entrenched Catholic moral, spiritual, and psychological values and the dream of
American capitalism. The picture is further complicated by sporadic Afro-Caribbean beliefs and superstitions. They strive to remain a proud people,
seeking not the machinations of colmilludos (dishon-
est politicians) and buchiplumas (pretentious persons), but a world which is indeed ¡chévere! (African for wonderful, great). Many of them are not in
quest of hand-outs from continentales (mainland Americans); instead, they avidly seek a middle ground in
which all of the problems of the clash between the
Old and New Worlds somehow find their solutions. In
short, they make every effort to hold their heads
high despite the obvious lack of chabo (money). They
are "New World" enough to be cognizant of the differences of race and gente de color (colored people) and
Spanish enough to attempt to confront the many issues
facing them with dignity and equanimity. When faced
with such issues, they often lift their hands heaven-
ward and pronounce their age-old answer to such prob-
lems--"el que no tiene dinga tiene mandinga."[188] The
particular flavor and intonation of Puerto Rican
Spanish are very pleasant. Indeed the version of the
language spoken on the Island is often a matter of
socioeconomic background and education rather than
any intrinsic "correctness" or "incorrectness" per
se. Many aspects of Island speech are carried over
into the Hispanic communities in the United States,
but the degree of transfer and resistance to English
interference is directly related to language consciousness and loyalty which are more a result of individual linguistic sensitivity and formal training
than other linguistic traits.[189]

MAINLAND PUERTO RICAN PHONOLOGY. The phonology of
Puerto Rican speakers in the United States has certain features resulting from Island speech habits as
well as English interference. These are found primarily in the areas of vocalic and consonantal production.

Vowels which are considerably open like [ɛ],
[ɔ], and [ʊ] tend to lose their openness when followed by the liquid r in closed syllables. There are
many such examples--[bérdə], [klérᵏ], [sérdᴐ], [bér-
bᴐ], [lérdᴐ], [férı], [nᴧyórᵏ], [kórtᴐ], [qórdᴐ],
[sórdᴐ], [tórpə], [búrlɛ], [kúrsᴐ], [túrnᴐ], [fᴧrnı-
túrɛ].190 Initial /e/ followed by a nasal tends to
be articulated weakly or is absorbed, so a word like
enfermo is produced either as [ᴧɱférmᴐ] or [ɱférmᴐ];
entierro>[ᴧⁿtjéfᴐ] or [ⁿtjéfᴐ]; enlace>[ᴧnlásə] or
[nlásə]. Perhaps the influence of English is even
more obvious in the articulation of medial a--pala-
talized before velar sounds as in [bák], [mãǽqᴐ], [lá-
qᴐ], [trᴁǽqᴐ], [tráкˢ], [fᴁáкaᵗ]. Often initial weak
vowels are reduced--[əsкúrᴐ], [əmíqᴐ], [ıléⁿɛ], [ᴧnı-
wéi].191 Other variations in vocalic production are
also found in the speech of the Island.192

The articulation of consonants coincides with
Island pronunciation although some minor divergences
are encountered. Here, in Puerto Rico, more often
than not, sibilants are produced with varying degrees of nasalization; that is to say, esta cesta
ehta cehta or ejta cejta. These nasalizations are
typical of the Caribbean--ehto/ejto, dehde/dejde,
ehtán/ejtán, ehtudia/ejtudia, ehtéril/ejtéril, ehta-
ble/ejtable. While this practice continues in Puerto Rican, the influence of English often produces an
exaggeration in the articulation of sibilants--eSta,
ceSta, eSto, deSde, eStán, eStudia, eStéril, eStable.
The same takes place with the articulation of l as a
velar [ł] in lieu of the normally alveolar sound [l].
Instances such as [fáⁱdɛ], [eⁱfıⁱér], [eⁱdéɛ], [áⁱ-
tᴐ], [blókə], [pᴐlíˢ] are good examples of interfer-
ence.193

The production of r is rather unique both on the

298

Island and the Mainland. Typical of certain areas of
Puerto Rico and Cuba, uvular or dorsal velar r [ř̃]
has a very high frequency. Typically, the single and
multiple vibrations give way to a very posterior or
guttural consonant--[kářɔ], [pɔtɔř̃ɔ], [ɛʃř̃ɛ], [sɛ́ř̃ɔ].
This velar dorsal r is heard a great deal, ranging
from exclusive use to very sporadic occurrences. Also typical of Puerto Rico is the originally Andalusian substitution r>l and l>r. Observe the shifts in
these consonants

	r>l		l>r
harto	[kált:]	caldo	[kárdɔ]
pardo	[pǎˑldɔ]	balde	[bárða]
puerto	[pwéltɔ]	último	[úrtımɔ]
marca	[málkɛ]	alfombra	[ɛrfɔ́mbrɛ]
dorso	[dɔ́ʃsɔ]	quitar	[kıtáʔ]

The more retroflex r /ř̃/ might be viewed as a result
of interference on the Island in most cases and as a
carry-over to the Mainland--[řářɔ], [ářmı], [ř̃ıʔıʔt],
[řɛ́ɔı], [ř̃ʑlı].[194]

The inconsistency of the articulation of b and v
(be grande and be pequeña) is another instance of English interference. Traditionally, one makes no distinction between orthographic b and v, but Puerto Ricans vacillate between the bilabial and the labiodental articulations as a result of obvious interference. Observe the following possibilities:

Word	Standard Spanish	Puerto Rican Spanish
tuvo	[túβɔ]	[túβɔ] or [túvɛ]
vaca	[bákɛ]	[bákɛ] or [vákɛ]
verde	[bérðə]	[bérðə] or [vérðə]
vaina	[bájnɛ]	[bájnɛ] or [vájnɛ]
nave	[náβə]	[náβə] or [návə]
navy	_____	[néjβı] or [néjvı]
groovy	_____	[qrúβı] or [qrúvı]
vano	[bánɔ]	[bánɔ] or [vánɔ]
lavado	[lɛβáˑɔ]	[lɛβáˑɔ] or [lɛváˑɔ]
avería	[ɛβəríɛ]	[ɛβəríɛ] or [ɛvəríɛ]

MAINLAND PUERTO RICAN MORPHOLOGY. Morphological changes are frequently linked with uses of word formations which seldom have any real meaning for monolingual speakers of Spanish. Such forms are used with the appropriate grammatical application, but their phonemic version is frequently distorted as in ⌐crájt˥, ⌐səkəŋhánd˥, ⌐qʌɓáj˥, ⌐sᵊlóŋ˥, ⌐šᵊɾóp˥, ⌐ajmín˥, ⌐wanwéy˥. These expressions are good examples of the impact which language contact can have upon common speech since they are often used without the speakers' awareness of code switching.

The verb-forms adapted to the Spanish sound system are probably the most outstanding morphological variations. Many of these are simply English verbs Hispanized with or without phonetic changes in the English root.

English	Puerto Rican Spanish
to back (up)	bakear
to bluff	blofear
to hold up	holopear
to vacuum	vacunear
to heat	heatear
to freeze	frezear
to clip	clipear
to type	taipear
to check	chequear
to watch	wachar
to wax	waxear
to leak	likear
to mop	mopear
to weld	weldear
to talk	tokear[195]

Syntax is also affected by contact with English. For example, the omission of the definite article in standard positions is a clear case of intrusion--"ella tiene ojos braun," "el muchacho pone manos en el vidrio," "el hombre paga cuentas con cheques."[196] In the same way, the indefinite article may function as a pronoun not normally required in standard Spanish-- "el plan parecía uno muy costoso," "la casa daba la impresión de ser una muy grande," "el carro que com-

300

pró era uno muy caro."[197]

While standard Spanish admits prenominal and postnominal adjectival placement as in el chico po-bre and el pobre chico with differing meanings or nu-ances, the influence of English is such that prenomi-nal placement often follows the non-Hispanic pattern, such as el alto costo de la vida, esto es un rush job, el pasado año, la pasada semana, quiere un jamón sandwich.[198] One might argue that these are not only examples of adjectival placement but rather incorpor-ations of entire English expressions and lexicon. However, on this level it is difficult to determine exactly at which point one aspect ends and the other begins.

A word frequently misplaced is como. In expres-sing to know how (Spanish saber + complementary in-finitive), como is never utilized. The addition of this adverb is pure English syntax, and this con-struction is heard quite often: él sabe hablar in-glés>él sabe como hablar inglés; ella sabe cocinar> ella sabe como cocinar.

Undesirable or ambiguous uses of the present participle are observable in the speech of many Spanish speakers, but in the case of Puerto Ricans, English contact seems to reinforce such construc-tions. For example, "un libro conteniendo seleccio-nes de las mejores novelas" is used in place of stan-dard "un libro que contiene;" "era un hombre de baja estatura, color trigueño, tostado del sol, vistiendo pantalones de dril" instead of "que vestía;" "la ca-bellera flotando al viento" in place of "que flota-ba;" "la ley asignando la suma de cien mil dólares" in lieu of "que asignaba;" "un cofre de madera con-teniendo tierra puertorriqueña" in place of "que con-tiene."[199] These constructions are not explained solely on the level of interference since there is a tendency in Spanish, in practice if not in theory, to be much more casual about the use and placement of participles. Whatever the origin, this calque from English seems to flow more smoothly than some other more standard constructions.

Progressive forms like estoy haciendo, estaré hojeando, iba paseándose, estuvo mirando, vendría mejorando, vaya diciendo, viniera contando are part and parcel of everyday speech. However, Spanish syntax avoids such forms with semiauxiliary verbs (querer, deber, poder), verbs of obligation (tener que, verse obligado), of supposition (haber de, deber de), and ser, estar, and ir. Nonetheless, the periphrastic use of ser, estar siendo followed by the past participle in the passive voice, is not atypical in Puerto Rican. An utterance like "la casa está siendo pintada" ("the house is being painted") is a form rejected by standard norms which require a pseudo-passive construction in such cases ("se pinta la casa," "se está pintando la casa") or a true passive construction ("la casa es pintada por el carpintero"). Other examples of this type of construction are: "el edificio está siendo demolido" (in place of "se demuele el edificio"); "la fruta estaba siendo comida por los gusanos" (instead of "era comida por"); "los cursos están siendo desarrollados con precisión" (in lieu of "se están desarrollando"); "el programa de música está siendo considerado por las autoridades" (instead of "es considerado por"); "su última publicación ya está siendo olvidada" (in place of "se está olvidando").[200] Related to this use of progressive forms is the use of the latter with extended time value--once more a clear case of English interference. Utterances like "le estoy mandando el paquete por correo" are heard in place of "le mando el paquete por correo," and "José está trabajando en el banco" is used in lieu of "José trabaja en el banco."

PUERTO RICAN LEXICON IN THE UNITED STATES. English interference is extremely common in the lexicon of most Puerto Ricans on the Mainland. In some instances, lexical items are extensions of the significations of traditional words, and in others totally new meanings are given to standard Spanish vocabulary as in factoría (factory), unión (labor union), récord (record, disc), cuarto (quarter), pie (twelve inches), metro (parking meter).[201] Many forms of American cur-

rency and units of measurement are assimilated totally or partially as Spanish words moni (money), cuora and peseta (quarter). The words daime and vellón
(old Spanish coin) are given the meaning of dime.
Similarly incorporated words are níkel, níquel, peni,
yarda, galón, busel, token and tokensito, and tostón
(half dollar). Many terms referring to cars, automo-
tive parts, and related topics are obvious phonetic
renderings of English words supplanting more traditional terms--carro (for auto, automóvil, coche),
troc (for camión or camioneta), tope (for techo), es-
tárter (for arranque), raid (for paseo), ribersa (for
contramarcha, marcha atrás), fénder (for guardafango,
guardabarro), breke or breque (for freno). Other
examples of this type of carry-over are grosería
(grocery), marqueta (market), tíket (ticket), bil
(bill), rufo (roof), mubi (movie), šo (show), bos,
bosa (boss), asemblijol (assembly hall)--most of
which are simply non-existent in standard Spanish.

Terms related to housing and living quarters are
also taken in as Hispanized English terms at various
stages of assimilation--cuarto fornido (furnished
room), bórdin (boarding house), bordante (boarder),
lanlord, lanledi, sink, tóilet, tob (tub), clóset
(closet), windo (window), eskrín or ejcrín (screen),
blain (blinds), benšembláin (Venetian blinds), yarda,
set (TV set), silin (ceiling), pláster (plaster),
cárpet (carpet), chinero (china closet), cuilta
(quilt), blanket or frisa (blanket), plag (plug), só-
ket (socket), stim or estim (steam), estimhit or
stimhit (steam heat), fornas (furnace), kol (coal),
beismen (basement), faireskeip (fire escape), súper
(superintendent), párler (parlor), bildin (building).

Words used having to do with articles of clothing are also frequent although many of these are used
popularly elsewhere. Frequently, names of synthetic
fabrics are assimilated variously as in nailan (for
nilón), poliéster (for poliester), waš en wer (for de
fibras sintéticas), reyón (for rayón). Other terms
on this level are oberoles (overalls), ko or co
(coat), eslípers (slippers), payamas (pajamas), sué-
ter and suerita (sweater), síper (zipper), yin

303

(jeans), sai (size), sute (suit).

Names of foods also reflect considerable American influence--sereales (cereals), cornfleika (cornflakes), donas (doughnuts), rollos (rolls), keik and keke (cake), pay (pie), candi (candy), chuingón (chewing gum), pikles (pickles), aiscrim (ice cream), sonde (sundae), yelo (jello), pudin (pudding), frankfurters (frankfurters), hot dog and perro caliente (hot dog), bequin (baking powder), yin (gin), scoch (Scotch), wiski (whiskey).

Sports terms reflect the popularity of such activities. These are in the main pure loans with little or no phonological change--hit, béisbol, fúbol, básquetbol, straik, ring, fil (field), flay, ron or run (run), suímimpul, pícer and pícer, cácer and cácer. Many verbs come into the language reflecting obvious English roots such as trainear, bowlear, straiquear, cacear and cacear, picear and picear. As might be expected in both cultures, these lexical borrowings have a high frequency. On the illegal side of things, a bolita is a numbers game.

Drug culture is one of the activities carried over into the ghettos where they reach epidemic proportions. A tecato or moto is a drug addict or junkie; estofa, stuff, drugs, narcotics. The word bate is used for drugs in general, and yerba is usually grass or marijuana. A joint is called a grifo, moto, or peto; a cura, any type of fix. Any person who is arrebatao is high on drugs, and a trip in this sense is a gira. The word trip itself is a pure loan, from which the verb tripear is derived. The verb disparar is the term heard most often to convey to shoot up drugs. In this ambience limpio connotes clean, without drugs on one's person, and chotas refers to squealers or rats.

The area of vulgar and taboo language is in no way diminished in the barrios. The term hijo de (la gran) puta (SOB) is extremely common on this level, while pato, chingona, corbejo, cabra, cabrita, gata, cheva, tusa, and guisa range in meaning from discreet

304

to not-so-discreet whore. A tetona (teta, breast) refers to an attractive woman with large breasts. A
mamota, flama, or condominia normally has the force
of beautiful woman, and hembrota, a sexy one. The
basic term for homosexual is pato (male) and pata
(female). In addition, the nouns loca, marica, and
mariquita mean queen, and maricón, queer. The terms
tortillera and cachapera are vulgar use for female
homosexuals. The expression tener sello is used to
express being a dead giveaway in the homosexual
sense. The ubiquitous cabrón basically means a
cuckold or complaisant husband but is often extended
on this level to mean buck or stud--similar to a güe-
bon or huevón. In the same way, a mistress of a married man may be called an izquierda. The taboo verb
to have intercourse is joder, but the latter is often
replaced by chingar, chichar, or echar polvo. The
adjectives jodido or chingado have the semantic force
of screwed or messed up, and jodienda is a real mess
or a source of annoyance. The verb encojonarse, of
strictly taboo origin, means to be extremely annoyed.
The expressions hacer cocolía and hacer puñeta are
also taboo, both expressing the concept of masturba-
tion. Caca, excrement, becomes cagarreta when it
signifies diarrhea. The vulgar expression for menstruation is caer mala or venir doña Rosa. Culo, cu-
lito (ass) is basically vulgar, but it is used affectionately with children. This level of language is
used by less fortunate Hispanics far down on the socio-economic scale and forced to live in ghettos of
which this type of language is an undesirable by-
product.

Life in the barrio can produce other types of
terminology. One of the many results of ghetto
dwelling is the sad practice of transferring children
from their natural parents to "economic godparents"
who take in poor children in a foster home setup.
The institutional channels referring to this practice
of child placing are known collectively as compadrazgo. In this fairly loose structure, the foster par-
ent--often without a partner--is known as a padrino
or madrina. Those of a slightly more elevated socio-
economic status who open their doors to the children

305

of others are generally known as compadres and comadres. Often parental rights are given to relatives who take in such children as hijos de crianza. At times the transaction has legal status, but in far too many instances these agreements are not legally binding and are merely another reflection of the grimness of the barrio.[202]

SEPHARDIC SPANISH IN THE UNITED STATES. The foreign born and United States Sephardics are associated with the patois learned either in their native land or in small American enclaves. But there is an obvious drifting away from their language habits and social customs as time passes and exposure to non-ethnic dominance continues. In order to stay the total acculturation process, attempts have been made to maintain their language, known also as "Ladino," in the "Talmud Torah" by having Bible passages translated into Judaeo-Spanish from Hebrew.[203] Sadly enough, as is often the case in such language-culture maintenance projects, the basic aims gradually weakened and in many instances the grasp of the language became rather superficial or disappeared. Although Sephardic Jews were originally Spanish-Portuguese, they immigrated to the United States from various parts of Europe--the Turkish Empire, the Balkans, Holland, North Africa, and Greece--and most of them settled in New York City, New York State, Los Angeles, and even Atlanta, Georgia.[204] From the beginning there were marked differences in dialect according to the place of origin--Rhodes, Sofia, Constantinople, Salonica, Smyrna, Cairo, Alexandria, and Palestine, to mention only some of the main centers. As frequently occurs in highly fractionated subminority linguistic groups, a levelling process eventually emerged leading to a more standard Judaeo-Spanish for purposes of oral and written communication, especially in matters religious and literary.[205] Although Sephardics probably number about a million world-wide, there are only about 5,000 in the United States. As might be expected in such immigrant situations, many of the Sephardics have yielded to larger minority pressures, espe-

cially to their Ashkenazic coreligionists, who out-
number them many times over. This is further complicated by influences of other ethnic and professional
groups in a totally Anglo-dominant society.

SEPHARDIC SPANISH SOUNDS. Ladino vowels are articulated more openly than standard Spanish ones. All
<u>a's</u> are pronounced medially regardless of stress or
position--<u>caza, algo, palavra, año</u>. Stressed <u>e</u> is
also quite open--[mέze], [tjέmpʌ]; however, this
sound becomes a rather high front vowel in absolute
final position or when followed by <u>n</u> or <u>s</u>--<u>prove</u>
[próvə]-[próvɪ], antes [ántəs]-[ántɪs], <u>comen</u> [kó-
mən]-[kómɪn].207 The articulation of <u>o</u> is similar
in that it is open in closed syllables [zmɔ́r],
[əskɔ́ŋdə], [sɔ̆n]) and in the monosyllabics <u>yo</u> and <u>no</u>
but tends to be high back in final position ([mɔːzɔ̆-
trʌs], [ɔlvídʌ], [tóʊns]).208

The consonants generally do not differ from the
norm, with some few exceptions. Consonants [b] and
[v] arc fully distinct, the former occurring initially and after m (<u>bien, blanko, ombre, embezar</u>), the
latter, elsewhere (<u>kavesa, avlar, bivir, barva</u>).209
The consonants [s] and [z] are voiceless and voiced
respectively (<u>pasar, caveza</u>). Voiceless [ʃ] and
voiced [ʒ] are a distinct pair as well ([ʃʒvɔ́n] and
[ʒʌrnə́l]).210 Unlike standard Spanish, all initial
r's are single vibrants. The characteristic Sephardic consonantal clusters are as follows: initial
/ué/>/qüé/ <u>güevo, güerta</u>; medial /-sk-/>/-ʃk-/
bu<u>ʃkar</u>, mo<u>ʃka</u>; -rd->-dr- <u>tadre, vedre</u>.211

ENGLISH INTERFERENCE IN UNITED STATES SEPHARDIC
SPANISH. The passage of time and socioeconomic and
linguistic pressures due to living in an Anglo-dominant society have affected Judaeo-Spanish in a number
of ways, the principal areas of influence being articulation and lexicon.

The intrusion of English in articulation has

been minimal compared to some other groups. Nonetheless, some few instances of contact interference are observable. Frequently, the voiceless velar /k/ becomes aspirated as in English in the obviously unassimilated loans bookkeeper [búkʰɪpɐ] and bookkeeping [bújkʰɪpɪŋk].²¹² The typically interdental fricative /ð/ yields sooner ·or later to the oclusive articulation [déðʌ]>[dédʌ]ˌ [táðrɪ]>[tádrɪ].²¹³

The area of greatest influence, as is to be expected, is the lexicon. Although there may be resistance of various kinds, eventually code switching leads to the incorporation of unassimilated, partially 'assimilated, or totally assimilated loans. Occasionally, one finds forms still in competition-- ebreo and ibru (Hebrew, Jew), Nueva York and Nuyork, presidente and prézident (president and President of the U. S.).²¹⁴ Other types of borrowings are a result of interference or lapsing into forms of expression which do not exist in the patois or which are no longer recalled actively afterol (after all), so (so), biznes (business), bloko (block of tickets), čekers (checkers), imigreyšen (immigration), kankes (concourse), mítink (meeting), parti (party), rayt (right), sítizen (citizen), skaleršip (scholarship), θíyeta (theatre), tibí (TB), tuins (twins), yuθ (youth), wánderful (wonderful), kara (care), plano (airplane), dipis (D. P.'s), čermen (chairman), čuíngam, (chewing gum), daym (dime), dil (deal). In the same way, new verbs are coined from English roots angašarse (to become engaged), delivrar (to deliver), edukasionar (to educate), to mention only a few.²¹⁵

CUBAN SPANISH IN THE UNITED STATES. Although Cubans have settled in many parts of the country from 1962 on, their major concentration is in Florida, chiefly in Miami and surrounding counties. Much of their business and social life is conducted in Spanish, and the Miami area has a more solid bilingual curriculum than most school districts in the United States.

Although the Cubans have been in the country for

almost two decades, thus far little has been done
with reference to investigation and analysis of linguistic change as a result of contact. Although
there has been a relatively firmly rooted Spanish enclave in the Tampa area since the end of the nineteenth century,[216] none has been so powerful or numerous as the Cuban immigration in Miami, where
first- and second-generation speakers of Spanish
cling tenaciously to their original tongue despite
their amazingly rapid adjustment to American life.
Interferences have occurred and continue to take
place since Cubans enjoy greater participation in
American life on all levels--social, political, and
professional. Moreover, due to the proximity of Cuba
to the United States and the rather high-level social
and intellectual life in the urban centers of Cuba,
"americanismos" and "extranjerismos" were not foreign
to the language of the Island. One may assume, then,
that the basic features of language in contact--pho-
netic, lexical, and syntactical interference--are already operative in this case, if not firmly rooted.
To date, however, few if any significant conclusions
have been reached.[217] Perhaps the latest influx of
its population will provide an impetus for greater
linguistic research in the area of interference.

THE FUTURE OF SPANISH IN THE UNITED STATES. The presence in this country of so many Hispanics of different backgrounds and levels of education and attainment brings to mind a consciousness struggle--one resulting from Spanish-speaking, basically Catholic and
conservative people residing in an Anglo-dominant society based on democracy, capitalism, and free enterprise. What is the future of the Spanish language in
the United States? If it is true that one may predict
the future by studying the past, Spanish as a primary
means of expression is doomed to the same fate as all
the other immigrant languages. Nonetheless, there
are certain truths which point to the possibility of
the survival of this ethnic language, even though pre-
dictability on this level is merely conjectural.

    The areas in which ethnic-language reinforcement

is taking place are the bilingual programs throughout the country and increasing ethnic awareness and the sociopolitical movements which derive from it. Bilingual-bicultural programs would not be possible were it not for extensive government funding which will probably not be appropriated indefinitely. What is more, many of the "assimilation-type" programs exist primarily to serve only as stop-gap measures at best. Sociopolitical organizations are growing steadily as political clout is progressively conceived as a source of power through ethnic cohesiveness. And yet, in the case of Hispanics there are certain factors to be considered that have not been typical of other immigrant groups.

The waves of immigration in this country to the present have generally been handled as temporary groups awaiting total "Americanization," and geographical distances and economic necessity have generally reinforced the traditional American handling of such problems. In the latino situation, however, there are certain basic differences which provide a fairly strong and continuous "re-Hispanization." First, Puerto Ricans are automatically American citizens and move freely from the Island to the Mainland and back again. Secondly, many Puerto Ricans, whether they were born on the Island or the Mainland, visit their "spiritual home" regularly. Thirdly, there is a great deal of movement between the American Southwest and Mexico. Fourthly, there are close to 2,000 miles of border shared by the United States and Mexico, and illegal entry is definitely on the upswing (illegal aliens are estimated at almost 12,000,000).

Unlike most immigrant groups in the past, the native language of Hispanics is reinforced either continuously or sporadically by these four fairly strong sources of native or near-native contact. Despite obvious and painful differences, the one bond cherished by all is their Spanish language. In fact, many Hispanics would have their tongue become the second official language of the United States--similar to the status of French and English in Canada and French and Flemish in Belgium. On the other

hand, there are many who are opposed to official bilingualism on the grounds of the divisiveness and
bitterness which coequality of languages has often
fostered. Other Americans, deeply entrenched in the
values of the "Anglo-Saxon" tradition, are strongly
opposed to any notion of official bilingualism. For
still others fairly far down on the social scale, a
form of Spanish remains their only means of communication, and it is not viewed as a means of expression to be pitted against any other. Some Hispanics
who enjoy a very latino orientation are quite mili-
tant about the survival of their language on a functional level. The solution probably lies somewhere
between the two extremes.

While knowledge of Spanish is extremely valuable, we are faced with the problems of survival in
a society in which the main business of life is carried on in English, which, in any case, should be
learned thoroughly as the main tool of self-expres-
sion in this society. If one wishes to add a further dimension in the form of "bilingualism," the approach should be a very sound one which is both
broad in perspective and intensive in approach, so
that the second language is removed from the context
of an academic discipline and becomes the dynamically
meaningful and useful tool in communication which
Spanish has become elsewhere.

EXERCISES

THEORY
A. ANSWER THE QUESTIONS BRIEFLY.
1. What were the two points of entry in the area
   which was to become the United States and its
   possessions in the sixteenth century?
2. What did the Spanish-American War (1846) cost
   Mexico in northern territory?
3. What language guarantees were included in the
   Treaty of Guadalupe (1848)?
4. Why do illegal aliens enter into the American
   Southwest with such apparent ease?
5. What are the two basic Hispanic patterns of immigration into the United States?
6. Aside from Chicanos and Puerto Ricans, what are
   some smaller groups of Hispanics in the United
   States?
7. What are some examples of the existence of Spanish
   in American English?
8. What are the possible significations of the word
   "barrio" in traditional Spanish? What overtones
   does it have in the United States?
9. What does "bilingual-bicultural education" mean?
10. What is meant by "languages in contact"?
11. What are the two basic models of "bilingual edu-
    cation" to which most American educators sub-
    scribe?
12. What do the terms "Anglo-dominant" and "ethnic-
    dominant" speakers of English mean?
13. What is a "pure loan"? An "unassimilated loan"?
    A "wholly assimilated loan"?
14. Among Mexican-American speakers of Spanish, what
    do the terms "pachuco," "Tex-Mex," and "pochismo"
    connote?
15. Which level of speech is most readily affected by
    contact with another language?
16. What is meant by a "calque"? Give some examples.

B. FILL IN THE BLANKS ACCORDING TO THE SENSE OF THE
   STATEMENT.
1. The _____ of the American Southwest has provided words like arroyo, meseta, and peninsula.

312

2. Words like vamoose, calaboose, and hoosegow are clearly derived from _____ Spanish.
3. Interference generally occurs on phonetic, grammatical, and _____ levels.
4. The verbs put, set, and burst are examples of _____ verbs in English.
5. The periphrastic form of the Spanish lo diré is _____ decirlo.
6. Spanish admits normal and _____ negation.
7. The words pantimedia, minifalda, and discount tienda are good examples of compound _____.
8. The prefixes reque-, rede-, and requete- are adverbial _____ used most often in Chicano and Caribbean Spanish.
9. The expressions ¡ay bendito! and ¡chévere! are associated with _____ Spanish.
10. The form of Spanish in which ⌈b/v⌉ and ⌈ʃ/ʒ⌉ are fully distinct is _____.

C. DEFINE THESE ITEMS BRIEFLY.
1. Sephardic Spanish
2. the barrio
3. bilingual education
4. language contact
5. loan words
6. language interference
7. loanblends
8. pachuquismo
9. Hispanic clout
10. Puerto Rican r's

D. IDENTIFY THE GROUPS OF WORDS ACCORDING TO THE PLACE OF ORIGIN OR THE HISPANIC GROUP MOST APT TO USE THEM.
1. coyote, mustang, rodeo _____
2. tortilla, enchilada, chile con carne _____
3. compadre, madrina, compadrazgo _____
4. Corona, Los Altos, Los Angeles _____
5. you better say, you better don't say _____
6. birria, bongue, sanga _____
7. atole, planta de huevo, tomate de fresadilla
8. tripa ida, sangre débil, óvulo _____
9. boricua, comemierda, arrebatao _____
10. matasanos, trotaconventos, aguafiesta

E. TRUE OR FALSE.
1. There is absolutely no difference between the

313

Spanish of Puerto Rico and the Spanish of Central
Spain. _____
2. Boricua and boricano are words of Taino Indian origin. _____
3. Words like batata, turpial, and ardilla reflect
objects native to the island of Puerto Rico. _____
4. The words manoseador, manoseada, and manosadera
are Chicano and refer to sexual matters. _____
5. The expressions chingar and mandar a la chingada
are taboo expressions of Cuban derivation. _____
6. Forms like toxido, londri, sinque, and pinche are
Chicano words having to do only with clothing.
_____
7. Verbs like responsabilizar, auspiciar, and finali-
zar are not necessarily limited to Puerto Rican
and Chicano usage. _____
8. Articulations such as ⌈mfrjár⌉ and ⌈láq:⌉ are
typical of Chicano articulation. _____
9. Words like tecato, estofa, and yerba reflect the
drug culture and might readily be used by Mexican
Americans and Puerto Ricans.
10. Forms like Buferín, Anacín, Entoral, and aspirina
are strictly limited to Puerto Rican usage. _____
11. Preterite forms such as llegates, hablates, and
cantates are strictly Chicano. _____
12. The aspiration of internal final -s- as in ehtan-
que is characteristic of Puerto Rican pronunciation. _____
13. Subjunctive forms with an archaic flavor as in
vaiga, caiga, and creiga are strictly Sephardic.
_____
14. The shift in stress in all first-person plural
subjunctive forms (hiérvamos, puédamos, séamos)
is typical of Chicano Spanish. _____
15. The forms so, salo, sabo are typically Puerto Rican. _____
16. The shift from e>i in unstressed positions (le-
ón>lión, señor>siñor) are more frequently than
not Chicano. _____
17. Forms like kaveza, bivir, embezar are strictly
Judaeo-Spanish in common usage. _____
18. Sports borrowings like béisbol, fúbol, básquet-
ball, hit, jomrón are not limited to any specific

314

Spanish-speaking group. _____

19. The Chicano forms bompa, pompear, and traque are normally replaced by the more traditional para-golpe, bombear, and vía del ferrocarril. _____

20. The terms gringos and gabachos are used by Puerto Ricans to refer to members of the out-group.

F. GIVE THE MEANING OF THESE WORDS AS THEY ARE USED BY UNITED STATES HISPANICS.

1. waxear _____
2. ribersa _____
3. lanledi _____
4. chinero _____
5. agüelo _____
6. tostón _____
7. tokensito _____
8. cuete _____
9. mopear _____
10. feri _____
11. weldear _____
12. cuora _____
13. erjostes _____
14. cadilec _____
15. caubói _____

16. yuθ _____
17. šerife _____
18. edukasionar _____
19. atrompillar _____
20. oberoles _____
21. tomatera _____
22. cabrita _____
23. malamé _____
24. yin _____
25. hijos de crianza _____
26. lana Morado _____
27. huevón _____
28. hacer tiempo _____
29. atole _____
30. mancornilla _____

G. GIVE A STANDARD SPANISH VERSION OF THESE CON-STRUCTIONS.

1. La lección está siendo leída.

_____

2. Ella se puso su blusa waš en wer.

_____

3. Hago mi mente pa' arriba.

_____

4. Ella sabe como tocar el piano y la guitarra.

_____

5. La jeba parecía una muy hermosa.

315

6. Platicaba por teléfono polque quería ŷamar al plomero.

7. Pa' poder desmanchar la ropa le puso un quitamanchas.

8. ¡Ese mardito maricocaimorfi anda tirriado todo el día!

9. La infeliz tiene sangre débil pero se esfuerza por trabajar de trabajanta.

10. Los familiares trataban de darle un levantón a la pobre viuda.

11. ¡Estoy harto!   ¡Cuidado que te juro que te meto a la ley!

12. ¡Pobre de Lupita!   Se ve que le tocó la de malas.

13. Mientras yo me pongo mi abrigo, ponte tu chaqueta.

14. Paco yúnier me confesó que le hubiese gustado pasar un rato en aquella casa de borde.

ASI SE DICE.
REPEAT EACH SEGMENT AS GIVEN AND FINALLY THE COMPLETE
UTTERANCE.

```
Cada                       ..........
Cada chango                ..........
chango a                   ..........
a su mescate               ..........
Cada chango a su mescate   ...............
y a darse                  ..........
y a darse vuelo            ..........
Cada chango a su mescate y a darse vuelo.
                           ..........................

Tú sabes                   ..........
Tú sabes quien             ..........
quien trae                 ..........
trae las llaves            ...............
las llaves, Chávez         ...............
trae las llaves, Chávez    ...............
Tú sabes quien trae las llaves, Chávez.
                           ..........................

Te casaste                 ..........
casaste, te                ..........
te fregaste                ..........
Te casaste, te fregaste.   ..........................

Salir                      ..........
Salir de                   ..........
de Guatemala               ..........
de Guatemala para          ..........
Guatemala para ir          ...............
para ir a                  ..........
para ir a Guatepeor        ...............
Salir de Guatemala para ir a Guatepeor.
                           ..........................

Comer                      ..........
Comer frijoles             ..........
frijoles y                 ..........
```

317

```
frijoles y repetir        ..........
y repetir pollo           ..............
Comer frijoles y repetir pollo.
                          ........................

No                        ..........
No importa                ..........
No importa que            ..........
que nazcan                ..........
que nazcan chatos         ..............
chatos con tal            ..........
con tal que               ..........
con tal que tengan        ..........
que tengan resuello       ..............
No importa que nazcan chatos
                          ..................
con tal que tengan resuello
                          ...................
No importa que nazcan chatos con tal que tengan re-
suello.                   ........................

Más                       ..........
Más vale                  ..........
Más vale que              ..........
vale que haiga            ..............
haiga un                  ..........
haiga un tonto            ..............
un tonto y                ..........
tonto y no                ..........
y no dos                  ..........
Más vale que haiga un tonto y no dos.
                          ........................

Nunca                     ..........
Nunca falta               ..........
falta un                  ..........
un yoloví                 ..........
Nunca falta un yoloví.    ........................

Pon                       ..........
Pon, pon                  ..........
Pon, pon, pon             ..........
pon un                    ..........
pon un nicle              ..........
pon un nicle pa'          ..........
```

318

pon un nicle pa' jabón   ....
jabón, pa'   ....
jabón, pa' lavar   ....
pa' lavar tu   ....
pa' lavar tu calzón   ....
Pon, pon   ....
pon un nicle pa' jabón   ....
pa' lavar tu calzón   ....
Pon, pon, pon un nicle pa' jabón, pa' lavar tu calzón.   ....

Ya   ....
Ya te   ....
te conozco   ....
conozco Mosco   ....
Ya te conozco Mosco.218   ....

Meter   ....
Meter el   ....
Meter el pie   ....
el pie en   ....
pie en el   ....
en el bote   ....
Meter el pie en el bote.   ....

No   ....
No es   ....
No es lo   ....
No es lo mismo   ....
es lo mismo llamar   ....
mismo llamar al   ....
llamar al diablo   ....
al diablo que   ....
que verlo   ....
que verlo venir   ....
No es lo mismo llamar al diablo
                                ....
que verlo venir   ....
No es lo mismo llamar al diablo que verlo venir.
                                ....

Te   ....
Te gusta   ....
Te gusta más   ....
Te gusta más meter   ....

```
más meter la                ..........
meter la cuchara            ..........
la cuchara en lo            ..........
cuchara en lo ajeno         ..........
ajeno que al                ..........
que al puerco               ..........
al puerco el            ·   ..........
al puerco el josico         ..........
el josico en                ..........
josico en agua              ..........
en agua de sancocho         ..........
Te gusta más meter la cuchara en lo ajeno
                        ..................
que al puerco el josico en agua de sancocho
                        ..................
Te gusta más meter la cuchara en lo ajeno que al
puerco el josico en agua de sancocho.
                        ..........................

Calma                       ..........
Calma, piojo                ..........
piojo, que                  ..........
que el peine                ..........
el peine llega              ..............
Calma, piojo, que el peine llega.
                        .......................

Ser                         ..........
Ser más                     ..........
Ser más feo                 ..........
más feo que                 ..........
feo que un                  ..........
que un pleito               ..........
un pleito de menores        ..............
Ser más feo que un pleito de menores.
                        ..........................

Tener                       ..........
Tener más                   ..........
Tener más golpes            ..............
más golpes que              ..........
golpes que un baile         ..............
que un baile de             ..........
un baile de bomba           ..............
```

320

Tener más golpes que un baile de bomba.[219]

....

321

FOOTNOTES

140 "It's Your Turn in the Sun," Time, 16 Oct. 1978, pp. 48-61.

141 Robert MacNeil and Jim Lehrer, Latino Power, The MacNeil/Lehrer Report Library, 795; Griffin Smith, Jr., "The Mexican Americans, A People on the Move," National Geographic, 157, 6 (1980), 780-809.

142 Joshua Fishman, Robert L. Cooper, and Roxana Ma, et al., Bilingualism in the Barrio (The Hague: Mouton & Co., 1971), pp. 13-14.

143 "It's Your Turn," p. 55.

144 F. C. Hayes, "Anglo-Spanish Speech in Tampa, Florida," Hispania, 32 (1949), 48-52.

145 Denah Levy, "La pronunciación del sefardí esmirniano de Nueva York," Nueva revista de filología hispánica, 6 (1952), 277-281.

146 Albert H. Marckwardt, American English (New York: Oxford University Press, 1958), pp. 40-47.

147 "It's Your Turn," p. 49.

148 Chester Christian, Jr., ed., Reports: Bilingual Education: Research and Teaching (Bethesda, Maryland: Educational Document Reproduction Service, 1967), #016 434.

149 Henry J. Casso, "Ya Basta, The Siesta Is

Over," in Educating the Mexican American, eds. Henry
Sioux Johnson and William J. Hernández M. (Valley
Forge, Pa.: Judson Press, 1970), pp. 93-99.

150 Rolf Kjolseth, "Bilingual Education Programs
in the United States: For Assimilation or Plural-
ism?," in Bilingualism in the Southwest, ed. Paul R.
Turner (Tucson: University of Arizona Press, 1973),
pp. 3-27.

151 Kjolseth, p. 9.

152 Kjolseth, pp. 15-16.

153 See James E. Alatis, ed., Monograph Series
on Languages and Linguistics. Twenty-first Annual
Round Table (Washington, D. C.: Georgetown University Press, 1970); also, Turner, Bilingualism.

154 Joshua Fishman, "The Politics of Bilingual
Education," in Monograph Series, ed. Alatis, p. 53.

155 J. L. Dillard, All-American English (New
York: Vintage Books, 1976), p. 81.

156 For an excellent analysis of the phenomena
of contact and interference, see Uriel Weinreich,
Languages in Contact, 8th ed. (The Hague: Mouton,
1974), pp. 14-62; also, Juan B. Rael, "Associative
Interference in New Mexican Spanish," in El lenguaje
de los chicanos: Regional and Social Characteristics
Used by Mexican Americans, eds. Eduardo Hernández-
Chavez, et al. (Arlington, Va.: Center for Applied
Linguistics, 1975), pp. 19-29.

157 Weinreich, pp. 18-20.

323

158 Robert P. Stockwell, J. Donald Bowen, and John W. Martin, The Grammatical Structures of English and Spanish (Chicago: The University Press, 1965), pp. 121-128.

159 Einar Haugen, ·The Norwegian Language in America (Bloomington: Indiana University Press, 1969), p. 390.

160 Richard V. Teschner, "Anglicisms in Spanish. A Cross-Referenced Guide to Previous Findings, Together with English...," Diss. University of Wisconsin 1972, Vol. I, 114-117.

161 Teschner, I, 114.

162 Teschner, I, 116.

163 Haugen, p. 390.

164 See Teschner, I, 1-34.

165 See Daniel N. Cárdenas, "Mexican Spanish," in El lenguaje, eds. Hernández-Chavez et al., pp. 1-5.

166 See George C. Barker, "Pachuco: An American-Spanish Argot and Its Social Function in Tucson, Arizona," in El lenguaje, eds. Hernández-Chavez et al., pp. 183-201.

167 Aurelio Espinosa, Estudios sobre el español de Nuevo Méjico, trans. A. Alonso and A. Rosenblat (Buenos Aires: Universidad de Buenos Aires, 1930),

vol. I, 53.

168 Marie Esman Barker, Español para el bilingüe (Skokie, Illinois: National Textbook Company, 1972), pp. 176-177.

169 Barker, Español, p. 70.

170 Barker, Español, p. 71.

171 Espinosa, vol. II, 14-15.

172 Donald M. Lance, "Dialectal and Nonstandard Forms in Texas Spanish," in El lenguaje, ed. Hernández-Chavez et al., pp. 37-51.

173 Robert Phillips, "Variations in Los Angeles Spanish Phonology," in El lenguaje, eds. Hernández-Chavez, pp. 52-60.

174 Rael, pp. 21-29.

175 Barker, Español, pp. 209-215.

176 Cárdenas, pp. 1-5.

177 Eighty percent of the Mexican-American lexicon is based on the findings of Teschner, "Anglicisms in Spanish," and Roberto A. Galván and Richard V. Teschner, El diccionario del español chicano. The Dictionary of Chicano Spanish (Silver Spring, Maryland: Institute of Modern Languages, Inc., 1977); all other entries are based on investigations and conversations with and interviews of native speakers by the authors.

[178] Barker, "Pachuco," p. 190.

[179] Barker, "Pachuco," p. 187.

[180] See Pauline Barker, Español para los hispanos (Dallas: Banks Upshaw and Co., 1953), pp. 42-45; also, Barker, "Pachuco," pp. 187-188.

[181] "It's Your Turn," pp. 55-56.

[182] Oscar Lewis, La vida (New York: Vintage Books, 1960), xxvii.

[183] See Harold J. Alford, The Proud Peoples. The Heritage and Culture of Spanish-Speaking Peoples in the United States (New York: New American Library, 1972).

[184] See fn. 142.

[185] See the works of Lefty Barretto, Nobody's Hero. A Puerto Rican Story (New York: New American Library, 1976); Piri Thomas, Seven Long Times and Down These Mean Streets (New York: New American Library, 1974); Paulette Cooper, ed. Growing Up Puerto Rican (New York: New American Library, 1972); Susan Sheehan, A Welfare Mother (New York: New American Library, 1975).

[186] Weinreich, pp. 3-4.

[187] Rubén del Rosario, El español de América (Sharon, Conn.: Troutman Press, 1970), pp. 59-61.

188 McDonough, see entry mandinga; this term implies that everyone has some degree of African blood.

189 Joshua A. Fishman, "Puerto Rican Intellectuals in New York: Some Intragroup and Intergroup Contrasts," Canadian Journal of Behavioral Science, 1 (1969), p. 225.

190 Lucrecia Casiano Montañez, La pronunciación de los puertorriqueños de Nueva York (Bogotá: Ediciones Tercer Mundo, 1975), pp. 32; 112-114.

191 Casiano Montañez, p. 41.

192 See pages 222-225 of the text.

193 Casiano Montañez, p. 85.

194 See Casiano Montañez, pp. 86-88.

195 Charles W. Kreidler, "A Study of the Influence of English on the Spanish of Puerto Ricans in Jersey City, New Jersey," Diss. University of Michigan 1957, pp. 119-120.

196 See Rose Nash, "Spanglish: Language Contact in Puerto Rico," American Speech, 45, 3-4 (1970), 225.

197 Nash, 225

198 Nash, 225-226.

199 Washington Llorens, El habla popular de Puerto Rico (Río Piedras: Editorial Edil, 1971), pp. 77-80.

200 Llorens, pp. 73-81.

201 All forms of Puerto Rican lexical borrowings and related materials are based on Kreidler, Nash, McDonough, and Morgan L. Jones, "A Phonological Study of English As Spoken by Puerto Ricans Contrasted with Puerto Rican Spanish and American English," Diss. University of Michigan 1962, and interviews of native speakers by the authors.

202 See J. M. Stycos, "Family and Fertility in Puerto Rico," in The Puerto Rican Community and Its Children on the Mainland, eds. Francesco Cordasco and Eugene Bucchioni (Metuchen, N. J.:   The Scarecrow Press, Inc., 1972), pp. 76-88.

203 Max A. Luria, "Judaeo-Spanish Dialects in New York City," Todd Memorial Volumes, 2 (1930), 9.

204 Frederick B. Agard, "Present-Day Judaeo-Spanish in the United States," Hispania, 33 (1950), 203-204.

205 Agard, p. 204.

206 Levy, p. 278.

207 Levy, p. 278.

208. Levy, p. 278.

209 Agard, p. 205.

210 Agard, p. 205.

211 Agard, p. 205; also see pages 233-235 of the text.

212 Ruth Hirsch, "A Study of Some Aspects of Judeo-Spanish by a New York Sephardic Family," Diss. University of Michigan 1951, p. 24.

213 Hirsch, pp. 24-25.

214 Hirsch, pp. 98-99.

215 Hirsch, pp. 97-100.

216 See Hayes; Carmelita Louise Ortiz, "English Influence on the Spanish of Tampa," Hispania, 32 (1949), 300-304; D. Lincoln Canfield, "Tampa Spanish: Three Characters in Search of a Pronunciation," Modern Language Journal, 35 (1951), 42-44.

217 See Adrian Cherry, Tampa Spanish Slang (Tampa: Lamplight Press, 1966); Jorge Manuel Guitart, "Markedness and a Cuban Dialect of Spanish," Diss. Georgetown University 1973; Anthony J. Lamb, "A Phonological Study of the Spanish of Havana, Cuba," Diss. University of Kansas Press, 1968.

218 Galván and Teschner, El diccionario, p. 135.

219 Llorens, El habla, p. 95.

APPENDIX ONE

SELECTED TEXTS
AND
PHONETIC TRANSCRIPTIONS

PRELIMINARY NOTES ON PHONETIC TRANSCRIPTIONS

The phonetic transcriptions are presented in relatively large phonic segments rather than syllabic divisions since the large units seem more accurately reflective of the natural flow of human speech. For purposes of graphic clarity, all diphthongs and triphthongs have not been transcribed as relaxed even though it is understood that in actual articulation they are normally relaxed except in stressed segments. Identical word-end and word-initial vowels are joined by the notation ⌒ above the line. Word-end and word-initial vowels which are not identical are linked by the notation ⌣ below the line.

Although Spanish has medial a and palatal a, the distinction has not been made in the transcriptions.

As a general rule, the following parts of speech are stressed: nouns, adjectives, verbs, adverbs; also, disjunctive, demonstrative, indefinite, quantitative, and interrogative pronouns. In compound nouns and adverbs, only the second element has been stressed. Compound adjectives, however, normally carry a double stress. On the other hand, articles, prepositions, conjunctions, and conjunctive pronouns are unstressed.

All major pauses are indicated by the notation // , and all minor pauses are noted as / .

The transcriptions are phonemic in that sound, meaning, and local variations are focused upon in each case. The general label in parenthesis after each text provides a clue as to the variant of Spanish being described: General Hispanic American, Ceceo, Seseo, River Plate Variety, Mexican, and Puerto Rican.

332

ENTRETELONES DEL IDIOMA (General Hispanic American)

La historia de los movimientos literarios es
la historia del desarrollo de las palabras, y en
cierto sentido es el crisol de la civilización. En
el vértice del análisis, en el último examen se o-
frecen a la crítica diferencias de tono y expresión.

La prosa y el verso de la lengua española se
enriquecen desde sus primeros autores hasta los más
modernos y contemporáneos. Esto justifica el concepto tan conocido que el idioma es algo vivo y por
lo tanto en constante evolución. Especialmente la
lengua hablada se modifica continuamente. Sancio-
nada por el uso, esas modificaciones pasan después
al lenguaje escrito; de populares se transforman en
cultas y aún los más rígidos puristas deben terminar
por aceptarlas. La mayoría de estas modificaciones
son aportes debidos a la capacidad creadora del pueblo, a su imaginación, a su capacidad de encontrar
voces inéditas que vengan a significar y expresar
más vivamente nuevos conceptos.

Si es propio de los pueblos de fuerte persona-
lidad tener una intensa acción en este sentido, in-
dudablemente los pueblos de Hispanoamérica son en
tal aspecto especialmente vigorosos y creadores.

Por ejemplo, la palabra jaiba en Puerto Rico se
aplica a la persona astuta, lista, mientras que en
Cuba quiere decir en cambio persona perezosa. De
jaiba deriva jaibería, que es, por supuesto, astu-
cia. En el mismo Puerto Rico juez, además de cangrejo de tierra, es en su segunda acepción persona
codiciosa, avara y la expresión hacerse el juez dormido no es otro que un sinónimo de hacerse la mosquita muerta. Ser un juez dormido es, consecuente-
mente, en el lenguaje figurado y familiar ser hipó-
crita. Jurutungo, también en el mismo país centro-
americano, es lugar lejano. Una idea similar expre-
sa asimismo en Puerto Rico y en Cuba una voz tan di-
versa de la anterior como quimbámbaras o quimbambas.
Así en las quimbambas quiere decir en sitio lejano
o impreciso. También sínsoras es un lugar lejano.

333

¿Cómo haremos para designar a un natural de la ciudad mexicana Monterrey? Pues invirtiendo el orden de las dos palabras de que se compone ese nombre monte y rey, de lo cual saldrá regiomontano, a quien se llama también reinero.

// aŋtratalónaz ða liðjómɐ //

// laɪ̯stórja ða loz motimjéntoz litarárjo
séz laɪ̯stórja ðaļ dasarɔ́yo ða lɐs polábrɐs/yan
sjérto sanṭíðo le léŋgwa é sol krisóḷ ða lɐ
siɓilisɐsjón// a mol bértisa ða lɐnálisis/a
no lúḷtimo aksámɐn se əfrésa ne lɐ krítikɐ
difɐrénsjaz ða tóno yɐsprasjón//
// lɐ prósɐ yɐl bérsɐ ða lɐ léŋgwa əspɐɲóla
sanfikésɐŋ dézða sns primérɐ saxtóra sáṣtɐ loz
máz modérnɐ si kontamporánɐɐs//éṣto xnṣtifí-
kɐ ɐl komséªto táŋ konosíðɐ ka liðjómɐ é
sálgɐ ɓiɓɔɪ por lɐ táŋtɐ əŋ konṣtáŋtɐ əbɐ-
losjón// əspəsjalméŋta lɐ léŋgwa əɓláðɐ sa
modífíkɐ kontinwaméŋta//sansjonáðɐs pɐ
ra lúsɐ /ésəz modifikɐsjónas pásəŋ dɐspwé sɐl
loŋgwáxɐ əskrítɐ/də pɐpnláros sa transfórmɐ
noŋ kúḷtəz yɐýn loz ma fíxlðɐs pɐrúṣtpz déɓəŋ
tɐrminár pɐ rɐsɐrtárlɐs// lɐ mɐyɐríɐ ða éṣtəz
modifikɐsjónɐs só nɐpórtaz ðaɓíðɐ sɐ lɐ
kɐpɐsiðá krɐɐðórɐ ðal pwéɓlɐ/ə swimɐxi-

335

nesjón/ e sn kɔpɔsiðá ðə ðŋkɔŋtrár ბósə sinéðites
kə béŋgɔ nɔ signifikár jɛᵏsprasár máz ბიbɔméŋtə
mwéბɔs kɔnséᵖtɔs//

//sjés própjo ðə lɔs pwéბlɔz ðə fwértə parsɔnɔ-
liðá tané rɔmaiᵢ ténsɔ ɛᵏsjó nə néṣtə sɔŋtið/
iŋdɔðɔბlaméŋtə lɔs pwéბlɔz ðə ispɔnɔɔmérikɔ
só naᵢ ta' lɔspéᵏtɔ ɔspɔsjalméŋtə ბიgɔrósɔ si
krɔɔðórɔs//

//pɔ raxémplɔ/lɔ pɔláბrɔ/xái̯ბɔ/əm pwértɔ r̃ɛ́kɔ
sə ɔplíkɔ ɔ lɔ parsónɔ ɔʂtútɔ/liʂtɔ/mjéŋtrɔs
kɔ ðŋ kúბɔ kjérə ðɔsír/aŋkámbjo/parsónɔ pɔ-
rɔsósɔ//ðə xái̯ბɔ ðɔríბɔ xaiბɔríɔ/kɔ és/pɔr
snpwéṣtɔ/ɔʂtúsja//ə nɔl míẓmɔ pwértɔ r̃ɛ́kɔ/
xwés/ɔðɔmáz ðɔ kɔŋgréxɔ ðə tjéɾɔ é sɔn sn
sɔgýŋdɔ ɔsaᵖsjón parsónɔ kɔðisjósɔ/ɔბárɔ/i
lɔ ɔsprɔsjón/ɔsérsə əl xwéz ðɔrmíðɔ nɔ é
sótrɔ kéxn sinónimɔ ðə ɔsérsə lɔ mɔskítɔ
mwértɔ//sé rɔŋ xwéz ðɔrmíðɔ és/kɔnsakwɔŋ-
tɔméntə/ə nɔl laŋgwáxə fignráðɔᵢ femiljár sé
ripókritɔ//xɔrɔtý̞ŋgɔ/tɔmbjé nə nɔl míẓmɔ

336

pwés séntroemorikáno/éz lngár laxáno//n naidéo
similá rosprésp psimjzmo om pwérto r̜íko yoy
kúbo/nno b̌ój táŋ dibérsp ðo le pŋtorjór kómo
kimbámbpro so kimbámbps//psí_on les kimbám-
bps kjéro ðosír /on sítjo laxáno ðimprosíso//
tombjén sínsorp sé snn lngár laxáno//

//¿ kómo_prémos pero ðosigná ráṇn nptn-
rá̦l do le sjuðá moxikáno/mоŋtor̜éi̦?//pwé
simbirtjéŋde_o lórðoŋ do lez ðós polátrez
ðo ka so kompóno éso mо́ŋtei̦ r̜éi̦/do lo
kwál soḷdrá r̜éxjomоŋtáno/o kjén so rámo
tombjén r̜ei̦mérо//

337

EN EL AEROPUERTO (General Hispanic American)

Un grupo de estudiantes conversan mientras esperan los respectivos anuncios de vuelos.

Pepe-   Yo creía que llegaríamos tarde con lo despacio que se movía el autobús por esa maldita autopista.

Perico-   No te aflijas, aunque se supone que los aviones siempre salen a tiempo. Hemos salido con mucha anticipación y créase o no, aún tendremos que esperar un par de horas.

Dirigiéndose a Josefina e Inés, estudiantes también.
Chicas, ¿no quieren tomar un refresco con nosotros para matar el tiempo?

Josefina- Déjame asegurarme del horario de mi vuelo. Si hay algún retraso podré hacerlo. Si no lo hay debo prepararme para embarcar.

Parte para leer el horario.

Pepe-   Inés, ¿tú viajas con la misma compañía que Josefina?

Inés-   No, porque ella tiene vuelo directo a Buenos Aires y yo permaneceré en Río visitando a unos parientes. Era más conveniente por la hora de llegada elegir un vuelo con Varig.

Dirigiéndose a los muchachos.
Y Uds., ¿volarán juntos a Madrid?

Perico-   No, Pepe va directamente a Madrid pero yo voy a Bruselas, así que también viajamos separados. Pepe va con Iberia y yo de aquí voy a Londres con TWA y luego cruzaré a Bruselas.

Josefina de regreso.

Josefina- El vuelo 230, que es el mío, saldrá con una hora de atraso; así que acepto la invitación para tomar un refresco.

Los cuatro se dirigen al bar automático.

338

//ə na leəropwérto//

//ʌŋ grúpo ðə aʂtnðjáŋtas Kombérsen mjéŋ-
tre saspéren lo r̄aspaktíbo senýnsjoz ðə ᵬwélos//
//pépa //dʒó kraíe ka yageríemos tárða kon lo
ðaspásjo ka sa mobíe a lȧxtobýs po rése
meldíte ȧxtopíste//
//paríko//no to eflíxes/áxŋka sa snpóna ka lo se-
ᵬjónas sjémpra sála na tjémpo/émos se-
líðo kon múêe eŋtisipesjó ni/kréesə o
nó/eýŋ taŋdrémos ka ospará rnm pár
ðə óres//
//dirixjéŋdosa e xosafíne eines/aʂtnðjáŋtas tem-
bjén//
//paríko//êíkes/¿no kjéraŋ tomá rnn r̄afrésko
kon nosótros pera metá ra tjémpo?//
//xosafíne//déxema esagnrárma ðə lorárjo ðə mi
ᵬwélo//sjá yelgýn r̄atráso/poðré esérlo//
si no lo ái/débo proparárma pera em-
barkár//
//párta pera laé ra lorárjo//

//pépa// ¡nés/¿ tú bjaxes kon le mízme kompa-
níe ka xosafíne?//

//¡nés// nó/pórka ére tjéne bwélo firéᵏtə e bwénc
sáira si dʒó pormonosaré ən ríe bisitán-
de e únos perjéntas//ére más kombanjénta
por le óre fa yagáfe aləxí rnm bwélo kom
bári!//

//dirixjéndosa e loz mñãâôs//
jusṭéðos/¿ boleráŋ xúŋto sp meðrí?//

//paríko// nó/pépa ḃá fira⸍teménta e meðrí
paro dʒó ḃój e brnséle sesi ka tembjém
bjaxámos saperáðos//pépa ḃá ko nibérjai
dʒó ða ekí ḃój e lóŋdros koŋ tú ai
lwégo krnseré b brnsélos//

//xosafíne ða ãgréso//

//xosafíne// al bwélo ðosjéntos tréiŋte/ka é sal
múo/seḷdrá ko nnne óre fa etrá-
so esi ka esé⸍to laimbitesjón pere
temá rnn ãfré⸍ko//

//los kwátro so firíxa nel ba´ raxtomátiko//

340

LOS MAESTROS (Ceceo)

Cuando alguien desea aprender algo puede realizarlo por uno de estos tres métodos: observar, leer o acudir a la enseñanza de un maestro. En la mayoría de los casos, los dos primeros sistemas resultan insuficientes, erróneos. Desde el principio de la civilización, el maestro significó la verdad, por lo dicho. De allí que fuese venerado y su voz y nada más que ella enseñó a quienes se le acercaban para ser sus discípulos por la palabra. Durante el medioevo la repetición y el estudio de los textos de los maestros eran, prácticamente, la única forma de enseñanza. Rompiendo el esquema pero sin revolucionarlo mucho, en 1631 un libro titulado Didáctica del pedagogo checo Juan Amos Comenius intenta valerse de objetos y de imágenes para acompañar la voz. ¿Audiovisuales? Sí, pero este nombre es nuevo. El maestro checo ni siquiera soñó que su método habría de imponerse tres siglos más tarde. Es necesario llegar al 1800 para que la infalibilidad del profesor, la enseñanza forjada a puro libro y memoria, fuese superada. La sociedad de Herbart, en boga a fines del siglo diecinueve, preconizó cinco rígidas etapas: preparación, exposición, asimilación, generalización y aplicación. Los partidarios de Rousseau, Pestalozzi y Froebel se opusieron a este modelo mecánico, inhumano de enseñanza. Tres pedagogos fueron quienes, separadamente, llevaron a su expresión más adulta el arte de formar niños y modelar personas: la italiana María Montesori, el belga Decroly y el estadounidense Dewey. Reunida en un compendio universal, la técnica que formularon se conoce como enseñanza activa. ¿De qué se trata? En primer lugar, del conocimiento integral del niño, en lo físico y lo síquico. Así, midiendo su interés fisiológico y mental, se sabe cuándo y hasta dónde se puede enseñar. Su grado de concentración, su vocación, su salud, todo preocupa. En segundo lugar, la forma de enseñar es la otra clave de la enseñanza activa. Ordenes, amenazas, premios y castigos se archivan para siempre. Nunca sirvieron para informar ni para formar a mentes jóvenes. Así se supo que las fantasías y los juegos varían según la edad. En

341

volcar las lecciones según un atrayente cuento o re-
creación estaba el gran misterio de interesar a los
aburridos o en entusiasmar aún más a los ya ganados
por el saber. A medida que el conocimiento sicoló-
gico se ahondó, a partir de las experiencias freu-
dianas en el año de 1900, la enseñanza se encarriló
hacia nuevas concepciones. La sicología, como
ciencia ya madura, afirmó que un conocimiento queda
más firme en nuestra mente cuantos más sentidos hayan intervenido en el aprendizaje. Todo lo sensible
debe cooperar, pues en el acto de aprender ojos, oídos, tacto, gusto, olfato. Durante siglos la visión
y la audición fueron las únicas vías para dominar
una lección. Se sabe que si no hay además partici-
pación manual en aquélla, la clase está a medio hacer. Aprender haciendo según centros de interés muy
bien estudiados llevó al maestro de hoy a crear una
escuela para la vida, por la vida. Este es el lema
enarbolado por las jóvenes generaciones de educado-
res de este siglo.

//loz meéṣtros//

//kwándo álgjeņ daseá eprandé rálgo
pweéða ã̄ərliθárlo po romo ða éṣtoș tréz méto-
ðos/ctsarbár/loér/o eknðí re lə ansanánθə ðéxn
meéṣtro//ən lə meyoríə ða los Kásos/loz ðos pri-
méros sistéme ãsúǃtə ninsnfiθjéņtos/ãrṍnoss//
dazðə ol prinθípjo ða lə θibiliθaθjón/əl meéṣtro
siᵍnifikó lə tərðáᵗ/por lo ðíəs//ða ?ļí ko fweésə tə-
norɔ̣ɔ̣ sn tɔ́θ/! náðə más Ka él?/ansanó ə Kjénos
sə lə eθarkábem perə sér snz ðísθípnlos por lə pə-
lábrə//dnrántã ol madjoétso/lə ãrapatiθjón je lastú-
ðjo ða los tẽᵍᵗtoz ða loz meéṣtro sérem/preᵍti-
kəméņto/lə únike fórme ða ãnsanánθə//ãom-
pjéņdo ə laskéme pərə sin ãrəbolnθjonárlo múés/
ən míl seịᵗθjéņtos treịntəyúno/nn líbro titolóð
ðiðáᵍtike ðəl pafegóᵍs ĉéKo xwá námos Kəménju
sinténte trlérso ða otsxéto si ðẹịmáxonos
perə ekompenár lə tɔ́θ//axðjobiswálas?//sí/
porə éṣto nómbrə éz nweéts//əl meéṣtro
ĉéKo ni siKjére sonó Ko sn métoðo ątríé
343

δειmpɔnérsə tres síglɔz maȝ tárδə // éz nəθə-
sárjo ləgá rɐl mí lɔɛ̃ʹθjéɳtɔs pɐrɐ kə laįm-
fɐlį·ƀį·ƌáƌ ƌal prɔfɐsór / lɐ ənsənáɳθɐ fɔrxáδɐ̃ ɛ̃
púrɔ líƀrɔį məmórja / fwésə snpəráδɐ // lɐ sɔ-
θjeδáƌ ƌə érbɐr / əm bóȷ̃ɛ̃ ɛ̃ fínəz ƌal sí-
glɔ δjeθįnwéƀə / prakɔn!θó θį̃ŋkɔ r̄į́x!δɐ sə-
tápɐs / prəpɐrɐθjón / ə⁹²pɔs!θjón / ɐs!m!lɐθjón / xə-
nərɐl!θɐθjón japl!kɐθjón // lɔs pɐrt!δárjoz ƌə
r̄nsó / pəştɐlós! ! fréƀal sə ɔpɔsjérɔ np eştə
mɔδɐlɔ makán!kɔ / !nɔmánɔ ƌə ənsənáɳθɐ // tres
pɔδɐgóȷɔs fwérɔɳ kjénəs / səpɐrɐƌeméɳtə / ləƀárɔ
rɔ np swə⁹²prəsjón má sɐδį́ltɐ ə lártə ƌə
fɔrmár nínɔ s! mɔδɐlár pərsónɐs / laįtɐljánɐ mɐríɐ
mɔɳtəsór! / əl bélgɐ ƌɐkról! yə ləştáƌɔɣn!δénsə
δúw! // r̄ɐɣnįδɐ ə mɳ kɔmpéɳdjo ɳn!ƀɔrsá'l / lɐ
téᵍn!kɐ kə fɔrmnlárɔn sə kɔnóθə kómɔ ənsə-
ɳáɳθɐ ɐᵍtíƀɐ // ɛ̨ da ké sə trátɐ? // əm prįmér
lngár / dal kɔmɔθ!mjéɳtɔįɳ təgrá! dal nínɔ /
ən lɔ fís!kɔį lɔ sík!kɔ // ɐsí / m!ƌjéndɔ swiɳ-
tarés f!sjolóx!kɔį məɳtá! / sə sáƀə kwáɳ-

de yáste fínde se pwéðoˆensenár//sn gráðe ðe
kenθentreθjón/ sn ðekeθjón / sn selúð / tóðe
proskúre//en segúnde lngár / le fórme
ðoˆensemá réz le ótre kláðe ðe le ense-
máðoˆeltíte//órðenes / emenáðes / prémjos!
keştíges se erθíðem pere sjémpre//áŋke
sirðjérem pe raˌmformár ni pere fermá re
méntes xóðenes//esí se súpe ke les fentesíe si
les xwéɣez ðeríen según le eðáˆ//em belkár le
laˆθjónes segú nn netreyénte kwénteˆ ə ʔe-
kreeθjó naştáðeˆel grán miştérjo ðeˌntere-
sá re le seðnáˌðes/ˆeˆe nantnsjazmá reˌn
má se lez yá ɣenáðes pe rel seðér//e me-
ðíðe keˆel kenceθimjénteˆ sikelóxike se ʔendó/e pertír ðe le sesperjénθjas freˌðjáne
se na láne ðe míl netaθjéntes/ le ense-
máðoˆ seˆeŋkeˌiló ˆðja nweðes ken-
θeˆθjónes//le sikeloxíe/ kóme θjénθja yá
meðúre/efirmó kéˌŋ kenceθimjénte kéðe
más fírma en nwéştre ménte kwántez

más saṇtíðc sáγe niṇtorɓəmíðc ə mə le-
prəṇdiθáxə//tóðc lə sənsíɓlə ðéɓə Kəpə-
rár/pwé sə mə láʔtc ðə eprəṇdér/ɔ́xcs/
cíðcs/táʔtc/gýstc/clfátc//dnráṇtə síglcz le
ɓisjó mi laɣðiθjón fwércm le súnikez ɓíps
pere ðcminá rnne laʔθjón//sə sábə Kə si
nó ái eðəmás pertiθipeθjón mənwá lə ne-
Kéle/le Klásə əʂtáʔ e méðjo eθér//eprəm-
dé reθjéṇdc/səgýn θéṇtrez ðéiṇtəréz múi
ɓjé məʂtnðjáðcs/ləɓó al meéṣtrc ðə ʄi e
Krəá rnne əskwéle pere le ɓíðe/pór le
ɓíðe//éʂtə é səl léme ənerɓcláᵒ pcr les
xóɓəməs xəməreθjónəz ðə əðnkeðórəz
ðe éʂtə síglc//

CONVERSACION TELEFONICA (Ceceo)

Suena el teléfono y contesta Julia.

Julia-   Dígame.
Alberto- ¿Hablo con Julia?
Julia-   Sí, la misma.
Alberto- Este es Alberto. Dime ¿qué programa tie-
          nes para mañana?
Julia-   Pues nada de especial. ¿Por qué?
Alberto- Porque tengo unas entradas para el teatro
          y, si quieres, puedes venir conmigo.
Julia-   ¿Qué es lo que dan?
Alberto- Dan la zarzuela de Manuel de Falla El som-
          brero de tres picos.
Julia-   ¡Formidable! ¿Dónde nos encontramos y a
          qué hora empieza?
Alberto- Comienza a las diez y nos encontraremos en
          la Plaza Mayor, donde tomaremos un café y
          luego vamos a la función en el Centro Cul-
          tural de Madrid.
Julia-   Muy bien. Pues hasta las nueve y gracias.
Alberto- De nada. Estaré esperándote con mucho
          gusto.

347

//kombarsaθjóŋ talafóniko//

/swéno al teléfonox kontéste xúlja//
//xúlja // dígema //
//albérto// ¿áblo koŋ xúlja?//
//xúlja/ sí/ lo mízmo//
//albérto//ésta e selbérto// díma ¿ké prográmo
tjénos pere menáno?//
//xúlja// pwéz naðe ðe ospaθjál// ¿porké?//
//albérto//pórka téŋgox ne santráðos pere al
taátro/! si kjéros/pwéðoz banír konmíɣo//
//xúlja//¿ké éz lo ko ðán?//
//albérto//dán lo θerθwélo ðo menwél da fáljo/al
sombréro ðe trés píkos//
//xúlja//¡formidáblo!//¿dónda no saŋkontrámoz
ya ké óro ompjéθo?//
//albérto//komjénθo e loz ðjéθ! mo saŋkontrerémo
san lo pláθo meyór/dónda tomorémo san
kaféɫ lwéɣo ðámo se le fnŋθjó no nal θén-
tro kaltorál da moðríð//
//xúlja//múɫ bjén//pwé sáɫto loz nwéðeɫ grá-

θjas//
//ɘlbértɘ// dɘ náðɘ// ɘsterẽ ɘspɘráɲdɘtɘ kɛm
múê͡ɘ gýʂtɘ//

LAS DROGAS (General Hispanic American)

Cuidar y recomponer el organismo tiene antece-
dentes simultáneos con la aparición del hombre en la
Tierra. Una constante de investigaciones y sacrifi-
cios engalana un friso en que el ser humano puede
observar satisfecho el proceso; el triunfo sobre las
enfermedades es casi total. Probablemente el primer
gran estudio científico de los medicamentos se en-
cuentra en la labor desarrollada por el ilustre fi-
siólogo Harvey (1578-1657). Christopher Wren, ar-
quitecto inglés, realiza un aporte trascendental en
la historia de la farmacología sugiriendo la posibi-
lidad de inyectar medicamentos en las venas de los
animales. Hasta ese momento, los remedios y tóxicos
eran asimilados a través de la boca. Un enriqueci-
miento vital para esta teoría de Wren lo realizó
Robert Boyle. Por vía endovenosa aplicó opio y compuestos de antimonio a perros. La confirmación fue
total; los elementos eran activos al ser inyectados.
La deducción es inevitable; las drogas tomadas por
boca obran después de haber sido absorbidas y pasa-
das al torrente circulatorio. Se hace necesaria una
delimitación de riesgos, y Juan Wepfer la realiza a
través del primer tratado de farmacología Historia y
toxicidad de la cicuta. Wepfer expone claramente
los peligros que se producen con el uso indiscrimi-
natorio de ciertos elementos como el mercurio y el
arsénico. Sin embargo, se hacen imprescindibles estos puntos de apoyo para todos los aportes de la
química y la fisiología. A mediados del siglo diecinueve, ambos pilares adquieren un óptimo desarrollo. El alemán Serturner y el francés Pelletier
descubrieron y aislaron las primeras drogas química-
mente puras. En forma simultánea, los grandes vivi-
sectores franceses de principio de siglo experimen-
tan y fundamentan los métodos de la fisiología. El
camino se ensancha. Claude Berhard, tal vez uno de
los más grandes fisiólogos de todos los tiempos, realiza su aporte máximo al descubrir que la inyección
de curare produce la paralización muscular. Los a-
lemanes llevan cierta cuota de gloria al establecer
la ciencia de los medicamentos como disciplina inde-
pendiente. La resultante de toda esta evolución se
puede verificar en la farmacología actual. Las ten-

dencias de hoy se dedican a investigar las relaciones entre la estructura química de los medicamentos y sus actividades farmacológicas. El camino es largo pero con un final previsto: el triunfo de la inteligencia humana sobre los males que aquejan al hombre.

//lꜫz fróğꜫs//

//kwiδá rꞎ ř̄ak꞉mp꞉né ra l꞉rgenꞏꜧzm꞉
tjéna entasaδénꞏt꞉s sꞏmaꞏtánaꞇs k꞉n l꞉ ꜟperꞏsjón da lómbra꜀ꞏn l꞉ tjéꞁꞁꞃn꞉ k꞉nꞎtánꞏta
δꞃꞏmbaꞎtꞏg꞉sjóna sꞏ sꞋkrꞏfꞏsjo saꞃ꞉ꞁámaꞃꞃ frꞏꞇ꞉꞉ꞃ k꞉꜀꞉l sé r꞉mán꞉ pweδꞃꞋꞋꞏsarꞇár
sꞋtꞏsfꞋꞇꞋ꞉꞉l pr꞉sꞋꞇ꞉/aꞎ trꞏꞋꞁꞏmf꞉ s꞉꜀r꞉ l꞉ saꞃꞁ꞉rma꞉δáδ꞉ sꞋꞇꞎ kásꞏ t꞉tál//pr꞉꜀aꞇ꜀lamḗnꞏtā ꞉l prꞏmḗr grá naꞎtꞏ꞉δjo sjꞋꞁꞏtꞏꞁꞏk꞉ δ꞉ l꞉z
maδꞏkꞋmḗnꞏt꞉s s꞉꜀꞉ꞁkwḗꞁꞏtre꞉꜀n l꞉ lꞋꞇ꞉ꞃꞁ δasꞋꞃ꞉yáδꞃ p꞉꜀꞉ r꞉ lꞏlꞇꞎtra fꞏsjól꞉gꞃ xárꞇꞏ//mꞏꞎl kꞏꞋꞏmjḗꞁꞏt꞉s saꞇaꞁꞏteꞃóꞇ꞉/mꞏꞎl sꞋꞇꞏsjḗꞁꞏt꞉ sꞏꞁꞁkweꞁꞏtaꞏꞋꞁsjé꞉t꞉//krꞏꞏꞎꞋꞇ꞉f꞉r ř̄ḗn/ꞃꞏꞋꞁꞋꞇꞃ toꞏꞁꞁꞁleꞎ/ř̄aꞇꞃlꞏsaꞃ naꞃ꞉r꞉t꞉ trasaꞁꞃꞋꞁꞏtá l꞉n laꞏꞎtóꞃꞁja δ꞉ l꞉ fꞋrmꞋk꞉l꞉xꞏꞁꞃ snxꞏꞃꞁꞋꞁꞏt꞉ l꞉ p꞉sꞏꞇꞃlꞏδá δꞃꞏꞁꞁy꞉꜀tár maδꞏkꞋmḗnꞏt꞉ san lꞋz ꞇꞃꞁꞋz δ꞉ l꞉ sꞋꞁꞏmꞁál꞉s//
ásꞏt꞉꜀és꞉ m꞉mḗnꞏt꞉/l꞉ ꞃꞃmḗδjo sꞏ tósꞏk꞉ séꞃa naꞋsꞏmꞏꞎlꞁáδꞃ saꞁrꞃꞇḗz δ꞉ lꞃ ꞇꞁóꞁk꞉꜀ꞁ naꞁꞁꞏꞁkasꞏꞋmjéꞁnꞏt꞉ ꞇꞏꞏꞁꞁál parꞃꞃéꞎꞏt꞉ ta꞉rꞏꞋꞏ δ꞉ ꞃḗn l꞉ ꞃaꞃlꞏsó ꞃꞏ꞉꜀꞉r ꞇ꞉ꞎꞎꞎl//par ꞇꞏꞋꞃ꜀ꞁꞁ꞉d꞉꜀Ꞌꞁꞁáꞃ꞉
352

əpliko ópjɔi kɔmpwéʃtɛz ða entimónjo e pé-
ʀɔs // lə kɔɱfirmɛsjón fwe tɔtál // lɛ sɔlɑméɲtə
sére nektíbə sɛl se ʀiɲɔʀtáðɛs // lə ðɑðnʰsjó ne
simɑbitáblɑ / lɛz ðróɟɛʂ tɔmáðɛs pɔʀ bókə óbʀɛɲ
dɑspwéz ðə ʀbéʀ síðɛ esɛʀbíðɛ si pesáðɛ sɛl
tɔʀéɲtə siʀknlətórjo // sə ásə nɑsɑsárja nnə ðə-
limitɛsjóɲ də fjézɡɛs / i xwáɱ wéʷfɔʀ lə fɑʒlí-
sə ʀtʀɔbéz ðɑl pʀiméʀ tʀɔtáðɛ ðə fɛʀmɔkɛlɔ-
xíɛ / iʂtórjɑi tɛsisiðá ðə lə siκútə // wéʷfɔʀ ɑspónə
kleʀɛméɲtɑ lɛs políɟʀɛs kə sə pʀɔfúsɑɲ kɛ nɑ lúsɔiɲ
diskʀiminɛtórjo ðə sjéʀtɛ sɑlɑméɲtɛs kɛmɛ ɑl mɑʀkú-
ʀjo yɑ lɛʀsénikɛ // si nɑmbáʀɟɛ / sə ásə nimpʀɑsiɲdí-
blɑ séʂtɛs péɲtɛs ðə ɛpóyɛ pɛʀɛ tóbɛ lɛ sɛpóʀtɛz ðə
lɛ kímikɑi lə fisjolɛxíɛ // ɛ mɑðjáðɛz ðɑl síɟlɛ ðjɛ-
sinwébɑ / ámbɛs pílɑʀɑ sɛʷkjéʀɑ nn nóʷtimɛ ðɑsɛ-
ʀóyɛ // ɑ lɑlɑmáɲ sɑʀtúʀnə ʀjɑl fʀɛnsés pɑlɑtjéʀ
ðɑsknbʀjéʀɛn jɑizlóʀɛn lɛs pʀiméʀɛz ðróɟɛs kimi-
kɛméɲtɑ púʀɛs / ɑɲ fórmɛ simɑltánɑɛ / lɛz ɡráɲ-
dɛz bibisɑʷtóʀɑs fʀɛnsésɑz ðə pʀinsípjo ðə síɟlɛ ɑspɑʀiméɲtɛ ni fnɲdeméɲtɛn lɛz métɛðɛz

353

ða lə fisjoloxíe//al kəmíno sə ònsánĉe//klóð
borár/təl bé súno ða loz máz grándos fisjólo-
gos ða tóðo loz tjémpos/fəəlíse swapórtə má-
simo əl dəskonbrír kə laɲĝe'sjóɲ də knrárə
profúsə lə pərəlisesjóɲ mnskníár//lə səlamánaz
rében sjérte kwóte ða glórjâ ə ləʂteblasér lə
sjénsjə ða loz maðikeméntos kómo ðisiplínaɲn-
dəpəndjéntə//lə rəsnʃtántə ða tóðe esʃte əbolo-
sjóɲ sə pwéðə barifiká ran lə fərmakoloxíe ə-
twəl//ləʂ təɲdénsjaz ða ʃí sə ðaðíkə naɲmbəs-
tigár lə rələsjónə sənʃrə lə əʂtronʳtúrə kímɪkə ða
loz maðikeméntə sɪ sn səʳtɪ!bɪ!ðəðəs fəmpkolóxɪkes//
al kemíno éz lárgo pərə ko mnɲ finál
prəbéʃto/al trjémfo ða laɲtalixénsjə nmánə
sobro loz máles kə əkéxə nə lómbrə//

UN MATRIMONIO TURISTA VISITA AL PRADO (Ceceo)

Los señores Reguero visitan al Museo del Prado.

Sr. Reguero-   Apresúrate, mujer; el guía que da ex-
                plicaciones está para salir.
Sra. Reguero-   ¡Ya voy! ¡Ya voy! Déjame ponerme
                las gafas; si no, no veré nada.
Sr. Reguero-   Bueno, tómate el tiempo que quieras
                porque el grupo acaba de salir y te-
                nemos que hacer la visita por nuestra
                cuenta.
Sra. Reguero-   ¿Por dónde quieres empezar?
Sr. Reguero-   Siempre he tenido interés especial en
                las pinturas de Goya de manera que
                quisiera dedicarme a estudiarlas en
                detalle.
Sra. Reguero-   Sería bien consultar el catálogo para
                ver en qué salas quedan.
Sr. Reguero-   Vamos a la sala donde está la Maja
                Desnuda y luego me interesaría ver su
                autorretrato.
Sra. Reguero-   Pues la primera sí pero la otra queda
                en la Academia de San Fernando.
Sr. Reguero-   Si el tiempo nos alcanza, iremos allí
                también.

355

//ʊn mɛtrimónjo tɾɛ́stɘ ɓisítɘ ɘl práɗɔ//

//lɔs saɲóɾa ɾaɠéɾɔ ɓisítɘ ɘl mʊséɔ ɗal práɗɔ//

//saɲóɾ ɾaɠéɾɔ// ɘprasúɾɘta/mɐxéɾ/ɘl ɡíɘ kɐ ɗá ɔs-
plikɘθjónɘ sɘçtá pɘɾɘ sɘlíɾ//

//saɲóɾɘ ɾaɠéɾɔ//¡yá ɓɔ́x!//¡yá ɓɔ́x!//déxɘmɘ
pɘnéɾmɘ lɐz ɡáfɘs/si nó/mɘ
ɓaɾé náɗɘ//

//saɲóɾ ɾaɠéɾɔ// bwénɔ/tómɘtɘ ɘl tjémpɔ kɐ
kjéɾɘs pórkɐ ɘl ɡɾúpɔ ɘkáɓɘ
ɗa sɘlíɾ/¡ tanémɔs kɐ ɘθéɾ lɘ
ɓisítɘ pɔɾ nwéçtɾɘ kwéɲtɘ//

//saɲóɾɘ ɾaɠéɾɔ//¿pɔɾ ɗóɲdɘ kjéɾɘ sɘmpɘθáɾ?//

//saɲóɾ ɾaɠéɾɔ// sjémpɾɘ é taní ɓɔɪ̃ɲtaɾé sɘspɘ-
θjá lɘn lɘs pɪ̃ɲtúɾɘz ɗa ɡóyɘ
ɗa manéɾɘ kɐ kɪsjéɾɘ ɗɘɗikáɾ-
mɘ ɘ açtɘɗjáɾlɘ sɘɲ ɗatálɘ//

//saɲóɾɘ ɾaɠéɾɔ//saɾíɘ ɓjéŋ kɔnsɘlta ɾɘl katálɘɡɔ
pɘɾɘ ɓé ɾaŋ ké sálɘs kéɗɘn//

//saɲóɾ ɾaɠéɾɔ//bámɔ sɘ lɘ sálɘ ɗóɲdɘ ɘçtá lɘ
mɐ́xɘ ɗɘznúɗaɪ̣ lwéɡɔ meɪ̃ɲtɘɾasɘ-

356

ríe ðér swéɥterátráte//

//sonóre ñagére// pwéz le priméra sí/para le ótre

kéðe en le ekeðémja ða sám

fornánde//

//sanór ñagére// sjeḷ tjémpe me seḷkánðe/

¡réme seḷí tembjén//

EL CASTELLANO EN ARGENTINA (Hispanic American--River Plate Variety)

La lengua castellana ha encontrado en Argentina algunos de sus más excelsos cultores y cuenta con nombres que figuran entre los primeros de aquéllos. El pueblo mismo habla y describe con soltura y no escasa belleza un idioma cuyos orígenes se confunden con los principios de nuestra civilización. Las naturales modificaciones y evoluciones que los tiempos, las circunstancias geográficas y sociales y la pluralidad de razas y nacionalidades han determinado no desmerecer esta herencia, sino enriquecerla. Es verdad que mucho queda por mejorar y perfeccionar, pero el balance no es en conjunto negativo. Los modernos medios de comunicación tienen, en este sentido, una fuerza incomparable y no siempre positiva tanto que es obra estéril la que los maestros y profesores pueden cumplir en las aulas si aquellos medios tan poderosos deshacen implacablemente su labor.

No se trata, por cierto, de defender la afectación, la pureza gramatical propia de otros ámbitos y ni siquiera de evitar la fresca y vital renovación que el habla común y los fenómenos propios del desarrollo histórico introducen en la estructura de la lengua.

El idioma es un cuerpo vivo, cuyo engrandecimiento y cuyas variaciones son prueba de fortaleza y hasta de grandeza espiritual. Pero lo que debe impedirse es la ramplonería, el mal gusto, la deformación consciente e innecesaria, la trasformación, en fin, de un noble instrumento en una pobre y envilecida herramienta.

Claro está que este tipo de situación sociológico-lingüística no es fácil de resolver. Frente a la justificada inquietud de aquellos envueltos en la enseñanza, y también de un buen sector de la población, lo mejor es iniciar una acción tendiente a obtener una comprensión del problema por parte de los responsables directos, hasta que se logren decisiones voluntarias para poner fin a tanta y tan innecesaria corrupción idiomática como a diario invade nuestros ambientes. Inclusive podría llegarse a verdaderas competiciones que otorgaran galardones a quienes más hayan hecho, en determinado período, por la elegancia y la pureza de esta lengua que los argentinos sienten tan suya y tan hermosa.

//əl kəṣtəžánⁿ* ə nⁿrxəɲtínɐ//

//lɐ léⁿgwa kɐṣtəžáⁿ á əɲkoⁿtráðə ə
nⁿrxəɲtíⁿ ɐlgúⁿɔz ðə snz má səᵏsélsɔs kəl-
tórəs /¡ kwéⁿtɐ kɔn nɔ́mbrəs kə fᵢgúrɐ
nəɲtrə lɔs prᵢmérɔz ðə ɐkéžɔs//əl pwéblɔ
mízmɔ áblaᵢ ðəskríbə kɔn sɔltúraᵢ nɔ əs-
kásɐ təžésəᵢ nᵢðjómɐ kúžɔ sɔrᵢxənəs sə
kɔ m fúⁿdə ŋ kɔn lɔs prᵢnsípjɔz ðə nwéṣtrɐ
sᵢbᵢlᵢsɐsjɔ́n//lɐz nⁿtⁿrálɔz mɔðᵢfᵢkɐsjónəz
yəbɔlⁿsjónəs kə lɔᵢ tjémpɔs /lⁿs sᵢrkⁿnⁿ ṣ-
tánsjəs xɔɔgráfᵢkⁿ sᵢ sɔsjálɔs/¡ lɐ plⁿrɐlᵢðá
ðɔ ⁿásⁿ sᵢ nⁿsjonⁿlᵢðáðɔs /áⁿ datərmᵢnáðɔ nɔ
ðɔz marəsé réṣtⁿ ərénsja /sᵢnó ⁿanᵣᵢkⁿsér lⁿ//
éz tərðá kə múĉɔ kéðⁿ pɔr maxⁿrá rᵢ pⁿr-
fɔᵏsjonár /pⁿrɔ əl bⁿlánsə nɔ é səŋ kⁿŋ-
xúⁿtɔ nəgⁿtíbɔ// lɔz mɔðérnɔs méðjɔz ðə

* Note that in the River Plate area, 11 and y
are palatalized [ž]--a **lleísmo** variant.

360

komunikesjón tjénon/a néṣtə saṇtíδc/ine
fwér saiŋkomperáblej nc sjémprə positíδe
taṇtə ka é sóbre aṣtéril le ka lcz meéṣtrc
si prcfasóras pwéδaŋ kamplí ran le saᶍlez reké-
žez meδjaṣ tem paδaróscz δasása nimplekeδlə-
méṇtə sn leδór//

//nc se tráte/per sjértc/da δafaṇdér.
le efaᵏtesjón/le pnrése gremetikál própja
δə ótrc sámbitcs/ ni sikjére δə aδitár le
fréskai δitál ranctesjón ka a láδle kcmýn/!
lcs fanómancs própjəz δeḷ daserś žaᶎṣtóríkc,
iṇtreδúsa nan le aṣtrᵏtúre δa le léṇgwa//

//a liδjóme é say kwérpc δíδc/kúžc aŋ-
greṇdesimjéṇtəi kúžez δerjasjónes sóm
prwéδe δa fcrtelése yáṣte δa greṇdése aspi-
ritwál//parc lc ka δéδeim paδírsa éz le rem-
plenaríe/al mál gýstc/le δafcrmesjón kcn-
sjéṇtə einnasasárja/le trensfcrmesjón/am
fᶍn/déᶍn nóδlein ṣtrnméṇtc a none pó-
δrə yambilasíδe aremjéṇte//

361

//kláro aṣtá /ka éṣto típo ða sitwasjón sosjo-
lóxiko liŋgwéṣtike/ no és fásil da ꭓaselbér//
fréṇta e le xnṣtifikáðaịn kjetú ða ekéꭓo som-
bwéịto san le ansanánse/ı tembjéṇ déxm
bwén saᵏtór ða le poblesjón/lo maxó ré
sinisjá rnne ᵉᵏsjóṇ taṇdjéṇto e otané rnne
kompronsjóṇ dal probléme por párto ða lo
ꭓospensábloz ðiréᵏtos/áṣte ka so lógraṇ
dasisjónoz bolnṇtárjas perp ponér fi ne táṇ-
taị tá ninnasosárja koꭓnsjó niðjomátike kómo e ðjárjoịmbáðo nwéṣtro sembjéṇtos//
ıŋklnsíbo poðríe žagárso e barðeðéres
kompatisjónos ka otorgáreŋ golorðóno se
kjénoz ma sáže néꭓo/aṇ datormináðo po-
ríoðo/por le alagánsjaị le pnrése ða éṣto
léŋgwe ka lo serxaṇtínos sjéṇtoṇ tán
súžaị tá normóse//

362

UN RESTORAN DE LA ZONA ROSA DE MEXICO (Mexican)

Dos amigos comparten una mesa al aire libre.

Marcelo- ¿Qué prefieres primero, un aperitivo o un refresco?
Juan-   Hace tanto calor que prefiero una limonada. ¿Y tú?
Marcelo- Yo probaré un poco de tequila.

Ordenan las bebidas al camarero y luego miran el menú.

Marcelo- ¿Qué te parece si probamos estas enchiladas?
Juan-   No es mala idea pero los tacos y el guacamole me gustan más.
Marcelo- Pidamos platos diferentes así probamos de todos un poco.
Juan-   O.K. pero pide unos bolillos también. ¿Tienes alguna preferencia para el postre?
Marcelo- Sí, yo quiero pay y luego un cafecito.
Juan-   Y yo un poco de queso de Chihuahua con una <u>Corona</u>.

‖ɑn ʔɑ̧ʂtɔɾáŋ də lə sónɐ ɾ̄ɔ̄ʂɐ ðə mɛ́xıkɔ‖

‖dó səmíɡɔs kɔmpártə nɑnə mésɛ̃ ɛ̃ lɑ́ʃɾɔ
líðɾɔ‖

‖mɐɾsélɔ‖ ¿ké pɾɑfjéɾɑs pɾıméɾɔ/n nəpɑɾıtí-
tɔ ɔ́xn ʔɑfɾéʃkɔ*‖

‖hwán‖ ásə tán̩tɔ kɐlɔ́ɾ kɔ pɾɑfjéɾɔx nɐ
lımɔnáðɐ/ ¿! tú?‖

‖mɐɾsélɔ‖ ɾó pɾɐðɐɾéɣm pókɔ ðə tɑkílɐ‖
‖ɔɾðénɐn lɐz ðɐðíðɐ sɐl kɐmɐɾéɾɔ̧ lwéɡɔ
míɾɐ nɑl mɑnú‖

‖mɐɾsélɔ‖ ¿ké tɐ pɐɾéʃə s! pɾɔðámɔ̄ʰ éʃtɐʰ
ɑnĉ!láðɐs?‖

‖hwán‖ nɔ éz mɑ́lɑ̧ ðéɐ pɑɾɔ lɔʰ tákɐʰ ɣɑl
ɡwɑkɐmólə mɑ ɡ/ʃtɐn más‖
‖mɐɾsélɔ‖ p!ðámɔʃ plátɐʰ ðıfɑɾéntɔ sɐʃí
pɾɔðámɔʃ ðə tóðɔ sɑm pókɔ‖

---

* Mexicans often articulate sibilants rather
strongly--[S] or [Ṣ].

364

//hwán// ɔkɛí / pɔrɔ píðɛx mɔh tɕɔlíɔ̀;*
　　tɛmbjén//ɛ̀ tjénɔ sɛlgúnɛ
　　prɔfɔrénʃjɔ pɛrɛ ɔl póʃtrɔ?//
//mɔrsélɔ// sí / ɣó kjérɔ paí! lwéɣɔxɳ kɛfɔ-
　　ʃítɔ//
//hwán// ! ɣó nm pókɔ ðɔ kéʃɔ ðɔ ĉiwáwɔ
　　kɔ nɔmɛ kɔrónɛ//

---

* An example of the [ʒ] variant of yeísmo,
typical of Mexican articulation.

365

IDIOMAS EXTRANJEROS (General Hispanic American)

Cuando llega el momento en que tienen que tomar
una decisión en cuanto a su futuro trabajo, casi todos los estudiantes que se especializan en idiomas
extranjeros tienen el mismo problema. Sienten la
obligación de escoger un empleo que les parezca a-
gradable y útil ya que se supone que van a desempe-
ñarlo por toda la vida. Si por acaso escogieran algo que poco les agradara, que no les diera satisfac-
ción alguna, pronto se aburrirían y seguirían trabajando relativamente mal. Desde luego hay otros aspectos de la vida del trabajo--las condiciones dia-
rias, el sueldo, la aprobación social, los benefi-
cios, y otros tantos.

Antes de matricularse en las distintas universidades de nuestro país, algunos habrían pensado seriamente en las múltiples profesiones que iban a poder
escoger algún día. Otros, menos entusiasmados por la
vida estudiantil y menos por la del trabajo, se habrían matriculado sin pensar seriamente en su futuro.
En cambio, los que se decidieron bastante temprano a
estudiar lenguas extranjeras tienen que encarar un
problema no muy agradable y una situación económica
y profesional bastante grave. ¿Qué van a poder hacer después de graduarse y a qué podrán aplicar sus
conocimientos de lenguas por modestos que sean? Algunos tienen pensado relacionar el estudio de lenguas
con el comercio de una manera u otra. Otros tienen
proyectada la carrera de intérprete en los tribunales
o, quizás, en las Naciones Unidas. Desgraciadamente
debemos ser realistas hasta cierto punto, y en muchos
casos lo del intérprete no sería nada más que un sueño, una ilusión. Hay, además, un pequeño núcleo de
estudiantes que sueñan con llegar a ser catedráticos
cuando hayan acabado sus estudios de ampliación. Este es otro sueño en muchos casos, sea porque no tienen la capacidad de alcanzar tal nivel intelectual,
sea por la actual situación económica, sea por el estado decaído en que se encuentran los estudios de
lenguas en la actualidad. Otros tantos quisieran ser
maestros de escuela secundaria porque les encanta la
idea de poder estimular la mente de los chicos y con-
ducirlos hacia un interés bastante dinámico en el es-

tudio del español o de otros idiomas. Los universitarios bien dedicados a la enseñanza de idiomas creen entenderse bastante de los métodos más recientes y de la pedagogía más moderna. Estos futuros profesores de idiomas ven la enseñanza de lenguas como combinación de lo vivo y lo correcto y lo dinámico a la vez y se aplican con gravedad a su trabajo futuro. Pero ¿qué les impide que desempeñen tal misión cultural y lingüística? Los que están verdaderamente envueltos en la actual situación pedagógica se sentirían obligados a contestar en seguida--la sociedad. Desafortunadamente vivimos en una época en la que los valores culturales, humanos y artísticos están mal vistos. Por consecuencia, los estudiantes de hoy realmente dedicados a tal enseñanza tienen la doble misión de tratar de colocarse dondequiera que puedan y de seguir luchando, trabajando y enseñando los altos valores de la comunidad universal de todos los seres humanos a fin de que las generaciones futuras puedan gozar de un aprecio más profundo y más significativo de las distintas culturas y tengan conocimientos bien arraigados de los valores inacabables del "hombre colectivo" a través del globo.

// ¡ðjóme saˠstreɲxéros //

// kwándo ɣéɣe al momento aɲ ka tjénaɲ
ka tomá rone ðasisjó. naɲ kwánto e sa fntúro
treβáxo / kási tóðoz lo saꟅtnðjáɲtas ka sa aspa-
sjalíse na niðjóme saꟅtreɲxéros tjéna nol míz-
mo probléme // sjéɲtan le obligesjóɲ da askexé
rn namplée ka las peréske egreðáβla yútil ye
ka sa sn póna ka βá ne ðasampaɲárlo por tóðe le βíðe // si po rekáso askexjére nálgo ka
póko la segreðáre / ka no laz ðjére setisfeksjó
nelgúne / próɲto sa ebnñiríe ni sagiríeɲ tre-
βexándo ñaletiβeménta mál // dézðo lwégo /
aí ótro sespéˠtoz ðo le βíðe ðal treβáxo / las
Kondisjónoz ðjárjas / al swéldo / le eprobesjóɲ
sosjál / loz banafísjoz rótroz táɲtos //

// eɲtaz ða metriknlársa an lez ðistíɲte
snnibarsiðáðoz ða nwéꟅtro peís / elgúno sebríem
pansáðo sarjaméɲto an lez múltiplas prefasjó-
nas ka íβe ne poðé raskexé relgúɲ díe //
ótros / méno saɲtnsjazmáðos por le βíðe aꟅ-

tndjantí li ménos por la ðaj trebáxo /sə ztríən
metrikuláðo sim pansár sarjaménta ən sn fntúro //əy
kámbjo /lós kə sə ðasiðjérom beṣtánta tampráno ə əṣ-
tndjár léŋgwa sastrənxéres /tjénəy kə ənkwrá
rnm prɔblémə nɔ múi̯ egreðáblə ynnə sitwasjó
nəkɔnómikai profasjonál beṣtántə grábə /i ké ðá nɔ
pɔðé resér dəspwéz ðə grɛdwársə yɛ ké pɔðrá
mɛplikár sns kɔmɔsimjéntɔz ðə léŋgwas por mɔ-
ðéṣtɔs kə séɛn? //ɛlgúnɔṣ tjénəm pansáðɔ Falɛsjo-
ná rə laṣtúdjo ðə léŋgwas kɔ nal kɔmérsjo ðɛunə
mɛnéro wótro //ótrɔṣ tjénəm prəyaktáðɛ lɛ
kɛréro ðɛintérprətə ən lɔṣ tribnnálas /ɔ/kisás/
ən lɛz nɛsjónə snmiðɛs //dəzgrɛsjaðəméṇtə/
dəðémɔs sér Faɛliṣtə seṣtə sjérto púṇtɔ /jen
múĉɔs kásɔs lɔ ðə liṇtérprətə nɔ saríɛ náðə
más kɛun swéno /n maẖlnsjón //áẖ /ɛðəmás/
nm pakéno núklɔ ðə əṣtndjáṇtas kə swénəy
kɔn ɣagá rɛ sér kɛtaðrátikɔs kwáṇdɔ áyɛ nɛ-
kɛðáðɔ sn saṣtúðjoz ðə ɛmpljasjón //éṣtə é sótrɔ swéno ən múĉɔs kásɔs /séɛ pɔrkə nɔ

tjénan lə kəpəsiðá ðə əlkənsár tál niðé liŋ-
talaᵏtwál/sée pər lə ə̃ᵏtwál sitwasjó nakənómikə/
sée pə rə laʂtáðə ðakəíðə əy kə sə əŋkwéŋ-
trən lə saʂtúðjoz ðə léŋgwa san lə ə̃ᵏtwaliðá//
ótrəʂ táŋtəs kisjérən sér məéʂtrəz ðə əskwélə
sakəndárja pórkə lə saŋkáŋtə laiðé'ə ðə pəðé
raʂtimnlár lə méŋtə ðə ləs ɛ́ikə si kəndasírlə
sásjəx niŋtərés bəʂtáŋtə ðinámikə ə nə
laʂtúðjo ðə laspəŋól/ə ðə ótrə siðjómes//lə
snmiðarsitárjəz bjéŋ dəðikáðə sə lə ansəŋánsə
ðeiðjómes kréə nəŋtəndérsə bəʂtáŋtə ðo ləz
métəðəz má rəsjéŋtə si ðə lə pəðəgəxíə máz
məðérnə/óʂtəs fntúrəs prəfasórəz ðeiðjómez béŋ
lə ansəŋánsə ðə léŋgwəs kómə kəmbinesjóŋ
də lə ðíðəi lə kərɛ́ᵏtəi lə ðinámikə ə lə bés/
i sə əplíkəŋ kəŋ grəbəðáə sn trəbáxə fntú-
rə//pərə ¿ké la simpíðə kə ðasampéŋəŋ tál
misjón kultnrá li liŋgwéʂtikə?//lós kə əʂtám
bərðəðarəméŋtə əmbwéltə san lə ə̃ᵏtwál
sitwasjóm pəðəgóxikə sə saŋtiríə nəbligáðə sə

370

kontaştá ransagíðe/le sosjeðá//dasefortonpeðe-
ménta bibímo sa none époke an le ka loz ße-
lóras kultorálas/nmános/jartíştiko saştán
mál bíştos//por konsakwénsja/lo saştnðjántaz
ða ói ñaelménta ðaðikáðo se tá lansanán-
se tjénan le ðóbla misjón da tretár ða ko-
lokársa ðondakjére ka pwéðe ni ða sagír
lncánde/treßexándo yansanánde lo sáltoz
ßelóraz ða le komnmíðá nmißarsál da tóðoz los séra snmáno se fín da ka les xa-
maresjónos fntúres pwéðen gosár ða nne-
présjo más profúndo más simifikatíbo
ða lez ðiştíntes knltúre si téngen ko-
nosimjéntoz bjé neñaigáðoz ða loz ßeló-
ra sinekeßáblaz ða lombra kolaktíbo e-
treßéz ðal glóbo//

EN EL MERCADO DE RIO PIEDRAS, PUERTO RICO (Puerto
    Rican)

    Ana y Rosa van al mercado.

Ana-   ¿Recuerdas todo lo que debemos comprar?
Rosa-   Sí, pero si veo algo que me gusta y está a
        buen precio lo compraré también.
Ana-   ¡Chévere! Mira que buenas chinas tienen en
        este puesto.
Rosa-   Y los guineos tampoco son malos. Compremos
        una docena de cada uno.
Ana-   Ya tenemos la fruta. Vamos al puesto de aves.
Rosa-   O.K. Si encontramos un pollo grande lo com-
        pramos. Así podemos hacer arroz con pollo.
Ana-   Tienes razón porque si nos sobra luego podemos
        preparar un asopao.
Rosa-   No olvidemos comprar habichuelas y garbanzos;
        siempre es bueno tener algo extra.
Ana-   Realmente a mí me gustaría preparar una pae-
        lla a la valenciana pero cuesta bastante di-
        nero y trabajó.
Rosa-   Sí, es verdad. Quedémonos con éstos y pensa-
        remos en las comidas de lujo otro día.

//ə nal markáðɔ ðə r̃ɛ́ɔ pjéðres/pwέrtɔ r̃íkɔ//

//ánai̯ r̃ósɐ t̆á nɐl markáðɔ//

//ánɐ// ¿r̃akwérðeʰ* tóɔ lɔ kə ðət̆émɔʰ kɔmprár?//

//r̃ósɐ// sí/parɔ sı̣ t̆éɔ álgɔ kə mə gų́ʰtɐ yɔʰt̆á ɐ
t̆wém présjo lɔ kɔmprɐré tɐmbjéŋ**//

//ánɐ//¡cĕt̆ara!//mírɐ kə t̆wénɐʰ ĉı́nɐʰ tjé-
mɔ mɔ néʰta pwéʰtɔ//

//r̃ósɐ//¡lɔʰ g̣! méɔʰ tɐmpókɔ sɔ́ŋ málɔs//
kɔmprémɔ ʰnnɐ ðɔsénɐ ðə káðɐ únɔ//

//ánɐ//dʒá tanémɔʰ lɐʰ frútɐʰ//bámɔʰ ɐl
pwéʰtɔ ðə át̆əʰ//

---

* The apico-alveolar multiple vibrant [r̃] is
frequently rendered a retroflex [r̃] in Puerto Rico
and elsewhere in the Caribbean. The aspiration of
internal-final and absolute-final sibilants is also
fairly normal in the Caribbean; i.e., estos>ehtoh.

** Final -n, especially in plural verb-forms
but frequently elsewhere, is typically velarized
[ŋ].

//ɾóse//ɔkéi̯//sjeŋ kɔŋtrámɔ ʰnm póɾɔ gránda
lɔ kɔmprámɔʰ//esí pɔðémɔ ʰɐsé ɐ̃ɔ̃ʰ
kɔm póɾɔ//
//áne//tjénə ře sɔ́ŋ/pólka sɪ nɔʰ sóbre lwégɔ
pɔðémɔʰ prɔpɐrá rn nɐsɔpáɔ//
//ɾóse//nɔɔ́lbiðémɔʰ kɔmprá reɐ̯bi̯ ĉwélɐ sɪ gɐr-
ɓánsɔʰ//sjémprə éʰ ɓwémɔ tané rálgɔ
ékstre//
//áne//řɐɐlméŋta ɐ mí ma gnʰtɔríɐ prɔpɐ-
ɾá rnne pɐéɣɐ ɐ lɐ ɓɐlɔnsjáne parɔ
kwéṣte ɓɐʰtáŋta dɪnérɔi treɓáhɔ//
//ɾóse// sí/éʰ ɓarðá//kɔðémɔnɔʰ kɔ néʰtɔ
sɪ pɔnsɐrémɔ ʰan lɐʰ kɔmíðeʰ ðə
lýhɔ ótrɔ ðíɐ//

374

EL PAIS DE LOS GAUCHOS HA CAMBIADO (Hispanic Ameri-
can--River Plate Variety)

Hace un siglo y medio la pampa no era de nadie--
una inmensidad de tierra buena y virgen donde los
gauchos y los indios cazaban reses salvajes. Hoy la
Argentina silvestre pertenece a la historia. Los
agrónomos seleccionan con criterio científico las
variedades de cereales más aptas y productivas. Los
cabañeros se esmeran continuamente en el mejoramiento
de las razas, que todos los años son examinadas y
juzgadas en múltiples exposiciones rurales. No ob-
stante, a pocos kilómetros de Buenos Aires, hombres
de campo argentinos mantienen viva la tradición del
gaucho. El orgullo de su historia los lleva a enjaezar sus caballos con adornos de oro y plata. A veces el conjunto de cabalgadura y arreos vale tanto
como un automóvil de lujo.

Buenos Aires es una ciudad para todos. Nació
dos veces: una en 1536 y otra en 1580, después de
su destrucción a manos de los indios. Durante cen-
turias creció con la obstinación de los que se saben
fuertes. Hoy es la ciudad más importante del hemis-
ferio meridional y uno de los centros más activos y
sofisticados del mundo. Buenos Aires, como el país
entero, creció gracias al esfuerzo de hombres y mujeres de todas las nacionalidades. Españoles, ita-
lianos, portugueses, franceses, ingleses, alemanes,
eslavos, rusos, turcos, árabes y judíos llegaron al
Río de la Plata en busca de paz y trabajo.

Sin pausa, el asfalto cubre los viejos empedra-
dos donde, a fines del siglo pasado, rodaron las notas de los primeros tangos, tocados por organilleros
ambulantes. Hoy Buenos Aires es una de las ciudades
más evolucionadas del mundo. Los productos de con-
sumo y el medio cultural sorprenden al viajero por
su excelencia. Por eso es una meca de la calidad y
el buen gusto y un lugar ideal para comprar. Es también un lugar encantador para descubrir los perfiles
más gratos de la vida. En diez kilómetros de una so-
la de sus avenidas se encuentran lugares para comer
y beber, almacenes de comestibles, clubes nocturnos,

canchas de minigolf, negocios de venta de automóvi-
les y lanchas, estaciones de servicio y tiendas de
ropa. Se trata de la Avenida del Libertador, que
une Buenos Aires con uno de sus suburbios, San Isi-
dro. Un poco más al norte, la desembocadura del Río
Paraná se enriquece con un delta lleno de encanto del
que los porteños gozan los fines de semana.

La cultura cosmopolita ha fraguado, al cabo de
un siglo y medio, un alma definida e impar. Un alma
explorada y descubierta día a día por los artistas,
los escritores, los poetas y los músicos. Al militar en la vanguardia del arte occidental, el país se
enorgullece de ser una gran fuente cultural de habla
hispana.

//əl pɐɪ́z ðə lɔz gáx̌ĉɔ sá kɐmbjáðɔ//

//ásə‿ɐn síɣlɔɪ méðjo lɐ pámpɐ nɔ‿érɐ ðə
máðje/n maɪnmɔnsíðá ðə tjéře bwénaɪ b̌írxəŋ
dɔ́ndə lɔz gáx̌ĉɔ sɪ lɔ sɪ́ndjos kɐsáben r̄ésəs sɐlbáxɔs//
óɪ lɐ‿ɐrxəntínɐ sɪlbéštrə pərtənésə‿ɐ laɪstórja//
lɔ sɐɣrónɔmɔs sɔlɐksjónɐʒ kɔŋ krɪtérjo sjɐntífikɐ
lɐʒ b̌erjɐðáðɔʒ ðə sɐrɐáləʒ má sáɐtɐ sɪ prɔðn̄tí-
b̌ɐs//lɔs kɐbɐɲérɔs sɐ‿ðʒmérɐŋ kɔntɪnwaméŋtɐ‿ə
nəl maxɔrɐmjéŋtɔ ðə lɐ r̄ásɐs/kɐ tóðɔ lɔ sáŋɔs só
nɐksɐmɪnáðɐ sɪ xnʒgáðɐ sɔn mýltɪplə sɐ‿ʒpɔsɪ-
sjónə r̄nráləs//nɔ‿ɔ̌ʃtántə/ɐ pókɔs kɪlómətrɔz
ðə bwénɔ sáɪrɐs/ɔ́mbrɔz ðə kámpɐ‿ɐrxəntínɔz
mɐŋtjénəm bíbɐ lɐ trɐðɪsjóŋ dəl gáx̌ĉɔ/ə lɔ-
gúx̌ɔ ðə swɪštórja lɔz žéb̌ɐ‿ə‿əŋxɐasár sɐs
kɐb̌áx̌ɔs kɔ nɐðórnɔz ðə‿órɔɪ plátɐ/ɐ b̌ɐ-
sɐ səl kɔŋxýŋtɔ ðə kɐb̌ɐlgɐðúrɐ yɐr̄ész b̌álə
táŋtɔ kómɔx nɐxtɔmób̌ɪl də lýxɔ//

//bwénɔ sáɪrɐ sé sɐnɐ sjuðá pɐrɐ tóðɔs//
nɐsjó ðɔ́z b̌ésɔs/n nɐ‿ɐn mɪ́l kɪnjéŋtɔʒ trɐɪ̯n
taɪséɪʒ yótrɐ‿ɐn mɪ́l kɪnjéŋtɔ sɔčéŋtɐ/dəspwéz

ða sn ðaʂtrⁿksjó me máⁿɔz ða lɔ síⁿdjɔs//dn-
ráⁿtɔ saⁿtúrjas krasjó kɔn lɒ_ɔʂtinɛsjóⁿ dɔ lɔs kɒ
sɒ sábɔm fwértɔs//ɔ̞į éz lɒ sjuðá má simpɔrtáⁿ-
tɔ ða lamisférjo mariðjonál junc ða lɔs séⁿtrɔz
má sɒᵏtíbc si scfiʂtikáðcz ðal múⁿdc// bwénc
sáįrɔs/kcmc̣ɔl pɛí saⁿtérc/krɔsjó grásja sɒ
lɔsfwérsc ða ɔ́mbrɒ si mɒxérɔz ða tóðɒz lɒz
mɛsjonɒli ðáðɒs//aspɒⁿólɒs/iteljáncs/pcrtnɡésɔs/
frɒnsésɔs/inɡlésɔs/ɒlɒmánɒs/ɒzláðcs/r̄ýscs/
túrkcs/árɒbɒ si xnðícs/žɒɡárc nɒl r̄íc ða lɒ
plátɒ_ɒmbúskɒ ða pá si trɒbáxc//
//sim páųsɒ/ɒ lɒsfáįtc kútbrɒ lcz bjéxc
sɒmpɒðɒráðcz ðóⁿdɒ/ɒ fínɒz ðɒl síɡlc pɒsáðɒ/
r̄cðárcn lɒz nótɒz ða lcs priméɔcʂ tánɡcs/tɒ-
káðcs pc rcrɡɒmižérc sɒmbnláⁿtɒs//ɔį bwénc
sáįrɒ sé snnɒ ða lɒs sjuðáðɒz má sɒbɒlnsjonáðɒz
ðɒl múⁿdc// lcs prcðýᵏtcz ða kcnsúmc yɒl méðjo knįtnrál scrpréⁿdɒ nɒl bjɒxérc pcr swɒᵏsɒ-
lɒⁿsja//pc résc é snnɒ mékɒ ða lɒ kɒliðáį
ðɒl bwéⁿ ɡýįtc rnn lnɡá riðaál pɒrɒ kcmprár//

éş tembjé nnn lngá raŋkeʂteðór pɛrɛ ðasknbŗír
lɔs parfílaz máz grátɔz ða lɛ ɓíðɛ//aʂ djés kilō-
matrɔz ðɛχnɛ sólɛ ða sn sɛɓaníðɛs sã ãŋkwéʂ-
trɛn lngárɔs pɛrɛ Kɔmé rı ɓaɓér/ɛlmɛsénaz
ða Kɔmaştíɓlɔs/klúɓaz nɔʳtýrnɔs/kánɛɛz ða
mınıgɔlf/naɡósjɔz ða ɓéʂtɛ ða aχtɔmóɓılɔ sı
lánɛɛs/aʂtɛsjónaz ða sarɓísjɔi tjéʂdɛz ða ɾ̃ō-
pɛ//sɔ trátɛ ða lɛ̃ ɛɓaníðɛ ðɔl lıɓartɛðór/ka ũna
ɓwénɔ sáiɾɔs kɔ nnmɔ ða sns snɓúrɓjɔs/sɛnısí-
ðrɔ//nm pókɔ má sɛl nórtɔ/lɛ ðasambɔkɛðúrɛ
ðɔl ɾ̃ı̨ɔ pɛrɛná sã ãnꞃıkésɔ .kɔ nnŋ déιtɛ žénɔ
ða ãŋkáʂtɔ ðɔl ka lɔs pɔrténɔz ɡósɛn lɔs
fínɔz ða samánɛ//
//lɛ knιtúrɛ kɔzmɔpɔlítɛ̃ á frɛɡwáðɔ/ɛl
kaɓɔ ðɛχn síɡlɔi méfjɔ nnálmɛ ɓatıníðɛ ɛιm-
pár//n nálmɛ aʳsplɔráðaι ðasknbjértɛ ðíɛ̃ ɛ̃
ðíɛ pɔr lɔ sɛrtιštɛs/lɔ saskrıtórɔs/lɔs pɔé-
tɛ sı lɔz músıkɔs//ɛl mılıtá rɔn lɛ ɓɛŋ-
gwárðja ða lártɔ ɔʳsıðaʂtȧl/ɔl pɛιs sã ãnɔꞃn-
žésɔ ða sé rnnɛ ɡrám fwéʂtɔ knιtnrái̯ da áɓlɛ
_ıspánɛ//

379

EN LA AGENCIA DE VIAJES (Hispanic American--River
   Plate Variety)

   Dos argentinos se encuentran con un chileno,
amigo de ambos.

Carlos y Guillermo
   (al mismo tiempo)-   Hola, Martín, ¿qué hacés* por
                         aquí?
Martín-   Tengo que comprar un pasaje de
                         avión para mi hermana. ¿Y
                         Uds.?
Carlos-   Yo vengo también a comprar un
                         pasaje, y Guillermo me acompa-
                         ña.
Martín-   No sabía que pensabas regresar
                         este año.
Carlos-   Yo tampoco pero vos sabés como
                         corre el dinero y ya casi estoy
                         sin fondos.
Guillermo-   Che,** no exagerés, lo que pasa
                         es que a vos te gusta vivir muy
                         bien y así a cualquiera se le
                         acaba prohto la plata.
Carlos-   No seas macaneador, es la pura
                         verdad y vos lo sabés mejor que
                         yo.
Martín-   No se agiten por tan poca cosa.
                         Ya se arreglarán los asuntos.
                         ¿Qué tal si al terminar aquí

   * Hacés and similarly stressed verb-forms are
typical of voseante Spanish; see fn. *, p. 382.

   ** A commonly used interjection in this area;
see fn. **, p. 382.

nos vamos a un café para char-
lar un rato?

Carlos y Guillermo— Buena idea.
Martín— Pues vamos.

//ən lɐ ɐxénsja ðə ɵjáxəs//

//dó sɐrxəŋtínɵs sə əŋkwéŋtrɐŋ kɵ nnn ɵi-
lénɵ/ɐmígɵ ðə ámbɵs//

//kárlɵ si gizérmɵ//ɐl mízmɵ tjémpɵ//ólɐ/mɐrtín/
¿ké ɐsés* pɵ rɐkí?//

//mɐrtín//téŋgɵ kə kɵmprá rnm pɐsáxə ðə ɐbjóm
pɐrɐ mjɐrmánɐ//¿jʋstéðəs?//

//kárlɵs//zó béŋgɵ tɐmbjé nɐ kɵmprá rnm pɐ-
sáxə/! gizérmɵ mə ɐkɵmpánɐ//

//mɐrtín//nɐ spbíɐ kə pənsábɐ fagrəsá réstə ənɵ//

//kárlɵs//zó tɐmpókɵ pɐrɵ bós sɐbés kɵmɵ kóraɵ|
dinérɵi zá kási əstói sim fóndɵs//

//gizérmɵ//ĉé** /nɵ əsɐxərés/lɵ kə pásɐ és
kə ɐ bós tə gʋstɐ bibír múi tjén/

* This is an example of the Argentinian variety
of _voseo_, in which verb-forms like hacés, ponés, decís, sabés are typical in the second-person singular--
vos--generally used with standard second-person singular pronouns as in vos te lavás, a vos te gusta.

** A frequently employed interjection used in
Argentina to get someone's attention, as an exclamation, and as an intensifier.

jasí e kwalkjére se le ekáɹe
próŋto le pláte//
//kárlos// no sée² mekenaedór/éz le púre
ɓardáȷ ɓɔ́z lo seɓéz moxón ka ɮó//
//martín// no se exítem por tám póke kóse//
ɮá se eɾaglerán lo sesýŋtos//¿ke tál
sjaȷ torminá reki noz ɓáme saɹɜ
keɾé pere ĉedá ron ɾáto?//
//kárle si ǵ!ɮérme// bwénaȷ ɗéʔe//
//mertín// pwéz ɓámos//

EL ARTE DE MEDIR EL TIEMPO (Ceceo)

Es imposible imaginar la vida actual sin reloj. Nos servimos de él continuamente para medir y coordinar nuestras actividades en cualquier orden, ya sea en el hogar, la escuela o en la oficina. Consultamos nuestros relojes a cada momento para controlar la producción en las fábricas y los talleres, la marcha de los ferrocarriles, aviones y vapores, o para determinar la duración de procesos físicos y químicos en los laboratorios de investigación de nuestras universidades.

Nosotros, hijos de este prodigioso siglo veinte, poseemos una bien definida noción del tiempo. Pensamos a veces en lapsos que abarcan meses y años, y otras veces calculamos en minutos y fracciones de segundo. Pero no siempre fue así. Nuestros remotos antepasados prehistóricos no conocieron el "tiempo." Les bastaba la salida del sol para tomar arco y flecha y largarse en busca de caza. Así como la caída de la tarde les indicaría, tal vez, que había llegado el momento de acudir a la cita con la bella de la tribu del valle vecino. Se referían a los acontecimientos pasados o futuros de la manera más vaga, tal como aún hoy se expresan algunos pueblos primitivos diciendo "cuando cambie la luna."

Durante milenios el hombre ha dejado correr así sus días entregado a vivir el momento. ¿Cómo llegó entonces a adquirir la consciencia del tiempo? Por ser curioso, por tener memoria, y por saber reflexionar. Y debemos agregar dos razones más: la inquietud que sentían los pobladores de la tierra frente a la oscuridad de la noche, y la necesidad de poder orientarse en sus largas excursiones motivadas por la escasez de alimentos que les obligaba a invadir nuevas y desconocidas regiones. Estas causas los impulsaron a observar la trayectoria de la luna, la marcha de las estrellas y el curso del sol. Hasta que un buen día se apercibieron de que todo se repetía a intervalos regulares: el crecer y menguar de la luna, el alargarse y acortarse del día solar, como el florecer y morir de las plantas y hierbas. De la experiencia así recogida, fue surgiendo lentamente el concepto "tiempo," y el hombre descubrió la gran ley que gobierna a nuestro mundo, más aún al universo--el ritmo. Pero ¿qué es el tiempo? Es la consciencia del "antes" y del "después" en el cambio o movimiento de los objetos y formas perceptibles. Para poder transformar el tiempo originado por el movimiento en conceptos mesurables, se observan movimientos rítmicos que se repiten uniformemente, y se elige uno de ellos, poniéndolo en relación con otros fenómenos del movimiento, ya sean más cortos o más largos. Así se origina la medición del tiempo, en forma parecida como se mide el espacio con el metro. Es la comparación relativa de movimientos diferentes, tal como la medición del espacio es una confrontación de diferentes longitudes. Una completa rotación de la tierra en torno a su propio eje (llamada "día") se compara con la rotación de la tierra alrededor del sol (denominada "año"), y se llega a los 365 días del año. El día es comparado con movimientos de menor duración y subdividido de acuerdo. Para orientarse en el tiempo, la división del día en intervalos regulares constituyó la meta principal de la medición del tiempo. El reloj de precisión de hoy día es la coronación de ese afán.

//ə lártə ðə maðí raj tjémpo//

//e' simposíbleĩ maxinár lə ƀiðẽ e'twál sin
ɾaló//mos sarƀímoz ðə él kontinwaméņtə parə
maðí ri kordinár nwéștrə seⁿfibiðáðə say
kwalkjé rórðən/yá séə a na logár/lə askwéle/
ə ən lə ofiθínə//konsnļtámoz nwéștro ɾalóxə se
káðə moméņto parə kontrolár lə proðn̄θjó nan
les fáƀrikə si loȝ taļéras/lə márðə ðə los ɾaɾo-
kaɾrílas/eƀjónə si ƀapóras/o parə ðatarminár lə
ðnraθjóņ də proθésos físikə si kímikə san loz
laƀoratórjoz ðeimbaștigaθjóņ də nwéștrə snmi-
ƀarsiðáðəs//mosótros/íxoz ðə éștə proðixjóso síglo
ƀéiņtə/posaémo snnə ƀjéņ dafiníðə noθjóņ dal
tjémpo//pansámo sə ƀéθə san láƀsos kə eƀárkən
mésaz ɾámos/jótrez ƀéθas kalknlámo san
minúto si freⁿθjónaz ðə sagúņdo//poro mo
sjémprə fwé esí//nwéștro ɾamóto sentapesá-
ðos preiștórikos mo konoθjéro naļ tjémpo//laz
ƀeștáƀə lə selíðə ðal sól parə tomá ráɾkoi Flé-
ðə/! largársə am býskə ðə káðə//así komo

386

le kɾíþe ða le tárða la sɪndɪkeríe/telbéθ/
ka ebíe lagáðe al moméṇte ða eknðí re le θíte
ten le béle ða le tríbn ðal bále baθíne//
se ɾafaríe ne le sekoṇtaθɪ mjéṇtes pesạ̈e se
fntúrez ða le memére máz báge/tạ̈l kóme
eú nɔ́ɪ sa aᵍᶻprése nelgúmes pweblos prɪmi-
tíþez ðɪθjéṇde/kwáṇde kámbje le lúne//
dnráṇte mɪlénjo sa lómbre á ðaxáe keɾ́
resí snz ðíe saṇtragáðe e bɪbí ral momém
te//¿kóme lagó aṇtíṇθe se ebkɪrír le
keṇθjéṇθja ðel tjémpe?//por séɾ knɾjóse/
pcɾ tanéɾ memórja/! por sebéɾ ɾaflagzjonár//
! ðabéme segragáɾ ðɔ́ ɾeθónez máz//laɪn-
kjetúd ka saṇtíen les peblɐðóraz ða le tjéɾe
fréṇte e le eskɾɪðáᵈ ða le móᵈa/! le naθe-
sɪðáᵈ ða peðé rɔɾjeṇtársɐ ən snz lárge
saᵍᶻknɾsjónez metɪbáðes por le askeséz
ða elɪméṇtes ka la sebligábe aɪmbeðír
nwébe sɪ ðaskeneθíðe ɾaxjónas//éstes káɥ-
sez le sɪmpnlsáɾe ne etsarbáɾ le treɾeɾtó.

rja ða le lúne/le márɛe ða le saʂtréɭez yal
kýrsɔ ðal sól//áʂte ka nm bwén díe se epar-
θiðjérɔŋ da ka tóðe se r̄apatíe ãiŋtarbálc
r̄ãɡnláras/al kraðé ri maŋgwár ða le lúne/
a lelerɡársɔ yekɔrtársɔ ðaɭ díe solár/kóme
ɔl flɔraðé ri morír ða les plánte si yérbes//
da le aɡzparjénθja esí r̄akɔxíðe/fwé snɾxjén-
dc lɔŋtəméntə əl kɔnθéᵗtə/tjémpɔ/je lómbrɔ
ðaskntɾjó le grán léx ka gɔðjérne e nwéʂtrɔ
mýŋdɔ/má súv ne lnniɓérsɔ/al ríᵗme//parɔ/
¿ke é saɭ tjémpɔ?//éz le kɔnθjénθja ða láŋtɔ
si ðaɭ daspwé sa nɔl kámbjɔ e mɔɓimjéntɔ
ða le sɔᵗxéᵗc si fórmes parðeᵗtéᵇlas//pare/
pɔðér trensfɔrmá raɭ tjémpɔ crixináðc pe
ral mɔɓimjéntɔ əŋ kɔnθéᵗtez masnráblas/
sə ɔᵗsérɓen mɔɓimjéntɔ r̄íðmikes ka sə r̄apí-
tə nnnifɔrmaméntə/i sə əɭéxa úne ða élɔs/pɔ-
njéndɔlɔ əŋ r̄aleθjón ke nótrɔs fanúmanɔz ðal
mɔɓimjéntɔ/yá séen más kórtc se máz lárɡcs//
esí se crixíne le maðiθjóŋ dəɭ tjémpɔ/əm fór-

me pəraθíðe kómo sə mífə ə laspáθjo kə nəl

métro//éz lə kompərəθjóŋ rələtíbe ðə motí-

mjéntoz ðiforéntəs/tál kómo lə məðiθjóŋ də

laspáθjo é sənə komfrontəθjóŋ də ðiforéntaz loŋ-

xitúðəs//nə mə kompléto rotəθjóŋ də lə tjérə əntórno-

mo e sə própjo éxə/ləmáðe ðíə/sə kompárə

kon lə rotəθjóŋ də lə tjérə əlrəðəðór ðəl sól/

dənominádə áno/! sə legə e los traθjéntos

sasəntaiθíŋko ðíez ðə láno//ə! díə és komp-

perádo kon motimjéntoz ðə mənór ðərəθjóni!

sə ðibidídə ðə ekwérðə//pərə ərjentársə ə

nə! tjémpo/lə ðibisjóŋ dəl díə ə nintərbá-

lə rəgnlárəs konstitnyó lə métə prinθipál

də lə məðiθjóŋ dəl tjémpo//əl rəlð ðə prəθi-

sjóŋ də ói díə ez lə korənəθjóŋ də ésə

əfán//

EN EL BANCO (<u>Seseo</u> and <u>Ceceo</u>)

Empleado- ¿Qué desea, señorita?
Señorita- He llegado ayer y desearía cambiar algu-
nos cheques de viajero. ¿A cuánto está
el cambio?
Empleado- A doscientas pesetas por un dólar.
Señorita- Pero ayer estaba más bajo. ¿Qué pasó?
Empleado- Bueno, el cambio varía de un día para el
el otro. Y ésta es la última cotización.
Señorita- ¿Puede, por favor, cambiarme cien dóla-
res?
Empleado- Sí, como no. ¿En qué más puedo servirle?
Señorita- Bueno, necesito hacer un giro. ¿Lo puedo
hacer aquí?
Empleado- Lo siento mucho pero para un giro debe ir
a la oficina de correos.
Señorita- ¿Es muy lejos de aquí?
Empleado- No, solamente unas pocas cuadras.
Señorita- ¿Puedo ir caminando?
Empleado- Ciertamente. Sale Ud. del edificio, do-
ble a la derecha y camine tres cuadras.
En la misma esquina encontrará la oficina
de correos.
Señorita- Muchas gracias. Adiós.
Empleado- Adiós.

//ə nəl báŋkɔ//

//amplaáðɔ//ɛ ké ðaséɛ/saŋɔríte?//
//saŋɔríte//é ɣaɣáðɔ eyé rɪ ðasaɛríɛ kɛmbjá
rɛlgúnɔs čékaz ða bjaxérɔ//ɛ kwáŋ-
tɔ aṣtá əl kámbjo?//
//amplaáðɔ//ɛ ðɔsθjéŋtɔs pasétɔs pɔ rɑŋ dólɛr//
//saŋɔríte//parɔ eyé raṣtábɛ máz bạ̈xɔ//ɛ ké
pɛsó?//
//amplaáðɔ//bwénɔ/əl kámbjo bɔríɛ ðɛuŋ díɛ
pɛrɔ ə lótrɔ//jéṣtɛ éz lɛ ýltɪmɔ
kɔtɪθɛθjón//
//saŋɔríte//pwéða/pɔr fɛbɔ́r/kɛmbjárma sjéŋ
dólɛras?//
//amplaáðɔ//sí/kómɔ nó//ɛ əŋ ké más pwéðɔ
sɛrbɛ́rla?//
//saŋɔríte//bwénɔ/masasítɔ ɛsé rɑŋ xírɔ//ɛlɔ
pwéðɔ ɛsé rɛkí?//
//amplaáðɔ//lɔ sjéŋtɔ múčɔ pɔrɔ pɛrauŋ xírɔ
ðébɛ í rɛ lɛ ɔfiθínɛ ða kɔfɛ́ɔs//
//saŋɔríte//ɛéz múi léxɔz ðɛ ɛkí?//

//əmplaáðɛ// nó/ sɔlɛméⁿtə únəs pókəs kwáðras//

//səŋɔríte// ¿pweðɛ ír kemináⁿdɛ?//

//əmplaáðɛ// θjɛrteméⁿtə//sálə ŋ̩stéᵈ ðə ləðifí-

θjo ɛ lə ðaréčai keminə tres

kwáðras//ən lə mízmə əskínə əŋ-

kɛⁿtrərá lə əfiθínə ðə kɔ̃rɛ́ɔs//

//səŋɔríte// múčez grásjəs//ɛðjós//

//əmplaáðɛ// ɛðjós//

ORACIONES

PADRE NUESTRO (Ceceo)

Padre nuestro, que estás en los cielos: santificado sea el tu nombre; venga a nos el tu reino; hágase tu voluntad así en la tierra como en el cielo. El pan nuestro de cada día dánosle hoy; y perdónanos nuestras deudas, así como nosotros perdonamos a nuestros deudores. Y no nos dejes caer en la tentación, mas líbranos del mal. Amén.

AVE MARIA (Ceceo)

Dios te salve, María, llena eres de gracia, el Señor es contigo, bendita tú eres entre todas las mujeres y bendito es el fruto de tu vientre, Jesús.

Santa María, Madre de Dios, ruega por nosotros pecadores, ahora y en la hora de nuestra muerte. Amén.

GLORIA AL PADRE (Seseo)

Gloria al Padre, y al Hijo y al Espíritu Santo. Como era en el principio, ahora y siempre, y por los siglos de los siglos. Amén.

‖ páðrə nwéʂtrə ‖

‖ páðrə nwéʂtrə / kə əṣtá san les θjéles / sẹṇti-
fikáðə séə əl, tn nómbrə / béŋgéə ne saɟ tn réɟ-
nc / ágesə tn ɓəlṇtáð esí ən lə tjéře kómə ə
maɟ θjéle ‖ əl pán nwéʂtrə ðə káðə ðíə ðánes-
lə ɔ́ɟ /ˌ parðónənəz nwéʂtrez ðéxðes / esí kómə nesótres parðenámə se nwéʂtrez ðexðórəs /ˌ
ne mez ðéxəs kəé ran lə təṇteθjón / máz líɓre-
nez ðəl máɟ ‖ ə mén ‖

‖ áɓə məríə ‖

‖ djós tə səɟlbə / məríə / léʾnə érəz ðə grá-
θja / əl sanó rés kəṇtígə / bəṇdítə tú érə səṇtra
tóðez lez mnxérə sɟ bəṇdítə é səl frútə ðə
tn ɓjéṇtrə / xəsýs ‖
‖ sáṇte məríə / máðrə ðə djós / řwégə pər nesó-
trəs pəkəðórəs / əírə yən lə órə ðə nwéʂtrə mwér-
tə ‖ ə mén ‖

//glórja el páðra//

//glórja el páðra/ja léxo ja laspíritn
sáŋtc//kómc ére a nal prinsípjo/eóraí
sjémpra/ı por los síglez ða los síglos//
//e mén//

EN EL CONSULTORIO DEL DENTISTA (General Hispanic
    American)

    La sra. de Carrillo (paciente), una enfermera
y el dentista.

Sra. de Carrillo-   Tengo hora con el doctor a las
                     diez.
Enfermera-   Por favor, tome asiento. Estamos
                     un poco retrasados con el horario,
                     y posiblemente tendrá que esperar
                     unos quince minutos.

En la sala de espera hay varias revistas y la sra.
de Carrillo hojea una. Pasa un rato, sale el paciente anterior y la enfermera, dirigiéndose a la
sra. de Carrillo, dice:
Enfermera-   ¿Quiere pasar, por favor?

La señora entra en el consultorio.
Sra. de Carrillo-   Buenos días, ¿cómo está, doctor?
Dentista-   Bien, gracias. ¿Y Ud.?
Sra. de Carrillo-   No tan bien como quisiera. Tengo
                     un problema doble; se me ha roto
                     un diente y he perdido la emplo-
                     madura de una de mis muelas.
                     ¿Cree que me los podrá arreglar
                     todos hoy?
Dentista-   Déjeme ver.
Examina la boca de la paciente.

Sra. de Carrillo-   ¿Qué le parece?
Dentista-   Para decirle la verdad es un tra-
                     bajo bastante grande y que lleva-
                     rá tiempo. No lo podré hacer to-
                     do hoy. ¿Qué le molesta más, el
                     diente roto o la carie?
Sra. de Carrillo-   Ahora ninguno, pero como el diente
                     roto queda tan feo y como Ud. sa-
                     be, soy muy coqueta, le agradece-
                     ría si me arreglara primero el
                     diente y luego la carie.
Dentista-   Bueno, entonces hoy empezaré con
                     el diente. Al salir, haga una

cita con la enfermera para otra
visita pero, si llegara a tener
dolor muy fuerte, llámeme en se-
guida por teléfono y trataré de
verla inmediatamente.

Sra. de Carrillo- Muy bien, así lo haré. Un millón
de gracias. Adiós.

Dentista- Adiós y cuídese.

//ə nəl kɛmsəlˈtórjo ðəl dənˈʈíʃtə//

//le saŋóre ða keříyɔ/pesjénta/n ne‿əmfar-
mére yəl dənʈíʃtə//
//saŋóre ða keříyɔ// téŋgɔ‿ɔ̃re kɔ nəl dɔktóre
lɛz ðjés//
//əmfarmére// pɔr febɔ́r/tóme‿esjéntə//əʃtámɔ
sɑm pókɔ ɾatresaðɔs kɔ mɑ lɔrá-
rjo/! pɔsɪblaméntə taŋdrá kɑ‿ɔ̃s-
pará rúnɔs kɣ́nsə mɪmútɔs//
//ən le sáłe ða‿ɔ̃spére áɪ̯ ʈárja ɾatɣíʃtə sɪ le saŋóre ða keříyɔ‿ɔxéé‿úne// páse‿ɑn ɾátɔ/sálə‿əl pe-
sjéntə‿ɛntarjó rɪ le əmfarmére/dɪrɪxjéndɔsə‿e
le saŋóre ða keříyɔ/dísə/
//əmfarmére//¿ kjéra pɔsár/pɔr febɔ́r?/
//le saŋóre‿éntre ə nəl kɛmsəltórjo//
//saŋóre ða keříyɔ// bwénɔz ðíes/¿ kómɔ‿əʃtá/
dɔktór?//
//dənʈíʃtə//bjén grásjas/¿ juʃté?//
//saŋóre ða keříyɔ//mɔ tám bjén kómɔ kɪsjére//
téŋgɔɣm prɔbléme ðóbla//sə mɑ‿á
398

r̄ótoʊɲ djéɲta ɣé parðíðo lɐ̯am-
plɐmeðúrɐ ðɛʊnɐ ðə mɪz mwélɐs//
¿Kreá kə mə lɔs pɔðrá ẽr̄aglár
tóðɔ sɔ̞ɪ̞?//

//dəɲtíṣtɐ// déxəmə bér//
//aᵏsɐmínɐ lɐ bókɐ ðə lɐ pɐsjéɲta//
//səɲórɐ ðɐ kɐr̄ɪ̞ɣɔ// ¿Ké lə pɐrésə?//

//dəɲtíṣtɐ// pɐrɐ ðasɪ̞́rlɐ lɐ bórðá é sɐɲ trɐ-
báxɔ bɐṣtáɲtɐ ɣráɲdei kə yɐbɐrá
tjémpɔ//nɔ lɔ pɔðré ɐsér tóðɔ ɔ̃i̞//
¿Ké lə mɔléṣtɐ máṣ/əɬ djéɲtɐ r̄ótɔ ɔ
lɐ kárje?//

//səɲórɐ ðɐ kɐr̄ɪ̞ɣɔ// ɐ́rɐ nɪ̞ɲɡúnɔ pɔrɔ kómɔ əɬ
djéɲta r̄ótɔ kéðɐ táɱ féɔ/!
kómɔ ɐ̯ɲṣté sába/sɔ̞ɪ̞ mú̞ɪ̞ kɔkéʈ-
tɐ/lɐ ɐɣrɐðɐsaría sɪ mə ɐr̄aɡlárɐ
prɪmérɔ əɬ djéɲtei lwéɡɔ lɐ kár̄je//
//dəɲtíṣtɐ// bwénɔ/əɲtɔ́nsə sɔ̞ɪ̞ ɐmpasɐré kɐ nəɬ
djéɲta//ɐl sɐlí ráɣɐ ɐnɐ sítɐ kɐn
lɐ̯ɐɱfarmérɐ pɐrɐ ótrɐ bisítɐ/pɔrɔ

399

si yagáre̯ e̯ tanér δolór mú̧i
fwérta/yámama ansagíδe̯ por ta-
léfoноi tretĕré δa δér lai^maδja-
teménta//
//saŋóre̯ δa keríγɔ// mú̧i tjén/esí lɔ eré//nn m!-
yóŋ da grásjes/eδjós//
//daŋtíște//eδjó si kwíδasa//

APPENDIX TWO

TRANSLATIONS OF:
PROVERBS
SAYINGS
IDIOMS
FIGURATIVE EXPRESSIONS

CHAPTER I

Al pan pan y al vino
vino.

(Literally, "To bread bread
and to wine wine.")
To call a spade a spade.

A lo hecho pecho.

(Literally, "To that which
has been done, chest
(courage).")
To face the music.

En un plato de trigo
comen tres tigres.

A tongue twister. (Lit-
erally, "In a plate of
wheat eat three tigers.")

El dar es honor, y el
pedir dolor.

It is better to give than
to receive.

Cada cabeza es un
mundo.

Each man is an island.

CHAPTER II

Cada loco con su te-
ma.

To each his own.

Tres grandes tigres
tragantones tragan
trigo y se atragan-
tan.

A tongue twister. (Lit-
erally, "Three gluttinous
tigers gobble wheat and
choke.")

A perro viejo no hay
tus tus.

You can't teach an old dog
new tricks.

A Dios rogando y con
el mazo dando.

(Literally, "Praying to God
and beating with the mal-
let.")
God helps those who help
themselves.

Haz bien y no mires a
quien.

(Literally, "Do good and
don't concern yourself
about whom you do it to.")
Virtue is its own reward.

CHAPTER III

No decir uno esta bo-

(Literally, "For one not to

402

ca es mía.	say 'This mouth is mine'.") Not to utter one word.
Volver uno pie atrás.	To take a backward step, to go backwards.
Menester es no meterse entre marido y mujer.	One must never interfere between husband and wife.
Más vale tarde que nunca.	Better late than never.
Perro que ladra no muerde.	A barking dog never bites.
Hombre prevenido vale por dos.	(Literally, "A man with foresight is worth as much as two people.") Foresight is better than hindsight.
Por la boca muere el pez.	(Literally, "The fish dies by its mouth.") Silence is golden. To be one's Achilles' heel.
A cada puerco le llega su San Martín.	(Literally, "To each pig comes the day of retribution.") Each dog has its day.

CHAPTER IV

No tener pelos en la lengua.	Not to mince words.
Pagar con la misma moneda.	To pay back in kind.
Andarse por las ramas.	To beat around the bush.
Buscar una aguja en el pajar.	To look for a needle in a haystack.
Ir con la corriente.	To follow the crowd.
Ir viento en popa.	To go very well.
Hacer pucheros.	To pout.
Estarse en sus treces.	To be persistent.
Ser el brazo derecho de.	To be the right arm of.

Ser la piel de Judas.	To be the devil himself.
Creerse la octava maravilla del mundo.	To be extremely conceited.
Ser un cero a la izquierda.	Not to count.
Dormirse sobre los laureles.	To rest on ones laurels.
Hacer de las suyas.	To be up to ones old tricks.
Consultar con la almohada.	To sleep on it.
Hacérsele a uno agua la boca.	To have ones mouth water.
Hacerse un ovillo.	To recoil.
Hacerse el zorro.	To play dumb.
Calentar la silla.	To keep the seat warm.
Tomar a pecho.	To take to heart.
No venir al caso.	Not to be opportune.
Ser más conocido que la ruda.	To be known by everyone.
Estar uno en (sobre) ascuas.	To be worried to death.
Tomar a mal, llevar a mal.	To take the wrong way, to take offense at.
No digas nunca de esta agua no beberé.	Never say never.
Genio y figura hasta la sepultura.	(Literally, "Temperament and countenance until the grave.") It is impossible to teach an old dog new tricks.
Con las glorias se olvidan las memorias.	Time heals all wounds.
Poco a poco se anda lejos.	(Literally, "Little by little one goes far.") Haste makes waste.

CHAPTER V

Aunque la mona se vista de seda, mona se queda.	(Literally, "Even though the monkey dresses in silk, it remains a monkey.")

El ojo del amo engorda al caballo.

You can't make a silk purse out of a sow's ear.
(Literally, "The eye of the owner fattens the horse.")

Quien siembra vientos recoge tempestades.

When the cat's away, the mice play.
(Literally, "He who sows winds reaps tempests.")

A quien madruga Dios le ayuda.

What you sow you shall reap.
(Literally, "He who rises early is helped by God.")

Agua pasada no muele molinos.

The early bird catches the worm.
(Literally, "Water which has passed does not turn the windmill.")

That's water over the dam. You can't cry over spilled milk.

Quien mal anda mal acaba.

(Literally, "He who goes (through life) badly, winds up badly.")

You get out of life what you put into it.

No se ganó Zamorra en una hora.

(Literally, "Zamorra was not won in an hour.")
Rome was not built in a day.

No hay mal que por bien no venga.

(Literally, "There is no evil which is not wrought for good.")

Everything happens for the best.

Por todas partes se va a Roma.

All roads lead to Rome.

CHAPTER VI

A la tierra que fueres haz lo que vieres.

When in Rome do as the Romans do.

Cuando a Roma fueres haz lo que vieres.	When in Rome do as the Romans do.
Haz como Blas, come y te vas.	(Literally, "Do as Blase does, eat and you leave.") It is perfectly alright to eat and run.
Donde una puerta se cierra, otra se abre.	(Literally, "When one door is closed, another is opened.") There are other fish in the sea.
El amor es ciego.	Love is blind.
Matrimonio y mortaja del cielo baja.	(Literally, "Marriage and shroud (death) descend from heaven.") Marriages are made in heaven.
Saber es poder.	Knowledge is power.
Quien poco lee poco aprende.	(Literally, "He who reads little learns little.") Books are your best friends.
Un hoy vale más que dos mañanas.	(Literally, "One today is worth more than two tomorrows.") Don't put off until tomorrow what you can do today.
Dios cura y el médico se lleva el dinero.	Literally, "God cures (you) and the physician carries away the money."
Cría cuervos y te sacarán los ojos.	(Literally, "Raise crows and they will gouge out your eyes.") Children should be reared properly.
La experiencia es madre de la ciencia.	Experience is the best teacher.
Lo barato cuesta caro.	You get what you pay for.

CHAPTER VII

A buen hambre no hay pan duro.	When you are hungry, everything tastes good.

Las flores contentan pero no alimentan.	Literally, "Flowers are satisfying but they don't provide nutrition."
Pájaro en mano vale por cien volando.	A bird in hand is better than two in the bush.
Quien supo olvidar no supo amar.	True love lasts forever.
Con pan y vino se anda el camino.	(Literally, "With bread and wine the journey is accom- plished.") You can't work a starving horse.
Hoy por ti, mañana por mí.	(Literally, "Today for you, tomorrow for me.") Each dog has its day.

CHAPTER VIII

Cada chango a su me- cate y a darse vue- lo.	(Literally, "Each monkey on his own rope and start swinging.") Every man for himself; let each person do his own thing.
Tú sabes quien trae las llaves, Chávez.	You know who runs the show around here.
Te casaste, te fre- gaste.	A man's troubles begin the day on which he gets mar- ried.
Salir de Guatemala para ir a Guatepeor.	To go from bad to worse; to go from the frying pan into the fire.
Comer frijoles y re- petir pollo.	Weak to perform though mighty to pretend.
No importa que nazcan chatos con tal que tengan resuello.	(Literally, "It doesn't mat- ter if they are born flat- nosed so long as they can breathe through it.") Handsome is as handsome does; you can't judge a book by its cover.
Más vale que haiga un tonto y no dos.	(Literally, "It is better that there be one fool and

not two.")
Two wrongs never make a
right.

Nunca falta un yolo-
ví.
There is always someone out
there watching.

Pon, pon, pon un ni-
cle pa' jabón, pa'
lavar tu calzón.
Every little bit helps.
(This saying is used fre-
quently when soliciting
public funds for benefits,
charities, etc.)

Ya te conozco, Mos-
co.
I've seen right through
you; I've got your number.

Meter el pie en el
bote.
To put one's foot in it.

No es lo mismo llamar
al diablo que verlo
venir.
(Literally, "It is not the
same to call upon the devil
as it is to see him com-
ing.")
It is more easily said than
done. It is one thing to
hear about it and another
to experience it.

Te gusta más meter la
cuchara en lo ajeno
que al puerco el jo-
sico en agua de san-
cocho.
You like to put your nose
where it doesn't belong.

Calma, piojo, que el
peine llega.
Take it easy, help is on its
way.

Ser más feo que un
pleito de menores.
To be as ugly as sin.

Tener más golpes que
un baile de bomba.
To be very sharp-tongued;
never to be at a loss for
words.

408

BIBLIOGRAPHY

Agard, Frederick B. "Present-Day Judaeo-Spanish in the United States." Hispania, 33 (1950), 203-210.

Alarcos Llorach, Emilio. Gramática estructural. Madrid: Editorial Gredos, 1951.

Alatis, James E., ed. Monograph Series on Languages and Linguistics. 21st Annual Round Table. Washington, D. C.: Georgetown University Press, 1970.

Alford, Harold J. The Proud Peoples. The Heritage and Culture of Spanish-Speaking Peoples in the United States. New York: New American Library, 1972.

Almasov, Alexey. "Vos and Vosotros as Formal Address in Modern Spanish." Hispania, 57 (1974), 304-310.

Alonso, Amado. Estudios lingüísticos: temas españoles. Madrid: Editorial Gredos, 1951.

----------. Estudios lingüísticos: temas hispanoamericanos. Madrid: Editorial Gredos, 1953.

Alvar, Manuel. El dialecto aragonés. Madrid: Editorial Gredos, 1953.

Azcárate, Andrés, ed. Misal diario para América. Buenos Aires: Guadalupe, 1946.

Barker, George G. "Pachuco: An American-Spanish Argot and Its Social Function in Tucson, Arizona." In El lenguaje de los chicanos: Regional and Social Characteristics of Language Used by Mexican Americans. Eds. Eduardo Hernández Chávez, et al. Arlington, Va.: Center for Applied Linguistics, 1975, pp. 183-201.

Barker, Marie Esman. Español para el bilingüe. Skokie, Illinois: National Textbook Company, 1972.

Barker, Pauline. Español para los hispanos. Dallas: Banks Upshaw & Co., 1953.

Barretto, Lefty. Nobody's Hero. A Puerto Rican Story. New York: New American Library, 1976.

Baugh, Albert C. A History of the English Language. New York: D. Appleton-Century Co., 1935.

Beinhauer, Werner. El español coloquial. Trans. Fernando Huarte Morton. Madrid: Editorial

Gredos, 1963.
Belasco, Simon, ed. Manual and Anthology of Applied
  Linguistics. Washington, D. C.: U. S. Depart-
  ment of Health, Education and Welfare, 1960.
Bowen, J. Donald, and Robert P. Stockwell. Patterns
  of Spanish Pronunciation. A Drillbook. Chi-
  cago: University of Chicago Press, 1960.
Brown, Roger, and Albert Gilman. "The Pronouns of
  Power and Solidarity." Style in Language. Ed.
  Thomas A. Sebeok. Cambridge: The M. I. T.
  Press, 1960, pp. 253-276.
Buchanan, Cynthia D. A Programmed Introduction to
  Linguistics. Lexington, Mass.: D. C. Heath &
  Co., 1963.
Burling, Robbins. Man's Many Voices: Language in
  Its Cultural Context. New York: Holt, Rine-
  hart, and Winston, Inc., 1970.
Cammarota, Federico. Vocabulario familiar y del lun-
  fardo. Buenos Aires: Peña Lillo, 1970.
Canfield, D. Lincoln. La pronunciación del español
  en América. Bogotá: Instituto Caro y Cuervo,
  1962.
----------. "Tampa Spanish: Three Characters in
  Search of a Pronunciation." Modern Language
  Journal, 35 (1951), 42-44.
----------. "Trends in American Castilian." Hispa-
  nia, 50 (1967), 912-918.
Cárdenas, Daniel N. "Mexican Spanish." In El len-
  guaje de los chicanos: Regional and Social
  Characteristics of Language Used by Mexican
  Americans. Eds. Hernández-Chavez, et al. Ar-
  lington, Va.: Center for Applied Linguistics,
  1975, pp. 1-5.
Casiano Montañez, Lucrecia. La pronunciación de los
  puertorriqueños de Nueva York. Bogotá: Edi-
  ciones Tercer Mundo, 1975.
Casso, Henry J. "Ya Basta, The Siesta Is Over." In
  Educating the Mexican American. Eds. Henry
  Sioux Johnson, and William J. Hernández-M. Val-
  ley Forge, Pa.: Judson Press, 1970, pp. 93-99.
Castro, Américo. Lengua, enseñanza y literatura.
  Madrid: Victoriano Suárez, 1924.
Castro Rawson, Margarita. El costumbrismo en Costa
  Rica. Costa Rica: Imprenta Lehmann, 1971.

410

Cherry, Adrian. Tampa Spanish Slang. Tampa: Lamp-
    light Press, 1966.
Christian, Jr., Chester, ed. Reports: Bilingual
    Education: Research and Teaching. Bethesda,
    Maryland: Educational Document Reproduction
    Service, 1967. #016434.
Cooper, Paulette, ed. Growing Up Puerto Rican. New
    York: New American Library, 1972.
Cuervo, José R. Apuntaciones sobre el lenguaje bogo-
    tano. Bogotá: Instituto Caro y Cuervo, 1939.
Dalbor, John B. Spanish Pronunciation: theory and
    practice. New York: Holt, Rinehart, and
    Winston, 1969.
Decamp, David. "Introduction: The Study of Pidgin
    and Creole Languages." In Pidginization and
    Creolization of Languages. Ed. Dell Hymes.
    Cambridge: University Press, 1971, pp. 13-39.
Decker, Donald. Mastering the International Phonetic
    Alphabet. New York: Simon & Schuster, 1970.
Delattre, Pierre, Carroll Ulsen, and Elmer Penock.
    "A Comparative Study of Declarative Intonation
    in American English and Spanish." Hispania, 45
    (1912), 233-241.
Dillard, J. L. All-American English. New York:
    Vintage Books, 1976.
Espinosa, Aurelio. Estudios sobre el español de Nue-
    vo Méjico. Trans. A. Alonso and A. Rosenblat.
    Buenos Aires: Universidad de Buenos Aires,
    1930. Vol. I; 1946. Vol. II.
Fallas, Carlos Luis. Marco Ramírez. Costa Rica:
    Imprenta Lehmann, 1975.
Fishman, Joshua A. "The Politics of Bilingual Edu-
    cation." Ed. James E. Alatis. Report of the
    Twenty-first Annual Round Table. Washington,
    D. C.: Georgetown University Press, 1970,
    pp. 47-58.
----------. "Puerto Rican Intellectuals in New
    York: Some Intragroup and Intergroup Con-
    trasts." Canadian Journal of Behavioral Sci-
    ence, 1 (1969), 215-226.
----------, Robert L. Cooper, and Roxana Ma, et al.
    Bilingualism in the Barrio. The Hague: Mouton
    & Co., 1971.
Galván, Roberto, and Richard V. Teschner. El dic-
    cionario del español chicano. The Dictionary

of Chicano Spanish. Silver Springs, Md.: In-
    stitute of Modern Languages, Inc., 1977.
García de Diego, Vicente. "Dialectismos castella-
    nos." Revista de filología española, III
    (1916), 305-308.
----------. Manual de dialectología española. Ma-
    drid: Instituto de Cultura Hispánica, 1946.
Gobello, José, and Luciano Payet. Breve diccionario
    lunfardo. Buenos Aires: Peña Lillo, 1959.
Guitart, Jorge Manuel. "Markedness and a Cuban Dia-
    lect of Spanish," Diss. Georgetown University
    1973.
Hall, Jr., Robert A. Introductory Linguistics.
    Philadelphia: Chilton Books, 1965.
Haugen, Einar. The Norwegian Language in America.
    1953; rpt. Bloomington: Indiana University
    Press, 1969.
Hayes, F. C. "Anglo-Spanish Speech in Tampa, Flo-
    rida." Hispania, 32 (1949), 48-52.
Henríquez Ureña, Pedro. El español en Santo Domin-
    go. Buenos Aires: Coni, 1940.
----------. Sobre el problema del andalucismo dia-
    lectal de América. Buenos Aires: Instituto de
    Filología, 1932.
Hirsch, Ruth. "A Study of Some Aspects of Judeo-
    Spanish by a New York Sephardic Family." Diss.
    University of Michigan 1951.
Hoyer, W. M. A Little Guide to English-Papiamento.
    Curaçao: Boek Handel Bethencourt, 1958.
"It's Your Turn in the Sun." Time, 16 Oct. 1978,
    pp. 48-61.
Jones, Daniel. An English Pronouncing Dictionary.
    London: J. M. Dent & Sons, Ltd., 1937.
Jones, Morgan E. "A Phonological Study of English
    as Spoken by Puerto Ricans Contrasted with
    Puerto Rican Spanish and American English."
    Diss. University of Michigan 1962.
Kany, Charles E. Semántica hispanoamericana. Trans.
    Luis Escolar Barreño. Madrid: Aguilar, 1969.
----------. Sintaxis hispanoamericana. Trans.
    Martín Blanco Alvarez. Madrid: Editorial Gre-
    dos, 1969.
Kjolseth, Rolf. "Bilingual Education Programs in the
    United States: for Assimilation or Pluralism?"

In Bilingualism in the Southwest. Ed. Paul R. Turner. Tucson: University of Arizona Press, 1973, pp. 3-27.

Kreidler, Charles W. "A Study of the Influence of English on the Spanish of Puerto Ricans in Jersey City, New Jersey." Diss. University of Michigan 1957.

Kuy, Harold. "Outline of Mexican Spanish Phonology." Studies in Linguistics, 10: 3 (1952), 51-62.

Kvavik, Karen. "An Analysis of Sentence-Initial and Final Intonation Data in Two Spanish Dialects." Journal of Phonetics, 2 (1974), 181-191.

Labov, William. Sociolinguistic Patterns. Philadelphia: University of Pennsylvania Press, 1972.

Lamb, Anthony J. "A Phonological Study of the Spanish of Havana, Cuba." Diss. University of Kansas 1968.

Lance, Donald M. "Dialectal and Nonstandard Forms in Texas Spanish." El lenguaje de los chicanos: Regional and Social Characteristics of Language Used by Mexican Americans. Eds. Eduardo Hernández Chavez, et al. Arlington, Va.: Center for Applied Linguistics, 1975, pp. 37-51.

Lapesa, Rafael. Historia de la lengua española. 7th ed. Madrid: Escelicer, 1968.

Lehiste, Ilse. Suprasegmentals. Cambridge: The M. I. T. Press, 1970.

Lehmann, Winfred P. Descriptive Linguistics: An Introduction. New York: Random House, 1972.

Lenz, Rodolfo. Diccionario etimológico de las voces chilenas derivadas de lenguas indígenas americanas. Santiago de Chile: Imprenta Cervantes, 1904-1910.

Levy, Denah. "La pronunciación del sefardí esmirniano de Nueva York." Nueva revista de filología hispánica, 6 (1952), 277-281.

Lewis, Oscar. La vida. New York: Vintage Books, 1966.

Lope Blanch, Juan M. El español de América. Madrid: Ediciones Alcalá, 1968.

----------. Estudios sobre el español de México. México: Universidad Nacional Autónoma de Méxi-

413

co, 1972.

----------. El léxico indígena en el español de
México. México: El Colegio de México, Centro
de Estudios Lingüísticos y Literarios, 1969.
Luria, Max A. "Judeo-Spanish Dialects in New York
City." Todd Memorial Volumes, 2 (1930), 7-16.
Llorens, Washington. El habla popular de Puerto Ri-
co. Río Piedras: Editorial Edil, 1971.
MacNeil, Robert, and Jim Lehrer. Latino Power. The
MacNeil/Lehrer Report Library, #795, Show #4075.
McDonough, James. Guide to Puerto Rican Slang. San
Juan: Publishers Group, Inc., 1972.
Mafud, Julio. Psicología de la viveza criolla. Bue-
nos Aires: Américaleer, 1971.
Malmberg, Bertil. La fonética del español en Para-
guay. Lund: C. W. K. Gleerup, 1947.
----------. Phonetics. New York: Dover Publica-
tions, Inc., 1963.
Marckwardt, Albert H. American English. New York:
Oxford University Press, 1958.
Matluck, Joseph. "Entonación hispánica." Anuario
de letras, 5 (1965), 5-32.
Mörner, Magnus. Race and Class in Latin America.
New York: Columbia University Press, 1970.
Moulton, William J. A Linguistic Guide to Language
Learning. 2nd ed. New York: Modern Language
Association, 1970.
Nash, Rose. "Spanglish: Language Contact in Puerto
Rico." American Speech, 45, 3-4 (1970), 223-
233.
Navarro Tomás, Tomás. Manual de pronunciación espa-
ñola. 5th ed. New York: Hafner, 1957.
Oroz, Rodolfo. La lengua castellana en Chile. San-
tiago: Universidad de Chile, 1966.
Ortiz, Carmelita Louise. "English Influence on the
Spanish of Tampa." Hispania, 32 (1949), 300-
304.
Palmer, F. R. Semantics. Cambridge: University
Press, 1976.
Pei, Mario. The Story of Language. New York: The
New American Library, Inc., 1966.
Perrin, Noel. "Old Macberlitz Had a Farm." New
Yorker, 27 Jan. 1962, pn. 28-29.
Phillips, Robert. "Variations in Los Angeles Span-

414

ish Phonology." In El lenguaje de los chica-
nos: Regional and Social Characteristics of
Language Used by Mexican Americans. Eds.
Eduardo Hernández-Chavez, et al. Arlington,
Va.: Center for Applied Linguistics, 1975,
pp. 52-60.
Rabanal, Manuel. Hablas hispánicas. Temas gallegos
y leoneses. Madrid: Ediciones Alcalá, 1967.
Rael, Juan B. "Associative Interference in New
Mexican Spanish." In El lenguaje de los chica-
nos: Regional and Social Characteristics of
Language Used by Mexican Americans. Eds.
Eduardo Hernández-Chavez, et al. Arlington,
Va.: Center for Applied Linguistics, 1975,
pp. 19-29.
Robe, Stanley L. The Spanish of Rural Panama.
Berkeley: University of California Press, 1960.
Rona, José Pedro. Geografía y morfología del "vo-
seo." Porto Alegre: Pontifícia Universidade
Católica do Rio Grande do Sul, 1967.
Rosario, Rubén del. América: lengua y cultura.
Río Piedras: Ediciones de la Universidad de
Puerto Rico, 1961.
----------. El español de América. Sharon, Conn.:
Troutman Press, 1970.
Rosenblat, Angel. Castellano de España y castellano
de América. Montevideo: Editorial Alfa, 1968.
Saubidet, Tito. Vocabulario y refranero criollo.
Buenos Aires: Editorial G. Kraft, 1952.
Sheehan, Susan. A Welfare Mother. New York: New
American Library, 1975.
Smalley, William A. Manual of Articulatory Phone-
tics. Tarrytown, New York: Practical Anthro-
pology, 1963.
Stockwell, Robert P., J. Donald Bowen, and John W.
Martin. The Grammatical Structures of English
and Spanish. Chicago: University of Chicago
Press, 1970.
Stycos, J. M. "Family and Fertility in Puerto Ri-
co." In The Puerto Rican Community and Its
Children on the Mainland. Eds. Francesco Cor-
dasco, and Eugene Bucchioni. Metuchen, N. J.:
The Scarecrow Press, Inc., 1972, pp. 76-88.
Tejada, Leonor. Hablar bien no cuesta nada. Mexi-

co: Organización Editorial Novaro, 1974.
Teschner, Richard V. "Anglicisms in Spanish. A
Cross-Referenced Guide to Previous Findings
with English Lexical Influence on Chicago
Mexican Spanish." Diss. University of Michi-
gan 1972.
Thomas, Piri. Down These Mean Streets. New York:
New American Library, 1967.
----------. Seven Long Times. New York: New
American Library, 1974.
Toranzo, Gloria. Un elemento de interés en la foné-
tica española. Pamplona: Ediciones Universi-
dad de Navarra, 1974.
Toscano Mateus, Humberto. El español en el Ecuador.
Madrid: Escelicer, 1953.
Trudgill, Peter. Sociolinguistics. Middlesex, En-
gland: Penguin Books, Ltd., 1974.
Wagner, Max Leopold. Lingua e dialetti dell'America
spagnola. Florence: Edizioni "Le Lingue Este-
re," 1949.
Weinreich, Uriel. Languages in Contact. 8th ed.
The Hague: Mouton, 1974.
Whinnon, Keith. "Linguistic Hybridization and the
'Special Case' of Pidgins and Creoles." In
Pidginization and Creolization of Languages.
Ed. Dell Hymes. Cambridge: University Press,
1971, pp. 91-115.
Zamora Vicente, Alonso. Dialectología española.
Madrid: Editorial Gredos, 1960.

SUGGESTED READINGS

I. MAJOR WORKS

Abercrombie, David. Studies in Phonetics and Linguistics. London: Oxford University Press, 1965.

Brown, R. Words and Things. Glencoe, Ill.: Free Press, 1958.

Chomsky, Noam. Syntactic Structures. The Hague: Mouton, 1957.

----------, and Morris Halle. The Sound Patterns of English. New York: Harper and Row, 1968.

Dillard, J. L. American Talk. New York: Vintage Books, 1977.

Gumperz, John J. "Types of Linguistic Communities." Anthropological Linguistics, 4 (1962), 28-40.

Hakes, David. "Psychological Aspects of Language." Modern Language Journal, 49, No. 4 (1965), 220-277.

Heffner, R. M. S. General Phonetics. Madison: University of Wisconsin Press, 1949.

Jespersen, Otto. Language. New York: W. W. Norton & Co., Inc., 1964.

Joos, Martin, ed. Readings in Linguistics. 4th ed. Chicago: University of Chicago Press, 1966.

Kooij, J. C. Ambiguity in Natural Language. Amsterdam: North Holland Publishing Co., 1971.

Laird, Charlton. Language in America. New Jersey: Prentice-Hall, Inc., 1970.

Lehman, Winifred P. Glossary of Linguistic Terminology. Garden City, N. Y.: Doubleday and Company, 1966.

Lyons, J., ed. New Horizons in Linguistics. Baltimore: Penguin, 1970.

Martín, Eusebia. ¿Qué es la investigación lingüística? Buenos Aires: Editorial Columba, 1972.

Martinet, André. Elements of General Linguistics. Trans. Elizabeth Palmer. Eds. Faber & Faber. Chicago: University of Chicago Press, 1964.

Mounin, Georges. Claves para la lingüística. Trans. Felisa Marcos. Barcelona: Editorial Anagrama, 1976.

Newman, Edwin. Strictly Speaking. New York: The
    Bobbs-Merrill Co., Inc., 1974.
O'Connor, J. D. Better English Pronunciation. Cam-
    bridge: Cambridge University Press, 1967.
Palmer, Frank. Grammar. England: Penguin Books,
    Ltd., 1971.
Pei, Mario. Glossary of Linguistic Terminology.
    Garden City, N. Y.: Doubleday and Co., 1966.
Sapir, Edward. Language. An Introduction to the
    Study of Speech. New York: Harcourt, Brace &
    World, 1949.
Sebeok, Thomas, ed. Style in Language. Cambridge:
    The M. I. T. Press, 1968.
Trager, G. L., and H. L. Smith, Jr. An Outline of
    English Structure. Washington: American
    Council of Learned Societies, 1956.

II. LINGUISTIC STUDIES

Aguero, Arturo. El español de América y Costa Rica.
    Costa Rica: Imprenta Antonio Lehmann, 1962.
Alonso, Amado. Castellano, español, idioma nacional:
    historia espiritual de tres nombres. Buenos
    Aires: Instituto de Filología, 1938.
----------. "Substratum, superstratum." Revista de
    filología hispánica, 3 (1941), 185-218.
Arango, Guillermo. "Nuevos anglicismos en el espa-
    ñol peninsular." Hispania, 58 (1975), 498-502.
Benvenutto Murrieta, Pedro M. El lenguaje peruano.
    Lima: Sanmartí and Co., 1936.
Birdwhistell, Ray L. Kinesics and Context: Essays
    on Body Motion Communication. Philadelphia:
    University of Pennsylvania Press, 1970.
Bloomfield, Leonard. Language. London: Allen and
    Unwin, 1933.
Bolinger, Dwight. Aspects of Language. New York:
    Harcourt, Brace & World, Inc., 1968.
Bright, William, ed. Sociolinguistics. The Hague:
    Mouton, 1966.
Canfield, D. Lincoln. East Meets West, South of the
    Border. Carbondale: Southern Illinois Univer-
    sity Press, 1968.
----------. An Introduction to Romance Linguistics.

Carbondale: Southern Illinois University Press, 1975.
----------. "Observaciones sobre el español salvadoreño." Filología, 6 (1960), 29-76.
Cárdenas, Daniel. El español de Jalisco. Madrid: Rivadeneyra, 1967.
Cassano, P. V. "The Fall of Syllable- and Word-Final /s/ in Argentina and Paraguay." Revue des Langues Vivantes, 38 (1972), 282-283.
----------. "Retention of Certain Hiatuses in Paraguayan Spanish." Linguistics, 109 (1973), 12-16.
Chomsky, N. Aspects of the Theory of Syntax. Cambridge: M. I. T. Press, 1965.
Crystal, David. Linguistics. England: Penguin Books, Ltd., 1971.
Cuervo, Rufino José. Apuntaciones críticas sobre el lenguaje bogotano. 7th ed. Bogotá: Editorial el "Gráfico," 1939.
Donni de Mirande, Nélida E. El español hablado en Rosario (Argentina). Rosario: Universidad Nacional del Litoral, 1968.
Ewton, R. W., and J. Ornstein, eds. Studies in Language and Linguistics. El Paso: Texas Western Press, 1970.
Fernández-Galiano, Manuel. "Algunas consideraciones sobre etimología." Español actual, 24 (1973), 1-6.
Fishman, Joshua A., ed. Readings in the Sociology of Language. The Hague: Mouton, 1968.
Flores, Luis. Apuntes de español. Bogotá: Instituto Caro y Cuervo, 1977.
Fries, Charles C. The Structure of English. New York: Harcourt, Brace and Company, 1954.
Gifford, D. J. "Latin-American Studies: Language, American-Spanish." Year's Work in Modern Language Studies, 35 (1973), 350-354.
Gleason, H. A., Jr. An Introduction to Descriptive Linguistics. New York: Holt, Rinehart and Winston, 1961.
----------. Linguistics and English Grammar. New York: Holt, Rinehart and Winston, 1965.
Goilo, E. R. Hablemos Papiamento. Aruba, N. A.: De Wit Stores n. v., 1974.
Henríquez Ureña, Pedro. "Observaciones sobre el es-

pañol de América." Revista de filología española, VIII (1921), 357-390.
Hockett, G. F. A Course in Modern Linguistics. New York: Macmillan, 1958.
Hoijer, Harry, ed. Language History from Language. By Leonard Bloomfield. New York: Holt, Rinehart and Winston, 1965.
Hymes, Dell. "Models of the Interaction of Language and Social Setting." Journal of Social Issues, 23 (1967), 8-28.
----------, ed. Pidginization and Creolization of Languages. Cambridge: University Press, 1971.
Labov, William. The Social Stratification of English in New York City. Washington, D. C.: Center for Applied Linguistics, 1966.
Lacayo, Heberto. Como pronuncian el español en Nicaragua. Mexico: Universidad Iberoamericana, 1962.
Lado, Roberto. Lingüística contrastiva: Lenguas y culturas. Trans. Joseph A. Fernández. Madrid: Ediciones Alcalá, 1973.
----------. Linguistics Across Cultures: Applied Linguistics for Language Teachers. Ann Arbor: University of Michigan Press, 1957.
Lope Blanch, Juan M. El español de América. Madrid: Ediciones Alcalá, 1968.
Maccurdy, Raymond R. "Louisiana-French Loan Words for 'Water Fowl' in the Spanish of St. Bernard Parish, Louisiana." In Romance Studies Presented to W. M. Day. No. 12. Chapel Hill: University of North Carolina, 1950, pp. 139-142.
----------. "A Spanish Word-List of the 'Brulis' Dwellers of Louisiana." Hispania, 42 (1959), 547-554.
Magnusson, Walter L. "The Orthographic Code of Spanish." Linguistics, 82 (1972), 23-51.
Marías, Julián. El uso lingüístico. Buenos Aires: Editorial Columba, 1966.
Martinet, A. Economie des Changements Phonétiques. Berne: Francke, 1955.
----------. Phonology as Functional Phonetics. London: Oxford University Press, 1949.
Murphy, S. "Notes on Anglicisms in American Spanish." Hispania, 37 (1954), 457-459.

Nash, Rose, ed. Readings in Spanish-English Con-
    trastive Linguistics. San Juan: Inter American
    University Press, 1973.
Navarro Tomás, Tomás. "Observaciones sobre el papia-
    mento." Nueva revista de filología hispánica, 7
    (1951), 183-189.
O'Connor, J. D. New Phonetic Readings. Berne:
    Francke, 1967.
----------. Phonetics. Harmondsworth: Penguin
    Books, Ltd., 1973.
Pike, K. L. Phonetics: A Critical Analysis of Pho-
    netic Theory and a Technic for the Practical
    Description of Sounds. Ann Arbor: University
    of Michigan Press, 1943.
Politzer, Robert L., and Charles N. Staubach.
    Teaching Spanish: A Linguistic Orientation.
    Boston: Ginn, 1961.
Quesada, J. Daniel. La lingüística generativo-
    transformacional: supuestos e implicaciones.
    Madrid: Alianza, 1974.
Risco, Antonio. "Las ideas lingüísticas de Larra."
    Boletín de la Real Academia Española, 52 (1972),
    467-501.
Rona, José P. "Normas locales, regionales, naciona-
    les, y universales en la América Española."
    Nueva revista de filología hispánica, 22 (1973),
    310-321.
Rosenblat, Angel. La lengua del "Quijote." Madrid:
    Editorial Gredos, 1971.
----------. Nuestra lengua en ambos mundos. Este-
    la: Biblioteca General Salvat, 1971.
Seco, Manuel. Arniches y el habla de Madrid. Ma-
    drid y Barcelona: Alfaguara, 1970.
Tello, Jaime. "Algunas peculiaridades del castellano
    en Venezuela." Thesaurus, 27 (1972), 128-131.
Tessen, Howard W. "Some Aspects of the Spanish of
    Asunción, Paraguay." Hispania, 57 (1974), 935-
    937.
Vidal de Battini, Berta Elena. El español de la Ar-
    gentina. Buenos Aires: Ministerio de Educa-
    ción de la Nación, 1964.
Wise, C. M. Introduction to Phonetics. Englewood
    Cliffs, N. J.: Prentice-Hall, 1958.
Zamora Vicente, Alonso. "Para el uso del dicciona-
    rio." Revista del Occidente, 34 (1971), 327-334.

III. DIALECTOLOGY

Alvar, M. El dialecto aragonés. Madrid: Biblioteca Románica Hispánica, 1953.

Alvarez, George R. "Caló: the 'other' Spanish." A Review of General Semantics, 24 (1967), 7-11.

Arias, Amable Veiga. "Fonología gallega. Fonomática: la sílaba." Grial, 44 (1974), 157-172.

Danesi, Marcel. "The Case for Andalucismo Re-Examined." Hispania, 45 (1977), 181-193.

García de Diego, Vicente. "El castellano como complejo dialectal y sus dialectos internos." Revista de filología española, XXXIV (1950), 107-124.

----------. Manual de dialectología española. 2nd ed. Madrid: Cultura Hispánica, 1959.

González, Ollé F. "Vascuence y romance en la historia lingüística de Navarra." Boletín de la Real Academia Española, 50 (1970), 31-76.

James, Herman C., and Julio Ricci. "The Influence of Locally Spoken Italian Dialects on River Plate." Forum Italicum, 1 (1967), 48-59.

Lope Blanch, Juan M. "El léxico de la zona maya en el marco de la dialectología mexicana." Nueva revista de filología hispánica, 20 (1971), 1-63.

Maccurdy, Raymond R. The Spanish Dialect in St. Bernard Parish, Louisiana. Albuquerque, N. M.: University of New Mexico Press, 1950.

Martínez Alvarez, Josefina. "El cambio /-as/ɔ/-es/ del asturiano central." Archivum, 22 (1972), 291-303.

Neira Martínez, Jesús. "Los prefijos es-, des-, en aragonés." Archivum, 19 (1969), 331-341.

Seward, Thomas A. "Old Leonese Morphophonemic Assimilations: An Analysis and Geographical Study." Revista de estudios hispánicos, 5 (1971), 291-306.

Whinnon, Keith. Spanish Contact Vernaculars in the Philippine Islands. London: Hong Kong University Press, 1956.

IV. LEXICOGRAPHY

Bermudo de Tiberio, María del Pilar. "El movimiento estudiantil y su léxico." Español actual, 21 (1972), 18-22.

Bershas, Henry N. Puns on Proper Names in Spanish. Detroit: Wayne State University, 1961.

García, Antonio F. "Sport y deporte: compuestos y derivados." Filología moderna, 4041 (1970-1971), 93-110.

García de Diego, Vicente. "Nombres de acción." Boletín de la Real Academia Española, 50 (1970), 19-29.

Kany, Charles E. American-Spanish Euphemisms. Berkeley: University of California Press, 1951.

Lorenzo Vázquez, Ramón. "Contribución al léxico gallego: palabras de Amaía y aledaños." Cuadernos de estudios gallegos, 24 (1969), 172-193.

Malaret, Augusto. Lexicon de fauna y flora. Madrid: Comisión Permanente de la Asociación de la Academia de la Lengua Española, 1970.

Malkiel, Yakov. "En torno al cultismo medieval: Los descendientes hispánicos de dulcis." Nueva revista de filología hispánica, 24 (1975), 24-45.

Megenney, William W. "Apuntes sobre el léxico de la costa colombiana: frecuentes locuciones, verbos y modismos característicos." Hispania, 56 (1973), 1065-1071.

O'Hare, Philip J. "Gallicisms in Modern Spanish." Modern Languages, 57 (1976), 182-186.

Pratt, Chris. "El arraigo del anglicismo en el español de hoy." Filología moderna, 40-41 (1970-1971), 67-92.

Rodríguez Bou, Ismael. Recuento de vocabulario español. Vol. I. Río Piedras: Universidad de Puerto Rico, 1952.

Rosenblat, Angel. Buenas y malas palabras en el castellano de Venezuela. 2nd ed. Caracas-Madrid: Ediciones Edime, 1960.

Sánchez-Rojas, Arturo. "Crudeza y eufemismo en el habla popular." Hispania, 57 (1974), 498-500.

Senabre, Ricardo. "El eufemismo como fenómeno lingüístico." Boletín de la Real Academia Española, 51 (1971), 175-189.

423

Tejera, Emiliano. Palabras indígenas de la isla de Santo Domingo. Ciudad Trujillo, R. D.: Editora del Caribe, 1951.

V. PHONOLOGY

Alarcos Llorach, Emilio. Fonología española. 4th ed. Madrid: Editorial Gredos, 1965.
----------. "El sistema fonológico español." Revista de filología española, XXXIII (1948), 265-296.
Alonso, Amado. De la pronunciación medieval a la moderna en español. Madrid: Biblioteca Romana Hispánica, 1955. Vol. I; 1969. Vol. II.
Bishop, Dorothy Sword. Mi primera fonética. Illinois: National Textbook Co., 1970.
Bjarkman, Peter Christian. "Natural Phonology and Loanword Phonology (with Selected Examples from Miami Cuban Spanish)." Diss. The University of Florida 1976.
Boleño e Isla, A. Manual de la lengua española. Mexico: Porrúa, 1959.
Bolinger, Dwight L. "Secondary Stress in Spanish." Romance Philology, 15 (1962), 273-279.
Boyd-Bowman, Peter. "La pérdida de vocales átonas en la altaplanicie mexicana." Nueva revista de filología hispánica, 6 (1952), 138-140.
----------. "Sobre la pronunciación del español en el Ecuador." Nueva revista de filología hispánica, 7 (1953), 221-233.
----------. "Sobre los restos de lleísmo en México." Nueva revista de filología hispánica, 6 (1952), 69-74.
Canfield, D. Lincoln. "Andalucismos en la pronunciación hispanoamericana." Kentucky Foreign Language Quarterly, 8 (1961), 177-181.
Cárdenas, Daniel N. "The Geographic Distribution of the Assibilated R, RR in Spanish America." Orbis, 7 (1958), 407-414.
----------. Introducción a una comparación fonológica del español y del inglés. Washington, D. C.: Center for Applied Linguistics, 1960.

Cassano, Paul. "The Influence of Guaraní on the Phonology of the Spanish of Paraguay." _Studia Linguistica_, 26 (1973), 106-112.

Chavarría-Aguilar, O. L. "The Phonemes of Costa Rican Spanish." _Language_, 27 (1951), 248-253.

Corominas, J. "Para la fecha del yeísmo y del lleísmo." _Nueva revista de filología hispánica_, 7 (1953), 81-87.

Cuéllar, Beatriz V. "Observaciones sobre la 'rr' velar y la 'y' africada en Cuba." _Español actual_, 20 (1971), 18-20.

Delattre, Pierre. _Comparing the Phonetic Features of English, French, German and Spanish: an Interim Report_. London: Harrap, 1966.

Dreher, B. B. "Phonological Development in Formal and Informal Environments." _Hispania_, 56 (1973), 421-425.

Entrambasaguas, Joaquín. _Síntesis de pronunciación española_. Madrid: Aldecoa, 1966.

Espinosa, Jr., Aurelio M., and Juan Rodríguez Castellano. "La aspiración de la 'h' en el sur y oeste de España." _Revista de filología española_, XXIII (1936), 226-254; 337-378.

Fernández, Joseph A. "La anticipación vocálica en español." _Revista de filología española_, XLVI (1963), 437-440.

Flórez, Luis. _La pronunciación del español en Bogotá_. Bogotá: Instituto Caro y Cuervo, 1951.

Fontanella de Weinberg, María B. "Comportamiento ante -s de hablantes femeninos y masculinos del español bonaerense." _Romance Philology_, 27 (1973), 50-58.

Gili Gaya, Samuel. _Elementos de fonética general_. Madrid: Editorial Gredos, 1961.

Granda, Germán de. "La velarización de RR en el español de Puerto Rico." _Revista de filología española_, XLIX (1966), 181-227.

Honsa, Vladimir. "The Phonemic Systems of Argentinian Spanish." _Hispania_, 68 (1965), 275-283.

International Phonetic Association. _The Principles of the International Phonetic Association_. London: IPA, 1957.

Jones, D., and L. Dahl. _Fundamentos de escritura fonética según el sistema de la Asociación Fo-_

nética Internacional. London: University Col-
    lege, 1944.
Jones, Willis K. "What Spanish Pronunciation Shall
    We Teach?" Hispania, 24 (1941), 253-260.
Kortlandt, F. H. H. "Sur l'identification des uni-
    tés phonologiques du castillan." Linguistics,
    iii (1973), 43-50.
Kvavik, Karen H. "Research and Pedagogical Material
    on Spanish Intonation: A Re-Examination."
    Hispania, 59 (1976), 406-417.
Ladefoged, Peter. Preliminaries to Linguistic Pho-
    netics. Chicago: University of Chicago Press,
    1971.
Macpherson, I. R. Spanish Phonology. New York:
    Barnes & Noble Books, 1977.
Marden, G. Carroll. "La fonología del español en la
    ciudad de Méjico." Biblioteca de dialectología
    hispanoamericana, IV (1938), 86-187.
Mel'cuk, I. A. "On the Phonemic Status of 'Semi-
    Vowels' in Spanish." Linguistics, 109 (1973),
    35-60.
Moreno de Alba, José G. "Frecuencias de la asibila-
    ción de /R/ y /RR/ en México." Nueva revista
    de filología hispánica, 21 (1972), 363-370.
Navarro Tomás, Tomás. Manual de entonación española.
    New York: Hispanic Institute, 1945.
----------, and Aurelio M. Espinosa. A Primer of
    Spanish Pronunciation. New York: Benj. H.
    Sanborn & Co., 1926.
O'Connor, J. D. Phonetics. England: Penguin
    Books, Ltd., 1973.
Resnick, Melvyn C. Phonological Variants and Dia-
    lect Identification in Latin American Spanish.
    The Hague: Mouton, 1975.
----------, and Robert Hammond. "The Status of
    Quality and Length in Spanish Vowels." Lin-
    guistics, 156 (1975), 79-88.
Rodríguez de Montes, María L. "Oclusivos aspirados
    sordos en el español colombiano." Thesaurus,
    27 (1972), 583-586.
Saporta, Sol. "A Note on Spanish Semi-Vowels."
    Language, 32 (1956), 287-290.
----------, and H. Contreras. A Phonological Gram-
    mar of Spanish. Seattle: University of Wash-

ington Press, 1962.

Silva-Fuenzalida, Ismael. "La entonación en el español y su morfología." Boletín de filología, 9 (1956-1957), 177-187.

Stockwell, R. P., J. D. Bowen, and I. Silva-Fuenzalida. "Spanish Juncture and Intonation." Language, XXXII (1956), 641-665.

Trager, George L. "The Phonemes of Castilian Spanish." Travaux du Cercle Linguistique de Prague, 8 (1939), 217-222.

VI. SEMANTICS

Aid, Frances M. Semantic Structures in Spanish: A Proposal for Instructional Materials. Washington, D. C.: Georgetown University Press, 1973.

Bergen, John J. "The Semantics of Spanish Count and Measure Entity Nouns." Language Sciences, 44 (1977), 1-9.

Berney, T. D., and R. L. Cooper. "Semantic Independence and Degree of Bilingualism in Two Communities." Modern Language Journal, 53, No. 3 (1969), 182-185.

Bernstein, J. S. "On the Semantics of Certain Phrasal Verbs and Their Renderings Into Spanish." The Bilingual Review/La Revista Bilingüe, 1 (1974), 59-66.

----------. "The Semantics of Emphasis: 'Act' and 'Scene' in English and Spanish." The Bilingual Review/La Revista Bilingüe, 1 (1974), 159-169.

Bishop, Ann. "A Semantic Analysis of Diminutives in Spanish with Their Comparatives in English." Lenguaje y ciencias, 14 (1974), 35-46.

Carrasco, Félix. "Ser y estar y sus repercusiones en el sistema." Thesaurus, 29 (1974), 316-349.

Chafe, Wallace. Meaning and the Structure of Language. Chicago: University of Chicago Press, 1970.

Chomsky, Noam. Studies on Semantics in Generative Grammar. The Hague: Mouton, 1972.

Ervin, Susan. "Semantic Shift in Bilingualism." American Journal of Psychology, 74 (1961), 446-451.

Granda, Germán de. "Análisis semántico y diacronía
(sobre un ejemplo criollo-atlántico)." Boletín
de la Real Academia Española, 54 (1974), 315-
323.
Huberman, Gisela B. "Los horizontes de la semántica
española." Cuadernos Americanos, 180 (1972),
99-103.
Klein, Philip W. "Semantic Factors in Spanish Mood."
Glossa, 11 (1977), 3-19.
Leech, Geoffrey. Semantics. England: Penguin
Books, Ltd., 1974.
Lo Coco, Verónica Gonzáles-Mena de. "A Semantic Analysis of Third Person Se Construction." Hispania, 59 (1976), 887-890.
Perl, Matthias. "Teoría de valencias e investigacio-
nes semánticas de verbos españoles." Lenguaje
y Ciencias, 15 (1975), 47-56.
Temoche-R., Felipe. "Analísis semántico de las cláu-
sulas condicionales en inglés en comparación con
sus equivalentes en español." Lenguaje y Cien-
cias, 14 (1974), 24-34.
Tobón de Castro, Lucía, and Jaime Rodríguez Rondón.
"La relación verbo objeto, un hecho semántico."
Thesaurus, 31 (1976), 512-522.
Trujillo, Ramón. Elementos de semántica lingüísti-
ca. Madrid: Ediciones Cátedra, 1976.
Youngren, W. H. Semantics, Linguistics, and Literary
Criticism. New York: Random House, 1971.

VII. SYNTAX

Alarcos Llorach, Emilio. "Adimento, adverbio y cues-
tiones conexas." Archivum, 19 (1969), 301-329.
----------. Estudio de gramática funcional del es-
pañol. Madrid: Editorial Gredos, 1970.
Albor, Hugo R. "Da + gerundio, ¿un quechuísmo? Y
otras maneras de atenuar los imperativos."
Hispania, 56 (1973), 316-318.
Almasov, Alexey. "Special Uses of tú and usted."
Hispania, 57 (1974), 56-57.
Alonso, Amado, and Pedro Henríquez Ureña. Gramática
castellana, primer curso. 4th ed. Buenos Ai-

res: Editorial Losada, 1944.
----------. Gramática castellana, segundo curso.
    4th ed. Buenos Aires: Editorial Losada, 1944.
Bastianutti, D. L. "Tendencias en el empleo del im-
    perfecto de subjuntivo en sus dos formas en el
    teatro español de las últimas décadas." Espa-
    ñol actual, 22 (1972), 11-18.
Bolinger, Dwight L. "Adjective Position Again."
    Hispania, 55 (1972), 91-94.
----------. "Again--One or Two Subjunctives." His-
    pania, 59 (1976), 41-49.
----------. "The Position of the Adverb in English:
    a Convenient Analogy to the Position of the Ad-
    jective in Spanish." Hispania, 26 (1943), 191-
    192.
----------. "Prepositions in English and Spanish."
    Hispania, 40 (1957), 212-214.
Chart, Ira E. "The 'Voseo' and 'Tuteo' in America."
    Modern Language Forum, 28 (1943), 17-24.
Contreras, Heles. "Grammaticality Versus Accepta-
    bility: The Spanish se Case." Linguistic In-
    quiry, 4 (1973), 83-88.
De Bruyne, Jacques. "The Past Participle in Span-
    ish: Problems of Construction." Linguistica
    Antverpiensia, 6 (1972), 27-50.
Gili Gaya, Samuel. Curso superior de sintaxis espa-
    ñola. 11th ed. Barcelona: Departamento Edi-
    torial, 1976.
----------. Nuestra lengua materna: observaciones
    gramaticales y léxicas. San Juan: Instituto
    de Cultura Puertorriqueña, 1965.
Hadlich, Roger L. A Transformational Grammar of
    Spanish. Englewood Cliffs, N. J.: Prentice-
    Hall, 1971.
Hart, Peggy D. "The Use of the Preposition por When
    It Means 'to fetch'." Hispania, 56 (1973),
    646-647.
Jordán, Pablo G. "La forma se como sujeto indefini-
    do en español." Hispania, 56 (1973), 597-603.
Kvavik, Karen H. "Spanish Noun Suffixes: A Syn-
    chronic Perspective on Methodological Problems,
    Characteristic Patterns, and Usage Data." Lin-
    guistics, 156 (1975), 23-78.
Lott, Robert E. "Frases populares y pintorescas em-

pleadas en Córdoba, Colombia." Hispania, 55 (1972), 506-510.
Marín, Diego. "El uso de 'tú' y 'usted' en el español actual." Hispania, 55 (1972), 904-908.
Morreale, Margherita. "Aspectos gramaticales y estilísticos del número." Boletín de la Real Academia Española, 51 (1971), 83-138.
Otero, Carlos, and Judith Springer. "Linguistic Analysis and the Teaching of se." Hispania, 56 (1973), 1050-1054.
Rivero, María-Luisa. "Estudio de una transformación en la gramática generativa del español." Español actual, 17 (1970), 14-22.
Solé, Yolanda R. "Sociocultural Determinants of Symmetrical and Asymmetrical Address Forms in Spanish." Hispania, 61 (1978), 940-949.
Weber, Frida. "Fórmulas de tratamiento en la lengua de Buenos Aires." Revista de filología hispánica, 3 (1941), 105-139.
Zavala, Víctor Sánchez de. Estudios de gramática generativa. Barcelona: Labor Universitaria, 1976.

VIII. BIBLIOGRAPHIES

Aveleyra A., Teresa, and Beatriz Garza Cuarón, eds. "Bibliografía." Nueva revista de filología hispánica, 23 (1974), 163-244; 431-476.
Barrios, Ernie, ed. Bibliografía de Aztlán: An Annotated Chicano Bibliography. San Diego: Centro de Estudios Chicanos Publications, 1971.
Beardsley, Theodore S., Jr. "Bibliografía preliminar de estudios sobre el español en los Estados Unidos." Boletín de la Academia Norteamericana de la Lengua Española, 1 (1976), 49-73.
Bleznick, Donald W. A Sourcebook for Hispanic Literature and Language. Philadelphia: Temple University, 1974.
Brenni, Vito J. American English: A Bibliography. Philadelphia: University of Pennsylvania Press, 1964.
Bruno, Lidia N., and Elena L. Najlis. "Bibliografía

430

argentina de filología y lingüística, 1965-
1968." Anales de la Universidad del Salvador,
N. 6. Buenos Aires: Universidad del Salvador,
1969.
Cortés, Carlos E. Mexican American Bibliographies.
New York: Arno Press, 1974.
Davis, Jack Emory. "The Spanish of Argentina and
Uruguay. An Annotated Bibliography for 1940-
1965, VI." Orbis, 20 (1971), 236-269.
Deal, Carl W., ed. Latin America and the Caribbean.
A Dissertation Bibliography. Ann Arbor, Michi-
gan: University Microfilms International, n. d.
Dossick, Jesse J. Doctoral Research on Puerto Rico
and Puerto Ricans. New York: New York Univer-
sity, 1967.
"El español en Puerto Rico: Bibliografía." Revista
de estudios hispánicos, 1 (1971), 111-124.
Fody, III, Michael. "The Spanish of the American
Southwest and Louisiana: A Bibliographical
Survey for 1954-1969." Orbis, 19 (1970), 529-
540.
Foster, David W., and Virginia Ramos Foster. Manual
of Hispanic Bibliography. Seattle: University
of Washington Press, 1970.
Frey, Herschel J. Teaching Spanish: A Critical Bib-
liographic Survey. Rowley, Mass.: Newbury
House, 1974.
Gifford, D. J. "Latin-American Studies: Language:
American Spanish." Year's Work in Modern Lan-
guage Studies, 38 (1976), 374-379.
Haugen, Einar. Bilingualism in the Americas: a
Bibliography and Research. Alabama: University
Press, 1956.
Hulet, Claude L. "Dissertations in the Hispanic Lan-
guages and Literatures." Hispania, 56 (1972),
386-399.
Jablonsky, Adelaide. Mexican Americans: An Annota-
ted Bibliography of Doctoral Dissertations.
New York: Columbia University Teachers College
and Washington, D. C.: ERIC, 1973.
Keightler, R. G. "Spanish Studies: Language."
Year's Work in Modern Language Studies, 33
(1971), 231-238.
López Morales, Humberto. "El español de Cuba: si-
tuación bibliográfica." Revista de filología

española, LI (1968), 111-137.

Maccurdy, Raymond P. A History and Bibliography of Spanish-Language Newspapers and Magazines in Louisiana, 1808-1949. Albuquerque, New Mexico: The University of New Mexico Press, 1951.

Millán Orozco, Antonio. "Bibliografía de lo publicado en México de 1961 a 1971." Español actual, 25 (1973), 24-28.

Nichols, Madaline W. A Bibliographical Guide to Materials on American Spanish. Cambridge, Mass.: Harvard University Press, 1941.

Nogales, Luis, ed. The Mexican-American: A Selected and Annotated Bibliography. 2nd ed. Stanford, Ca.: Stanford University: Center for Latin American Studies, 1971.

Pottier, Bernard. "Publications récentes sur l'espagnol et le portugais en Amérique." Travaux de l'institut d'Etudes Latino-Américaines de l'Université de Strasbourg, 11 (1971), 33-35.

Rohlfs, Gerhard. Manual de filología hispánica. Guía bibliográfica crítica y metódica. Bogotá: Instituto Caro y Cuervo, 1957.

Rona, José Pedro. Aspectos metodológicos de la dialectología hispanoamericana. Montevideo: Universidad de la República, 1958.

Saunders, Lyle. Spanish Americans and Mexican-Americans in the U. S.: A Selected Bibliography. New York: Bureau for Intercultural Education, 1944.

Serís, Homero. Bibliografía de la lingüística española. Bogotá: Instituto Caro y Cuervo, 1964.

Solé, Carlos A. Bibliografía sobre el español en América 1920-1967. Washington, D. C.: Georgetown University Press, 1970.

Teschner, Richard V. "A Critical Annotated Bibliography of Anglicisms in Spanish." Hispania, 57 (1974), 631-678.

----------, comp. Spanish-Surnamed Populations of the United States: A Catalog of Dissertations. Ann Arbor, Michigan: Xerox University Microfilms, 1974.

----------, Garland D. Bills, and Jerry R. Craddock. Spanish and English of United States Hispanos: A Critical, Annotated, Linguistic Bibliography.

Arlington, Va.: Center for Applied Linguistics, 1975.
Tully, Marjorie F., and Juan B. Rael. An Annotated Bibliography of Spanish Folklore in New Mexico and Southern Colorado. Albuquerque, N. M.: University of New Mexico: Publications in Language and Literature, 1950.
Vivó, Paquita. The Puerto Ricans: An Annotated Bibliography. New York: R. R. Bowker Company, 1973.
Woodbridge, Hensley C. "Central American Spanish: A Bibliography (1940-1953)." Inter-American Review of Bibliography (Revista inter-americana de bibliografía), 6 (1956), 103-115.
----------. "Spanish in the American South and Southwest: A Bibliographical Survey for 1940-1953." Orbis, 3 (1954), 236-244.
----------, and Paul R. Olson. A Tentative Bibliography of Hispanic Linguistics. Urbana, Illinois: University of Illinois Press, 1952.
Zubatsky, David S. "Hispanic Linguistic Studies in Festschriften: An Annotated Bibliography (1957-1975)." Hispania, 60 (1977), 656-717.

IX. DICTIONARIES AND REFERENCE WORKS

Alfaro, Richard J. Diccionario de anglicismos. 2nd ed. Madrid: Editorial Gredos, 1970.
Alonso, Martín. Enciclopedia del idioma. 3 Vols. Madrid: Aguilar, 1958.
Bentley, Harold W. A Dictionary of Spanish Terms in English with Special Reference to the American Southwest. New York: Columbia University Press, 1932.
Cabrera, Luis. Diccionario de aztequismos. Mexico: Ediciones Oasis, 1974.
Casullo, Fernando H. Diccionario de voces lunfardas y vulgares. Buenos Aires: Freeland, 1972.
Corominas, Joan. Breve diccionario etimológico de la lengua castellana. Madrid: Editorial Gredos, 1961.
De Toro y Gisbert, Miguel. Pequeño Larousse Ilus-

433

trado. Paris: Editorial Larousse, 1964.
Espasa-Calpe. Diccionario enciclopédico abreviado.
Madrid: Espasa-Calpe, S. A., 1972.
Gili Gaya, Samuel. Diccionario general ilustrado de
la lengua española. Barcelona: Editorial
Spes, 1961.
Malaret, Augusto. Diccionario de americanismos.
3rd ed. Buenos Aires: Emecé, 1946.
Martínez Amador, Emilio. Diccionario gramatical y
de dudas del idioma. Barcelona: Ramón Sopena,
S. A., 1961.
Mattoso Camara, Jr., Joaquim. Dicionário de linguís-
tica e gramática. 7th ed. Petrópolis: Editora
Vozes, 1977.
Millares, Luis y Agustín. Léxico de Gran Canaria.
Las Palmas: Tipografía "Diario de las Palmas,"
1924.
Moliner, María. Diccionario de uso del español. 2
vols. Madrid: Editorial Gredos, 1966.
Real Academia Española. Diccionario de la lengua
castellana de la Real Academia Española. 19th
ed. Madrid: Espasa-Calpe, 1970.
----------, Comisión de Gramática. Esbozo de una
nueva gramática de la lengua española. Madrid:
Espasa-Calpe, 1973.
Sainz de Robles, Federico Carlos. Ensayo de un dic-
cionario español de sinónimos y antónimos.
Madrid: Aguilar, 1969.
Santamaría, Francisco J. Diccionario de mejicanis-
mos. México: Editorial Porrúa, 1959.
----------. Diccionario general de americanismos.
Méjico: Editorial Pedro Robredo, 1942.
Seco, Manuel. Diccionario de dudas y dificultades
de la lengua española. Madrid: Aguilar, 1964.

X. BILINGUALISM AND RELATED AREAS

Anderson, Theodore, and Mildred Boyer, eds. Bilin-
gual Schooling in the United States. 2 vols.
Washington, D. C.: Government Printing Office,
1970.
Bowen, J. Dodd. "A Comparison of the Intonation
Patterns of English and Spanish." Hispania, 29

(1956), 30-35.

Burma, John H., ed. Spanish-Speaking Groups in the United States. Durham, N. C.: Duke University Press, 1954.

Burt, Marina K., and Heidi C. Dulay, eds. New Directions in Second Language Learning, Teaching and Bilingual Education. Washington, D. C.: TESOL, 1975.

Chreist, Fred M. Foreign Accent. Englewood Cliffs, N. J.: Prentice Hall, Inc., 1964.

Cormejo, Ricardo. "Bilingual Lexicon in Speech." In Bilingualism in the Southwest. Ed. Paul R. Turner. Tucson, Arizona: University of Arizona Press, 1973, 77-88.

Craddock, Jerry R. "Spanish in North America." In Linguistics in North America. Eds. William Bright, Dell Hymes, et al. Vol. 10 of Current Trends in Linguistics. The Hague: Mouton, 1973, pp. 305-339.

Croft, Kenneth. Readings on English as a Second Language. Cambridge: Winthrop Publishers, Inc., 1972.

Diebold, Richard A. "Incipient Bilingualism." Language, 37 (1961), 97-112.

Fernández-Shaw, Carlos M. Presencia española en los Estados Unidos. Madrid: Ediciones Cultura Hispánica, 1972.

Finocchiaro, Mary. Teaching English as a Second Language. New York: Harper, 1958.

Fisher, J. C. "Bilingualism in Puerto Rico, a History of Frustration." The English Record, 2, 2 (1971), 19-24.

Fishman, Joshua A. "Bilingualism in the Barrio." Modern Language Journal, 53 (1969), 151-155.

----------, ed. Language Loyalty in the United States: The Maintenance and Perpetuation of Non-English Mother Tongues by American Ethnic and Religious Groups. The Hague: Mouton, 1966.

----------. "A Sociolinguistic Census of a Bilingual Neighborhood." American Journal of Sociology, 45, 3 (1969), 323-339.

----------. "Some Things Learned; Some Things Yet to Learn." Modern Language Journal, 53, 4

(1969), 255-258.

González, George Adalberto. "The Development and
Preliminary Testing of a Theoretical Spanish
Language Instructional Model for Bilingual Education." Diss. The University of New Mexico
1973.

Greenfield, L., and J. A. Fishman. "Situational
Measures of Normative Language Views in Relation to Person, Place and Topic among Puerto
Rican Bilinguals." Anthropos, 65 (1975), 602-
618.

Gumperz, John J., and Eduardo Hernández-Chavez.
"Cognitive Aspects of Bilingual Communication."
In El lenguaje de los Chicanos: Regional and
Social Characteristics of Language Used by Mexican Americans. Eds. Eduardo Hernández-Chavez,
et al. Arlington, Va.: Center for Applied Linguistics, 1975, pp. 154-163.

Gutiérrez, Medardo. "A Description of the Speech of
Immigrant and Second Generation Gallego-Spanish
Speakers in New York City. A Study in Bilin-
gualism." Diss. Georgetown University 1971.

Haugen, Einar. "Schizoglossia and the Linguistic
Norm." In Georgetown Monograph Series on Languages and Linguistics, No. 15. Washington,
D. C.: Georgetown University Press, 1962,
pp. 63-73.

----------. "The Stigmata of Bilingualism." In The
Ecology of Language. Ed. Anvas S. Dil. California: Stanford University Press, 1972,
pp. 207-324.

Helm, June, ed. Spanish-Speaking People in the
United States. Proceedings of the 1968 Meeting
of the American Ethnological Society. Seattle:
University of Washington Press, 1968.

Lado, Robert. "A Comparison of the Sound Systems of
English and Spanish." Hispania, 39 (1956),
126-129.

Lambert, W. E. "Measurement of the Linguistic Dominance of Bilinguals." Journal of Abnormal and
Social Psychology, 50 (1955), 197-200.

Lance, D. M. "The Codes of the Spanish-English Bilingual." TESOL Quarterly, 4, 4 (1970), 343-
351.

436

Lowery, Woodbury. The Spanish Settlements within
the Present Limits of the United States. New
York: Russell & Russell, Inc., 1959.
Lugo, James Oscar. "A Comparison of Degrees of Bi-
lingualism and Measure of School Achievement
among Mexican-American Pupils." Diss. Univer-
sity of Southern California 1970.
MacNamara, J. Bilingualism in Primary Education.
Edinburgh: Edinburgh University Press, 1966.
Maiztegui, M. T., and J. Rivas. "A Contrastive
Study of the Article in English and Spanish."
English Language Journal/Revista de la Lengua
Inglesa, 2, 4 (1971), 291-303.
Marrone, Nila. "Investigación sobre variaciones
léxicas en el mundo hispano." The Bilingual Re-
view/La Revista Bilingüe, 1 (1974), 152-158.
Matilla, Alfredo, and Ivan Silen, eds. The Puerto
Rican Poets/Los Poetas Puertorriqueños. New
York: Bantam Books, 1972.
Mazeika, Edward John. "A Descriptive Analysis of
the Language of a Bilingual Child." Diss. The
University of Rochester 1971.
Murra, Elizabeth. "Learning a Second Language."
Journal of Educational Sociology, 28, No. 4
(1954), 181-192.
Nash, R. "Intonational Interference in the Speech
of Puerto Rican Bilinguals: an Instrumental
Study Based on Oral Readings of a Juan Bobo
Story." Journal of English as a Second Lan-
guage, 4 (1969), 1-42.
Ortega, Joaquín. The Compulsory Teaching of Spanish
in the Grade Schools of New Mexico. Albuquerque: The University of New Mexico Press, 1941.
Pimsleur, Paul, and Terence Quinn. The Psychology
of Second Language Learning. London: Cambridge University Press, 1971.
Ragsdale, J. D. "Predicting Pronunciation and
Listening Skills of Native Speakers of Spanish:
an Exploratory Study." TESOL Quarterly, 2
(1968), 33-38.
Rice, Frank A., ed. Study of the Role of Second Languages in Asia, Africa, and Latin America.
Washington, D. C.: Center for Applied Linguistics, 1962.

437

Shiels, Marie Eileen. "Dialects in Contact. A
Sociolinguistic Analysis of Four Phonological
Variables of Puerto Rican English and Black
English in Harlem." Diss. Georgetown Univer-
sity 1972.
Skoczylas, Rudolph V. "An Evaluation of Some Cogni-
tive and Affective Aspects of a Spanish-English
Bilingual Education Program." Diss. The Uni-
versity of New Mexico 1972.
Smith, William Carlson. Americans in the Making:
The Natural History of the Assimilation of Im-
migrants. New York: D. Appleton-Century Co.,
1939.
Steiner, Roger J. Two Centuries of Spanish and Eng-
lish Bilingual Lexicography 1590-1800. The
Hague: Mouton & Co., 1970.
Stockwell, Robert P., and J. Donald Bowen. The
Sounds of English and Spanish. Chicago: Uni-
versity of Chicago Press, 1965.
Teschner, Richard V. Spanish-Surnamed Populations
of the United States. Ann Arbor: Xerox Uni-
versity Microfilms, 1974.
Turner, Paul R., ed. Bilingualism in the Southwest.
Tucson, Arizona: University of Arizona Press,
1973.
Valdés-Fallis, Guadalupe, and Richard V. Teschner.
Español escrito: Curso para hispanohablantes
bilingües. New York: Charles Scribner's Sons,
1978.

XI. CHICANO

Alford, Harold J. The Proud Peoples. The Heritage
and Culture of Spanish-Speaking Peoples in the
United States. New York: New American Library,
1972.
Avendaño, Fausto. "Observaciones sobre los problemas
de traducción de la literatura chicana." The
Bilingual Review/La Revista Bilingüe, 2 (1975),
276-280.
Blanco, Antonio. La lengua española en la historia
de California. Madrid: Cultura Hispánica,
1971.

Bowen, J. Donald. "The Spanish of San Antonito,
New Mexico." Diss. University of New Mexico
1952.
Braddy, Haldeen. "The Pachucos and Their Argot."
Southern Folklore Quarterly, 24 (December,
1960), 255-271.
Canfield, D. Lincoln. Spanish Literature in Mexican
Languages as a Source for the Study of Spanish
Pronunciation. New York: Instituto de las
Españas en los Estados Unidos, 1934.
Clegg, Joseph Halvor. "Fonética y fonología del es-
pañol de Texas." Diss. The University of Texas
at Austin 1969.
Coltharp, Lurline H. The Tongue of the Tirilones.
Tuscaloosa: University of Alabama Press, 1965.
Domínguez, Domingo. "A Theoretical Model for Classi-
fying Dialectal Variations of Oral New Mexican
Spanish." Diss. The University of New Mexico
1974.
Espinosa, Aurelio M. Romancero de Nuevo Méjico.
Madrid: C. Bermejo, 1953.
----------. Studies in New Mexican Spanish. Chica-
go: The University of Chicago Press, 1909.
Floyd, Mary Elizabeth. "Verb Usage and Language
Variation in Colorado Spanish." Diss. The Uni-
versity of Colorado 1976.
Forbes, Jack D. Mexican Americans: A Handbook for
Educators. Washington, D. C.: U. S. Govern-
ment Printing Office, 1970.
----------. "The Mexican Heritage of the United
States: An Historical Summary." In Educating
the Mexican American. Eds. Henry Sioux Johnson
and William J. Hernández-M. Valley Forge, Pa.:
Judson Press, 1970, pp. 46-53.
Galván, Roberto A. "El dialecto español de San An-
tonio, Texas." Diss. Tulane University 1955.
Gamio, Manuel. Mexican Immigration to the United
States. New York: Arno Press, 1930.
Grebler, Leo, Joan W. Moore, and Ralph C. Guzmán.
The Mexican-American People: The Nation's Sec-
ond Largest Minority. New York: The Free
Press--MacMillan Company, 1970.
Guerra, Manuel H. "The Mexican-American Child:
Problems or Talents?" In Educating the Mexican

439

American. Eds. Henry Sioux Johnson, and William
J. Hernández-M. Valley Forge, Pa.: Judson
Press, 1970, pp. 64-79.
Hernández-Chavez, Eduardo, Andrew D. Cohen, and An-
thony Fred Beltramo, eds. El lenguaje de los
Chicanos: Regional and Social Characteristics
of Language Used by Mexican Americans. Arling-
ton, Va.: Center for Applied Linguistics, 1975.
Hoffer, Bates, and Jacob Ornstein. Sociolinguistics
in the Southwest. San Antonio, Texas: Dept.
of English/Trinity University, 1974.
Horgan, Paul. The Heroic Triad. Backgrounds of Our
Three Southwestern Cultures. New York: A Meri-
dian Book, 1971.
Johnson, Henry Sioux, and William J. Hernández-M.,
eds. Educating the Mexican American. Valley
Forge, Pa.: Judson Press, 1970.
Lawton, David. "Chicano Spanish: Some Sociolinguis-
tic Considerations." The Bilingual Review/La
Revista Bilingüe, 2 (1975), 22-33.
Lo Coco González-Mena de, Verónica. "The Salient
Differences between Chicano Spanish and Standard
Spanish: Some Pedagogical Considerations." The
Bilingual Review/La Revista Bilingüe, 1 (1974),
243-251.
Lozano, Anthony G. "Grammatical Notes on Chicano
Spanish." The Bilingual Review/La Revista Bi-
lingüe, 1 (1974), 147-151.
Ludvig, Ed, and James Santibáñez, eds. The Chicanos.
Mexican American Voices. Baltimore, Maryland:
Penguin Books, Inc., 1972.
McWilliams, Carey. North From Mexico, the Spanish-
Speaking People of the United States. Phila-
delphia: J. B. Lippincott Co., 1949.
Manuel, Herschel T. Spanish-Speaking Children of the
Southwest. Austin: University of Texas Press,
1965.
Martínez, Al. Rising Voices: Profiles of Hispano-
American Lives. New York: New American Li-
brary, 1974.
Matthiessen, Peter. Sal Si Puedes: César Chávez and
the New American Revolution. New York: Random
House, 1969.
Nava, Julián. Mexican Americans, Past, Present, and

Future. New York: American Book Co., 1969.
Ornstein, Jacob. "Toward a Classification of South-
    west Spanish Nonstandard Variants." Linguis-
    tics, 93 (1972), 70-87.
Ortega, Joaquín. The Compulsory Teaching of Spanish
    in the Grade Schools of New Mexico. Albuquer-
    que: University of New Mexico Press, 1941.
Peñalosa, Fernando. "Chicano Multilingualism and
    Multiglossia." Aztlán, 3 (1972), 215-222.
Peñuelas, Marcelino C. Lo español en el suroeste de
    los Estados Unidos. Madrid: Ediciones Cultura
    Hispánica, 1964.
Phillips, Jr., Robert Nelson. "Los Angeles Spanish:
    A Descriptive Analysis." Diss. The University
    of Wisconsin 1967.
Post, Anita C. "Some Aspects of Arizona Spanish."
    Hispania, 16 (1933), 35-42.
Ross, Lyle Ronald. "La lengua castellana en San
    Luis, Colorado." Diss. The University of Colo-
    rado 1975.
Samora, Julian, ed. La Raza: Forgotten Americans.
    Notre Dame: University of Notre Dame Press,
    1966.
Serrano, Rodolfo G. "Sociocultural Influences on the
    Development of Mexican American Language
    Styles." Diss. The University of Arizona 1972.
Simmen, Edward, ed. The Chicano: From Caricature to
    Self-Portrait. New York: New American Library,
    1971.
----------, ed. Pain and Promise: The Chicano To-
    day. New York: New American Library, 1972.
Steiner, S. La Raza: The Mexican Americans. New
    York: Harper and Row, 1969.
Teschner, Richard V. "Problems of Southwestern Span-
    ish Lexicography." Linguistics, 128 (1974),
    41-51.
Thurman, Herschel. Spanish-Speaking Children of the
    Southwest. Austin: University of Texas Press,
    1965.
Webb, John Terrance. "A Lexical Study of 'Caló' and
    the Non-Standard Spanish in the Southwest."
    Diss. University of California 1976.

441

XII. CUBAN

Bomse, Marguerite D., and Julián H. Alfaro. Practical Spanish for Medical and Hospital Personnel. Elmsford, N. J.: Pergamon Press, 1973.

Church, George J. "The Welcome Wears Thin." Time, 1 Sept. 1980, pp. 8-10.

Covington, James W. "Ybor City: A Cuban Enclave in Tampa." The Florida Anthropologist, 19 (1966), 85-90.

Fagen, Richard R., Richard A. Brody, and Thomas J. O'Leary. Cubans in Exile. Disaffection and the Revolution. Stanford: Stanford University Press, 1968.

Hammond, Robert M. "Phonemic Restructuring of Voiced Obstruents in Miami-Cuban Spanish." In 1975 Colloquium on Hispanic Linguistics. Eds. Frances M. Aid, Melvyn C. Resnick, and Bohdan Saciuk. Washington, D. C.: Georgetown University Press, 1976, pp. 8-12.

----------. "Some Theoretical Implications from Rapid Speech Phenomena in Miami-Cuban Spanish." Diss. The University of Florida 1976.

Meyer Rogg, Eleanor. The Assimilation of Cuban Exiles. The Role of Community and Class. New York: Aberdeen Press, 1974.

Ortiz, Carmelita Louise. "English Influence on the Spanish of Tampa." Hispania, 32 (1942), 300-304.

----------. "English Influence on the Spanish of Tampa." MA Thesis University of Florida 1947.

Ramírez, Manuel D. "Some Semantic and Linguistic Notes on the Spanish Spoken in Tampa, Florida." Revista Interamericana, 1 (1939), 25-33.

Research Institute for Cuba and the Caribbean Center for Advanced International Studies. The Cuban Immigration, 1959-1966, and Its Impact on Miami-Dade County, Florida. Health, Education and Welfare. Miami: University of Miami Press, 1967.

Sacks Da Silva, Zenia. "La Hispanidad en los Estados Unidos." Hispania, 58 (1975), 41-44.

Smith, M. Estellie. "The Spanish-Speaking Population of Florida." American Ethnological Society,

(1968), 120-133.
Vallejo-Claros, Bernardo. "La distribución y estra-
tificación de /r/, /r̄/ y /s/ en el español cu-
bano." Diss. University of Texas 1970.
Varela de Cuéllar, Beatriz. "La influencia del inglés en los cubanos de Miami y Nueva Orleans."
Español actual, 26 (April, 1974), 16-25.

XIII. SEPHARDIC

Armistead, S. G., and J. H. Silverman. "Hispanic
Balladry Among the Sephardic Jews of the West
Coast." Western Folklore, 19 (1960), 229-244.
----------. "A New Semantic Calque in Judeo-Spanish:
Reinado 'Belongings, Property'." Romance Philo-
logy, 26 (1972), 55-57.
Attías, Moshé, Arturo Capdevilla, and Carlos Ramos
Gil. "Supervivencia del judeo-español." Cua-
dernos Israelíes, 9 (1964), 15-31.
Benardete, M. J. Hispanic Culture and Character of
the Sephardic Jews. New York: The Hispanic
Institute, 1953.
----------. Hispanismo de los sefardíes levantinos.
Trans. Manuel Alvar. Madrid: Aguilar, 1963.
Besso, Henry V. "Dramatic Literature of the Spanish
and Portuguese Jews of Amsterdam in the 17. and
18. Centuries." Bulletin Hispanique, 39 (1937),
215-238.
----------. "A Further Contribution to the Refranero
Judeo-Español." Bulletin Hispanique, 37 (1935),
209-219.
----------. "Judeo-Spanish in the United States."
Hispania, 34 (1951), 89-90.
----------. "Judeo-Spanish Proverbs." Bulletin
Hispanique, 50 (1948), 370-387.
Danon, A. "Les éléments grecs dans le judéo-espa-
gnol." Revue des Études Juives, 75 (1922),
211-216.
Díaz-Plaja, Guillermo. "Aportación al cancionero
judeo-español del mediterráneo oriental." Bo-
letín de la Biblioteca Menéndez Pelayo, 16
(1934), 44-61.
Estrago, José M. Los sefardíes. La Habana: Edito-

443

rial Lex, 1958.

Hassán, Iacob M. "Activadades en torno al judeo-es-
    pañol." Boletín de filología española, 4
    (1964), 15-17.
----------. "El Simposio de Estudios Sefardíes."
    Sefarad, 24 (1964), 327-355.
Levy, Denah. "El sefardí de Nueva York. Observa-
    ciones sobre el judeo-español de Esmirna." MA
    Thesis Columbia University 1944.
----------. "El sefardí esmirniano de Nueva York."
    Diss. University of Mexico 1952.
Menéndez Pidal, Ramón. "Catálogo del romancero ju-
    deo-español." Cultura española, 1 (1906),
    1045-1077; 2 (1907), 161-199.
Pulido y Fernández, Angel. Los israelitas españoles
    y el idioma castellano. Madrid: Tipografía
    "Sucesores de Rivadeneyra," 1904.
Renard, Raymond. "Le Système Phonique du Judéo-Espa-
    gnol." Revue de Phonétique Appliquée, 1 (1965),
    23-33.
Sephipha, Haim Vidal. "Problématique du Judéo-espa-
    gnol." Bulletin de la Societé de Linguistique
    de Paris, 69 (1974), 159-189.
Tovar, R. "Estudios dialectológicos. Supervivencia
    del arcaísmo español." Boletín de la Academia
    Argentina de Letras, 13 (1944), 493-659.
Wagner, Max L. "Algunas observaciones generales so-
    bre el judeo-español de Oriente." Revista de
    filología española, X (1923), 225-244.
----------. Caracteres generales del judeo-español
    de Oriente. Madrid: Imprenta de la Librería
    y Casa Editorial Hernando, 1930.

XIV. PUERTO RICAN

Acosta-Belén, Edna. "On the Nature of Spanglish."
    The Journal of Contemporary Puerto Rican
    Thought, 2, 2 (1975), 7-13.
----------. "Spanglish: A Case of Languages in
    Contact." In New Directions in Second Language
    Learning, Teaching and Bilingual Education.
    Eds. Marina K. Burt and Heidi C. Dulay. Wash-
    ington, D. C.: TESOL, 1975, pp. 151-158.

Alvarez Nazario, Manuel. El elemento afronegroide
   en el español de Puerto Rico. San Juan: Insti-
   tuto de Cultura Puertorriqueña, 1961.
----------. La naturaleza del español que se habla
   en Puerto Rico. San Juan: Instituto de Cultu-
   ra Puertorriqueña, 1963.
Battlé, Anna, et al. The Puerto Ricans: A Resource
   Unit for Teachers. New York: The Anti-Defama-
   tion League, 1973.
Berle, Beatrice B. 80 Puerto Rican Families in New
   York City. New York: Columbia University
   Press, 1958.
Betancourt, Francisco. "Language Attitudes and Lan-
   guage Education in Arecibo, Puerto Rico."
   Diss. The University of Texas 1976.
Brameld, Theodore A. The Remaking of a Culture:
   Life and Education in Puerto Rico. New York:
   Harper, 1959.
Cabiya San Miguel, Carmen Rosa. "Estudio lingüístico
   de la zona de Santurce (Puerto Rico)." MA The-
   sis Universidad de Puerto Rico 1967.
Carrillo, Ricarda de Carle. "Estudios lingüísticos
   de Vieques." Diss. University of Puerto Rico
   1967.
Chenault, Lawrence R. The Puerto Rican Migrant in
   New York City. New York: Russell & Russell,
   1970.
Colhoun, Edward R. "Local and Non-Local Frames of
   Reference in Puerto Rican Dialectology." Diss.
   Cornell University 1967.
Cordasco, Francesco. "The Puerto Rican Child in the
   American School." Kansas Journal of Sociology,
   II (Spring, 1966), 59-65.
----------, and Eugene Bucchioni. Puerto Rican Chil-
   dren in Mainland Schools: A Source Book for
   Teachers. Metuchen, N. J.: The Scarecrow
   Press, Inc., 1968.
Doob, Christopher Bates. "Family Background and Peer
   Group Development in a Puerto Rican District."
   The Sociological Quarterly, 11 (1970), 523-532.
Epstein, Erwin H. Politics and Education in Puerto
   Rico. Metuchen, N. J.: The Scarecrow Press,
   Inc., 1970.
Fitzpatrick, Joseph P. Puerto Rican Americans.

445

Englewood Cliffs, New Jersey: Prentice—Hall, 1971.

Gallardo, J. M. "Language and Politics in Puerto Rico." Hispania, 30 (1947), 38-44.

Gladwin, E. Changing Caribbean. New York: Collier-MacMillan, 1970.

Glazer, Nathan, and Daniel P. Moynihan. Beyond the Melting Pot. Cambridge: M. I. T. Press, 1965.

Golding, J. A Short History of Puerto Rico. New York: New American Library, 1974.

Granda, Germán de. "Notas sobre léxico palenquero de origen bantú." Boletín de filología española, 40-41 (1971), 9-13.

----------. Transculturación e interferencia lingüística en el Puerto Rico contemporáneo. San Juan: Ateneo Puertorriqueño, 1969.

Handlin, Oscar. The Newcomers. Cambridge: Harvard University Press, 1959.

Lewis, Gordon. Puerto Rico: Freedom and Power in the Caribbean. New York: Harper and Row, 1968.

Lewis, Oscar. A Study of Slum Culture. New York: Random House, 1968.

Malaret, Augusto. Vocabulario de Puerto Rico. 2nd ed. New York: Las Américas, 1967.

Marden, Charles F., and Gladys Mayer. Minorities in American Society. New York: Van Nostrand-Reinhold Co., 1968.

Milan, William G. "Patterns of Sociolinguistic Behavior in Puerto Rican Spanish." Diss. Temple University 1974.

Mills, C. Wright, Clarence Senior, and Rose Goldsen. The Puerto Rican Journey. New York: Russell & Russell, 1967.

Mintz, Sidney W. Worker in the Cane. A Puerto Rican Life History. New Haven: Yale University Press, 1960.

Montalvo, David, et al. The Puerto Ricans: A Brief Look At Their History. New York: The Anti-Defamation League, n. d.

Morrison, Cayce J. The Puerto Rican Study. 1953-1957. New York: Oriole Editions, 1972.

Narváez Santos, Eliezer. La influencia taína en el vocabulario inglés. Barcelona: Ediciones Rumbos, 1960.

Nash, Rose. "Englañol: More Language Contact in Puerto Rico." American Speech, 46, 1-2 (1971), 106-122.

----------. "Orthographic Interference in Pronunciation." In Readings in Spanish-English Contrastive Linguistics. Ed. Rose Nash. San Juan: Inter-American University Press, 1973, pp. 123-135.

Navarro Tomás, Tomás. El español en Puerto Rico: contribución a la geografía lingüística hispanoamericana. 2nd ed. San Juan: Universidad de Puerto Rico, 1948.

Padilla, Elena. Up From Puerto Rico. New York: Columbia University Press, 1958.

Pérez-Sala, P. Interferencia del inglés en la sintaxis del español hablado en la zona metropolitana de San Juan. San Juan: Inter-American University Press, 1973.

Rand, Christopher. The Puerto Ricans. New York: Oxford University Press, 1958.

Rosario, Rubén del. La lengua de Puerto Rico: Ensayos. 7th ed. Río Piedras, P. R.: Editorial Cultural, 1971.

----------. Vocabulario Puertorriqueño. Sharon, Conn.: The Troutman Press, 1965.

Schorer, G. E. "English Loan Words in Puerto Rico." American Speech, 28 (1953), 22-25.

Senior, Clarence. The Puerto Ricans: Strangers-- Then Neighbors. Chicago: Quadrangle, 1965.

Sexton, Patricia Cayo. Spanish Harlem: An Anatomy of Poverty. New York: Harper, 1965.

Silen, Juan Angel. We, The Puerto Rican People. New York: Monthly Review Press, 1971.

Stewart, Julian Haynes, ed. The People of Puerto Rico. Urbana, Illinois: University of Illinois Press, 1956.

Wagenheim, Kal. Puerto Rico: A Profile. New York: Praeger, 1971.

Wolf, H. "Partial Comparison of the Sound System of English and Puerto Rican Spanish." Language Learning, 3 (1950), 38-40.

VOCABULARY

The following abbreviations are used: adj.,
adjective; adv., adverb; Cub., Cuban; fig., figurative; id., idiom; interj., interjection; L. A., general Latin-American; Lunf., Lunfardo; Mex., Mexican
or Chicano; nf., noun feminine; nm., noun masculine;
pl., plural; P. R., Puerto Rican; prep., preposition;
pron., pronoun; s., singular; theat., theatre; vi.,
verb intransitive; vr., verb reflexive; vt., verb
transitive. Radical-changing verbs are indicated by
(ie), (ue), (ie, i), (ue, u), and (i).

A

abarcar   vt.   to embrace, include, take in
abey   nm.   jacaranda
abnegar   (ie)   vt.   to abnegate, renounce
abotonar   vt.   to button
abrigo   nm.   coat; shelter
abulia   nf.   apathy, indifference
acarrear   vt.   to transport, carry
acertar   (ie)   vt.   to hit the bull's eye; to guess
aclamar   vt. & i.   to acclaim, applaud
aclarar   vt.   to clarify, explain
acostar   (ue)   vt.   to put to bed; lay down
acta   nf.   minutes, record of proceedings
actor   nm.   actor
actuador   nm.   performer
acudir   vi.   to come to the rescue; to respond; to
   turn to
acusar recibo   id.   to acknowledge
achaque   nm.   pretext, excuse
achicharrar   vt.   to scorch; to bedevil
adminículo   nm.   adminicle, aid, auxiliary; gadget
adquirir   (ie, i)   vt.   to acquire
afán   nm.   hard work; anxiety
afecto   nm.   love, affection
afligirse   vr.   to be grieved; to get upset
afuera   adv.   outside; _____ s   nf. pl.   outskirts
agradecer   vt.   to show gratitude for; to thank for
agrónomo   nm.   agronomist

449

agua nf. water
aguacate nm. avocado
aguafiestas nm. party pooper
aguardiente nm. brandy
aguja nf. needle; buscar una ____ en el pajar
    to look for a needle in a haystack
aguzar los oídos id. to prick up one's ears
ahijado nm. godchild; protégé
ahinco nm. zeal, ardor
ahogar vt. to drown, smother, suffocate
ahondar vt. to deepen, make deeper
ahorcar vt. to hang, execute
ahorrar vt. to save; put away
ahuyentar vt. to drive away, cast off
airar vt. to anger
aire nm. air
ajeno adj. alien, foreign
ajo nm. garlic
ajonjolí nm. sesame
ala nf. wing
al cabo de id. at the end of
alabanza nf. praise
alabar vt. to praise, exalt
alameda nf. poplar grove; tree-lined walk
álamo nm. poplar tree
alberca nf. pool; pond; reservoir
alcachofa nf. artichoke
alcahuete nm. go-between, entremetteur
alcalaíno (-na) nm. or f. a native of Alcala
alcanzar vt. to reach, attain; id. si el tiempo
    nos alcanza if we have enough time
aldea nf. village, hamlet
alejarse vr. to go away, withdraw, separate
alentar (ie) vt. to encourage, inspire
alfil nm. bishop (chess)
alfombra nf. carpet, rug
alhaja nf. jewel
alianza nf. alliance
alimento nm. food; foodstuff; nutrition
al militar en id. as a result of participating in
almohada nf. pillow, cushion; consultar con la
                 ____ to sleep on a matter
almorzar (ue) vi. to lunch, have luncheon
alquiler nm. rent, hire
alzar vt. to lift, hoist

450

amarrar vt. to lash, tie up
amate nm. rubber plant
amortiguar vi. to deaden, lessen
ancho adj. broad, wide
andar vt. to go, move, walk; ____se por las ramas
   to beat around the bush
andén nm. railway platform; side path
ánima nf. soul
ánimo nm. soul, spirit, mind; courage, valor
anquilosarse vr. to become stiff in the joints; to
   grow creaky with age
ansia nf. anxiety, anguish
ante nm. elk; first course of a meal; suede
anteayer adv. the day before yesterday
anteojos nm. pl. eyeglasses
antimonio nm. antimony
anudar vt. to fasten; to tie; to knot
anular nm. ring finger; vt. to annul, nullify
año nm. year
apaciguar vt. to appease; edify
aparejo antihurto nm. security lock (system)
apercibirse vr. to perceive; to become cognizant
aplazar vt. to postpone; to fail in an examination
aporte nm. contribution
apostar (ue) vt. & i. to bet
apóstol nm. apostle
apoyo nm. support, leaning upon
aprehender vt. to apprehend, catch; seize
apresurar vt. to hasten, rush (someone)
apretar (ie) vt. to press, squeeze
apretón nm. shaking (of hands)
aprobado adj. passing; approved
aptitud nf. suitability; aptitude
apto adj. apt; suitable
aquejar vt. to grieve; weary
arado nm. plowshare, plough
arbusto nm. shrub, bush
arco nm. arch; bow; hoop
archivar vt. to file; deposit in archives
ardid nm. ruse, trick
argüir vi. to argue
armatoste nm. hulk
arranque nm. starter; starting
arre interj. giddyap
arreglar vt. to arrange, fix

451

arreglo nm. arrangement
arrendar (ie) vt. to rent; to tie (an animal)
arreo nm. adornment; appurtenance; trapping;
sin _____ without interruption
arroyo nm. stream, brook
arroz nm. rice
asar vt. to roast
ascender (ie) vi. to ascend
ascensor nm. elevator
aseo nm. toilette; rest room; neatness
asopao nm. rice based stew with chicken or seafood (P. R.)
astronauta nm. astronaut
asunto nm. subject matter; business, affair
ataúd nm. coffin
atrio nm. vestibule; atrium
atropellar vt. to trample upon, to run over
atún nm. tuna fish
aturdir vt. to stun, amaze; bewilder
auto nm. judicial act; religious play; auto, car
autopista nf. highway; expressway
autorretrato nm. self-portrait
auxilio nm. help
avaluar see evaluar
ave nf. bird, fowl
avería nf. aviary; breakdown; damage
averiguar vt. to ascertain, find out
avestruz nm. ostrich
azar nm. chance; fate; misfortune, hazard

B

babero nm. bib
bacalao nm. codfish
bacana nf. a person with money (Lunf.)
baga nf. head of flax; rope to tie burdens on the
back of beasts; tree of the Annonacea family
(Cub.)
bagual adj. untamed, wild; dull
bailar vt. & i. to dance
bailaora nf. Flamenco dancer
bala nf. bullet; bale
baladí adj. trivial, worthless
452

balbucear vi. to babble; to stammer, stutter; to mumble; to lisp
balde nm. bucket, pail; en ____ in vain
baratija nf. trifle, trinket
barco nm. boat, ship
barrer vt. to sweep, sweep clean
barril nm. barrel; water jug
barrio nm. ward, quarter, precinct
bastar vi. to suffice
bastimentar vt. to supply
bata nf. robe, house coat
bautizar vt. to baptize
beldad nf. beauty
bergamota nf. bergamot
boa nf. boa
bochinche nm. tumult, uproar
boda nf. wedding, marriage
bodegón nm. taproom, country bar
boina nf. beret
bolígrafo nm. ballpoint pen
boloñés adj. Bolognese
bolsillo nm. pocket
bondad nf. goodness
bordar vt. to embroider
bote nm. thrust; prance (animal); rowboat, boat
boto adj. dull, blunt
bou nm. fishing by casting a net between two boats
brillar vi. to shine, sparkle
brioso adj. spirited, sprightly
bruja nf. witch
brujo nm. wizard
buche nm. craw; crop; mouthful
buey nm. ox
buitre nm. vulture

C

cabañero nm. shepherd; drover
caber vi. to fit
cabrón nm. buck; cuckold
cacahuete nm. peanut
cacheo nm. search for weapons on suspects

453

caída nf. fall
caimán nm. alligator, caiman
cala nf. cove, inlet; a type of lily
caldo nm. broth, soup
calidad nf. quality
calor nm. warmth, heat
calvo adj. bald
calle nf. street
callejón nm. alley; _____ sin salida blind al-
    ley
callo nm. callous
camión nm. truck; jitney
cama nf. bed
camote nm. sweet potato; infatuation, love (Mex.)
cancha nf. field, ground; _____ de tenis tennis
    court (L. A.)
cangrejo nm. crab
caniste nm. canistel (fruit)
canoso adj. grey-haired
cantaora nf. folk singer; gypsy entertainer
cántaro nm. bucket, pail
cantidad nf. quantity
cantor nm. singer, minstrel
capa nf. cloak, mantle
capataz nm. foreman, overseer
captar vt. to capture, seize
caracol nm. snail
caray nm. tortoise, tortoise shell; interj. for
    goodness' sake; confound it
careto adj. marked with a blaze (said of animals)
cargar vt. to load, pack
caridad nf. charity
carmesí adj. crimson
carie nf. tooth decay, caries
carnero nm. ram; mutton
carnicero nm. butcher
caro adj. dear; costly
carpa nf. carp; tent (L. A.)
cartero nm. mailman
carraspear vi. to be hoarse
carreta nf. cart
carril nm. track; furrow; narrow road
carro nm. cart, wagon; truck; auto
casaquinta nf. country house
casar vt. to marry

454

_____ se   vr. to get married
cata   nf. taste, sampling
catedrático   nm. full professor
cauce   nm. channel; river bed
causa   nf. cause
cautela   nf. caution, care; craftiness
cava   nf. digging; cultivation
caza   nf. hunt, hunting
cazar   vt. to hunt
cebolla   nf. onion
celemín   nm. Spanish measurement; one-half peck
Cenicienta   nf. Cinderella
ceniza   nf. ash; _____ s   nf. pl. ashes
centauro   nm. centaur
centenar   nm. about a hundred
cepillo   nm. brush
cero   nm. zero; ser un _____ a la izquierda   to be
    of no account
cerrar   (ie)   vt. to close
cerrazón   nf. closure, closing; overcasting
cerro   nm. hill
cicuta   nf. hemlock, poison
ciervo   nm. stag, deer
cima   nf. summit, top
cinc   see zinc
circo   nm. circus
citación   nf. citation; quotation; summons
clavija   nf. pin, peg; plug
clavo   nm. nail, spike
coba   nf. tricks; cajolery
cocer   (ue)   vt. to cook, to bake;   vi. to cook,
    to boil
cocinero   nm. cook; chef
codornís   nm. quail
coger   vt. to pick, gather; collect
cogote   nm. back of the head
cohete   nm. rocket
cojear   vi. to limp
cojo   see cojear
col   nf. cabbage
cola   nf. tail; hacer _____ to stand in line
colchón   nm. mattress
colgar   vt. to hang, drape
colibrí   nm. hummingbird

455

coliflor nf. cauliflower
colmillo nm. eyetooth; canine tooth; tusk
coma nf. comma
comedido adj. courteous, polite; frugal
cometa nm. comet; nf. kite
compartir vt. to share, split
comunicador adj. communicating
concurso nm. contest, competition; concurrence
condado nm. county; earldom
conde nm. count
conductor adj. conducting, conductor
confesar (ie) vt. & i. to confess
conformador adj. conforming
conservador adj. conservative
constante adj. constant; nf. constant
constituir vt. to constitute
contaminación del aire nf. air pollution
contar (ue) vt. to tell, recount, narrate
contramarcha nf. reverse gear
contrapeso nm. counterbalance; counterpoise
convenir (ie) vi. to be suitable
convertir (ie) vt. & i. to convert; _____ se
          vr. to become
cónyuge nmf. spouse, mate
copa nf. glass (wine)
coqueta nf. coquette, flirt
corcho nm. cork
coreo nm. choreus
corso adj. Corsican; nm. Corsican dialect;
          festive parade (L. A.)
cortaplumas nm. penknife
cortar vt. to cut; _____ se vr. to become con-
          fused
corregidor nm. mayor
corregir (i) vt. to correct; grade
correo nm. mail
costear vt. to defray the cost of; sail along the
          coast of
cotización nf. stock quotation
crear vt. to create
criado nm. manservant
criar vt. to raise, bring up, rear
crisol nm. crucible
cruz nf. cross

456

cuadra nf. city block (L. A.); stable
cubo nm. bucket; hub (of wheel)
cuerda nf. cord, rope
cuero nm. leather
cueva nf. cave, cavern
cuidar vt. to take care of, look after
cuita nf. sorrow, worry, trouble
culpa nf. blame
cuota nf. quota, rate
cupo nm. quota, share
cura nm. priest; nf. cure, healing
curare nm. curare
curro adj. sporty, flashy

CH

chaparro adj. short, stubby (L. A.); nm. ever-
        green oak
chato adj. flat, blunt; flat-nosed
chévere interj. marvelous, wonderful (P. R.)
chicano nm. Mexican American
chiflar vt. to hiss (theat.); to gulp down (li-
        quor); to whistle
chillón adj. shrieking, whining
china nf. Chinese woman; orange (L. A.)
chinche nmf. bedbug
chiquitín adj. very small, tiny
choclo nm. clog, wooden shoe; green ear of
        maize (L. A.)

D

dar vt. to give
dar miedo a vt. to be frightening to
dardo nm. dart
dato nm. datum; fact
deber vi. & t. should, ought; to owe
dedo nm. finger
delantal nm. apron
deleite nm. delight, pleasure

457

denominar vt. to name; indicate
desabotonar vt. to unbutton
desamparar vt. to abandon
desarraigar vt. to uproot, to dig up; to extirpate
desaseo nm. untidiness, disarray
desaventajado nm. & adj. disadvantaged
desbrozador adj. clearing (of brush)
descender (ie) vi. to descend
descubrirse vr. to remove one's hat
desdecir vt. to contradict, differ; retract
desembocadura nf. mouth (river); opening, outlet
desempeñar vt. to fulfill, carry out, practice; to take out of pawn
desenvainar vt. to unsheathe
desmerecer vt. to become unworthy of (praise, etc.); to take away from
despacio adv. slowly
despedir (i) vt. to hurl, throw; dismiss; se vr. to take leave
destituir vt. to deprive; to dismiss
destornillador nm. screwdriver
deuda nf. debt
diario adj. daily
diezmar vt. to decimate; vi. to tithe
diferenciador adj. differentiating
dintel nm. doorhead; threshold
discernir (ie; i) vt. to discern
discípulo nm. disciple, follower
discorde adj. discordant
disminuir vt. & i. to diminish, decrease
diurno adj. daily, diurnal
divisibilidad nf. divisibility
doler (ue) vt. to ache, hurt
don nm. gift, talent
donaire nm. wittiness; gracefulness; bon mot
dormilón nm. sleepyhead
dorar vt. to gild, palliate; to brown (a cookie)
dorso nm. back, dorsum
drogadicto nm. drug addict
dudar vt. to doubt
duende nm. goblin, elf
dueño nm. owner, boss
duomo nm. dome

E

echar vt. to throw, cast away; to discharge; to
    utter; vi. to tend (in a certain direction),
    to lean
eje nm. axis; core; axle
ejote nm. tender bean pod; string bean (Mex.)
ello pron. it
emergencia nf. emergency; emergence
empanada nf. meat pie
empezar (ie) vt. & i. to begin, commence
emplomadura nf. filling (tooth)
enaltecer vt. to exalt, extol
enano nm. midget, dwarf
enarbolado adj. hoisted; hung out
enardecer vt. to inflame; to excite
encarar vt. to face
encarrillar vt. to put back on the rails; to put
    on the right track
encima adv. above, at the top; overhead
endovenosa adj. intravenous
enfadar vt. to anger
enfermizo adj. sickly
enfoque nm. focus; approach
enfriar vt. to cool, make cold
engalanar vt. to adorn, bedeck
engañar vt. to deceive
engaño nm. deceit, deception; fraud
engrandecer vt. to make large, aggrandize; to
    exalt
enjaezar vt. to trap; harness
enorgullecerse vr. to pride oneself on; boast
    about
enredar vt. to confuse, entangle; to embroil
    vi. to fiddle, trifle
enredo nm. entanglement; complication
ensalzar vt. to extol, exalt
ensancharse vr. to widen, expand
ensanche nm. widening, extension; turn-in of a
    seam
enseñar vt. to teach; show
ensimismado adj. self-absorbed
ensueño nm. dream; daydream
entablar vt. to board, board up; to splint; to
    bring up a topic (in a conversation)

459

ente nm. being
entender (ie) vt. to understand
entenderse (ie) vr. to know a great deal about;
        specialize
entrada nf. entrance; ticket
envejecer vi. to grow old
envidioso adj. covetous, greedy
epazote nm. tea (Mex.)
errar (ie) vi. to wander
esbelto adj. slender, thin
escaparse vr. to flee, escape; run away
escasez nf. scarcity, paucity
escoger vt. to choose, select
escorpioide nm. scorpion grass
escorbuto nm. scurvy
escudero nm. shield bearer; nobleman
esfuerzo nm. effort, attempt
esmerarse vr. to take pains to or for
espalda nf. back
especiería nf. spice store; spice business
esperma nf. sperm
esquema nm. scheme; schema; diagram
estafiate nm. a type of medicinal plant
estanque nm. reservoir, basin; pond, pool
estar embarazada see estar encinta
estar encinta id. to be pregnant
estar preñada see estar encinta
estiércol nm. dung, manure
estudio nm. study
_____ de ampliación graduate work
excelso adj. lofty, elevated
exclamar vt. & i. to exclaim, applaud
éxito nm. success
exponer vt. to expose

F

fábrica nf. factory, plant; mill
fabricar vt. to build; produce
facción nf. feature; faction
faisán nm. pheasant
fámula nf. maidservant
fanfarrón nm. braggart, "show off"
460

```
farol    nm.  lantern; headlight
fastidiar vt.  to annoy, sicken
fealdad  nf.  ugliness
ferrocarril nm.  railroad
feudo    nm.  feud; fief
fiar     vt.  to entrust, give credit for
         vi.  to trust
fidedigno adj.  reliable, trustworthy
fidelidad nf.  fidelity, faithfulness
fiel     adj.  faithful
flaco    adj.  thin, gaunt; weak
flecha   nf.  arrow
flojo    adj.  loose, limp
florecer vi.  to blossom; flourish
florero  nm.  florist (L. A.); flower pot
flotar   vi.  to float
focino   nm.  goad
fogoso   adj.  fiery, spirited; vehement
folio    nm.  folio; folder
fontanero nm.  plumber
fraguar  vt.  to forge; brew
freno    nm.  brakes
friso    nm.  freize, wainscot
frotar   vt. & i.  to rub
fuero    nm.  law; statute
fumador  nm.  smoker
fusilar  vt.  to shoot, execute


G

gafas    nf. pl.  eyeglasses
gaita    nf.  bagpipe
gala     nf.  festive dress
galgo    nm.  greyhound
gallina  nf.  chicken; "coward"
gallo    nm.  rooster
gama     nf.  gamut; doe
gamba    nf.  shrimp
ganar    vt.  to earn
ganoso   adj.  desirous
garbanzo nm.  garbanzo bean, chick pea
garrón   nm.  spur, talon
```

gasa nf. gauze; chiffon, crepe
gaveta nf. drawer; glove compartment
gente nf. people
girasol nm. sunflower
gola nf. gullet
golpear vt. to strike, beat, hit
goma nf. eraser; gum, rubber; elastic band
gorra nf. beret, peasant's cap
gorrión nm. sparrow
gota nf. drop; gout
gozar vt. to enjoy
graduar vt. to graduate, grade
gratuito adj. gratuitous, free
grilo nm. pants, trousers (Lunf.)
gris adj. gray
groenlandés adj. of Greenland
guacamole nm. avocado salad
guajalote nm. turkey (Mex.)
guapo adj. nice-looking; handsome; pretty
guara nf. tree similar to a chestnut tree (Cub.)
guardafango nm. fender
guerra nf. war
guerrero nm. warrior
guiar vt. to guide, lead
guineo nm. banana (P. R.)
guiño nm. wink; grimace
guión nm. pennant; outline; hyphen; script
       (theat.)
guisado nm. stew

H

haba nf. bean; coffee bean
habichuela nf. kidney bean
hábil adj. clever; handy
hábito nm. habit, custom
hablador adj. talkative, loquacious
hacer vt. to do, make
_____ se el juez dormido to play dumb
_____ la mosquita muerta to play dumb
hacia prep. toward, about
hacha nf. axe, torch

hada nf. fairy
halcón nm. falcon
hallar vt. to find
hallazgo nm. discovery; find
hambre nf. hunger
harén nm. harem
hartar vt. to stuff, satiate; gratify
harto adj. full, fed up with
        adv. quite enough
haz nm. bundle, sheath
hechizado adj. bewitched, enchanted
hecho nm. fact, deed, act
helado nm. ice cream
helar (ie) vt. to freeze
hembra adj. female
henchir (i) vt. to fill, stuff
hendir (i) vi. to cleave, crack
herida nf. wound
herir (ie, i) vt. to wound
hermandad nf. brotherhood
hervir (ie, i) vi. to boil
herramienta nf. tool; instrument
herrar (ie) vt. to shoe (horses, etc.);
        brand (cattle)
hidalgo adj. noble, illustrious
        nm. nobleman
hielo nm. ice
hierro nm. iron
higo nm. fig (fruit)
higuera nf. fig tree
hijastro nm. stepchild, stepson
hilar vt. & i. to spin (wool, etc.)
hilo nm. thread; yard; filament
himno nm. hymn; anthem
hincar vt. to stick, drive, thrust
hinchar vt. to swell, inflate
hinojo nm. knee; fennel
hioides nm. hyoid
hípico adj. horse, equine
hiriente adj. stinging; cutting
hirviente adj. boiling
hispanohablante nm. Spanish-speaking person
hispanoparlante nm. Spanish-speaking person
hoja nf. leaf; sheet (paper)

463

holandés adj. & nm. Dutch
holgar (ue) vi. to idle, rest up
holgazán adj. lazy, indolent
hollín nm. soot
hombro nm. shoulder
horchata nf. orgeat, beverage made from barley
hormiga nf. ant
horquilla nf. hairpin
hoz nf. sickle
huelga nf. strike
huella nf. trace, sign, step
hueso nm. bone
huir vi. to escape, flee
humo nm. smoke, steam; fume
hundir vt. to sink, destroy
huracán nm. hurricane
huraño adj. diffident, shy, bashful
hurí nf. Arabian woman
hurtar vt. to steal, rob

I

idem adj. & pron. idem
ijada nf. flank (of an animal); stitch (pain)
ijar nm. flank, loin
impecabilidad nf. impeccability
imperscrutabilidad nf. inscrutability
imprescindible adj. essential, indispensable
incluir vt. to include
inédito adj. unpublished; new, unknown
ínfimo adj. lowest, humblest
ingles nf. pl. groins
injurioso adj. offensive, insulting
inspirar vt. to inspire
instruir vt. to instruct, teach; to inform
invertir (ie, i) vt. to invert; reverse; invest
inyección nf. injection
inyectar vt. to inject
isleño adj. island; of Spanish-speaking dweller of
       Louisiana; nm. islander; Spanish-speaking
       dweller of Louisiana
item nm. item; article

J

jabalí nm. wild boar
jabón nm. soap, cake of soap
jabonera nf. soap maker, dealer; soap dish
jalapeño nm. native of Jalapa; a kind of pepper
jalar vt. to pull, haul
jaleo nm. brawl, rumpus
jazmín nm. jasmine
jebo nm. guy, man, fellow (P. R.)
jefe nm. chief; leader; boss
jira nf. tour, spin
jorobado adj. hunchbacked; nm. hunchback
jugo nm. juice; substance
juramento nm. oath, curse

K

kan nm. khan
kepis nm. s. & pl. kepi
kilate nm. carat
kirie nm. kyrie
kiwi nm. kiwi
klaxson nm. horn
kurdo nm. Kurd, Kurdish

L

labrador nm. farmer, peasant
lada nf. rockrose (bot.)
lagaña nf. rheum
lago nm. lake
lama nm. lama (Buddhist priest); nf. slime; mud;
  lamé
lamer vt. to lick
lana nf. wool
lancha nf. barge; yacht
largarse vr. to move away, sneak away
lata nf. can; tin plate
lavandera nf. laundress; washerwoman

465

lealtad nf. loyalty
lema nm. motto
lento adj. slow
liar vt. to tie, bind, wrap
libertador nm. liberator
libresco adj. bookish
lima nf. file; sweet lime
limosna nf. alms
limosnita nf. (small) alms
limpio adj. clean, neat; tidy; pure
linaza nf. linseed, flaxseed
lintel nm. see dintel
liviandad nf. lightness; fickleness
loa nf. praise, panegyric
lobo nm. wolf
lóbrego adj. lugubrious, dark, gloomy
londinés nm. Londoner
loor nm. praise
lozano adj. exuberant; vigorous; verdant
luciérnaga nf. firefly, glowworm
luchador nm. fighter, struggler
lucir vi. appear, seem
lujo nm. luxury

LL

llaga nf. sore
llama nf. flame; passion; llama
llamar vt. to call
llano adj. smooth, even; paroxytone
llanto nm. crying; mourning
llanura nf. plain
llave nf. key; wrench; faucet
lleno · adj. full; filled; replete
llorar vi. to weep, mourn
llorón nm. & adj. cry baby; whining
llover (ue) vi. to rain
lluvia nf. rain

M

macaneador nm. storyteller, exaggerator (L. A.)
macharse vr. to get drunk (L. A.)
macho adj. male
maldad nf. evil, wickedness
maldito adj. cursed, damned
malecón nm. dyke, sea wall
malhechor nm. evil doer
malva nf. mallow; malva
mamar vt. to suck, suckle
manantial nm. source, spring; source (fig.)
manejar vt. to manage; handle; drive (auto)
manso adj. gentle, mild, meek
manto nm. mantle, cloak; robe, gown (priest, etc.)
maña nf. dexterity, cleverness
máquina nf. machine; clippers; engine
marino nm. seaman, sailor, mariner
marsellés adj. & nm. pertaining to or native of
          Marseilles
mascar vt. to chew; mumble
máscara nf. mask, masquerade
mata nf. brush, shrub; underbrush
matar vt. to kill
matricularse vr. to enroll, register
maxocote nm. shrub (Mascagnia scleriana) (Mex.)
mazorca nf. ear of corn (L. A.)
medicastro nm. quack doctor
medición nf. measurement
medio adj. half, mid; adv. half
_____ ambiente nm. environment (ecol.)
medir (i) vt. to measure; control
melocotón nm. peach
mendigo nm. beggar
menguar vt. to lessen, diminish
mentir (ie, i) vi. to lie, be false
mero adj. mere
mesón nm. inn, country tavern
meta nf. goal, aim
mezcla nf. mixture; mix; melee
miaja (migaja) nf. crumb
mico nm. long-tailed monkey
milicia nf. militia, military service
minusválido nm. handicapped person

467

mirra nm. myrrh
misil televidente nm. satellite telecast
mitad nf. half
mojado adj. soaking wet
molido adj. ground; "done in"
molino nm. mill; grinder
mono adj. nice-looking, cute
morcillo adj. reddish black (horses); nm. fleshy
     part of the arm
mortificar vt. & i. to mortify
mover (ue) vt. & i. to move, transport
mozo nm. lad, youth; waiter; servant
mudarse vr. to change (clothing, location)
muela nf. tooth, molar
murciélago nm. bat

N

nadar vi. to swim
nao nf. ship, vessel
nene nm. baby, boy
neutro adj. neutral, neuter
nevar (ie) vi. to snow
nido nm. nest
niño nm. child; ____ marginado nm. illegitimate
     child
nivelación nf. levelling process
nivelador adj. levelling
nopal nm. prickly pear (L. A.)
noramala (enhoramala) adv. unluckily; in an evil
     hour
norteño adj. northern
nudo nm. knot; tangle
nuera nf. daughter-in-law

O

obrero nm. worker, workman
oferta nf. offer
ofrecer vt. to offer
oír vt. & i. to hear

468

ojear vt. to eye, look over
olvidado adj. forgotten
olla nf. pot, bowl
onza nf. ounce
orador nm. speaker
orar vi. to pray; make a speech
orientador adj. orienting
orillarse vr. to skirt the edge; come up to the
shore
oveja nf. sheep
ovillo nm. ball of yarn; ball, heap; hacerse un
_____ to recoil, cower

P

padrino nm. godfather; sponsor
paella a la valenciana nf. saffron-flavored stew
of chicken, seafood and rice
with vegetables
pala nf. shovel; blade; scraper
pálido adj. pale
palmotear vt. to clap
pampa nf. pampa
panal nm. hornet's nest
pantano nm. marsh, swamp
paño nm. cloth; drapery
papa nm. pope; nf. potato (L. A.)
par nm. pair; a few
parar vi. to stop
pardo adj. brown; dub, dark
paridad nf. parity; comparison
parlanchín adj. talkative, loquacious
partidario nm. partisan, party member
partir vt. & i. to spill, crack; depart
pasar vt. & i. to pass, approve; go by
pata nf. paw; leg (of furniture); pocket flap
patata nf. potato
patalear vi. to kick, stomp
patinar vi. to skate
patria nf. native country, fatherland
patrocinar vt. to favor, sponsor
paulatino adj. slow, gradual

469

```
pauta    nf.  guide lines; ruler
pavor    nm.  fear
pay   nm.  pie; tart (L. A.)
peatón   nm.  pedestrian
pecho    nm.  chest, breast, bosom; a ____ seriously
pedir   (i)  vt.  to ask for, request
peine    nm.  comb
pelea    nf.  fight, quarrel; ____se  vr.  to fight
peligro  nm.  danger, peril
pelirrojo  nm.  redhead
pelo   nm.  hair, thread; nap
pellejo  nm.  hide, skin; rawhide
pellizcar  vt.  to pinch, take a pinch of
pena   nf.  anguish, pain
peña   nf.  rock
pepita   nf.  pip; melonseed; nugget
peral    nm.  pear, pear tree
perder   (ie)  vt.  to lose
perdiz   nf.  partridge
perejil  nm.  parsley
perfil   nm.  side; profile; view
perjudicar  vt.  to harm, damage
persignarse  vr.  to cross oneself
persona de edad  nf.  older person
pertrechos  nm. pl.  supplies, provisions
perro   nm.  dog
pésame   nm.  condolence
peso   nm.  weight, burden
peste    nf.  pest, plague; epidemic
picardía  nf.  crookedness; knavery
piedad   nf.  piety; pity
pila   nf.  basin, trough; holy-water font
pilar    nm.  basin, bowl; pillar
pintar   vt.  to paint, depict
piñata   nf.  a hanging pot of candy broken by
                children
piojo    nm.  louse
pique    nm.  pique, resentment
piragua  nf.  pirogue; tailflower
pisa   nf.  trampling, stamping; pressing of grapes
pito   nm.  whistle, horn; ni ____ ni flauto  not a
                single word
plantar  vt.  to plant; to stand someone up
platanal  nm.  plantation of plantains
```

```
plátano    nm.  plantain
playa      nf.  beach
pleito     nm.  lawsuit; litigation
plomo      nm.  lead; "bore"
poblador   adj. populating
polvo      nm.  dust; powder
popa       nf.  poop, stern; ir viento en ____ to get
           along famously, to go very well
porteño    nm.  native of Buenos Aires
pote       nm.  pot, jug; flower pot
potro      nm.  wild horse
preconizar vt.  to commend publicly; proclaim
prender    vt.  to catch, grasp; vi. to ignite
prestar    vt.  to lend
prieto     adj. dark; black; mean
probar     (ue) vt. to try, test
____se     vr.  to try on
profesor titular  nm.  associate professor
propina    nf.  tip, gratuity
proyectar  vt.  to project, plan
pseudomorfo nm.  pseudomorph
pseudónimo nm.  pseudonym, pen name
pseudópodo nm.  pseudopod
pseudoprofeta nm. false prophet
psicoanálisis nm. psychoanalysis
psicolingüístico adj. psycholinguistic
psicometría nf.  psychometry
psicosomático adj. psychosomatic
psicoterapia nf. psychotherapy
psiquiatría nf.  psychiatry
psiquis    nf.  psyche
puchero    nm.  pot, kettle; a dish of boiled meat and
           vegetables; hacer ____s to pout
pudor      nm.  modesty; virtue
puente     nm.  bridge
puerto     nm.  port, harbor
puerro     nm.  leek, scallion
pulir      vt.  to polish, refine
pulque     nm.  pulque
pulular    vt.  to pullulate
puma       nm.  puma, cougar
puna       nf.  bleak tableland in the Andes
puño       nm.  fist; punch; fistful
purga      nf.  purge, physic
```

471

purificador adj. purifying
puxchana nf. badly made bundle (Mex.)

Q

quedarse vr. to remain; _____ como una lechuga
    to remain undaunted
quemar vt. to burn
quepo see caber
quepis nm. kepi
querer (ie) vt. to want; to love
quilate nm. carat
quinina nf. quinine
quiosco nm. kiosque, newsstand
quitar vt. to remove, take away

R

rabiar vi. to rave, rage
rabo nm. tail
ramo nm. branch, limb; bouquet
ramplonería nf. coarseness; vulgarity
rana nf. frog
raptar vt. to abduct, kidnap
rasgar vt. to tear; scratch
rasgo nm. flourish; trait; characteristic
rata nf. female rat; installment
ratón nm. rat; como un _____ slyly and cleverly
recién llegado nm. new arrival
referir (ie, i) vt. to tell, narrate, refer
regatear vt. to haggle over, bargain
regir (i) vt. to rule, govern; be in force
reguera nf. irrigating ditch
reina nf. queen
reja nf. grille, grating
relampaguear vi. to lighten
relinchar vi. to neigh
remendar (ie) vt. to mend
renovar (ue) vt. to renew
reñir (i) vt. & i. to scold; quarrel, fight
replicar vi. to reply, answer
472

requerir (ie, i) vt. to summon, request, send for
res nf. head of cattle; beast
resbalar vi. to slide, skip
restituir vt. to restitute, give back
resultante adj. resultant
resultar vt. to result, prove to be, turn out
retransmisión nf. rerun (TV)
retrasado adj. delayed
retraso nm. delay
revoltijo nm. mess; confusion
rezar vt. to pray
riachuelo nm. rivulet; little stream
rima nf. rhyme
rito nm. rite; ceremony
rizo nm. curl, lock
robar vt. to steal, rob
roce nm. rubbing, contact
roer vt. to gnaw, to pick at (bones, etc.)
ronco adj. hoarse
rostro nm. face, countenance
roto adj. broken; torn
rubí nm. ruby
ruda nf. rue (bot.); más conocido que la ____ extremely well known

S

saber vt. to know
sacar dos bolillas vt. to draw two numbers for an
oral examination
sacapuntas nm. pencil sharpener
sagaz adj. wise, sagacious
sahumar vt. to smoke (meats)
sal nf. salt; wit
salchichón nm. large sausage
sancionar vt. to sanction, approve
sangre nf. blood
sauce nm. willow tree
____ llorón nm. weeping willow
secuestración de aviones nf. hijacking
semilla nf. seed
senda nf. walk, path

473

```
sentar   (ie)  vt.  to seat
seña  nf.  sign, mark
____s  nf.  pl.  address
sensible  adj.  sensible; perceptible; sensitive
separador  adj.  divisive, separating
serrado  adj.  sawed, jagged
serrar  (ie)  vt.  to saw; serrate
sien  nf.  temple
síquico  adj.  psychic
smoking  nm.  dinner coat, tuxedo
soba  nf.  kneading; massage
sobornar  vt.  to bribe
sobrar  vi.  to be excessive, be left over
sobre  nm.  envelope
sobrentender  (ie)  vt.  to assume
sobresaliente  adj.  outstanding
sofisticado  adj.  sophisticated
soler  (ue)  vi.  to be accustomed to
sonar  (ue)  vt.  to sound, sing, play
sonrisa  nf.  smile
sopa  nf.  soup
soso  adj.  insipid, tasteless; dull
subalterno  adj.  subordinate
subantártico  adj.  subantarctic
subarrendar  (ie)  vt.  to sublease
subcomendador  nm.  deputy
subcomisión  nf.  subcommission, subcommittee
subconsciencia  nf.  subconscious, subconsciousness
subcontratar  vt.  to subcontract
subdecano  nm.  subdeacon
subdesarrollo  nm.  underdevelopment
subentender  see  sobrentender
subestimar  vt.  to underestimate
subexposición  nf.  underexposure  (phot.)
subfluvial  adj.  underriver
subgénero  nm.  subgenus
subgobernador  nm.  lieutenant governor
subinquilino  nm.  subtenant
subjefe  nm.  assistant to the boss, sub-head
sublevar  vt.  to incite rebellion
suboficial  nm.  noncommissioned officer
subscribir  vt.  to subscribe, endorse
subsecretaría  nf.  undersecretaryship
subsidio  nm.  aid, help, subsidy
subsiguiente  adj.  subsequent
```

474

sudanés adj. Sudanese
suelo nm. ground; soil; land; floor
suspendido adj. flunked, suspended

T

taba nf. anklebone; knuckle
tabla nf. board, table, chart; slab
tacaño adj. stingy, parsimonious
taco nm. plug, wad; rolled maize tortilla; (high)
    heel (L. A.)
tálamo nm. nuptial bed
taller nm. shop, workshop
tamal nm. tamale
tapa nf. lid, cap, cover
tardar vi. to be long in; delay
tardío adj. late
tarro nm. milk pail; horn (Amer.)
telespectador nm. television viewer
telenovela nf. television novel, T. V. story
ternero nm. bull calf
tiburón nm. shark
tierno adj. tender; supple
tina nf. earthen jar; wooden tub or vat
toalla nf. towel; _____ de baño bath towel
toro nm. bull
torso nm. torso; bust
torrar vt. to toast; to parch, burn
torrente nm. torrent
    circulatorio nm. circulatory system
tos nf. cough
toxicidad nf. toxicity
tóxico nm. toxin; poison
trabajador adj. hard-working
traductor nm. translator
traer vt. to bring
transformista nm. female impersonator
transpirante nm. anti-perspirant
tratar vt. to deal with, treat; address; _____
    con guante blanco id. to treat with kid
    gloves
trayectoria nf. trajectory; path

trecho nm. stretch of time; interval
trigueño adj. dark, dark complexioned; olive skinned
tropezar vt. hit, strike; vi. to stumble; _____ con to bump into
tuétano nm. marrow
tuna nf. group of students; prickly pear
turrón nm. nougat candy
tutear vt. to address in the familiar form (tú)

U

ubicar vt. to position, locate
ultraje nm. outrage, insult
usura nf. usury
uva nf. grape

V

vademécum nm. manual
vagancia nf. laziness, idleness; vagrancy
vaina nf. scabbard; holster
valar adj. relating to an enclosure, to a rampart, hedge, or fence
valer vt. to defend, protect
_____ se de to make use of, to avail
vallado nm. fence; barricade
valle nm. valley
vara nf. twig, stick; rod; wand
variar vi. & t. to vary, change
varón nm. man, male
velo nm. veil; velum
velludo nm. velvet; plush; adj. shaggy, hairy
vendedor nm. seller, vendor
verter (ie) vt. to pour, shed
vértice nm. vertex
vestido nm. dress
vestir (i) vt. to dress
_____ se (i) vr. to get dressed
vidrio nm. glass; pane

virar vi. to turn; vt. to wind, twist
visa nf. visa
vislumbrar vt. to glimpse; foresee; surmise
viuda nf. widow
viudo nm. widower
volcar (ue) vt. to upset, tip, overturn
volver (ue) vi. to return, come back
vorágine nf. whirlpool; vortex; malestrom
votar vi. to vote

X

xola nf. turkey hen (Mex.)
xoxoco nm. shrub (Odostemon fascicularis) (Mex.)

Y

ya adv. already; longer
yanqui nm. yankee, North American
yegua nf. mare
yerba (hierba) nf. grass
yerbabuena nf. mint
yerno nm. son-in-law
yerro see errar
yeso nm. plaster; gypsum; chalk
yugo nm. yoke; burden
yunque nm. anvil

Z

zaga nf. rear, load carried in the rear
zagala nf. lass, maiden; shepherdess
zaguán nm. entry; vestibule
zambullida nf. dive, plunge
zapatera nf. shoemaker's wife, cobbler's wife
zapatilla nf. slipper
zeda nf. zed (letter)
zéjel nm. Spanish-Arabic verse form

Zelandia, la nf. Zealand
zenit nm. zenith
Zepita nf. village in Peru
zeugma nm. zeugma, zeuma
zigzaguear vi. to zigzag
zinc nm. zinc
zíngaro nm. gypsy (esp., Hungarian)
zinia nf. zinnia
zipizape nm. rumpus
zircón nm. zircon
zócalo nm. base of a column, baseboard; public
        square (L. A.)
zorro nm. male fox; stupid person; hacerse el
            to pretend ignorance, pretend not to
        hear
zozobra nf. anxiety, anguish
zueco nm. wooden shoe, clog
zumbar vt. to make fun of; to let have (kick, slap,
        etc.)
zumo nm. juice (of a fruit); profit
zurrar vt. to curry, dress (leather)
zus (sus) interj. get on; take heart

explosives, cont.,
83, 86, 88, 104,
128, 189, 190, 197,
221, 234, 283f.,
299
expressions, idiom-
atic, 143-145, 151,
161-162, 231, 232,
288-289, 293, 297
extremeño, 195, 202,
213

Filipinos, 235-237,
298
Flemish, 310
Florida, 255, 256,
259f., 295, 308-
309
forms, archaic, 216f.,
223, 225f., 233,
234-235, 283, 284-
285, 286-287
French, 192, 227,
229, 268, 310
fricatives, 43-44,
54-56, 58, 64, 66,
68-69, 70, 76-77,
80, 83, 86, 88, 90-
91, 128, 180-185,
189-190, 196, 197,
199, 200, 215, 221,
234, 270, 283, 299

gabacho, 281
Galician, 189, 190-
192, 193, 233
German, 127, 229, 264,
267
germanía (see jargon)
glides, 24, 30, 32,
33, 35, 37, 38,
271f., 284

Greek, 264, 267, 306
Guadalupe Hidalgo,
Treaty of, 256
Guarani (see substra-
ta, Indian)
Guatemala, 179, 220

hiatus, 12-13; (see
also 41-43)
Hispanics (see hispa-
nos)
hispano (see caste-
llano)
hispanos, 66, 144-
145, 148, 160-162,
163-164, 175, 178,
180-182, 188, 202,
256, 258-261, 264-
265, 268-269, 270,
280-282, 295-297,
337
Honduras, 179, 220-
221
hypercorrection, 216,
218

idiolect, 141
immigration, 256-261,
264-265, 272, 295-
296, 306-307, 308-
309, 310-311
interdentals, 53, 64,
66, 68-69, 180-184,
190, 200, 216, 218,
221, 270, 298-299,
307, 308
interference, 215,
225, 264, 269-273,
277, 284, 285, 287-
288, 289, 293-294,
296-297, 298-299,
300-302, 303-305,

484

vibrants, cont., 53-
54, 55, 70, 73,
128, 199, 200, 215-
216, 218, 220, 221,
222, 224, 226, 270,
283, 298-299, 307
vos, diplomatic, 188-
189
voseante (see voseo)
voseo, 185-189, 219,
229, 234-235
vowels, 23-24, 26,
29, 30, 32, 35, 37,
38, 43-45, 127,
195-197, 228, 271-
272, 282-283, 290,
307
vowels, back, 23, 26,
33, 35, 37-38
vowels, close, 5, 14,
23-24, 26, 28-29,
30, 33, 35, 37, 38
41, 190, 193, 195-
196, 200, 216, 226,
236, 282, 285, 298
vowels, epenthetic,
130, 197, 270, 284
vowels, front, 23,
26, 28-30, 32-33,
307
vowels, individual,
[a] medial, 24, 26;
(see also 41-46)
[a] velar, 26, 222
[ä] palatal, 26,
199, 298
[ɐ] lax, 26
[e] close, 26, 28-
30, 298
[ɛ] open, 29, 30,
298, 307
[ə] lax, 29-30, 193
[i] close, 24, 30,
41, 42, 43, 190,

[i], cont., 195,
227, 239, 283
[i] open, 30, 32,
33, 88, 193, 282
[ɪ] lax, 32, 33, 43,
219, 282
[i̯] semi-vocalic,
32, 33, 41, 42, 44,
187, 188, 189, 226,
228, 282
[j] semi-consonan-
tal, 33, 41, 43,
45, 232, 234, 271-
272, 282
[o] close, 23, 33,
35, 41, 44, 45,
195, 271, 298, 307
[ɔ] open, 35, 41,
44, 45, 93, 283,
298
[ɔ] lax, 35, 45
[u] close, 23, 24,
37, 38, 41, 42, 298
[ʊ] open, 37, 38,
41-42, 298
[ʌ] lax, 37, 38, 42,
193, 195-196, 234,
236, 239, 307
[u̯] semi-vocalic,
37-38, 41
[w] semi-consonan-
tal, 38, 41, 42,
44, 45, 195, 283,
307
vowels, length of,
127-128, 271, 284
vowels, loss of, 215,
219, 232, 234, 239,
282, 298
vowels, medial, 5,
23, 24, 26, 307
vowels, open, 5, 14,
23-24, 29, 30, 32-
33, 35, 37-38, 41,

490